WRITING AND ANALYSIS IN THE LAW

FOURTH EDITION

By

HELENE S. SHAPO
Professor of Law
Director of Legal Writing
Northwestern University School of Law

MARILYN R. WALTER
Professor of Law
Director of the Legal Writing Program
Brooklyn Law School

ELIZABETH FAJANS, Ph.D.
Associate Professor of Legal Writing
Writing Specialist
Brooklyn Law School

New York, New York
FOUNDATION PRESS
1999

 TEXT IS PRINTED ON 10% POST CONSUMER RECYCLED PAPER

DEDICATION

To our families—
Marshall, Benjamin, and Nathaniel Shapo
Ron, Amy, and Alison Walter
Bob, Nicholas, Rachel, and Paul Zimmerman
For the love, support, and advice they have given us
before and during the preparation of this book.

*

PREFACE

Many people find writing a difficult and frustrating process. As a result, they put off writing projects in the hope that they will eventually be struck by inspiration. Unfortunately, few professions, especially the legal profession, are willing to postpone business in anticipation of this happening.

This book is devoted, therefore, to taking control over the writing process away from chance and investing it in ourselves. We have tried to break the legal reasoning and writing process into manageable components to enable you to be conscious of that process and to be master of your thoughts and their expression. We hope this awareness of the writing process will also make you less anxious when writing and more satisfied with your work when finished.

Writing and Analysis in the Law is a collaborative effort. Decisions about the scope of the book and the focus of each chapter were made jointly. In addition, the authors edited each other's chapters extensively, making both substantive and stylistic contributions to each chapter. We have learned much from each other and hope the book confirms our belief in the benefits of editing and rewriting.

*

ACKNOWLEDGMENTS

We would like to acknowledge and thank our students. Their progress marks our success as teachers and their questions spur our own development. We would like to offer special thanks to those students and ex-students who have given us permission to use their work in this book: Robert Banozic, Dale Berson, Brian Blanchard, Robert M. Bornstein, Jacqueline Bryks, Gail Cagney, Anthony T. Cartusciello, Abigail Chanis, Barbara Curry, David Evans, Laura E. Ewall, Jennifer Franco, Katherine Frenck, Patricia Gennerich, Victor Gialleonardo, Rhonda Katz, Jane Levin, Kathleen Lewis, Philip J. Loree, Bruce E. Loren, Joseph Macaluso, Linda Mendel-owitz-Alpert, Donna A. Mulcahy, Bonnie M. Murphy, Anthony Rothschild, Ann Ruben, Alice F. Rubin, Concettina Sacheli, Thomas Skinner, Leslie Soule, Abby Sternschein, Douglas Tween, Heike Vogel, Roberta Wilensky, Eric Wunsch, Melissa Wynne, and Mona Zessimopoulos. Three research assistants from Northwestern University School of Law—Anne Meyer, Kevin Osborne, and Robert Sell—provided perceptive suggestions for many of our chapters for the first edition. Jim Groth was an invaluable editor for the second edition, Lee Garner helped with the third edition, and Jennifer Franco and Katherine Frenck with this edition. John Mandelbaum was kind enough to allow us to use the brief on which the brief in Appendix F was based.

We are also indebted to our colleagues, from whom we have learned much. Professors Ursula Bentele, Neil Cohen, Debra Harris, Will Hellerstein, Ann McGinley, Sara Robbins, and Jeff Stempel, Victoria Szymczak, faculty members at Brooklyn, and Professor Marshall S. Shapo of Northwestern read various chapters for us and made valuable suggestions. Professors Jim Haddad and John Elson of the Northwestern faculty gave their time to help teach appellate advocacy to the first-year class; their ideas have inevitably found their way into the final chapters of this book. Professor Cynthia Grant Bowman of Northwestern graciously provided us with the memorandum on which Appendix E is in large part based. Many legal writing instructors, past and present, and other colleagues have allowed us to base examples and exercises on problems they developed for their classes. We extend thanks to those from Brooklyn— Bob Begleiter, Stacy Caplow, Eve Cary, Cynthia Dachowitz, Martha Dietz, Mollie Falk, Philip Genty, Michael Gerber, Paul Green, Sharon Katz, Roseann MacKechnie, Kirsten Mishkin, Kate O'Neill, Pamela Perron, Susan Pouncey, Carrie Teitcher, Carol Ziegler—and to those from Northwestern—Ben Brown, Marion Gray, Peter

ACKNOWLEDGMENTS

Humphrey, Mardell Nereim, and especially, Judith Rosenbaum. Judy also did some valuable editing for us.

We would also like to express our gratitude to Brooklyn Law School and Northwestern University School of Law. These institutions not only gave us general encouragement, but also invested in our project by granting us research stipends.

Finally, Marilyn Walter and Elizabeth Fajans would like to thank Rose Patti for her efficiency and graciousness—even after interminable hours word processing. Similarly, Helene Shapo would like to thank Derek Gundersen for his fine work on the fourth edition.

TABLE OF CONTENTS

APPENDICES

*

WRITING AND
ANALYSIS
IN THE LAW

*

Chapter One

Introduction to the Legal System and Legal Writing

I. The Primary Sources of Law

Students decide to come to law school for many good and diverse reasons. However, despite our numerous years teaching in law schools, we have never heard new students say they have come to law school because they like to write. Yet lawyers write all the time. They write to colleagues; they write to clients; they write to adversaries in a law suit; they write to third parties requesting favors or information; they write to judges. They write documents for many different purposes: to persuade a court to rule in a client's favor; to answer a client's questions; to analyze a client's case; or to inform an adversary that a client is open to settlement but willing to litigate if pressed too hard. To be a good lawyer, you must be a good writer. And to be a good legal writer, you must have both a good understanding of law and a good grasp of principles of writing.

This book is about good writing. It introduces you to the sources of authority with which a lawyer works and upon which a lawyer's writing revolves. It introduces you to legal analysis and some forms of legal writing. Finally, it tries to integrate those lawyerly enterprises with that which all good writing must demonstrate, namely, a clear sense of audience, purpose, organization, and paragraph and sentence structure.

When you were an undergraduate or graduate student, you probably read a variety of primary and secondary sources to get the information you needed to write papers. You may have relied upon several secondary sources, such as books written by others about the topics of your papers. As a lawyer you will also use many different sources of information to acquire the necessary background information to analyze a legal question. A lawyer's most important sources of information, however, are primary sources.

Primary sources in law include both case law (judicial decisions) and enacted law (statutes, constitutions, and administrative regulations). These are the formal sources of enforceable legal rules in this country. Although you may not study administrative and constitutional law until the second or third year of law school, you will have to learn to use case law and statutory law throughout your first year and for almost all the writing that you do in your legal writing course. That is because in our legal system, analysis of a problem is controlled by enacted law that regulates the subject matter of that problem, and by the decisions of earlier cases that involved issues and facts similar to those in that problem. This year you will be learning how to find those legal authorities, how to use them, and how to write about them.

The first information you need concerns the origins of the primary authorities of the law. Because most of your first-year classes emphasize case law, this introduction will begin with judicial decisions. You should be aware, however, that enacted law forms a significant part of the body of law in our country. You must always consult these sources first when you do research for a problem because constitutional provisions and statutes take precedence over case law. However, even when you find an applicable statute or constitutional provision, you must also determine whether any case law is relevant to the problem. Your legal research will require you to search for cases that have interpreted the particular statute or constitutional provision. When you find these cases, you analyze how they are relevant to your problem or explain why the cases are not relevant. When no statute or constitutional provision applies, however, you must rely solely on earlier cases to provide the law on the subject. Those earlier cases provide a source of enforceable rules called the common law.

The United States is a common law country, in that rules of law come from the written decisions of judges who hear and decide litigation. The common law is judge-made law. Judges are empowered by statute or by constitutional provision in every state and in our federal system to decide controversies between litigants. When a judge decides a case, the decision attains the status of law, and it becomes a precedent for future legal controversies that are similar. Our common law system, like the English system from which it came, is a system of precedent. In the simplest sense, precedents are just the decisions of judges in previous litigation.

Those decisions, however, play a dual role. First, the decision resolves the litigation that is before the court. Second, if that decision is published, it becomes available for use by judges in later litigation. According to the doctrine of precedent, judges should resolve litigation according to the resolutions of similar cases in the past.

Many factors in addition to similarity determine how a case is used as a precedent, and this book will introduce you to some of those factors. For example, the value of a decision is affected by the court that decided the case. The purpose of this introductory section is to explain where our law comes from and how a decision's value as a precedent is affected by the nature of the court that decided the case. This information, in turn, is crucial to the analysis and organization of your written work.

II. Structure of the Court System in the United States

A. The Vertical Structure of Our Court System

Case law in the United States comes from litigation conducted in many court systems. Each state, as well as the District of Columbia and the federal government, has its own system of courts. Each is a separate jurisdiction. For our purposes, a jurisdiction is the area over which the courts of a particular judicial system are empowered to resolve disputes and thus to enforce their decisions. Jurisdiction is determined by a geographic area, like a state, and it can also be based upon subject matter. Subject matter jurisdiction is the authority of a court to resolve disputes in only a particular subject area of the law, such as criminal law.

The structure of the court system within each jurisdiction is a hierarchical one. Courts are organized along a vertical structure, and the position of a court within that structure has important consequences. Courts in which litigation begins are called courts of original jurisdiction. In many states, the lowest rung of the courts of original jurisdiction is occupied by a so-called court of inferior jurisdiction. This court has the power to hear only limited types of cases, such as misdemeanor cases or cases in which the amount of damages the complaining party (the plaintiff) demands from the party sued (the defendant) does not exceed a specified sum. These courts have various names, such as courts of common pleas or small claims courts. Other courts of inferior jurisdiction are limited to deciding cases about one particular subject matter, for example, juvenile or family law matters. Courts of inferior jurisdiction may be conducted informally. For example, the parties often represent themselves and the court does not follow the formal rules of evidence used in higher courts. The decisions of these courts are not published and they have no value as precedent to future litigants.

The next rung up from the courts of inferior jurisdiction is occupied by the trial courts. Litigation often begins at this level, and the trial courts are usually the courts in which the parties first litigated the cases that appear as appellate decisions in your case books. Trial courts are usually courts of general jurisdiction, that is, they may hear cases of all subject matters. Thus, a trial court may hear civil litigation, which is litigation between private parties who are designated as the plaintiff and the defendant. It may also hear criminal cases. Criminal litigation is brought by the state, which prosecutes the criminal charges against a defendant or defendants. There is no private party plaintiff in a criminal case.

A trial court is presided over by one judge. It is the particular province of the trial court to determine the facts of the case. The trier of fact, either judge or jury, "finds," that is, determines, the facts from the evidence at trial, the examination of witnesses, and the admissions of the parties. For example, one issue in a case may be the speed at which a vehicle was travelling. This fact may be disputed by the parties. The trial judge or the jury, if the question is put to a jury, will resolve the dispute and "find," for example, that a party traveled at 75 miles per hour. The court then decides the case by applying the applicable law to that fact.

Often the trial court judge will decide a case by procedures that preclude a trial. For example, one of the parties may bring a motion (a request to the court) for the court to take a particular action. Some types of motions, if granted, will result in a decision that eliminates the need for a trial. You will learn about those types of motions in your civil procedure course. If a case is not ended on a pre-trial motion, and the parties do not voluntarily settle their dispute, then the case will go to trial.

The next step up the hierarchy of courts from the trial courts is occupied by the appellate courts. The party that has lost at the trial level, either by motion or by a decision after trial, may ask for review by a higher court. This review is known as an appeal. The party who appeals is usually called the appellant and the other party, the appellee. The appellate court determines whether the lower court committed any error significant enough to require that the decision be reversed or modified, or a new trial be granted.

Most states provide two levels of appellate courts. The first is an intermediate court of appeals. The second is the highest court of appeals and is usually known as the state's supreme court, although some states use other designations. Sometimes a jurisdiction's highest court is described as the court of last resort. Generally, the intermediate appellate court hears appeals from the trial courts, and the supreme court hears appeals from the intermediate courts of appeals. In many states with intermediate courts of appeals, however, the supreme court must hear appeals for certain types of issues directly from the trial courts. There is no further appeal of the decisions of the state court of last resort as to matters of state law.

Some states, although a decreasing number, have no intermediate court of appeals. In those states, trial court decisions will be reviewed directly by the court of last resort. In either system, except for certain types of cases, the court of last resort need not hear every case for which an appeal has been requested. Rather, the court has discretion to choose which cases to hear.

In many states, the intermediate appellate level consists of more than one court. For example, the state may be geographically divided into appellate districts, with each district having its own court of appeals. That district will contain several trial courts, the appeals from which all go to the one court of appeals for that district. Each court of appeals in that state is a co-equal, that is, each occupies the same rung on the court hierarchy as the others. The state will have only one court of last resort, however, and that court is superior to all other state courts.

An appeal is heard by more than one judge, and because the appeal should be heard by an odd number of judges, all appellate courts require three or more judges. The judges decide the case by voting and usually one of the judges from the majority writes the decision. A judge who disagrees with the majority may write his or her own opinion, called a dissenting opinion (or just a dissent). In addition, a judge who has voted with the majority as to the outcome of the case may write a separate opinion to express his or her differing views about certain aspects of the case. This decision is a concurring opinion ("concurring" because the judge concurred in the outcome of the case). The name of the judge who writes an opinion appears at the beginning of that opinion. Sometimes the opinion of the court does not bear the name of an author, but is designated a "per curiam" decision. This means a decision "by the court" and may be used for a shorter opinion on an issue about which there is general unanimity.

The procedure of an appeal differs from proceedings before a trial court. An appeal does not involve another trial before the panel of appellate judges. That is, the parties do not submit evidence or examine witnesses, and the court does not empanel a jury. Rather, the parties' lawyers argue to the appellate judges to persuade them that the court below did or did not commit an error or errors. Typically, this argument is made by means of written documents called appellate briefs that the attorneys submit to the court. The attorneys may also argue orally before the judges, although not all appeals involve oral argument. In addition, the appellate court reviews the record of the proceedings below.

Most state trial court decisions do not result in explanatory judicial opinions and so are not published, but the verdicts are recorded in the court files. Many, but not all, of the appellate decisions, however, are published in volumes called case reporters.

B.   The System of Courts: The Federal Courts

We have explained the vertical system of courts and its hierarchy of higher and lower courts in terms of a state court system. In this country, we also have a system of federal courts that parallels the state courts. The systems also intertwine at certain points. Federal courts are empowered by federal statutes and the constitution to hear certain types of cases, and are limited to those cases. There is federal jurisdiction for cases that involve questions of federal law, such as federal statutory or administrative agency matters, for cases in which the United States is a party, and for cases that involve citizens of different states. The latter is known as diversity jurisdiction. These cases involve matters of state law that a party chooses to litigate in federal court. The court, however, must apply the law of the state.

The trial courts within the federal system are called district courts. There is at least one United States District Court within each state. A district court's territorial jurisdiction is limited to the area of its district. A state with a small population and a low volume of litigation may have one district court and the entire state will comprise that district; for example, Rhode Island has one district court called the United States District Court for the District of Rhode Island. The volume of litigation in most states, however, requires more than one court in the state and thus the district is divided geographically. For example, Illinois is divided into three federal district courts: The United States District Court for the Northern District of Illinois, the United States District Court for the Southern District of Illinois, and the United States District Court for the Central District of Illinois.

Each intermediate appellate court in the federal system is called the United States Court of Appeals. For appellate court purposes, the United States is divided into thirteen circuits, so there are thirteen United States Courts of Appeals, eleven of which are identified by a number. Thus, the complete title of one court is The United States Court of Appeals for the First Circuit. The eleven numbered circuits are made up of a designated group of contiguous states (and also may include territories). The United States Court of Appeals for the Seventh Circuit, for example, is made up of the states of Illinois, Wisconsin, and Indiana. The other two courts of appeals, designated without numbers, are the United States Court of Appeals for the District of Columbia Circuit, and the United States Court of Appeals for the Federal Circuit.[1] Appeals from the district courts within the area that makes up a circuit go to the court of appeals for that circuit. A case that was litigated in the United States District Court for the Northern District of Illinois, for example, would be appealed to the United States Court of Appeals for the Seventh Circuit.

The highest court in the federal system is the Supreme Court of the United States. This court hears cases from all the United States Courts of Appeals and, for certain issues, from federal district courts and from the highest courts of the state systems. The Supreme Court must hear certain types of cases and has discretion to hear other requests.[2]

III. *The Development of the Law Through the Common Law Process*

A. *Precedent and Stare Decisis*

The position of a court within the structure determines how its decisions are treated as precedent. Some precedents have greater authoritative value than others. In order to describe the weight of precedent, we must first discuss some important characteristics of the American system of precedent and its companion doctrine, stare decisis. That term is a shortened form of the phrase stare decisis et non quieta movere, which means "to stand by precedents and not to disturb settled points." In this country, stare decisis means that a court should follow the common law precedents. But the doctrine also means that a court must follow only those precedents that are binding authority.

Precedent becomes "binding authority" on a court if the precedent case was decided by that court or a higher court in the same jurisdiction. If precedents exist that are binding authority on the particular point of law then those precedents constrain a judge to decide a pending case according to the rules laid down by the earlier decisions or to repudiate the decisions. Cases decided by courts that do not bind the court in which a dispute is litigated, such as a court of another state, are persuasive authority only.

---

1. The United States Court of Appeals for the Federal Circuit hears certain specialized cases such as international trade, patents, trademarks, and government contracts.

2. The United States also has courts of limited jurisdiction, that is, courts that are competent to hear only specialized subject matters, such as tax courts. You will rarely read cases from these courts in your first year of law school and we will not include them in this discussion.

When an authority is persuasive, the court deciding a dispute may take into account the decision in the precedent case, but it need not follow that decision.

When you search for case authorities to help you answer the issue before you, you will search first for precedents that are binding on the court where the dispute will be decided because these cases provide the constraints within which you must analyze the problem. If the issue has never been litigated in the jurisdiction of the dispute (sometimes called a "case of first impression"), you should familiarize yourself with how courts in other jurisdictions have analyzed the problem. Those precedents, even though not binding on the court, may nevertheless persuade the court to decide your case in a particular way.

Even if there is relevant case law in the jurisdiction in which your dispute will be litigated, you may still want to familiarize yourself with case law in other jurisdictions. This is especially so if those cases are factually similar, or well-reasoned, or particularly influential decisions.

B.   *Binding and Persuasive Authority*

Because the United States is composed of many jurisdictions, including each of the states and the federal court system, it is important to determine which precedents a court in each jurisdiction must follow besides its own prior decisions.

1.   *State Courts*

A state court must follow precedents from the higher courts in the state in matters of state law. Thus, a trial court must follow the precedents of the state's highest court. If the state court system includes a tier of intermediate appellate courts, as most state systems now do, the trial court must also follow the precedents of the intermediate courts of that state. Depending upon the rules of procedure of the particular state, the trial court may be bound only by the intermediate court that has the authority to review its decisions, or it may be bound by the decisions of any of that state's intermediate courts of appeals that are not in conflict with the court that reviews its decisions.

An intermediate appellate court also must follow the decisions of the state's highest court, but it is not bound by the decisions of the other intermediate courts because those courts are not superior to it, although these decisions usually will be very persuasive.

In addition, a state court is bound by the statutes of that state, as interpreted by its courts. Like case law, the statutes of one state do not bind the decisions of the courts in another state. If another state has a statute that is the same as, or has language similar to, the statute that controls your case, the interpretations given to that statute by the courts of the other state may be persuasive to the court of your state, but they are not binding on it. That is, the court may, but does not have to, follow the other state's interpretation of the statute. If your case is not governed by either a statute or a judicial precedent from your jurisdiction, then look to precedents in other states. Remember those precedents are persuasive only. The courts of a state are not required to follow precedents from other states, but they will take those decisions into account in reaching their own decisions.

2. Federal Courts

The decisions of the Supreme Court of the United States are binding on all courts in all jurisdictions for matters of constitutional and other federal law. The decisions of the courts of appeals do not bind each other, even in cases in which the appellate court has interpreted a federal statute. For matters of federal law a court of appeals is bound only by its own decisions and those of the Supreme Court. A federal district court (the trial court) is bound by its own decisions, the decisions of the court of appeals of the circuit in which the district court is located, and the decisions of the Supreme Court. The district court is not bound by the decisions of any other district court, nor by the decisions of other federal courts of appeals. Again, as always, a court will take account of the decisions of other courts.

Questions of state law, either common law or statutory, often come to the federal courts in lawsuits between parties from different states, known as "diversity suits." In diversity suits, the federal court must apply state law and thus follow the state courts' decisions on state substantive law questions. A detailed discussion of problems related to federalism, that is, the relationship between state courts and federal courts and state law and federal law, is beyond the scope of this introductory explanation.

3. Writing About Legal Authority

Because the common law and statutes of a jurisdiction are binding on future litigation within that jurisdiction, when you write an analysis of a legal problem you should always first identify and explain the binding law on the issue of the problem. Begin first with relevant statutes, if there are any, and the cases that interpret the statutes. Explain relevant case law first from the highest court of the jurisdiction and then other reported decisions from that jurisdiction's lower courts.

If there is controlling law from the jurisdiction of the problem, you should not begin by writing about the law in other jurisdictions or with explanations from other sources such as legal encyclopedias or a law dictionary.

Read the two examples below, which are introductory sentences to a discussion about a false imprisonment problem in the state of Kent. What is the difference between them? Which is the better way to begin the discussion? The underlined words are the names of the cases from which the quotes were taken. All are cases from the state of Kent.

> 1. In most states, the definition of false imprisonment requires that the defendant intend to confine the plaintiff within boundaries set by the defendant. Some other jurisdictions also require that the plaintiff be aware of the confinement.
>
> The definition of false imprisonment in Kent is "the intentional unlawful restraint of another against that person's will." Jones v. Smith.
>
> 2. In Kent, false imprisonment is "the intentional unlawful restraint of an individual's personal liberty or freedom of locomotion against that person's will." Orange v. Brass. A person need not use force to effect false imprisonment, but may restrain by words alone. Arnold v. Rocky. "Against that person's will" requires that the person be aware of the confinement. Jones v. Smith.

Example 1 incorrectly begins with the law of other states. Example 2 correctly begins by setting out the law of the jurisdiction of the problem.

C.   *Stare Decisis and Overruling Decisions*

The standard definition of stare decisis implies that following precedent is mandatory and that precedent is binding authority within a particular jurisdiction. Yet the doctrine as applied in the United States does not produce rigid adherence to prior decisions. Instead, a court has freedom to overrule its previous decisions and thus decide a case by a rule different from the one it had previously adopted.[3] A court overrules its earlier decision by explicitly or implicitly deciding in a later case that it will no longer follow that previous decision.

One reason that a court may overrule a case is that the earlier decision has become outdated because of changed conditions. Other reasons are that the existing rule has produced undesirable results, or that the prior decision was based on what is now recognized as poor reasoning. Sometimes a changed interpretation

---

3. A court will not overrule the decision of a higher court, although cases exist in which a lower court did not follow a rule from a controlling higher court because that rule was very old and out-of-date. If a judge of a lower court were to refuse to follow the decision of a higher court, that judge's decision would no doubt be appealed.

reflects a difference in the views of the present judges on the court as compared with those of the previous court.

When a court overrules a previous case, that change in the law has no effect on the parties to the litigation that produced the prior decision, or on other parties whose rights have been determined under that precedent. The results between those parties became final at the time of the last decision in those cases. Indeed, sometimes the change in the law will not affect the parties in the very case in which the court overrules the earlier decision and announces its changed rule. This result occurs when the court makes the new rule prospective, that is, applicable in future cases only.

Another means of overruling a judicial decision is by legislation. The legislature may change by statute a rule that came from a particular decision or a common law rule of long standing. This change in the law binds the courts within that jurisdiction.

A more literal interpretation of stare decisis would lead to a more rigid system of law than now exists in this country, or would require frequent appeal to legislative bodies to correct by statute undesirable or outdated judicial decisions.

D. *Holding and Dicta*

A judge may decide to be bound by a precedent and to reach the same outcome in a case before the court when the causes of action are the same, the issues presented to the court for decision are the same, and the material facts are similar enough so that the reasoning of the earlier case applies. Even if there is such a similar case from a court that is binding on the judge's decision, that judge is bound only by the holding of the previous decision. This is another limitation on the binding force of precedents in addition to the limitation that arises from a judge's ability to overrule an earlier decision.

The holding of a case is the court's decision on the issue or issues litigated. The holding has been defined as the judgment plus the material facts of the case.[4] Several other definitions of the holding exist.[5] But whichever definition is used, the holding of a case must include the court's decision as to the question that was actually before the court. That decision is a function of the important facts of the litigated case and the reasons that the court gave for deciding the issue as it did based on those facts.

---

4. See Glanville Williams, Learning the Law 72 (8th ed. 1969).

5. See those in Edgar Bodenheimer et al., An Introduction to the Anglo-American Legal System 85–88 (1980).

Thus, the holding is different from general rules of law and from definitions. If a court in a contracts case says "a contract requires an offer and an acceptance," that is a rule that has come from many years of contract litigation, but it is not necessarily a statement of the decision in the particular contract case before the court. In deciding a case, a court identifies the particular rule that controls the issue being litigated.[6] Then it analyzes whether the facts of the case satisfy the requirements of the rule.

Rules come from many places. In addition to rules like the contracts rule just mentioned that comes from common law adjudication, rules may come from enacted law like statutes and administrative agency regulations. Rules also come from private documents like contracts, deeds, and leases.

For example, a particular contracts case may require the court to decide the issue of whether the defendant offered to sell goods to the other party. If the defendant did, and the other party accepted, then the general contracts rule of offer and acceptance requires the court to decide that the parties had entered into a contract. The court may also define some of its terms. If the court says, "an offer must manifest definite terms," the court is defining an offer, one in keeping with a long line of litigation, but is not giving its holding. The holding might be "the defendant's letter describing his goods and saying, 'I am considering asking 23¢ a pound,' was not an offer." This statement decides the question before the court in terms of the facts of the case. A holding that includes reasons would add, "because the defendant did not convey a fixed purpose and definite terms." The court is deciding that those facts did not fulfill the definition of an offer.

Not everyone will agree to any one formulation of a holding of a case. Indeed, there is no one correct way to formulate a holding. Formulating the holding can be a difficult task, and one that you will refine throughout your legal career. One source of difficulty is to determine which facts are essential to the decision. For example, in a false imprisonment case, the plaintiff may have been kept in a corner of a room by a black and white bulldog that growled and showed its teeth. Your statement of the holding would not include the dog's color because these facts would not have been necessary to the decision that the plaintiff was imprisoned. The breed of the dog may have been important, however, if its ferocity led the plaintiff to believe that the dog would bite if he moved out of the corner.

---

6. Sometimes the court first will have to decide what rule is the appropri-   ate one to apply to the case.

Another source of difficulty is how to describe the facts, that is, whether to describe them specifically as they were in the case or to describe them more generally. For example, a more general descriptive category for the growling bulldog is as a dog, or more generally as a household pet that made noises at the plaintiff. These terms are broader because they include more types of animals and behavior than do the more narrow categories "dog" and "growled." When you describe the facts too broadly, however, your description will include facts that may raise considerations that are different from those that the court took into account when it made its decision. For example, the description "household pet" includes a white rabbit. And although a rabbit may cause fear in a person who hates rodents, the issue of whether that person's fear is reasonable raises questions about phobia that are different from considerations about a dog's ferocity.

Frequently, common sense will take you a long way in deciding how to determine a holding. Common sense will tell you that the fact that the defendant's dog was black and white should not be important to the decision in the false imprisonment example, but that the breed of dog could be important because of its size or ferocity. Common sense will also tell you that "household pet" is probably too broad a description for false imprisonment purposes because the term includes white rabbits and goldfish. Beyond that, you will acquire the added experience and judgment that will come with being a law student and lawyer.

If you are recording the holding for objective purposes, such as in a case brief for class (see Chapter Two) or just to describe a case, then you may want to use more specific facts rather than broad categories. You may say, for example, that the defendant's letter said "I am considering asking 23¢ a pound." Often, however, you will describe a holding more generally. When you use cases as precedents for evaluating legal problems, or when you want to persuade a court that it is bound in a particular way by a precedent's holding, you may need to describe the facts more generally in order for them to encompass your client's situation. Courts have a good deal of freedom to decide what a precedent stands for, that is, what its holding was, and an important skill of the attorneys appearing before those courts is to formulate a holding in a way that is favorable to the attorney's case. As you will see, this is an important skill for your writing assignments, and one we will emphasize through the book.

Sometimes the court itself will announce its holding. You should not always accept that court's formulation, however. Make sure that the judge has not stated the holding too broadly or too narrowly and that the principle the judge has articulated was actually required for the resolution of that case. For example, if the court deciding the hypothetical false imprisonment problem had written, "We therefore hold that the defendant's dog's growling at the plaintiff was sufficient to constitute false imprisonment," that court would have stated its holding too broadly. A literal application of this statement of the holding would permit liability if a person's dog growled at someone on the street. The statement must be read in conjunction with the facts of the case that the plaintiff was kept immobilized in the corner of a room.

The binding nature of a statute is somewhat different from that of a case because the entire statute is binding authority, and all the statutory requirements must be satisfied. This is not always as simple as it sounds, however. As indicated earlier, there may be case law interpreting the statute that tells you how to interpret the statutory language. The statute may contain internal contradictions that a court may have reconciled, for example, or a court may have decided that the legislature meant an "or" instead of an "and" in part of the statute. These interpretations affect the manner in which the statutory language is binding. In this situation, the statute and the case law interpreting its language are binding.

There are many statements in a judicial decision that are not part of the holding and are not binding on later courts. These statements are called dicta. For example, the statement "but if the defendant's cat had trapped the plaintiff in the corner of the room, the defendant would not be liable," would not be part of the holding of the false imprisonment case we have hypothesized. This is so because the plaintiff was not trapped by a cat, and so that is not a material fact of the case. The court was illustrating the extent of its decision. Therefore, dicta about a cat in an earlier case concerning a dog would not bind a judge who had to decide a later case in which a defendant's hissing cat had kept a plaintiff in a corner of a room.

Statements that are dicta are not always unimportant, however. Sometimes the dicta in a case become more important in later years than the holding of the case. Dicta is analogous to persuasive authority in that the statements may be persuasive to a later judge, but the judge is not bound to follow them. If the court later had to decide a false imprisonment case involving a cat, the court's dictum in the earlier case would be very important to the later court's decision.

When you write about judicial decisions, you will have to describe the action that the court took by using a verb. For example, you will be saying that the court said something, or held something, or found something. You must be careful to use the correct verb. It would be incorrect to say "the trial court held that the defendant's car was traveling at ninety miles per hour" if this sentence states a finding of fact by a court. In that case, the sentence should be written, "the trial court found that the defendant's car was traveling at ninety miles per hour."

A sentence correctly describing the holding of this case might be written, "the court held that the defendant was guilty of reckless driving for driving ninety miles per hour in a forty-mile-per-hour zone."

To describe a court's dicta, you could use a verb such as "said," or "stated," or "explained." For example, the hypothetical dicta used in the false imprisonment example, "but if the defendant's cat had trapped the plaintiff in the corner of the room, the defendant would not be liable," should not be preceded by the inaccurate statement "the court held," but by a statement such as "the court said," or "the court hypothesized," or "the court limited its decision."

Read the case decision below. Then choose the best statement of the holding from the five choices.

In Re Gaunt

Terse, J.

John Gaunt was having coffee with his nephew Felix. John told Felix that he was giving him a gift of his gold watch, which he kept in a safe deposit box in his bank. He said he would get the watch for Felix the next time he went to the bank. John died that night, without going to the bank. Felix has demanded the watch be delivered over to him as his gift. The administrator of John's estate is keeping the watch as part of the estate.

Felix's demand must be refused. A completed gift requires first that the donor intend to give the gift, second, delivery of the item of gift, and third, acceptance by the donee. Only then does the intended donee have title to the item. John probably did intend that Felix have the watch. The watch had been John's grandfather's and Felix is the next male heir in that family. We can assume that Felix would have accepted the watch. Sentiment aside, it is a valuable piece of jewelry. John, however, never sent the watch to Felix, and Felix never had possession of the watch. If he had given him the key to the safe deposit box, that may have been a constructive delivery, effective to create a gift. As it is, without delivery, John made only an unenforceable promise. A court will not enforce an uncompleted gift.

Which is the best statement of the holding in In re Gaunt?

1. The court held that delivery of a key to a safe deposit box is a delivery of the item kept in the box because it is a constructive delivery.

2. The court held that there are three requirements for a valid gift: intent to give, delivery, and acceptance.

3.   The court held that a decedent's jewelry remains part of his estate at death if he has not given it away during his life.

4.   The court held that a decedent had not made an effective gift of personal property during his life where he made an oral promise of the gift but had not delivered possession of the item to the intended donee (the person receiving the gift).

5.   A court will not enforce an incomplete promise of a gift.

Sentence four is the best statement of the holding.

1.   Sentence 1 is a statement of dicta in In re Gaunt. John did not give the safe deposit key to Felix. The court used that fact as a hypothetical of what may have been a delivery for purposes of satisfying the requirements of a gift.

2.   Sentence 2 is the general rule of the three requirements for a gift which had been formulated before this case was litigated. Not all three were disputed in this case.

3.   Sentence 3 sounds as if it could be the holding, but it is really a general rule of property law that tells the result of the decision in this case.

4.   Sentence 4 is the holding that decides the question in this case of whether John Gaunt had given away the property during his lifetime if he had not delivered the watch to his nephew. If he had not, then John still owned the watch and the result described in Sentence Three occurs.

5.   Sentence 5 is a reason for the decision in the case.

The holding could be made broader or narrower by describing the intended item of gift differently. The gift could be described as

1.   property (which includes real and personal property)

2.   jewelry

3.   a gold watch

4.   a family heirloom

Which of these items is the broadest? Which is the most specific? Could you describe the parties involved as an uncle and nephew instead of a decedent and a donee?

Exercise 1–A

Read the following decision in the case Sosa v. Lowery.

The plaintiff John Sosa rented an apartment from Tim Lowery. Lowery required a security deposit of one month's rent. The lease provides that Lowery must return the security deposit within 30 days of the expiration of the lease, but could deduct for damage to the property beyond reasonable wear. Lowery deducted $400 from Sosa's deposit to replace the living room carpet, which, during Sosa's tenancy, suffered several cigarette burns. Sosa claims that the burns are the result of reasonable wear. We disagree. Cigarette burns result from a careless act rather than from accumulated use. Frayed spots from walking on the rug would be reasonable wear. Lowery properly deducted the $400.

    1.   What is the rule for when a landlord may deduct from the tenant's security deposit? Where does this rule come from?

    2.   The court used this rule to decide the question before it, that is, to reach its holding. What is the court's holding regarding Sosa's deposit?

    3.   What is the court's dicta about what type of use might be reasonable wear of the carpet?

Exercise 1–B

Beta v. Adam

Terse, J.

    Beta has sued Adam, the owner of a restaurant, for false imprisonment. Adam believed that Beta was leaving without paying her bill. Beta in fact had left the money on her table. Adam told Beta that she could not leave until someone verified that she had paid. Adam took Beta's pocketbook in which Beta had her keys, money, credit cards, and her checkbook. The restaurant was very busy and understaffed. Beta stayed with Adam for twenty minutes until Adam found an employee to see if Beta had left the money on the table.

    Although Adam never physically prevented Beta from leaving, and Beta could have walked out of the restaurant at any time, Adam is liable to Beta for falsely imprisoning her. A person falsely imprisons another by unlawfully confining her within fixed boundaries, if he acts intending to do so. Adam confined Beta in the restaurant by telling her she could not leave and by taking her purse. Confinement may be effected by duress, even duress that is not the product of threatening behavior. Beta could not leave the restaurant because she believed that she could have lost her pocketbook with its valuable contents if she did so. Thus, she was unlawfully confined. She acted reasonably by remaining in the restaurant until she recovered her possessions.

———

    Which is the broadest formulation of the holding? The most narrow?

    1.   The defendant falsely imprisoned the plaintiff by duress when he took an item from the plaintiff in order to have her remain on the premises.

    2.   The owner of a restaurant unlawfully confined his customer when he told her she could not leave and took her pocketbook and its valuable contents away for twenty minutes until he could verify her payment of her bill.

    3.   The defendant falsely imprisoned the plaintiff by means of duress although he did not use physical force when he took an item of value belonging to plaintiff in order to have her remain on the premises.

E.   *The Weight of Authority*

Besides the judgments involved in determining the holding and the dicta of a case, and therefore which part of that case is binding, you must make other judgments in using precedents. For example, where there are many relevant cases, you will have to decide which are most important to your problem and will have the most weight with the court deciding your own case. Several factors can determine the weight of an authority.

The precedents that are binding authority are of course the most important. Always begin your analysis with the cases on the same issue from the jurisdiction of your problem. Start with the cases from the highest court. In addition, the decisions of the courts within the jurisdiction, even if not binding (such as decisions of another court of appeals) generally will be the most persuasive authority to a court. As to the weight of authority of cases from all jurisdictions, the similarity of the facts between the precedent and your problem is important. The more similar the specific facts between the cases, the greater weight the precedent will have for your own problem.

Another important factor is the level of the court that decided the previous case. A case decided by a state's supreme court will be more authoritative than one decided by a lower state court.

An opinion written by a particular judge may be important because of the excellent reputation of the judge. In addition, decisions from a particular court in a particular era may carry extra weight because of the membership of the court during those years. Exemplary are the New York Court of Appeals (the highest court in New York) during the time when Benjamin Cardozo was a member of the court, and the California Supreme Court during the service of Justice Roger Traynor.

A case decided by a unanimous court or a nearly unanimous court may be more persuasive as a precedent than one in which the court was closely divided. And statements from concurring or dissenting opinions will usually not carry as much weight as statements from majority decisions, although exceptions exist.

Another factor to consider in evaluating the weight of a precedent is the year of the decision. If a case is old and the decision reflects policies or social conditions that are no longer as important as they once were, then the precedent will have little weight even if the facts of the case are very similar to your problem. If, however, the decision is based on reasoning that is still valid, the age of the case may not be important.

The courts in some states may favor decisions from states that are geographically close or have similar social or economic conditions that relate to the litigation. In addition, a decision that interprets a statute may be persuasive to another court in a case that involves a similar statute.

Very important is the depth and quality of the prior treatment of the relevant issue. A case in which the issue received the full attention of the previous court and was fully and articulately discussed will be more important than one in which the question received cursory attention. And well reasoned decisions with careful explanations will probably already have achieved deserved respect in the field.

No matter how many of these factors are present, however, a case from another jurisdiction is not binding on a court, and does not foreclose the decision of that issue.

IV. *Statutes and the Relationship Between Case Law and Statutes*

The preceding material in this introduction reflects the historic importance of case law to our legal system. You should be aware, however, that enacted law, especially statutory law, forms a greater part of the body of legal authority in our country than ever before. In fact, enacted law should be the first source in which you research a legal problem. In this section we will discuss enacted law in the form of statutory law and its characteristics and relationship with case law.

Statutes are enacted by legislative bodies that are constitutionally empowered to exercise the legislative function within a jurisdiction. The federal legislative body is the United States Congress. Each state has its own legislature and also has municipal and, perhaps, county forms of legislatures. In addition, state and federal administrative bodies may have limited legislative functions in that they are empowered to enact regulations concerning the subject matter of their administration. These regulations provide another form of enforceable law.

Enacted law, like case law, falls along a vertical hierarchy.[7] At the top of that hierarchy is the Constitution of the United States. Next are both federal statutes and treaties. Federal statutes, when enacted within the powers conferred by the Constitution, take precedence over statutes of other jurisdictions. Then come federal executive orders and administrative regulations, state constitutions (a constitution, however, is the highest authority within a state as long as it does not conflict with federal law), state statutes, state administrative regulations, and municipal enactments.

---

7. This hierarchy is taken from E. Allan Farnsworth, An Introduction to the Legal System of the United States 55–57 (1983).

A jurisdiction's constitution and its statutes are the highest authority within that jurisdiction, and the courts are bound by them. A legislature may change the common law by passing legislation that changes the common law rule. That change then supersedes the old rule. A court cannot in turn overrule that legislative enactment and say it will not follow it (although it can invalidate it on the ground of unconstitutionality). The legislature may also create new causes of action that were not available in the common law but which result from the legislation, such as worker's compensation laws and employment discrimination laws. A legislature may also enact a common law rule into statute; for example, many criminal statutes have codified what were previously common law crimes. Then the case law interpreting that common law rule may still be valid.

Because a jurisdiction's constitution is more authoritative than its statutes, the legislature may act only within its constitutional powers. Although a court cannot overrule legislation, that is, it cannot decide it will not follow the law imposed by the particular statute, a court may review a statute's validity. Legislation may be challenged in court on the ground that the legislature exceeded its constitutional powers. A reviewing court may then decide a statute is unconstitutional and is invalid.

Courts are constantly deciding statutory issues because statutes must be enforced and frequently must be enforced by litigation. A person's challenge to the constitutionality of a statute, for example, will usually arise during litigation in which the government attempts to enforce the statute against that person.

More often, however, a court must decide not the validity of the statute, but how to apply the statute. As a necessary step in this litigation, the court may have to interpret the meaning of the statutory language in order to apply and enforce it in a specific situation. Cases that interpret and apply statutes are case law and become precedents in that jurisdiction. But they are not common law because the legal rule that is being enforced originates with the legislature. Common law rules originate with courts.

By its nature, legislation is cast in general terms, that is, in broad categories, because it is law written to affect future conduct, rather than law written to decide a specific case. General legislative language must then be applied to individuals and to the particular controversy being litigated. Statutory language may also be vague; for example, businesses cannot act in "unreasonable restraint of trade." Thus, a good portion of a court's work is deciding questions that involve the interpretation of statutes. The legislature could still have the last word, however. If it does not agree with the court's statutory interpretation, it can amend the statute. In reality, however, a legislature rarely gives attention to the course of judicial interpretation of a statute, and even more rarely reacts to judicial interpretation by amending the statute.

When you are writing about a problem that is controlled by a statute of that jurisdiction, you should always include the exact statutory terms at issue and an explanation of those terms. The explanation usually should be at the beginning of your written analysis. Do not start writing about the problem as if the reader knows the statute's terms unless you have been instructed to do so.

Exercise 1–C

What is the difference between the two examples below? Which is the better introduction to a discussion of a statute?

1. Under the Wills Act of Kent, a person's will must be "in writing, signed at the end by the person, and attested by two competent witnesses". Smith fulfilled all these requirements when he executed his will, even though he signed the will with his initials only.

2. Smith's will is valid because he fulfilled the three requirements under Kent law. He fulfilled the second requirement even though he used only his initials to sign the will.

V. *Citation*

One consequence of relying on legal authorities in your written work is that you will have to provide citations to those authorities. In legal writing, you use citations for many purposes: You demonstrate that your assertions are supported by other authority; you supply the bibliographic information a reader needs if she wants to look up that source herself; and you attribute borrowed words or ideas to their sources, thus avoiding plagiarism.

A. *Citations to Provide Authority and Bibliography*

Citation is important to all types of writing, but you probably will use more citations in your legal writing than you are accustomed to using. Because of the doctrine of precedent, lawyers analyzing a common law action constantly rely on case law to prove that the legal theory offered as the governing rule of law is valid and has been applied in similar situations. In a statutory action, lawyers quote and thus cite the statute that supplies the governing rule of law. They also use cases to help interpret what the statute means. Thus, a legal argument requires identifying the sources of the governing principles of law as well as analyzing what they mean. The writer must cite to those sources each time they are mentioned or relied upon. Lawyers also use secondary authority, such as books and periodical articles, as support for their legal analysis. These sources also must be cited.

Legal citations tell the reader many things. As mentioned above, the presence of a citation tells the reader that the preceding text is based upon information from another source and is not original with the writer. A citation to a case also tells the reader that there is legal authority for the previous statement and where the reader can find that authority. A citation provides information that helps the reader evaluate the weight of the precedent. For example, the citation tells which court decided the case.

Most law schools and lawyers use a specialized citation form found in a book called A Uniform System of Citation, known as the Bluebook. Some lawyers adhere strictly to the requirements of the Bluebook; others make changes to suit their own practices or to comply with the rules of a particular court or agency. Most law schools require that students use Bluebook citation form in their writing.

Besides learning correct citation form, you should also become familiar with certain conventions of legal citation. In legal memoranda and briefs, which are typical law school writing assignments, you will put citations in the text right after the material for which they provide authority, rather than in footnotes. You should use citations to authority for direct quotations, for text that paraphrases the authority, and for text that is based on information in the authority, although not quoting or paraphrasing from it. Notice the citations in the following paragraph. See Appendix B for an explanation of the citation form.

> The law of battery in this state is adopted from the Restatement of Torts. Lion v. Tiger, 500 N.W.2d 10 (N.D. 1954). A person may be liable for battery if the person directly or indirectly causes a "harmful contact" with another's person, and the person intends to cause the contact. Id. at 12; Restatement (Second) of Torts § 13(b) (1977). Under this definition, Smith will not be liable because she did not act with the required intent.

The first citation, to the case of Lion v. Tiger, supplies the authority for the statement about the state's law of battery. It tells you that the court that decided Lion v. Tiger is the court that adopted the Restatement definition. The second citation provides the source of the definitions. These sources are the case already cited (Id. means that the citation is the same as the previous one) and the Restatement of Torts.

B. *Citations to Provide Attribution and Avoid Plagiarism*

Citation to sources is essential in legal writing not only to show authority for your reasoning, but to avoid plagiarism. Most of you are familiar with university honor codes prohibiting plagiarism. These concerns are especially important in law school because of the need to document precedents and supporting arguments. As indicated in Part A, citing to authority is essential in legal work. Indeed, although the Rules of Professional Conduct have no specific reference forbidding plagiarism, the Rules forbid dishonest, fraudulent, or deceitful conduct.[8]

Law schools use different definitions of plagiarism, and it is important that you become familiar with the one used by your school. In general, however, plagiarism occurs when you use another's ideas or words and pass them off as your own, that is, when you do not cite to the source. One important difference among definitions is whether plagiarism includes within its definition the element of intentional conduct. Some schools do not require the writer to have acted intentionally; careless research and notetaking that result in failure to attribute work is enough to sustain a charge. Some schools define the word plagiarism to include the requirement of intentional conduct, although some schools' prohibitions require "intentional plagiarism."

The basic rules of attribution require that you cite (i.e., attribute) the source of direct quotations and paraphrases. If you change some words of the text, you are paraphrasing and must cite. However, if the language remains very close to the original, you should consider quoting directly instead and citing. See Appendix A for the mechanics of quotations. If you use a line of analysis from a source but change all or a lot of words, you are still paraphrasing and must cite the source. To avoid unintentional nonattribution, be careful when you do your research and take notes. Include quotation marks and check the accuracy of the material you copy when you prepare your research notes and write drafts of your paper. See the suggestions in Chapter 12.

An important difference from most undergraduate definitions of plagiarism involves information that is "common knowledge," rather than ideas unique to an author. You did not have to attribute common knowledge in your undergraduate work.[9] Law school practice is to require citation for legal "common knowledge" as well as for unique ideas or language. For example, it is commonly known that a contract requires an offer and an acceptance, but were you to write that statement in a legal memorandum, you would cite one or more authorities. This is not really a matter of plagiarism, however, but of providing legal support for your proposition of law. Your writing professor will not likely report you to

---

8. Model Rules of Professional Conduct Rule 8.4.

9. See, e.g., H. Ramsey Fowler, The Little, Brown Handbook 482 (1980);

Sylvan Barnet and Marcia Stubbs, Practical Guide to Writing 231 (1975).

the school for violation of an honor code for failure to cite. She will probably note that the statement needs a citation to show its acceptability as a general rule of law.

You need not, however, turn your writing into a bibliography. If a book or an article leads you to cases and statutes and you yourself read those materials and discuss their facts or language in your written work, cite to the cases and statutes. You do not also have to cite the source that led you to the cases and statutes, even if that source describes their facts and language. You do cite the source for any of its ideas or theories that you use.[10]

When you become a lawyer in practice, you will find that attitudes toward plagiarism are different from those in an academic setting. In practice, lawyers cite to cases and statutes and to other materials to add precedential value to their arguments and so that their readers can find the sources. Lawyers also provide citations for quotations. However, lawyers typically use others' materials without attribution. One co-defendant's brief may include ideas and even verbatim material from another defendant's work without attribution. Indeed, judges often use material directly from a party's brief without attribution. The attorneys never accuse the judge of plagiarism; instead they feel complimented.

This does not mean that after you graduate from law school you will never be concerned with plagiarism again. Several years ago, a United States Senator's bid for his party's nomination for president was damaged in large part because he plagiarized a speech. It also became known that he had plagiarized on a law school paper written for a first-year legal writing course. The Senator explained, "I was wrong, but I was not malevolent in any way. I didn't know how to write a legal memorandum." [11] We hope, first, that you will never attempt to pass on others' work as your own, malevolently or not, and that after using this book, you will know how to write a legal memorandum, and other documents as well.

Exercise 1–D

Where do citations belong in the following paragraphs? Why?

1. The test for determining whether a plaintiff is entitled to attorney's fees involves four factors: whether the litigation provided a public benefit, whether the plaintiff gained financially from the litigation, whether the plaintiff had a personal interest in the materials sought, and

---

10. In more advanced writing, you should cite the source that has led you to other sources if the first source uses the other source in an unusual way and you use the other source in the same way. That type of citation is usually not necessary in memoranda and briefs, but may be.

11. Jon Margolis, Biden on quote furor: "I've done some dumb things", Chi. Trib., Sept. 18, 1987, at 3.

whether the government unreasonably withheld the materials. The factors usually have equal weight. However, if the government acted particularly unreasonably, the last criterion may be most important.

2. The Kent statute permits an unwitnessed will. This type of will is known as a holographic will. To be valid, a holographic will must be entirely written and dated by the testator. The courts have interpreted "dated" to mean month, day, and year.

————

Once you become accustomed to using legal citations, you will find that they can contribute to your legal writing style by keeping unnecessary information out of your text. For example, one common writing weakness of lawyers is to explain textually the information that is available in the citation, instead of using the citation to provide that information. Notice the differences in these three sentences.

1. In an old 1922 Massachusetts case, the Supreme Judicial Court held that the plaintiff must prove fraud in order to invalidate an antenuptial contract. Wellington v. Rugg, 243 Mass. 30, 136 N.E. 831 (1922).

2. In Massachusetts, a plaintiff must prove fraud in order to invalidate an antenuptial contract. Wellington v. Rugg, 243 Mass. 30, 136 N.E. 831 (1922).

3. Massachusetts is the only state that requires a plaintiff to prove fraud in order to invalidate an antenuptial contract, a rule that dates back to 1922. See Wellington v. Rugg, 243 Mass. 30, 136 N.E. 831 (1922).

The writer of sentence 1 has supplied two facts in the text that are provided in the citation, that the case was decided in 1922 and that the highest court in Massachusetts decided it. (If the citation does not specifically include the name of the court within the parenthesis and the court is not otherwise identifiable by the citation, the case was decided by the highest court of the state). Unless the writer had a particular reason to include those facts in the text, they are unnecessary, and the sentence is better written as in sentence 2. If the writer wanted to emphasize that the rule is an old one, sentence 3 provides more specific emphasis than sentence 1.

Although the examples may seem strange to you now, citation will become an important and familiar aspect of your writing about legal materials.

————

Exercise 1–E

1. You are doing research for a state law problem. Your research uncovers some cases similar to the case you are working on, which you are appealing to the intermediate appellate court of your state. These cases are from

    a. Another intermediate appellate court of the state

    b. A diversity suit in a federal district court in the state, applying the state's law on that issue

    c. The federal court of appeals for the circuit of your state in an appeal from a district court from a diversity suit applying the law of a different state

    d. A state trial court's judgment entered in a decision that was not published but which you know about

    e. The highest court of the state

What weight would you assign to these authorities? Evaluate how important each is as a precedent.

2. Because the domiciles of the parties permit, you have decided to litigate an Illinois property law question in the United States District Court for the Northern District of Illinois. In which sources of primary law would you do your research? Why? Evaluate these in terms of efficient use of your research time.

    a. United States Supreme Court cases

    b. Cases from the Illinois Supreme Court and intermediate appellate courts

    c. Cases from the United States Court of Appeals for the Seventh Circuit

    d. Cases from the other two United States district courts in Illinois

    e. Property law cases from other states

3. You are doing research for a state law problem about the liability of owners of recreational land to people who use those premises. There are two questions involved, whether the land your client owns is recreational land, and if so, whether your client did not fulfill his legal duties.

How relevant are the following authorities to your analysis of this problem?

    a. A newspaper article about accidents in parks

    b. A statute of the state that limits the liability of owners of recreational land

    c. The regulations of a state agency requiring safety features on recreational land that is open to the public

    d. A brochure printed by the owner of the recreational land

    e. Case law from the state's intermediate appellate courts interpreting the statutory term "recreational land"

f.   Case law from the highest court of another state that has an almost identical statute. These cases interpret the term "recreational land"

g.   A case from your state's appellate court that interprets the term "recreational area" in a different state statute about licensing for privately owned recreational areas

h.   The notes of the drafters of a uniform act about liability of owners of recreational areas, an act that your state has adopted

Chapter Two

Analyzing Legal Authority: Case Law

I. Introduction

In your first year of law school, you will be analyzing a case in two contexts. First, your professors may suggest that you "brief" (summarize) each case assigned for class. This type of brief is a written synopsis of the important points of the case. For this purpose, you consider each case in isolation, just trying to understand that particular case. In the second context, however, your concern is the impact that a previous case may have as a precedent for your own problem case, often a hypothetical fact pattern. There, you analyze the relationship between cases. Your success in both of these contexts will depend to some extent on how carefully you identify the significant parts of a judicial decision.

II. Briefing a Case: Finding the Parts of a Judicial Decision

You brief a case to help you understand its significance. There are different methods of briefing a case and the following format is meant to be only an example. Your professors may suggest a format to you, or you may devise your own system by identifying what helps you in your classes. Whatever method you use, read through the case once to get a general idea of what it is about before you start your brief.

The typical components of a case brief are explained below.

A. *Facts*

The fact section describes the events between the parties that led to the litigation and tells how the case came before the court that is now deciding it. Include those facts that are relevant to the issue the court must decide and to the reasons for its decision. You will not know which facts are relevant until you know what the issue or issues are. For example, if the issue is whether a minor falsely represented himself as an adult for the purpose of fraudulently inducing a car salesman to contract with him, relevant facts could include the minor's written and oral statements about his age, the minor's height and weight, and his manner of dress. These facts are relevant because they can help prove how the minor represented his age. However, the minor's eye color, the weather on the day the contract was signed, and the payment schedule in the contract would not be relevant to the issue of false representation.

The fact section should also include the relevant background information for the case, for example, who the plaintiff and defendant are, the basis for the plaintiff's suit, and the relief the plaintiff is seeking. Also include the procedural history, although you may put the procedural facts under a separate heading. Procedural facts should include any dispositive motions, such as a motion to dismiss for failure to state a claim. If the case is an appeal, state the lower court's decision, the grounds for that decision, and the party who appealed.

Often you will have to understand the procedural posture of a case in order to understand the court's decision. For example, if the appeal is from a successful motion to dismiss, then the appellate court will decide whether the plaintiff's pleadings stated a claim and whether the plaintiff should be permitted to continue the lawsuit. The appellate court will not decide who should win the lawsuit if it continues.

B. *Issue(s)*

The issue is the question that the court must decide to resolve the dispute between the parties in the case before it. To find the issue, you have to identify the rule of law that governs the dispute and ask how it should apply to those facts. You usually write the issue for your case brief as a question that combines the rule of law with the material facts of the case, that is, those facts that raise the dispute. Although we use the word "issue" in the singular, there can be and often is more than one issue in a case.

C. *Holding(s)*

The holding, as was explained in Chapter One, is the court's decision on the question that was actually before it. The court may make a number of legal statements, but if they do not relate to the question actually before it, they are dicta. The holding provides the answer to the question asked in the issue statement. If there is more than one issue, there may be more than one holding.

D. *Reasoning*

The court's reasoning explains and supports the court's decision. The court may explain why it applied the controlling rule as it did. Sometimes the issue in the case may involve the validity of the rule itself, and the court may have looked at two lines of authority and decided the case was more like one group of cases than another. Or the court may have decided that the policy justifying a rule was no longer valid, or may have concluded that the facts of this particular case required an exception to the rule. In any event, it is important to isolate the court's reasoning from the facts and the holding of the case.

E. *Policy*

Underlying legal decisions are the social policies or goals that the decision-maker wishes to further. When a court explicitly refers to those policies in a case, include that information in your case brief, since it will probably help you understand the court's decision. If the court does not explain the policies on which it based its decision, then try to identify them for yourself.

———

Read the following case. It is followed by a sample brief.

Paugh v. City of Seattle[1]

'The plaintiff is the father of two boys who died at ages six and eight when they drowned in a pond on city-owned land. Mr. Paugh sued the city for the deaths of his sons. The city successfully moved for summary judgment and this appeal followed.

The pond is about 100 feet wide at its widest point. It is shallow at the edges, and slopes gently to six feet at its deepest point. Its bottom is muddy and the water is murky. It is located in unimproved bushy terrain about 300 yards from the housing development where the plaintiff lives, and is accessible by a dirt road. The sheriff described it as an ordinary pond, just like the many others in the area. The pond is popular with nearby residents for

---

1. This example is based on and uses language from Ochampaugh v. City of Seattle, 588 P.2d 1351 (Wash. 1979).

fishing and swimming and the plaintiff himself had taken his sons there four or five times to fish. He had told them to go only with him and to stay out of the water. There are no witnesses to the drownings.

The city had not taken any measures against trespassers. There are no warning signs around the pond, and the evidence is that a fence all around would be prohibitive in cost and probably not possible without leveling the trees and the uneven ground. The city is now contemplating draining the pond and estimates the cost at $25,000.

The general rule is that a landowner owes no duty to trespassers except to not willfully cause their injury. Mail v. Smith Lumber Co., 287 P.2d 877 (Wash. 1955). There is an exception, however, for child trespassers, the attractive nuisance doctrine, which has been adopted in this state. Id. This doctrine reflects public concern for the welfare and safety of children. The requirements for this doctrine to apply are

(1) The condition must be dangerous in itself, that is, it must be likely to, or probably will, result in injury to those attracted by it;

(2) The condition must be attractive and enticing to young children;

(3) The children, because of their youth, must be incapable of understanding the danger involved;

(4) The condition must have been left unguarded at a place where children go, or where they could reasonably be expected to go; and

(5) It must have been reasonably feasible either to prevent access or to render the condition innocuous without destroying its utility.

Shock v. Ringling, 105 P.2d 838 (Wash. 1940).

In this case, we agree with the court below that the pond is not an attractive nuisance because it is not dangerous in itself. Thus summary judgment for the defendant is appropriate. Admittedly, ponds, like many bodies of water, are attractive to children, who love to fish and swim. Moreover, when ponds are located near people's homes, children could reasonably be expected to visit them. Nevertheless, although drowning is always a danger, it is a commonly known danger, and six- and eight-year olds are capable of understanding it. In addition, all the evidence is that the number of drownings a year is slight compared to the recreational use made of similar bodies of water. The evidence is that this sad event was the first drowning in this pond.

This state has miles of shoreline and numerous natural creeks, ponds, lakes, and rivers. These bodies of water, standing or flowing, are natural to all states and countries that are not deserts. Compared to the heavy use of these bodies of water, the number of drownings is so small that we must conclude that they are not dangerous. Moreover, it would be an undue burden to require owners to fence them or drain them in order to escape liability for the occasional drowning that occurs, and this duty would shift the responsibility of child care to the landowners from the parents. In addition, the environment, especially wildlife, would suffer and people would not be able to enjoy the recreational facilities. It is a policy of this state to encourage owners of recreational land to allow the public to use the land. Towards this end, the state's Recreational Land Act limits the land owner's liability to the public allowed to use the land for recreational purposes.

If, however, there were conditions that caused particular risk, like a concealed danger, our decision might be different. The trial court here correctly decided that the pond is not an attractive nuisance. Affirmed.

Sample Brief of Paugh v. City of Seattle

A. Facts

The plaintiff sued the city for the deaths of his six- and eight-year-old sons, who drowned in a pond on city-owned land. The trial court granted summary judgment for the city and plaintiff appealed. The pond is described as ordinary, shallow at the edges, gently sloping, and murky. It is about 300 yards from a housing development. The pond is accessible by a dirt road and is used by the community for fishing and swimming. The plaintiff, who lives in the adjacent community, had taken his sons there to fish 4 or 5 times and warned them not to go alone. The plaintiff's sons were the first drownings in the pond.

The court affirmed the trial court summary judgment for the city.

B. Issue

Is an ordinary pond located near residential property an attractive nuisance so that the property owner is liable for the drowning deaths of trespassing children?

C. Holding

The pond is not an attractive nuisance because it is not dangerous in itself.

D. Reasoning

The general rule in Washington is that a landowner (the city) owes no duty to a trespasser except not to willfully cause injury. There is an exception in favor of child trespassers for injury from an "attractive nuisance." If the landowner maintains an attractive nuisance on its land, it is liable for injuries caused by that condition. The state imposes 5 requirements:

1. The condition must be dangerous in itself, that is must be likely to or probably will, result in injury to those attracted by it;

2. The condition must be attractive and enticing to young children;

3. The children, because of their youth, must be incapable of understanding the danger involved;

4. The condition must have been left unguarded at a place where children go, or where they could reasonably be expected to go; and

5. It must have been reasonably feasible either to prevent access or to render the condition innocuous, without destroying its utility.

The court does not provide a detailed application of these elements, but seems to decide mainly on the ground that the plaintiff could not prove that the pond was dangerous in itself, the first element.

The statistics (not supplied) are that in relation to the many bodies of water in the state, there are few drownings. That is, a pond is not dangerous because its use is not likely to result in injury. These were the first drownings in this pond.

The court also mentions that it was not feasible to prevent access by fencing off the pond because of the terrain. The city may drain it for $25,000, which will destroy its utility for recreation and for the environment.

Finally, the plaintiff had warned his children about the danger of drowning and, at six and eight years, they were old enough to understand that warning. Thus, although ponds are attractive to children (second element) and although this pond was unguarded (fourth element), three of the five elements were not proven.

E. Policy

The purpose of the attractive nuisance doctrine is to protect the welfare and safety of children, who are unprotected under the general rule governing a landowner's liability to trespassers. However, the condition on the landowner's premises must be a dangerous one, that is, likely to cause injury. Ponds and other bodies of water are so common and widely used without injury that they are not dangerous.

Other considerations here are first that ponds are environmentally important; if the water is drained or fenced off, the water is neither available to wildlife, nor available for recreation for others. Moreover, this duty would be unduly burdensome on landowners, and would shift responsibility to protect children to them from the children's parents. The court will do that only if the condition is dangerous. Finally, the state by statute encourages landowners to allow the public to use recreational lands, not to fence them off or make them unusable.

———

After you identify these important parts of a court's opinion, you should spend some time evaluating what you are reading. This is the best preparation for your classes and for your writing. For example, think about the legal rule that the jurisdiction has adopted and that the court applies. Does the attractive nuisance rule (now often called the child trespasser rule) properly balance the policy of not unduly burdening the landowner with the policy of protecting minor children? Does it place the burden of protection on the correct party (among the landowner, the child, and the parents)? If the rule is based on the fact that we cannot expect children to be careful, in what circumstances should others be more careful for them? Also evaluate the court's application of the rule to the facts of the case and the logic of the court's opinion. Is an ordinary pond a dangerous agency? Should the city have drained the pond if its agents knew that children fished and swam there?

To prepare for class, think of how changes in the facts might change the court's decision.

III.   Using the Parts of a Judicial Decision

A.   Reasoning by Analogy

Under the doctrine of precedent, judges decide cases according to principles laid down in earlier similar cases, that is, the precedents. Lawyers (and law students) who are working on a legal problem must find those earlier cases and analyze the impact that those cases will have on the decision in their own problem. Thus, lawyers are always comparing cases by drawing analogies and making distinctions between them. By comparing their problem to decided cases, lawyers decide how the decisions of previous cases apply to the new problem. If the cases resemble each other in important ways, such as by their relevant facts, then they are analogous and should also resemble each other in their outcome.

Cases are analogous if they are alike in ways that are important to their outcome and if the differences between them are not enough to destroy that analogy.

The first precedents to look for are those that are binding authority on the court in which the case will be litigated. If that court, or a higher court in that jurisdiction, decided a case or cases on the issue before the present court, those cases become the precedents to which the present controversy will be compared, and those are the cases that the court will want to know about first. If there are no cases in that jurisdiction on that exact issue, cases on similar issues will be important if the court's reasoning and the underlying policies also apply to the facts of the present case.

If you decide, however, that the cases are different and that the decision in the precedent case should not control the outcome of your problem, you are "distinguishing" the cases. If you distinguish a prior case, you avoid its impact on your case. You may distinguish a case by establishing that the differences in the facts require that the court apply a different rule. Or you may decide that the same rule should be applied, but that the facts in your case require a different outcome.

Be careful not to distinguish cases too easily. Each case will have some differences from other cases. The distinguishing facts you select must be significant.

By comparing and contrasting your problem with the precedents, you will be able to show how well the rules of those cases fit your case. This in turn should enable you to predict the probable outcome of your own case. When you reason by analogy, though, you can only offer probable proof for your conclusions, not certainty. Your task is to assess all the possible applications of the relevant rules and to offer the best prediction of the outcome.

Although analogizing and distinguishing may sound like mechanical exercises, legal analysis is rarely analysis by rote. Comparing the similarities and contrasting the differences between cases is often a creative process and the ability to do this is one of the hallmarks of a skillful lawyer. You will become more sophisticated in this process as you gain experience.

B. *Applying Precedent*

1. *Issues*

To determine whether a case is controlling as precedent, the issue in the precedent should be essentially the same as the one in the new problem. However, sometimes you can define the issue in the precedent more broadly in order to reveal its significance for your problem case by describing the key facts more broadly. For example, if your attractive nuisance case involved a river, you would describe the dangerous condition in <u>Paugh</u> as a body of water, rather than as a pond.

The most relevant cases are those in which the issue is the same. However, sometimes you will not find a case in the jurisdiction with the same issue, but you will find a case or cases on similar issues. You may use those cases to draw analogies, but it is important that the reasoning and policies supporting those decisions are relevant to the current issue.

For example, a federal district court (a trial court) sitting in Pennsylvania had to determine whether it had diversity jurisdiction[2] in a personal injury suit (personal injury suits are typically litigated in state court under state law). The plaintiff, Ms. Last, sued a residential school for the developmentally disabled located in Pennsylvania. Ms. Last sued on behalf of her legally incompetent adult son who was injured when he was a resident of the school. Ms. Last was a domiciliary of New York. She argued that her son's domicile was also New York and not Pennsylvania, the defendant's domicile. (If Pennsylvania, the parties' domiciles would not be diverse.) A child's domicile is deemed to be that of the parents and an incompetent adult is deemed unable to form the intent to change domicile from that of the parents. The school's burden was to prove that the son had changed his domicile to Pennsylvania as a resident of the school.

The district court relied on an earlier case from its circuit, <u>Juvelis v. Snider</u>. <u>Juvelis</u> also involved the domicile of an incompetent adult, but the issue was different from that in <u>Last</u>. <u>Juvelis</u> raised the issue of domicile not to determine jurisdiction, but to determine whether the plaintiff qualified for benefits under a federal statute. Nevertheless, the court in <u>Last</u> used the rule developed in <u>Juvelis</u> to determine whether an adult incompetent had changed domicile from that of his parents. The court said there were no reasons why the difference in the issue (domicile for benefits under a statute and domicile for purposes of diversity jurisdiction) should change the inquiry into whether an incompetent adult changed domicile.

2. *Facts*

After you find cases on the same issue, or on issues that are sufficiently analogous, you compare the facts of those cases. When you brief a case, you concentrate on how the facts of that case are relevant to the issue in the case and the reasons for the court's holding. However, when you are considering the relationship between a precedent and your problem case, you view the facts

---

2. See Chapter One p. 9.

somewhat differently. Now, you also try to determine if the facts in the two cases are basically analogous or distinguishable.

The facts of one case need not be identical to the facts of another case for the cases to be analogous. Indeed, the facts will never be identical. A case can be a precedent for your problem, however, when the facts can be classified similarly. For example, the relative bargaining strength of a party to a contract is one factor the courts will consider in deciding whether a contract is unconscionable (so unfair as to be unenforceable). Thus, an analogy could be drawn between a case in which the owner of a small gas station dealing with EXXON claimed a contract was unconscionable and a previous case in which a consumer dealing with General Motors successfully claimed a contract was unconscionable. Although the station owner is a business person, both the station owner and the consumer are vulnerable buyers in a weak bargaining position relative to the defendant. On the other hand, if these plaintiffs were described at a lower level of abstraction, as a consumer and a commercial enterprise, then the case about the consumer contract might not apply to the gas station. Similarly, a rule for automobiles may apply equally to snowmobiles or even to mopeds if all are classified as motorized vehicles.

Another example involves the element of the tort of intentional infliction of emotional distress requiring that the defendant's conduct be outrageous. Suppose you were asked to analyze whether Olympia Department Store's conduct was outrageous if it made daily phone calls to a customer over a three-month period in attempting to collect payment for a debt. In the jurisdiction of this problem, there may be no cases about the issue of outrageous conduct in which a store made phone calls to a customer. But there may be a case in which a department store sent daily letters to a consumer over a three-month period in attempting to collect a debt. In that case, the court had decided that the conduct was not outrageous on the grounds that a creditor could use reasonable, if annoying, methods to collect a debt, and that the letters fell within reasonable limits.

You may decide that the two cases resemble each other because three months of daily telephone calls are like three months of daily letters. They both fit within a more general category of persistent communications from an outside source. You may, therefore, conclude that the cases are analogous and should resemble each other in result also. Under this reasoning, Olympia's conduct would not be characterized as outrageous.

On the other hand, you might argue that the cases are distinguishable because phone calls are a much more intrusive kind of communication than letters. Or you could distinguish the case if the basic facts were different, if, for example, the customer never actually owed the debt. Under this circumstance, the precedent would be distinguishable since the court's reasoning was premised on the existence of the underlying debt.

In applying precedent, as when briefing a case, you must first determine which facts are relevant to the issue that a court must decide and to the reasons for its decision.

Exercise 2–A

False imprisonment litigation often involves employment situations. The plaintiff's employer wants to question the plaintiff about some aspect of the plaintiff's job performance, and often does so in the employer's office with the door closed. The plaintiff claims that he was involuntarily confined, one of the elements of false imprisonment.

Suppose that Mr. Brown claims he was involuntarily confined in his employer's office for five hours. During this time, he was questioned about his methods of billing his time, and then fired. The door to the room was closed but not locked, and Brown was sometimes left alone in the room, where there was a telephone. He never tried to leave.

The defendant relied on Towls v. McGann, in which the court held that the plaintiff was not involuntarily confined when she was called to her employer's office and questioned about money shortages for three hours. Though the door had been locked, she was not prevented from leaving the room when she became upset and wanted to leave. Before that time, she had not been left alone in the room.

Brown points to differences in the facts that may be relevant to change the outcome. Evaluate his success.

    a.   The previous plaintiff had walked out of the room, but Brown had not.

    b.   The previous defendant had locked the door.

    c.   Brown had been left alone in the office where there was a telephone.

    d.   Brown was in the defendant's office for five hours; the previous plaintiff was in the defendant's office for three hours.

Exercise 2–B

1. Analogize or distinguish the following facts and those in the Paugh case (page 30) and decide if the factual difference changes the outcome of whether the defendant maintained an attractive nuisance. Explain why.

    a.   The plaintiff's sons drowned in a river on the city's property that ran near their home (not a pond).

    b.   They drowned in an artificial body of water, a pond created by filling in a gravel pit dug originally for commercial purposes, but now used by the neighborhood for recreation.

    c.   They drowned in a lake when they were swept over a small waterfall that was not visible until they were in the lake.

d. They drowned in an old, open, abandoned well located in an undeveloped lot in a subdivision. A path went by the well, over which children chased each other.

Exercise 2–C

Read the following case. Identify the issue in the case and make a list of the facts that are relevant to a court's decision on that issue.

In Re Estate of Winter

The heirs of Robert Winter seek to void a contract for the sale of land Mr. Winter made three weeks before his death. They allege that Winter was mentally incompetent to make a contract at that time. In this state, a contract may be voidable on grounds of mental incompetence if, because of a person's mental illness, he was unable to reasonably understand the nature and consequences of the transaction in question. Since Winter was incompetent under this standard, the contract he made for the sale of land is voidable and will not be enforced.

Mr. Winter had a stroke in 1992. He suffered from a vascular disease which resulted in partial amputation of his foot. As a result of this amputation, he became unable to continue to operate his farm himself. In 1993, Mr. Winter's wife died. Since he was unable to take care of himself, he moved in with one of his daughters, Sandra Bright. Another one of his daughters testified that from that point on, Winter seemed to lose interest in everything. He stopped managing his own affairs. Mrs. Bright handled all of his finances. She balanced his checkbook, deposited his social security checks, and managed the farm.

As time went on, Mr. Winter became easily confused and lethargic, spending much of his time sitting in a chair, staring out of the window. A family friend testified that when Winter described the farm, he sometimes said it was 200 acres and sometimes said it was 2,000 acres. (The farm is 2,000 acres.) Dr. Crabtree, Winter's longtime physician, said that in his opinion, from March 1994 until he died, Winter was totally incompetent to handle any of his own affairs, including taking care of his own body.

In May, 1994, while Mrs. Bright was out for the afternoon, Herbert Spencer paid Winter a visit. Mr. Spencer offered to buy the farm from Winter. Winter agreed and signed a contract for the sale of the farm to Spencer for what a local real estate agent said was far below its actual value. In addition, Winter did not reserve a right of way for himself and his family, creating a problem of access from the road to their other piece of property. Mr. Winter died three weeks after the sale of the farm.

The evidence suggests that at the time of the contract, Winter was unable to understand the nature and consequences of the transaction of the sale of land. He did not appear to have a clear idea of the number of acres in question. The price he received was below the fair market value of the property. He failed to reserve an important right of access for himself. His physician testified that he was incompetent to handle his own affairs. His daughter had, in fact, been taking care of his personal and business affairs before the sale took place, as Winter had lost interest in these matters. Under these circumstances, I hold that Winter was unable to understand the nature and consequences of the transaction, and, therefore, the contract for the sale of land is voidable.

Exercise 2–D

Using Winter as the only precedent, identify the issue and make a list of the relevant facts in the following problem case:

Richard Bower wants to void the contract his uncle Joseph Black made for the purchase of a car shortly before Mr. Black's death on the grounds that Black was mentally incompetent at the time he made the contract. Excerpts from the following depositions, taken in the case, will provide the factual background.

DEPOSITION: DR. MARTIN DREW

(By Ms. Jones, attorney for plaintiff, Richard Bower)

Q: Was Joseph Black a patient of yours?

A: Yes, he was my patient for six years until he died on April 10, 1996, of cerebral apoplexy, what you would call a stroke.

Q: What had you been treating Mr. Black for?

A: Mr. Black had cerebral arteriosclerosis. He suffered from a hardening and shrinkage of the arteries, which reduced the amount of blood that gets to the brain.

Q: What are the symptoms of cerebral arteriosclerosis?

A: Well, since this disease develops gradually, the symptoms develop gradually as well, becoming more and more intense. The most common early signs are memory loss, irritability, anger, confusion, and forgetfulness. In Mr. Black's case, the symptoms were becoming more and more severe. You see, as the amount of blood that got to his brain diminished because the arteries continued to shrink, the amount of his confusion and forgetfulness increased. He also became more stubborn as his memory became more uncertain.

Q: When did you last see Mr. Black?

A: I last saw him on January 31, 1996.

Q: How would you describe his condition?

A: I would say that his arteriosclerosis had become quite severe—not enough that he needed to be hospitalized, but enough so that he needed home nursing care. He would talk to me and then he would forget what he said and tell me the same things again and again. And he thought I was my father, who had been his physician 30 years ago. I asked him to tell me his name and where he lived. He remembered his name, but couldn't tell me where he lived.

Q: Doctor, in your opinion, was Mr. Black able to understand ordinary business transactions?

A: At this point in his life, I would say he would not.

DEPOSITION: RICHARD BOWER

(By Ms. Jones)

Q: Mr. Bower, what is your relationship to Joseph Black?

A: He was my uncle, my mother's brother.

Q: Did you accompany your uncle to Miller Motors on February 12, 1996?

A: Yes I did. He came next door, where I live, and asked me to go with him to Miller Motors, which is around the corner. I couldn't understand why, but I humored him and went with him. When we got there, a salesman came out and said, "Your car is ready, Mr. Black." My uncle had bought a Buick the day before and he wanted me to drive him home in it. I couldn't believe it because he hasn't driven in three years. I don't think he even has a valid license anymore. I asked him how he could do such a thing, because he only had $15,000 left to live on, except for Social Security, and the car cost around $14,000. He wouldn't even be able to make his mortgage payments and eat on what he had left. When I reminded him of that he said it was not a problem because he had only borrowed the car and it only cost a few hundred dollars. Then he said that he could give the car back in a few days. When I told him again that he had spent $14,000 on a car, he started yelling at me and making a terrible scene so I drove him home and put it in the garage beside his house. He never went near it. I started it once a week so that the engine wouldn't rot.

Q: What did you do after your uncle died?

A: I called Miller Motors and said I was my uncle's executor and that I wanted to give the car back. I said I would be willing to pay them for the two months' use of the car, even though we never even drove it. But they refused.

DEPOSITION: ROSE BROWN

(By Ms. Jones)

Q: Ms. Brown, were you employed by Joseph Black?

A: I took care of Mr. Black, though Mr. Bower actually paid me out of a joint checking account he had with Mr. Black.

Q: How long did you take care of Mr. Black?

A: I took care of him from February 3, 1996, until he died on April 10.

Q: What did your work consist of?

A: I did the shopping, cooked, cleaned, helped Mr. Black get dressed if he needed help.

Q: How did Mr. Black occupy his time?

A: He sat around, sometimes watched TV. He didn't read the paper anymore. I had to watch him very carefully because he would wander off, like he did the day he bought the car. But you had to be very careful how you talked to him, because he would get angry and use terrible language. He hated to hear that he had forgotten something and would just get more stubborn.

Exercise 2–E

Compare the facts in the Winter case and in the problem case to determine whether the cases are analogous or distinguishable. Under what general classifications would you compare the facts?

———

3. *Holding*

When you are considering the relationship between a precedent and your problem case, you might formulate a court's holding differently from the way you would if you were simply briefing the case. The holding of a mandatory precedent becomes a rule to apply in the next similar case. Nonetheless, as explained in Chapter One, you have some flexibility in formulating the holding in that you can choose how many facts to include as essential, and how to characterize those facts. If you describe the facts exactly as they were in the case, then the holding you state will be very narrow. This is sometimes called limiting a case to its facts, because the case cannot be used as a precedent for many other cases. If, however, you describe the facts more broadly, then the holding will apply to a larger number of future cases whose facts come within that broader description. The holding in the Paugh case, for example, might be stated in terms of the particular facts of that case, in terms of bodies of water in general, or, most broadly, in terms of any outdoor recreational facility. The holding in the Last diversity case could be stated in terms of the plaintiff in particular, in terms of incompetent adults, or more broadly in terms of any category of persons incapable of choosing a domicile.

The way you formulate the holding may depend on the result you want the court to reach in applying that case, the purpose of the document you are writing, and its intended audience. For example, if you are writing to a court and the decision in the precedent case is one that is favorable to your client, then you will try to formulate the holding broadly enough to encompass the facts of your client's case. Or, if the decision in the precedent is unfavorable, you will try to state the holding more narrowly so that it will not encompass the facts of your client's case. If your client is a parent whose child drowned in an artificial body of water then you might want to limit Paugh's holding to natural bodies of water. Of course, there are limits to formulating the holding broadly or narrowly. If you manipulate the facts to violate the sense of the case, you will be engaging in unethical behavior and faulty analysis.

Exercise 2–F

Reread Beta v. Adam in Chapter One, page 17. Suppose you represented the plaintiff in each of the following three false imprisonment cases.

How would you formulate the holding of Beta v. Adam to be most advantageous to your client?

Case 1:

Same facts as in the Beta case in Chapter One, but your client's pocketbook contains only a handkerchief, a comb, and makeup. Your client stays five minutes and leaves.

Which of these two statements would you use as the holding in Beta v. Adam?

a. In Beta v. Adam, the owner of a restaurant confined the plaintiff when he took her pocketbook and told her she could not leave the restaurant until he determined that she had paid her bill.

or

b. In Beta v. Adam, the owner of a restaurant confined the plaintiff when he took property of value from her in order to detain the plaintiff and detained her for twenty minutes.

Case 2:

Same facts as above but the restaurant owner tells your client that he does not believe that she left the money to pay her bill, and asks your client to wait while he gets someone to see if she left the money on her table. The owner does not take anything from her, but asks the restaurant hostess to keep an eye on your client. Your client waits for twenty minutes.

Which of these two statements would you use as the holding in Beta v. Adam?

a. In Beta v. Adam, the defendant confined the plaintiff by duress even though he did not engage in threatening behavior.

or

b. In Beta v. Adam, the defendant confined the plaintiff by duress by implied threats that if she left the premises she would lose her property.

Case 3:

Your client drove her car into a gas station for gas. An employee of the station who thought she was wanted for bank robbery drained the water from her car's radiator and called the police. Your client had to wait fifteen minutes for a police officer to come and identify her as not being the felon.

Which of these two statements would you use as the holding in Beta v. Adam?

a. In Beta v. Adam, the owner of a restaurant confined the plaintiff when he took her pocketbook, told her not to leave the restaurant, and took twenty minutes to determine whether she paid her bill.

or

b.   In <u>Beta v. Adam</u>, the defendant confined the plaintiff by duress when, although he did not threaten the plaintiff to remain, the plaintiff would have had to leave behind valuable property if she left the defendant's premises.

4.   *Reasoning*

The court's reasoning in the precedent case must apply equally well to the facts in your problem case. This would certainly happen when the facts are quite similar, as they would be if you were applying <u>Last</u>, a case dealing with the domicile of an incompetent offspring for diversity purposes, to another case involving the same issue and similar facts. However, the court's reasoning may also apply in a different context. The <u>Last</u> court found the reasoning of <u>Juvelis</u> applicable to the issue of domicile to establish jurisdiction even though that case involved establishing domicile to receive federal benefits.

5.   *Policy*

The court in the precedent may be basing its decision on an articulated (or unarticulated) policy. If the same policy would apply in your problem case, the result should be the same.

For example, suppose a state court has a well-established rule upholding releases in litigation involving race car drivers and bicycle racers. A release is a document in which the signing party (the participant in the race) agrees to release the operators of the activity from liability if their negligence injures the signing party. One policy behind that rule is the public interest in participating in and watching competitive racing. A rule invalidating the release would decrease the number of racing events because the operators would fear potential liability from injuries. Another reason for the rule is that the participants in the races are usually experienced racers who can calculate their risks.

This rule upholding releases for competitive racing is invoked by the operator of a cave exploration tour for tourists who requires participants to sign a release. The tour operator is sued by an inexperienced participant who was hurt in the cave because of the guide's negligence.

In this situation, a court may not enforce the release. Neither policy for upholding releases in competitive racing would apply: cave exploration is not a competitive spectator sport that involves the public, and the participants in these cave tours are not experienced spelunkers.

———

In general, then, under the principles of precedent and stare decisis, if your problem case is similar to the precedent, the result should be the same. When your problem case is different from the precedent in a significant way, the precedent should not be controlling. In making these comparisons, you will find a number of possibilities:

   —Your problem case and a precedent dealing with the same issue and with similar facts—the result should be the same (the case is analogous);

   —Your problem case and a precedent with the same issue but materially different facts—the result should be different (the case is distinguishable);

   —Your problem case and a precedent dealing with a completely different issue—there should be no impact;

   —Your problem case and a precedent with the same issue but based on a policy which is no longer persuasive or has not been accepted by another court—the result should be different.

Exercise 2–G

Consider whether a court would decide that the plaintiff in the following case could succeed in the described law suit. Use these five questions as a guide.

   a.   Is the issue the same or analogous to the issue in <u>Paugh</u>?

   b.   Are the relevant facts analogous or distinguishable?

   c.   Would the court's reasoning in <u>Paugh</u> lead to the same or a different result?

   d.   What impact, if any, would the policy behind the decision in <u>Paugh</u> have on this case?

   e.   In light of the answers to these questions, is it likely that the holding in <u>Paugh</u> will be followed?

———

From: Supervising Attorney, practicing in Tacoma, Washington

To: Law Associate

Date: October 10, 1998

Re: <u>Adam Dale Case</u>

I met last week with Susan and Robert Dale, Adam Dale's parents. They have retained this law firm to represent their son, Adam, in a lawsuit against the Tacoma Gardens Hotel. They will be bringing the case as guardians for their son who is six years old. I have attached a transcribed copy of my interview with them and notes of a phone conversation with the Hotel's lawyer. Please analyze whether Adam's lawsuit is likely to be successful.

Conversation with Susan and Robert Dale, October 5, 1998

Q. I just need to ask some very basic questions so please bear with me. Adam lives with you?

A. Yes, we all live in a house on 395 Thistle Drive in Tacoma. That's about a quarter of a mile away from the Tacoma Gardens Hotel.

Q. Now, as I understand it, Adam was injured when he tried to get inside the Hotel grounds.

A. Yes. He and some friends were playing outside the Hotel. They decided to scale the hedge and get inside the grounds.

Q. How is he doing? You said over the phone that his kneecap was seriously injured.

A. Adam was in a lot of pain, but he's feeling somewhat better now. But the doctors are saying that he will have a permanent disability.

Q. I'm very sorry to hear that. The poor kid. You must be very upset too.

A. We are, it's been awful.

Q. Could you tell me about the hedge?

A. Sure. The Hotel is surrounded by a very thick hedge, which is about six feet high. The hedge is very carefully trimmed. We were told that to facilitate the trimming and allow the hedge to grow straighter, the Hotel has installed thin poles of wood in the hedge at intervals of about one foot. The poles are colored so that they are virtually indistinguishable from the wood part of the actual hedge.

Q. You said that Adam was trying to get inside the Hotel grounds. Is that something that has happened before?

A. Not with Adam. But young children are constantly trying to get inside the Hotel grounds. Usually, the Hotel security force chases them away. The Hotel is very protective of the grounds because they are really beautiful and, we have heard, an important selling point to Hotel guests. We've seen the Hotel brochures and other advertising and the gardens inside are prominently featured.

Q. What happened on September 2, 1998?

A. Well, as we said, Adam was playing outside the Hotel grounds with some friends and they decided to try to scale the hedge. At first they thought that the Hotel security guards would chase them away, but nobody was there. The guards who were supposed to be on duty had gone inside the Hotel. Adam's two friends lifted him up on their shoulders and Adam jumped onto the top of the hedge. However, when he landed, he fell through the hedge, banging his right knee severely on one of the wooden poles that was in the hedge.

Q. And you said his kneecap was severely injured.

A. Yes. Not only was he hurt, but he won't ever regain the full use of his right leg. He is particularly upset because over the summer he had become actively involved in a gymnastics class in his elementary school gymnasium.

Summary of Phone Conversation with Charles Kelly, representative of the
    Tacoma Gardens Hotel, October 5, 1998

I spoke with Mr. Kelly today. He said that for $20,000 the Hotel could
have placed a fence around the hedge which would have prevented children
from trying to climb it. However, the Hotel felt this would be too expensive
and decided not to do it. He also said that his six-year old wouldn't be
wandering around with a bunch of other six-year olds getting into trouble,
and that if the parents had been doing their job, the injury would never
have happened.

———

Exercise 2–H

1. Read Smith v. Allen. Then write an answer applying Smith to the
problem in the Peterson case which follows Smith. How would a court
decide the issue of David Peterson, Sr.'s liability? Peterson would be
litigated in the same jurisdiction.

Smith v. Allen

Judith Smith alleges that James Allen owned a golf club which he left
lying on the ground in the backyard of his home. On April 12, 1995, his son
the co-defendant Jimmy Allen, age eleven years, was playing in the yard
with the plaintiff, Judith Smith, age nine years. Jimmy picked up the golf
club and proceeded to swing at a stone lying on the ground. In swinging
the golf club, Jimmy caused the club to strike the plaintiff about the jaw
and chin.

Smith alleges that Jimmy Allen was negligent since he failed to warn
her of his intention to swing the club and he swung the club when he knew
she was in a position of danger.

Smith also alleges that James Allen was negligent and that he is liable
for his son's actions. She alleges that although Allen knew the golf club
was on the ground in his backyard and that his child would play with it,
and that although he knew or "should have known" that the negligent use
of the golf club by children would cause injury to a child, he neglected to
remove the golf club from the backyard or to caution Jimmy against the
use of the golf club.

James Allen demurred, challenging the sufficiency of the complaint to
state a cause of action or to support a judgment against him.

The demurrer is sustained. A person has a duty to protect others
against unreasonable risks. A person who breaches this duty is negligent
and liable for injuries resulting from his negligence. No person, however,
can be expected to guard against harm from events which are not reasonably to be anticipated at all, or are so unlikely to occur that the risk,
although recognizable, would commonly be disregarded. A golf club is not
so obviously and intrinsically dangerous that it is negligence to leave it

lying on the ground in the yard. Thus, the father cannot be held liable on the allegations of this complaint.[3]

Aarons v. Peterson

David Peterson stored a tool chest on the floor in the basement of his suburban home. In it he kept three screwdrivers, two wrenches, a hammer and several boxes of nails. Last Tuesday afternoon, his eleven-year-old son, David, Jr., and a nine-year-old neighbor, Phil Aarons, were playing knock hockey in the basement. Their exertions were so strenuous they knocked the side rail loose from the baseboard. Phil, who was losing, was glad. He was tired of playing knock hockey and wanted to play with David's trains. David, however, wanted to continue the match. Spotting his father's tool chest lying on the floor in the corner, he decided to fix the board. He took a hammer and a large nail out of the chest and, while Phil was playing with the train set, quietly set about repairing the damage. At first the work went well. He placed the nail at the joint and hit it firmly on the head. It pierced the wood and held firm. Then disaster struck. On the next hammer blow, the nail flew out from the wood and struck Phil in the face, chipping his two front teeth, bloodying his nose, and gashing his cheek.

In an action for negligence, is David's <u>father</u> liable for the injuries to Phil?

2.   Read the following case summary of <u>Green v. Kermit</u>. This case was decided by a court in the same jurisdiction as <u>Smith v. Allen</u>. Does this decision change your analysis of <u>Smith</u> and <u>Aarons v. Peterson</u>?

Green v. Kermit

The plaintiff Lucy Green is suing for injuries she received on the Muni Golf course when she was struck in the knee by the defendant, John Kermit, who is eleven-years-old. Green was walking over a foot bridge about 150 yards from the eighth tee, when Kermit, who was playing in a foursome with his parents and sister, teed off the eighth tee without yelling "fore." The plaintiff was in clear view of the tee at the time Kermit teed off and hit her with the golf ball. The issue is the standard of care that the eleven-year-old defendant should be held to when he played golf.

A golfer should be required to use reasonable care. But whether John should be held to use the reasonable care of a reasonably prudent child or of a reasonably prudent adult depends on whether he used a dangerous instrument. Minors will be held to an adult standard of care if they used a dangerous instrument. A golf ball is a dangerous missile that can cause injury if it hits someone during its flight. Indeed, in some ways, hitting a golf ball is more dangerous than firing a gun or throwing a stone, because a person can have more control over the direction of a gunshot or a stone than over a golf ball.

Golf has become a very popular sport, and as golf courses have become more crowded, more accidents have occurred, especially accidents involving

---

3.   This example is based on and uses language from <u>Lubitz v. Wells</u>, 113 A.2d   147 (Conn. Super. Ct. 1955).

golf balls. Yet golf is an adult activity involving dangerous instruments. Since a child is, for practical purposes, on the course as an adult, he should be held to an adult standard. John could see the plaintiff, he did not yell fore, and he teed off with the plaintiff in sight. The judgment for the plaintiff is affirmed.

IV. *Synthesizing Cases*

You will rarely work on a problem for which there is only one case precedent. More likely, your research for a problem will turn up many cases relevant to the problem. In order to use the principles that those cases offer to resolve your problem, you must relate the cases to each other, that is, synthesize them. In that way, you can understand the applicable area of law and then use the synthesis to analyze your problem.

The courts will frequently have done some synthesis for you. Often, when you read cases, you will see definitions of a claim for relief, like the definition of battery by a court or in the Restatement of Torts. In Paugh, for example, the five elements of the attractive nuisance rule had already been formulated. Usually these definitions or rules have evolved as courts over the years have put together the decisions of many related cases. The judges who have formulated those definitions have worked inductively, that is, from the specific to the general. They have analyzed the outcome of each case and then combined those separate cases into a coherent rule. The rule is expressed at a level of abstraction that encompasses the particular holdings of all of the individual cases.

When you analyze a legal problem, such as one of your class assignments, you will do further synthesis of your own. Synthesizing is the step between your research and your writing. You do research by reading one case at a time. If in your writing you merely report each case, one at a time, then you have compiled a list of case briefs, but you have not analyzed a topic.

To analyze and write about a topic, you will engage in one of three types of case synthesis, or in a combination of these three types:

1) Grouping cases according to the rule they follow;

2) Defining the elements of an evolving claim or defense;

3) Identifying the factors (the general categories of facts) that courts use to determine how a particular cause of action can be proven.

The first type, which is perhaps the least difficult, essentially requires you to group cases. For example, if you read several cases from different states on the issue of whether to adopt the attractive nuisance rule, you will find that several states have adopted the rule, but that some have not.

In writing about your research, you would group the cases applying the rule, rather than list the cases one by one. You would work deductively, starting with the general proposition that unites the cases.

> The majority of the states have adopted the traditional rule that a landowner is liable for injuries to trespassing children if the landowner maintains an attractive nuisance on the property. See [cases applying this rule]. The reasons for this rule are that [explanation of reasons].

> A number of states, however, have rejected the rule and instead apply the traditional rule of a landowner's duty to trespassers. See [cases rejecting the rule and explanation of these cases].

This writer has identified two lines of decisions and described the basic characteristic of each in clear topic sentences. The two categories in this example were based on a legal rule that was explicit in the cases themselves.

A second, more difficult, type of synthesis is required when courts have not yet clearly or fully articulated the elements of a cause of action. This type of synthesis involves putting together a general principle of law that is evolving in the case law.

Suppose you are analyzing some cases on the question of whether parents are immune from tort suits brought by their children. In this situation you know part of the rule, that parents may be immune from suit. Read the four case summaries to synthesize the rest of the rule. All suits are in the jurisdiction where the age of majority is 18. (Full citations are omitted.)

Case 1:

Jack Abbott sued his father Joseph for negligently pouring hot liquids in the Abbott kitchen so that he burned Jack in the process. Jack is twelve years old. Held: Mr. Abbott is immune from suit. Abbott v. Abbott (1985).

Case 2:

James White sued his father Walter for battery, an intentional tort. Walter knocked James's baseball cap off his head because James struck out in the last inning of a Little League game. James is ten years old. Held: Mr. White is not immune from suit. White v. White (1990).

Case 3:

Joan Brown sued her father Matt for assault, an intentional tort, for brandishing a tennis racket at her after she lost her serve in the final set of the women's 25 and under local tennis tournament. Joan is twenty-four years old and lives at home. Held: Mr. Brown is not immune from suit. Brown v. Brown (1991).

Case 4:

George Black sued his father Paul for negligently burning him in Mr. Black's kitchen by handing him a large hot pot. George is a twenty-four-year-old business man and is married. Held: Paul Black is not immune from suit. Black v. Black (1992).

These cases involve two requirements of whether the parent is immune from suit. To analyze the topic, you should identify them and consider how they determine immunity. Look at the facts that evidently have led the courts to decide that the parent is immune, and at the facts that evidently have led the courts to decide that the parent is not immune.

In each case, the court mentions the child's age. In Case 1, the child was a minor and the parent was immune from suit. In Case 2, however, the child was a minor but the parent was not immune from suit. In seeking an explanation for this difference, you notice that a second requirement is involved, the type of tort, whether an intentional tort or negligence. In Case 4, the parent was negligent, but the child was not a minor and the parent was not immune from the suit. These two requirements now become part of the rule: 1) the child must be a minor, and 2) the child must sue for negligence.

You may find a chart helpful.

Number of Case	Type of Tort	Age of child	Result
1	negligence	12	immunity
2	intentional	10	no immunity
3	intentional	24	no immunity
4	negligence	24	no immunity

When you can characterize these facts in a way that explains the results, that is, the full parental immunity rule, you are ready to begin writing. You would then start your written discussion of these cases with a topic sentence that identifies the parental immunity rule.

Notice the difference between the following two discussions of the immunity topic. Which is more effective and why?

 1. Parents are immune from a tort suits brought by their children if the suit is for negligence and the child is a minor. First, parents are not immune from suits for intentional torts. The Kent Supreme Court has held that parents are not immune from their child's suit for assault, Brown v. Brown, and for battery, White v. White. But the court has held that parents are immune from a negligence suit brought by their child. Abbott v. Abbott. Second, in Abbott, the court held that a parent was immune from suit brought by a minor child for negligence. But in Black v. Black the parent was not immune

from the negligence suit brought by his twenty-four year old son.

2.   The Kent Supreme Court has decided four cases on parental immunity from tort suits by their children. In the first case in 1985, the court decided that a parent was immune from suit for negligence brought by his twelve-year-old son. Abbott v. Abbott (1985). However, in the next suit, in 1990, the court held that a parent was not immune from a suit for battery brought by a ten-year-old son. White v. White (1990). Only a year later in Brown v. Brown (1991), the court affirmed that a parent is not immune from suit for assault brought by a twenty-four-year-old daughter. The most recent case on this topic is Black v. Black, decided in 1992. In Black, the court decided another suit by a twenty-four-year-old against his parent, this time for negligence. The court still decided that the parent is not immune.

In the first discussion, the writer synthesizes the four cases and explains the two requirements for immunity. In thinking through the problem, the writer proceeded inductively by analyzing individual cases and then generalizing about these cases, i.e., by identifying two requirements that appear crucial on the issue of parental immunity. For the written product, however, the writer followed a deductive pattern. The writer put together a general rule to explain the law and started the discussion with that rule. Then she developed it, using the cases as authorities for her conclusion. However, the writer of the second discussion has not analyzed the problem. She has written no more than a historical narrative of the four cases. The paragraph's only organizing principle is one of chronological order. The writer has recreated her research process, but has left the job of making sense of the cases to the reader.

Exercise 2–I

Consider these cases along with the preceding cases about parental immunity.

Case 5:

Bob Peepe sued his father Larry for negligence for driving his car into Bob while Bob was riding his bicycle. Bob is nineteen and a senior in high school. He lives at home. Held: Mr. Peepe is immune from suit. Peepe v. Peepe (1989).

Case 6:

Marilyn Smith sued her father Richard for negligence for riding his bicycle into Marilyn while she was gardening. Marilyn is nineteen years old, unmarried, and a part-time college student who lives at home. She is not self-supporting. Held: Mr. Smith is immune from suit. Smith v. Smith (1994).

Case 7:

Gretel Andersen sued her father Hans Andersen for negligence for stumbling against Gretel and pushing her against the hot pottery she had just removed from her kiln. Gretel is seventeen, married and lives in another city. Held: Mr. Andersen is not immune from suit. Andersen v. Andersen (1995).

How might you synthesize these three cases and add them to the preceding four? What do these cases add to the rule?

————

The third type of synthesis is the kind you will be doing most often. It requires you to identify factors important to the application of a rule. Many of your assignments will involve claims for which courts have already synthesized a rule. To analyze the claim, you must apply the rule to your facts. Before you can do this, however, you must read the precedents you found, and identify the types of facts that courts consider significant in proving or disproving the elements of the rule. You then articulate a general category for each type of fact. These categories of facts are called factors.

For example, in cases dealing with the domicile of students, the courts determined the plaintiffs' domiciles by looking at a number of facts. One plaintiff had lived in the state for eighteen years, the other plaintiff for twenty years. The factor involved here can be described as length of time living in the state of the alleged domicile. In addition, one plaintiff received tuition payments from the state; the other received tutoring help. This factor can be described as benefits received from the state of alleged domicile. And, if one plaintiff returned to visit his parents in the alleged domicile at least once a month and the other plaintiff had friends and family living in that state, we can describe this as the factor of retaining personal commitments to the state of alleged domicile.

Exercise 2–J

The question is whether at the time one defendant committed a murder, the other defendant was "in immediate flight" from a robbery they had both committed, and therefore was also chargeable with the murder under the state felony murder law.[4] The murder was of a third felon of their group. Synthesize the holdings in these five cases in order to formulate the relevant factors in determining whether a defendant was "in immediate flight."

4. Under the criminal law, one whose conduct brought about an unintended death during the commission of a felony is guilty of murder.

Case 1:

The murder was committed by Alfred one day after Alfred and Bob robbed a store together. Bob was in another county 50 miles away. Held: Bob was not in immediate flight from the robbery.

Case 2:

The murder was committed by Delia as she and Gene were being chased by the police moments after they had robbed a store. Held: Gene was in immediate flight from the robbery.

Case 3:

The murder was committed by Adam one hour after he and Keith had robbed a store. Keith had gone to buy the two of them bus tickets to Atlantic City. They had agreed to divide the proceeds when Adam joined Keith at the bus terminal. Held: Keith was in immediate flight from the robbery.

Case 4:

The murder was committed by Barbara two hours after she and Dan had committed a robbery. One hour after the robbery, Dan had surrendered to the police and was in police custody. Held: Dan was not in immediate flight from the robbery.

Case 5:

The murder was committed by George at 10 p.m. At 5 p.m. George and Bert had divided the proceeds from the robbery that they had committed at 4 p.m. Held: Bert was not in immediate flight from the robbery.

Exercise 2–K

Read the following summaries of fourth amendment decisions. Under the case law interpreting the fourth amendment, the police need a search warrant if their activity invades a criminal suspect's reasonable expectation of privacy. You now want to know what types of situations involve a reasonable expectation of privacy. From the summaries, identify the factors that determine whether police violated the rule. (In these examples, the police acted without a warrant.)

1. Police broke down the door of the suspect's apartment and ransacked the suspect's bedroom. Police violated the fourth amendment.

2. Police knocked on the suspect's door, were admitted to his home, and strip-searched the suspect. Police violated the fourth amendment.

3. Police used binoculars to look through the windows of the suspect's home. No violation.

4. Police used dogs to sniff the suspect in an airport. No violation.

5. Police put a radar device into a package so it could be traced inside the suspect's home. Police violated the fourth amendment.

Chapter Three

Analyzing Legal Authority: Statutes

I.   Reading the Text of the Statute

Just as you should know how to read and analyze a judicial opinion, you should also know how to read and analyze a statute. And just as there are layers of analysis involved in analyzing case law, from briefing a single opinion to synthesizing a group of related cases, there are layers of understanding involved in statutory analysis.

The first step in statutory analysis, as with analysis of any written material, is to read the text carefully. Your analysis of a statute begins with its exact text; you must know what the statute says. Among other things, you must read the statute to know to whom it is addressed, the exact conduct it prohibits, requires, or permits, and how the parts of the statute relate to each other. Your next step is to isolate the issue in your problem by determining what question is raised by the statutory language in terms of the facts of your case.

Often, your assignment involves only one section of a larger statute. Even so, you should look at that section within the context of the statute as a whole. Federal statutes, for example, often include explanatory preliminary sections, some of which can be helpful to you in interpreting the section at issue. Start by reading the title of the statute, which can help you understand its area of application. For this same reason, read any preamble or statement of policy or purpose which appears at the beginning of many statutes. This statement may tell you, for example, that the statute was written to codify the existing common law. If so, then the case law decided prior to the enactment of the statute should still be authoritative. If the statute was written to change the common law, then that case law should no longer be controlling. Frequently overlooked, but important to know, is the date that the statute took effect. This information will be in the statute and it may be crucial; for example, the statute may not have been in effect at the time of the conduct at issue in your problem. Also, read through the other sections of the statute to see if any of them affect your problem. Look especially for a definition section, and determine whether any of the terms in the sections that apply to your case are defined there.

For example, a state statute, § 10 of the Probate Code, permits a person to revoke a will "by a subsequent will which revokes the prior will." Your client's mother left a will and a separate signed paper dated after the date of the will that said only, "I revoke my will." Your client wants to know if the revocation is valid. If you had read only § 10, you would have told your client that the revocation was not valid because the statute requires a person to revoke by means of a later will and the second paper is not a will. In order to advise your client correctly, however, you should also have read the Definitions section of the entire Probate Code. There you would have seen that the word "will" in § 10 is defined to include "any instrument that revokes another will." The second instrument is, thus, a valid revocation.

When you read the text of the sections with which you are concerned, look at the overall structure to see how one part of the text relates to the rest. If, for example, some language of the statute is in the alternative, that is, connected by the disjunctive "or," then only one of those parts needs to be proven. If, on the other hand, parts of a statute are connected by the conjunctive "and," then both parts must be proven. Consider this statute:

Burglary in the Third Degree

§ 1. A person is guilty of burglary in the third degree if he knowingly and unlawfully either enters or remains in a building, and

§ 2. Does so with the intent to commit a crime.

Under the language of § 1, the person charged needs either to have entered a building or to have remained there. He or she need not have both entered and remained in order to be guilty. And, according to the modifiers, the person must have both knowingly and unlawfully entered or remained. Thus if a person entered a building while it was open to the public, but knowingly remained unlawfully after the building had closed, the prosecutor will be able to prove § 1 of the definition of burglary.

Both § 1 and § 2 of the statute must be proven, however, because they are connected by the conjunction "and". The prosecutor must prove that the person charged with burglary in the third degree either entered or remained in a building knowingly and unlawfully, and also that the person did either of those with the intent to commit a crime. These statutory requirements are known as elements. Each element must be proven in order to determine whether someone has violated the statute.

Statutory requirements will not always be delineated the way they are in the burglary statute above. Sometimes, as in the Animal Control Act that follows, the statutory elements are drafted in paragraph form. In this statute, the plaintiff must prove all the elements, although the drafters did not use explicit conjunctive connectors.

Animal Control Act

> If a dog or other animal, without provocation, damages another's property or injures any person who is peaceably conducting himself in any place where the person may lawfully be, the owner of the dog or other animal is liable for the damages or injury caused.

Exercise 3–A

1. What are the alternatives within the Animal Control Act?

2. What are the required elements?

II. *Finding the Statutory Issues*

When you read a statute in light of the facts of your problem case, you determine first if the statute applies to your case at all. For example, one of the parties to litigation may rely on Article 2 of the state's Commercial Code, which applies to sales of goods. If the case concerns the leasing, rather than the sale, of goods then one issue is whether the requirements of Article 2 apply to a contract for the lease of goods.

Exercise 3–B

Do the following statutes apply to the sets of facts that follow them?

1. Statute: Deceptive Collection Practices Act

A collection agency or any employee of a collection agency commits a deceptive collection practice when, while attempting to collect an alleged debt, he or she adds to the debt any service charge, interest, or penalty, which he or she is not entitled to by law.

Facts 1:

John Brown, an interior decorator, loaned $3000 to his employee. When the employee had made no efforts to return the loan, Brown began harassing him for repayment and also claimed a usurious interest rate. The employee threatens to sue Brown under the Deceptive Collection Practices Act.

Facts 2:

Oscar Green, a secretary for Acme Collection Agency, plays poker with five friends every Tuesday evening after work. One night his friend Felix ran up a $500 debt that he couldn't pay, and Oscar loaned him the $500. Two weeks later, when he asked Felix to repay him, Oscar added a $25 charge.

What information about the statute's coverage might you want to know besides the section above?

2. Statute: The Animal Control Act on page 57 includes the following paragraph from the definitions section:

Owner means any person who has a right of property in an animal, keeps or harbors an animal, has an animal in his or her care, or acts as custodian of an animal.

Facts:

John Anderson, a home care provider, was injured when he walked his employer's dogs. One of the dogs nipped Anderson's leg, without provocation. Anderson wants to sue his employer.

———

Once you have determined that a statute applies to your case, then identify the elements of the statute that were violated. What conduct does the statute permit or not permit? Does your client's or the other party's conduct come within the statutory description?

Exercise 3–C

Identify the statutory issues in these problems.

1. Statute: Wills

In order for a will to be valid, the will must be signed by the testator (the person who executes a will) in the presence of two witnesses.

Facts:

Mr. Beal signed his will while one witness, Ms. Smith, stood next to him, and the other witness, Ms. Byrd, was in the adjoining room getting her pen. Ms. Byrd was facing Mr. Beal and saw him bend over the paper at the time he signed.

2. Statute: Solid Wastes

No garbage dump shall hereafter be established within the corporate limits of any city or town, nor shall any garbage dump be established within 250 yards of any residence without the consent of the owner of the residence.

Facts:

The People's Garbage Dump was opened by the city in 1950. Three years later, Tom Smith built a house on a lot near the dump. The city acquired a tract adjoining the dump and within 200 yards of Smith's residence. The city plans to enlarge the dump with the new tract of land. Smith opposes the enlargement.

3. Statute: Distribution of Damages in Wrongful Death Action: [2]

The jury in any wrongful death action may award such damages as may seem fair and may direct how the damages shall be distributed among the surviving spouse, the children, and grandchildren of the decedent.

Facts:

Martha Smith, for whose death a wrongful death action was brought, was survived by her husband, by a natural born child of the marriage, by an adopted child, and by her non-marital child.

4. Statute: Worker's Compensation

If an employee suffers personal injury by an accident arising out of and in the course of the employment, the worker is entitled to recover under this Act.

Facts:

Nathan Hail was employed by a university's tennis facility as a teacher at its tennis camp for children. The facility sold summer passes and also solicited people to contribute as subscribers. The director of the facility made clear that the teachers should be friendly to the subscribers. Sam Hardy, a subscriber, asked Nathan to play one afternoon after Nathan got off work teaching tennis classes. During the match, Nathan twisted his ankle and had to stop working for the rest of the season.

5. Statute: The Animal Control Act

If a dog or other animal, without provocation, damages another's property or injures any person who is peaceably conducting himself in any place where the person may lawfully be, the owner of the dog or other animal is liable for the damages or injury caused.

2. A wrongful death statute provides a civil recovery against a person who caused the death of another.

Facts:

   Joan Robinson brought her two young children, Missy and Eli, to visit her friend Jamie Meadows. Ms. Meadows owned two dogs, which stayed in the living room where they all were sitting. While they were there, the doorbell rang, and the dogs ran excitedly to the door, barking and jumping. When Eli started yelling at the dogs, the dogs ran back to the living room and one of them bit Missy.

   When you brief a case or write any legal analysis in which there is a statutory issue, your writing should reflect the statutory nature of the case. You should state the issue to reflect the exact question that the statute raised and you usually should include verbatim the operative language of the statute. Your statement of the holding of the case should answer that question, also in terms of the statute and its exact language.

   The following are examples of issues written for a case brief.

   1. Is a will "entirely written, dated, and signed by the testator" as required by the Probate Code if it is a handwritten will, dated with the month and year, but not the day?

   2. Does a person enter a "building" within the meaning of the burglary statute if she without authority goes into a tent pitched in a park?

   3. Is a signed writing that says only "I revoke my will," a "subsequent will which revokes the prior will" as required by the Probate Code?

Exercise 3–D

   Write the issues for the five exercises beginning on page 57 as you would write them for a case brief.

Exercise 3–E

   For the following exercise, read the statute and the facts to which you will apply the statute.

Statute: Theft of Lost or Mislaid Property

   A person who obtains control over lost or mislaid property commits theft if that person

   (1) Knows or learns the identity of the owner or knows of a reasonable method of identifying the owner, and

   (2) Fails to take reasonable measures to restore the property to the owner, and

   (3) Intends to deprive the owner permanently of the use of the property.

10 Kent Rev. Stat. § 20 (1985).

Facts:

Bill Smith saw a 14k gold locket on the ground of the park softball diamond at 1:30 p.m., just after a team from the YWCA had been practicing there. The diamond is located just west of a residential area of Kent and is in a large park that also contains children's playground facilities and tennis courts. The locket was engraved with three initials. Although he did not know the people on the team, Smith knew the name of the team because of the YWCA uniforms they wore. Smith was making deliveries for a nearby supermarket, where he worked a 10 a.m. to 4 p.m. shift. He also worked evenings for a newspaper.

Smith picked up the locket, looked it over, saw it was stamped 14k gold and saw that the initials were the same as those of his sister, who was in school 300 miles away. The locket needed polishing and had two pictures inside it. One was of a movie star. Smith pocketed the locket. He walked toward the street for his next delivery, in the opposite direction from the YWCA. About a block from the place where he picked up the locket, John Lyons robbed Smith of the groceries, Smith's own money, and the locket.

Someone who knows Smith saw him pick up the locket and gave his name to the police, who claim he violated the statute.

---

    a. What does the prosecutor have to prove in order to convict Smith of Theft of Lost or Mislaid Property?

    b. What are the statutory issues?

    c. What are the legally relevant facts?

    d. Write an analysis of whether Smith violated the statute.

III. *Techniques of Statutory Interpretation*

Once you identify the exact dispute about the application of the statute, you then analyze what the statute means in order to resolve how the statutory language applies to the facts of the case. Because a legislature enacts a statute to apply to future conduct, some of which is unforeseen at the time of enactment, rather than to a particular situation that has already occurred, legislative language is often more general than is the language in a judicial opinion. In written opinions, judges can tailor their language to apply specifically to the events that gave rise to the litigation. Statutory language may not be as specific to the events, however, and judges cannot rewrite the text of the statute, although they can direct its application.

In statutory litigation, then, the judge must often decide how the relatively general language of legislation, such as language that refers to a class of things, applies to a particular case. For example, a statute may require registration of motor vehicles. A court may have to determine which specific types of vehicles are included in that category, such as whether the requirement applies to a person's private airplane. Besides being general, statutory language may also be vague, sometimes purposely so. The statute may use terms like "fair use" or "reasonable efforts." The court must then determine the content of those vague terms within the framework of specific litigation. Statutory language, like all language, may also be ambiguous; it may have more than one meaning and the court may have to decide which meaning to apply. For example, a municipal ordinance revokes the license of a cab driver if he is convicted for a "second time of any offense under the Motor Vehicle Act." This statute may mean that the driver must be convicted twice of the same offense, but may also mean that the license will be revoked upon a conviction for a second but different offense. In all of these situations, a judge may be called upon to interpret what the text means.[3]

A. *Legislative Intent*

The court determines what statutory language means by asking what the legislature intended it to mean. The first source of the legislature's intended meaning is the language of the statute itself. Often, however, the court must examine other evidence about the statutory language. Moreover, a court may seek to determine what policy the legislature intended to pursue through the statute by determining the purpose of the statute. Then the court interprets the statute in a way that furthers that policy.

1. *Plain Meaning*

Courts employ a variety of approaches to determine what the legislature intended the statute to mean. The first step for most courts is to determine whether the statute has a single plain meaning. This process determines whether the parties may submit evidence besides the statute itself to support their interpretations of the language. If the court can interpret the statutory language according to a plain meaning, then it often will decide not to permit the parties to submit other evidence to explain the statute's meaning; it will use only the statute itself to indicate what the legislature meant.

For example, the Freedom of Information Act requires government agencies to disclose documents to any person who requests disclosure, subject to several statutory exemptions. One of those exemptions, Section 7, excludes from disclosure federal records that are compiled for law enforcement purposes if the production of those records would "disclose the identity of a confidential source." The plaintiff sought the production of documents from the govern-

---

3. See Reed Dickerson, The Fundamentals of Legal Drafting, 31–43 (1986).

ment which the government argued were exempt from production because they would disclose confidential governmental agency sources. The plaintiff argued that the exemption referred only to human sources and not to foreign, state or local law enforcement agencies. The court decided, however, that the plain and ordinary meaning of the language "confidential source" is any confidential source without distinction among types.

"Plain meaning" is often, but not always, the ordinary meaning, sometimes the dictionary meaning, rather than a technical meaning of the statutory words. However, words in some statutes, such as statutes that regulate a particular industry, may be interpreted according to their technical meanings in that industry. Some words may be interpreted according to their technical legal meaning. For example, if a lawyer drafts a document and uses the word "heir," that word will most likely be given its technical meaning (a person who inherits if the decedent died without a will). If a layman uses the word, it may be given its more colloquial meaning (a person's children).

Besides the "plain meaning" of the particular statutory language at issue, other internal aids to interpreting the scope of the disputed language can come from similar language in other parts of the same statute. If the exact language is used elsewhere in the statute, that use may provide the intended meaning of the words. If similar words are used, the difference in the wording may aid you in interpreting the disputed language. For example, if a statute refers to a person's "residence premises" in one section, but refers to "place of actual residence" in another section, a comparison of the terms indicates that the term "residence premises" is not restricted to the place at which the person is actually residing. Where the legislature intended that restriction, it used different wording. Of course, if the statute includes a definition section, that section should be the first place to look.

Exercise 3–F

The Right Times is an independent journal published by a student organization at a local university. The organization members distribute copies in stands located around the campus, and place signs inviting passersby to take a copy. The defendant Salter removed all the copies from the stands and threw them away.

　　1. Right Times sued Salter under one section of a mischief statute that prohibits a person from "intentionally damaging personal property contained in a structure located at a school or community center."

　　a. Is the university a school? A community center?

　　b. Does the term "school" have a plain meaning or do you need other evidence?

2. Right Times also sued for conversion. The conversion statute prohibits a person from "intentionally exerting unauthorized control over property of another person."

a. Were the journals in the distribution stands the "property" of Right Times?

b. Do you need other evidence to interpret this statute?

2. *Legislative History*

If the court cannot determine a plain meaning from the statutory language itself, but decides that the language is "ambiguous" (used in this sense to mean doubt exists about the meaning of the language), then it will permit the parties to introduce other evidence to show what the legislature intended the statute to mean. There is also considerable case law to the effect that these may not be exclusive steps, and a court can use other evidence as aids in construing the statutory language even if it can ascribe a plain meaning to the words. For instance, even if a plain meaning is discernible, a court will permit the parties to submit evidence explaining what the legislature intended in order to show that an ambiguity exists, or to show that enforcing the first meaning would lead to absurd or to unintended results.

For example, a federal statute prohibits importing aliens "under contract to perform labor or service of any kind in the United States." Has a church violated this statute by contracting and bringing from England an English minister to perform services as minister for the church? If it seems absurd to construe this statute to impose a monetary penalty on a church because it employed a minister from England, then the court will admit evidence to show that Congress did not intend the statute to prohibit that type of employment.

The most favored evidence that parties employ to determine the legislature's intended meaning is the legislative history of the statute. A legislative history consists of different elements. One part of a legislative history is the predecessor statutes to the one at issue. More importantly, legislative history consists of the documents that were produced during the statute's legislative journey from its beginning as a bill introduced in the legislature, through proceedings in the committee or committees to which it was assigned, and to its passage into law. You use this type of legislative history to find legislators' statements about what they meant by the disputed language. In the case of the statute that prohibits importing aliens, for example, the transcripts of committee hearings, the committee report, and the Congressional Record account of the debate on the floor of Congress all show that Congress intended to prohibit importation of contract labor crews to perform unskilled labor, not to prohibit hiring an individual from abroad to perform professional services.

If, however, the documents do not reveal the legislators' intended meaning or if they show that the legislators never thought about the application of the statute to the particular problem posed by the case, then you read the documents to try to find the more general purpose of the statute and you interpret the language in a way that promotes that purpose.

For federal statutes, the legislative history can be extensive, the most favored source being committee reports. For example, committee reports played a considerable role in one court's interpretation of Exemption 6 to the Freedom of Information Act. This section exempts from mandatory disclosure "personnel and medical files and similar files the disclosure of which would constitute a clearly unwarranted invasion of personal privacy." The section required judicial interpretation because of an ambiguous modifier. It is unclear which terms are modified by the phrase "the disclosure of which would constitute a clearly unwarranted invasion of personal privacy." The restriction could apply only to similar files or it could modify personnel files, medical files, and similar files.

If the restriction applies only to "similar files," then personnel and medical files are under a blanket exemption from disclosure regardless of whether their disclosure would constitute an invasion of privacy. A person requesting disclosure of personnel files would interpret the modifier to apply to all three descriptions of files. The government agency would interpret the modifier to apply only to "similar files."

Because of the ambiguous syntax of Exemption 6, the statute's plain language is unhelpful. Thus, the court facing this issue of statutory interpretation used the following information and reasoning to decide that the "invasion of privacy" language applied to all three types of files.

1. That court had already interpreted the policy behind the entire FOIA statute as one of disclosure, not secrecy.

2. The Congressional committee reports included language that applied to all of Exemption 6. That language requires a court to engage in a balance of the two policies of protecting an individual's private affairs from unnecessary public scrutiny and of preserving the public's right to governmental information. A court would not engage in that balance for medical and personnel files if those files were under a blanket exemption from disclosure.

3. The committee reports had no language about blanket exemptions in Exemption 6.

Thus, although the legislative history contains no explicit information, the court used these sources to decide that the limiting language modified the three types of files listed so that none was under a blanket exemption from the Act.[4] By doing so, the court interpreted the statutory language to promote the statute's policy of disclosure.

Unlike the materials available for federal statutes, the legislative materials available for state statutes may be meager. Even if considerable state or federal materials exist, however, they may be inconclusive as to what the legislature intended the litigated language to mean, or how the purposes of the statute bear on the application of the particular language to the facts of the case. The lawyer must assemble all the relevant pieces to form a coherent interpretation of legislative intent.

Exercise 3–G

Some of the relevant legislative history of the Freedom of Information Act § 7 exemption described previously is set out below. Based on this legislative history, did the court interpret the § 7 exemption correctly? Was the statute intended to mean only human sources?

1.   Original version of statute:

The original version of § 7 exempted records that would "disclose the identity of an informer." The committee to which the bill was referred amended the term "informer" to "confidential source."

2.   Committee Report:

The Committee Report contains the following statements:

a.   "The substitution of the term 'confidential source' in § 7 is to make clear that the identity of a person other than a paid informer may be protected if the person provided information under an express assurance of confidentiality."

b.   "The bill in the form now presented to the Senate . . . has been changed from protecting the identity of an 'informer' to protecting the identity of a person other than a paid informer. . . . Not only is the identity of a confidential source protected but also protected from disclosure is all the information furnished by that source to a law enforcement agency. . . ."

3.   Congressional debate:

The debate on the floor of the Senate recorded in the Congressional Record contains the statement by a senator on the committee, "we also provided that there be no requirement to reveal not only the identity of a confidential source, but also any information obtained from him in a criminal investigation."

---

4. Based on Department of Air Force
v. Rose, 425 U.S. 352 (1976).

How do you evaluate the following arguments in support of the court's plain meaning interpretation that § 7 applies to all sources including other law enforcement agencies and not human sources only?

    a.   The use of the word "person" in the Committee Report is similar to the use of any collective noun and refers to a variety of entities in addition to human beings.

    b.   The singular masculine pronoun, such as the "him" used by the senator, is often used where the sex of the referent is unknown or where it refers to a collective noun consisting of entities of more than one sex. A person using a pronoun during debates is not grammatically precise.

    c.   Congress was concerned that it not impair the ability of federal law enforcement agencies to collect information. The plaintiff's interpretation of § 7 would make other law enforcement agencies or other entities reluctant to share information with federal agencies.

    d.   The legislative history materials are themselves ambiguous and should not control the customary meaning of words in the statute.

Exercise 3–H

For the following exercise, read the facts of the problem. The case following the facts will provide some arguments relevant to the issue in the problem.

Facts:

The Oz Licensed Nursing Home Act § 15 provides a hearing for any licensee that has been charged with abusing a patient. The section provides "The Department shall commence a hearing within thirty days of the receipt of a nursing home's request for a hearing."

On April 10, 1986, the Department determined that TranQuil Nursing Home had abused a patient. TranQuil then requested a hearing on May 1, 1986. The Department, however, overlooked the request and did not schedule a hearing until December 1, 1986. At the hearing, the Department again determined that TranQuil was guilty of abuse. The home now seeks judicial review of that determination and has moved to dismiss the Department's proceedings for lack of timeliness because it was held after the thirty day period.

Adam v. Personnel Board

The Personnel Code of Oz § 20 requires that the Personnel Board provide a review for all state personnel protesting their discharge. Section 20 provides that the review "shall be held within 60 days of a discharged employee's request for review." Donald Adam requested review on September 1, 1980. The Personnel Board hearing, which confirmed his discharge, was held January 15, 1981. Adam has asked this court to void the Board's decision on the grounds that it was not timely.

The plain meaning of the word "shall" is that of a mandatory verb. The dictionary so defines it. The word has sometimes been construed as directory, however. That is, it has been interpreted as "may." If the statute states the time for performance but does not deny performance after a specified time, then "shall" is usually considered directory. If the time period safeguards someone's rights, it is mandatory.

Section 20 is designed to protect the rights of government employees who protest their discharge. A delay in their hearing could prejudice their rights. We therefore interpret the section as mandatory.

    a. Which statutory argument will the plaintiff TranQuil Nursing Home make?

    b. Which arguments will the state make?

    c. Which arguments are better?

Exercise 3–I

Acme Collection Agency sent three collection letters to the plaintiff Bass. The letters did not meet the requirements of the Fair Debt Collection Practices Act (FDCPA), and Bass wants to sue Acme under that statute. Bass had written a check at the supermarket to pay for his groceries, but the check bounced. The market ultimately sent the check to Acme for collection. The only issue is whether the payment obligation from the bad check is "a debt" as defined in the FDCPA.

The Act defines "debt" as "any obligation ... of a consumer to pay money arising out of a transaction in which the money, property ... or services which are the subject of the transaction are primarily for personal, family, or household purposes. . . . "

Acme has argued that the debt must flow from a specific type of transaction, that is, that the consumer transaction must be a credit transaction, and that the FDCPA does not apply to bad checks given in immediate payment for goods, because the goods were not sold on credit. How do you analyze this argument?

    1. Look first to the statutory language. Does the definition of debt have a plain meaning, and if so, does the definition include this transaction?

    2. Is there any ambiguity in the definition because it does not define "transaction"?

    3. Is a statement in the committee report definitive that "the Committee intends that the term 'debt' include consumer obligations paid by check or other non-credit consumer obligations"?

    4. Should the court consider the FDCPA's statutory structure? The FDCPA was passed as an amendment adding a subchapter to the Consumer Credit Protection Act. This Act, as its name suggests, applies to credit transactions only.

    5. Should the court defer to another federal appellate court that concluded, on a different issue, that the word "transaction" in the above definition does not include tort liability (the case involved a person sued for conversion[1] because he pirated microwave television

---

    1. Conversion is a taking of property   value.
that completely deprives the owner of its

signals). However, this court went on to say that "transaction" involves the offer or extension of credit to a consumer.

B. *The Canons of Construction*

Another long-standing—and frequently criticized—method of determining statutory meaning is to apply what are called "canons of construction." These canons are maxims or guides that suggest possible interpretations of certain verbal patterns in statutes and certain types of statutes. The canons, however, often yield inconclusive results.

A well-known canon used to interpret verbal patterns is the canon known as *ejusdem generis*. *Ejusdem generis* is applied to mean that whenever a statute contains specific enumeration followed by a general catchall phrase, the general words should be construed to mean only things of the same kind or same characteristics as the specific words (*ejusdem generis* means "of the same genus or class"). For example, in the language "no one may transport vegetables, dairy, fruit, or other products without a certificate of conveyance," the catchall words "or other products" could be interpreted to mean food products but not manufactured goods. However, the term may also be interpreted to include non-manufactured goods that are not foods, such as fresh flowers or lumber. To determine the scope of this phrase, it may be more important to know that the legislature's purpose in requiring a certificate of conveyance was to ensure sanitary conditions during transport.

Another example is a criminal code that makes illegal the shipment of obscene "books, pamphlets, pictures, motion picture films, papers, letters, writings, prints or other matter of indecent character." In a prosecution under the statute for mailing obscene phonograph records, application of the rule of *ejusdem generis* would require that the statute be interpreted to not include obscene phonograph records because the enumerated list includes matter taken in by sight, not by hearing.

The Supreme Court, however, did not use the canon to construe this statute because to have done so would have defeated the obvious purpose of the statute, which was to make illegal the use of the mails to disseminate obscene matter. The Court read the entire statute, beyond the portion under which the defendant was charged, to construe the statute as a "comprehensive" one that should not be limited by a mechanical construction.

Another well-known canon, which is again always referred to in Latin, is *expressio unius, exclusio alterius* (expression of one thing excludes another), usually shortened to *expressio unius*. *Expressio unius* is applied to mean that if a statute expressly mentions what is intended to be within its coverage, then the statute excludes that which is not mentioned.

For example, the statute that prohibits importing aliens contains a section that excludes actors, artists, lecturers, professional musicians, and domestic servants, but does not exclude ministers. A court applying *expressio unius* would interpret the list of exemptions as an exclusive one, yet the legislature may not have intended the enumerated exclusions to be exclusive or may not have thought about other categories of people who should also have been excluded from the statute's broad coverage.

A third well-known canon is "statutes in *pari materia* (on the same subject matter) should be read together," that is, they should be interpreted consistently with each other. For example, a section of the Family Law Code on the topic of adopted children provides, "the adopted child shall be treated for all purposes as the natural child of the adopting parents." A section of the Probate Code provides that the property of a person who dies without a will shall be distributed "one-third to the surviving spouse and two-thirds to the surviving children." If this statute and the section of the Family Law Code are to be read in *pari materia* so as to be consistent with each other, then the word "children" in the Probate Code should be interpreted to include adopted children of the person who died.

Of course, the statutory language of one or both statutes may show that the statutes should not be interpreted together. For example, the Family Law Code may provide that the adopted child be "treated for all purposes, including relations with the kin of the adopting parents, as the natural child of the adopting parents." The Probate Code, however, may provide only that "the adopted child shall inherit from the adopting parents as would a natural child." If the issue is whether the adopted child inherits from an adopting parent's mother (where the adopting parent has died), the differences in language between the statutes now make a difference. The Probate Code does not employ the specific language about "kin of the adopting parents," nor does it define the child as a natural child "for all purposes." Because the drafters of the Probate Code did not use that language, they may not have intended that the statute apply to all the situations to which the Family Law Code applies. Of course, the drafters also may not have read the Family Law Code, and had not thought about problems arising from interpreting the two statutes consistently. The court will have to decide if it should do so, or whether the more narrow language of the Probate Code should control because it is the statute that more specifically applies to this problem.

Some canons are used to help interpret types of statutes by the presumed policy behind those statutes. An example is "a penal statute should be strictly construed." This means that if it is not clear whether the language of a criminal statute (or a civil statute that imposes a penalty) applies to a particular defendant's conduct, the statute will be interpreted narrowly in favor of the defendant, that is, it will be interpreted not to apply. This type of construction is based on a policy that people should have fair warning of conduct that is punishable. Other canons of this type are "statutes in derogation of the common law should be strictly construed," which is a somewhat outdated canon, and "remedial statutes should be liberally construed." If the remedial statute is one that changes (is in derogation of) the common law, however, such as a worker's compensation act, then the two canons' presumptions conflict. You will find that the opposing lawyers often can supply a conflicting interpretation based on another canon.[5]

Canons do not explain what the legislature meant in enacting the particular statute being analyzed. Rather, they suggest what people usually mean by common language patterns. A canon such as "a penal statute should be strictly construed" supplies a presumption about how any legislature enacting that type of statute would intend the statute to be interpreted. Thus, because the canons do not analyze the reasons for the particular statutory language being applied, a canon should not by itself compel a particular interpretation. Indeed, in the case involving the criminality of sending obscene phonograph records through the mail, the Court did not interpret the statute according to this canon either. Instead, it read the statute as a whole to determine the enacting legislature's purpose. You should become familiar with the canons because many courts employ them as aids in construing language, especially if there is no legislative history available, but they are not conclusive about meaning.

Statutory interpretation often can be a difficult process of analyzing the language of text, the pre-enactment legislative history materials related to that text, other materials related to the statute, such as proposed amendments, and the canons of construction. But just as you apply case law to further the policies behind legal precedents, you use the techniques of statutory analysis to determine the legislative policy in enacting the statute and to interpret the text to further that policy.

---

5. As has been pointed out, many canons point to opposite conclusions. See Karl Llewellyn, Remarks on the Theory of Appellate Decision and the Rules or Canons About How Statutes Are To Be Construed, 3 Vand. L. Rev. 395 (1950).

C. *Stare Decisis and Statutes*

Once a court interprets a statute, the principle of stare decisis applies and the court will then follow the interpretation it has previously adopted unless it overrules it. For each new case with the same statutory issue, the court then reasons by analogy to the facts of the prior cases in order to apply the statute to the new case.

When you write about a problem that involves statutory analysis and arguments, you should include these analytic steps in your written analysis. Focus on the exact statutory language and its possible interpretations. Summarize the relevant legislative history, if any, and its interpretations, and, if the canons are relevant, explain how they apply to the language. If the statute has been interpreted by the courts, discuss the case law. If there is binding precedent interpreting the statute, explain how that interpretation applies to the facts of your problem. You will find that after a statute has been interpreted by the courts, its history becomes less important to its interpretation.

Exercise 3–J

The following two exercises are examples of constitutional issues for which a court has already applied the disputed constitutional provision in a precedent. For the purposes of these exercises, consider that the same principles of stare decisis apply to prior interpretations of constitutional language as to statutory language. Use Case 1 in each exercise as the controlling precedent for Case 2.

1. Does a city's display of a creche at Christmas time violate the establishment clause of the first amendment to the United States Constitution that says "Congress shall make no law respecting an establishment of religion"?

Case 1

A city owned and displayed a Christmas scene in a privately owned park located near a shopping area. The display consisted of many figurines and decorations, including a Santa Claus and sleigh, a decorated tree, several carolers, animals, clowns and a creche scene. The court decided that the display of the creche did not violate the establishment clause of the first amendment, which prohibits government activity that establishes religion. One part of the test of whether the establishment clause has been violated is whether the activity has the effect of advancing religion. The court decided that although the creche by itself is a religious symbol, within the overall context the display was a seasonal rather than religious display, and the creche demonstrated the historical origins of the holiday. Thus, the city did not act unconstitutionally by including the creche scene because the scene did not have the effect of advancing religion.

Case 2

Another city, one of the ten largest in the country, displayed a city-owned creche in the lobby of the City Hall. The city also decorated the lobby with Christmas wreaths above the elevators, a large Christmas tree just inside the entrance, and a Santa Claus and sleigh in the lobby, which it designated as the collection spot for food donations. These decorations are from ten to ninety feet away from the creche. Is this city's creche an unconstitutional endorsement of religion?

Compare Case 2 with Case 1. You must determine if Case 2 should be decided differently from Case 1 for purposes of whether the city endorses religion by displaying a creche. You do that by examining whether the facts are essentially analogous or distinguishable.

In Case 1 the creche is one part of a large diverse display. In Case 2 the creche is not side-by-side with other figures. Is it a self-contained religious exhibit because it is ten to ninety feet from other holiday decorations? Or is it just one element of an ensemble of seasonal holiday decorations? Are the two cases analogous or distinguishable on this point?

In Case 1, the holiday display was owned by the city but set up in a privately owned park. In Case 2, the city-owned display is in the lobby of City Hall. Does this difference in location and the ownership of the display make the cases distinguishable in terms of whether the two cities endorsed religion by setting up a creche at Christmas time?

2. Does the fourth amendment require that police acquire a search warrant in order to accomplish aerial observation of a person's premises within the fenced area around the person's home?

Case 1

Municipal police, acting without a search warrant, used a small airplane to fly 1000 feet over the house and backyard of the defendant. The yard was completely enclosed by a ten-foot fence. From the airplane, the officers saw marijuana plants growing in the defendant's yard. The court held that the police, although acting without a search warrant, did not violate the fourth amendment by their observation of the defendant's backyard. The fourth amendment is interpreted to mean that a person is entitled to its search warrant protections if he has a reasonable expectation of privacy in the object of the challenged search. This defendant's expectation of privacy from observation was unreasonable because the police were in an airspace open to public navigation, viewing what was visible to the naked eye.

Case 2

Municipal police acting without a search warrant flew in a helicopter at 400 feet over the defendant's premises. Police observed the defendant's greenhouse adjoining his house. The officers were able to look through openings in the greenhouse roof and sides to see marijuana growing inside the greenhouse. Did the officers violate the defendant's reasonable expectation of privacy and thus conduct an illegal search under the fourth amendment by observing the premises from a helicopter without getting a search warrant?

Does Case 1 require a decision that the police did not need a search warrant in Case 2? What are the analogies between these two cases?

What are the differences that are relevant to the question of whether the defendant had a reasonable expectation of privacy that was violated?

Exercise 3–K

John Hume is charged with violating 18 U.S.C. § 2114 (1988), which provides

> whoever assaults any person having lawful charge . . . or custody of any mail matter or of any money or other property of the United States with intent to rob or robs any such person of mail matter or of any money or other property of the United States shall be imprisoned. . . .

Hume assaulted an undercover Secret Service agent while attempting to rob him of $2000 of United States money entrusted to the agent to "purchase" counterfeit money from Hume.

Hume's defense is that the language in § 2114 "any money or other property" applies only to crimes involving robbery of postal money or postal property. The predecessor statutes to § 2114 all applied only to mail robbery and appeared in the section of the Criminal Code about offenses against the Post Office. The Postmaster General requested Congress to amend the statute to include robberies of money and other valuables as well as mail from a Post Office.

How would you evaluate the following arguments about the question of what the statutory language means? Which arguments would be used by the prosecutor and which by the defendant?

1. The statutory language is plain and unambiguous: the statute applies to any lawful custodian of three distinct classes of property. Nothing on the face of the statute limits its reach to offenses against custodians of postal money or postal property.

2. The principle of *ejusdem generis* demonstrates that the general terms "money" and "other property" should be limited by the specific term "mail matter" to postal money or postal property.

3. The bills introduced to amend the predecessor statute, which broadened its language, were referred to the Post Office Committees of both the Senate and the House of Representatives. A member of the House Post Office Committee said on the floor of the House that "the only purpose of the pending bill is to extend protection of the present law to property of the United States in the custody of its postal officials, the same as it now extends the protection to mail matter in the custody of its postal officials."

4. The Committee Reports of both the House and Senate Committees say that "the purpose of the bill is to bring within the provisions of the Penal Code the crime of robbing or attempting to rob custodians of government moneys."

5. The federal Criminal Code § 2112 contains a general statute penalizing thefts of government property with a much lesser sentence than the one imposed by § 2114.

6. In an earlier case, the Solicitor General of the United States conceded that § 2114 covered only postal crimes.

Chapter Four

Organization of a Legal Discussion: Large–Scale Organization

I. Introduction

In this chapter, you will learn how to identify the legal issues that are relevant to analyzing a problem and to use these issues to organize a written analysis of a legal problem, as it might appear, for example, in the Discussion section of a legal memorandum. See Chapter Seven. In Chapter Two, in the context of briefing a case, we used the word "issue" to describe the basic question that the court has to answer to resolve the dispute between the parties. Here we use the word "issue" to describe the points that must be discussed when you analyze a claim.

To write an analysis, you must break a subject into its component parts. To analyze a legal subject, you first identify the claims or defenses (which we will call the claims) in your problem. Then you break each claim down into its parts. Then where needed, you break each part down into its sub-parts. Once you have identified the parts and sub-parts, you arrange them in a logical order. This logical order forms the organizational structure of your discussion.

II. Organizing a Discussion

A. Overall Organization

The first organization, that of an entire discussion, is dictated by the topic of your problem. If your problem contains only one claim, then your entire discussion will be an analysis of that claim. If your problem contains more than one claim, then you discuss each separately. For example, if your client has two claims, one for assault and one for battery, you should divide the discussion into two main sections, one for assault, and one for battery.

The order in which you discuss the claims depends upon the particular problem. If the problem requires resolution of a threshold question, then logically you should analyze it first. A threshold question is one that the court will answer first because its decision on that issue will determine whether the litigation will continue or whether the court must decide the other issues.

An example of a threshold question is whether the plaintiff waited too long to file a complaint and whether the period for filing that type of complaint (governed by legislation known as a statute of limitations) has expired. A court will resolve this first, because if the plaintiff has waited too long to file, the court will dismiss the complaint. Therefore, you should discuss it first in your analysis. Your resolution of the threshold question, however, should not end the discussion. The judge may disagree with your conclusion on the threshold question, or your reader may want an analysis of the entire subject.

If there are no threshold questions, you may want to organize the claims by degree of difficulty. You may decide to analyze the simpler claim first to dispose of it quickly and then work toward the more difficult one. Or you may decide to attack the most complex claim first while you have the reader's attention, and then follow with the claim that you think is easier to establish.

B. Organization Within One Claim—Identifying the Issues

After identifying the claims in your assignment and deciding the order in which you will discuss them, you must break down each claim into its constituent parts, that is, into the legal issues raised by that claim. These issues may come from an established definition, such as the elements of a tort or crime. Or they may be factors that the courts have previously considered in determining how to decide particular cases. In any event, you need to identify these issues and analyze each separately. They will form the organizational framework for your analysis. The fundamental principle to remember is that when you analyze a claim, you organize your analysis around the issues that the claim raises, not around individual cases.

There are several different ways of finding these issues.

1. A court's opinion identifies the elements of a rule.

2. The terms of a statute identify the elements.

3. A rule may evolve over a series of opinions.

4. The rule is vague and you must extract the factors from an opinion or a series of opinions and balance them.

1. The Court's Opinion Identifies the Elements of a Rule

Sometimes, a court opinion will tell you what issues must be discussed in a claim by defining the claim, for example, the elements of a tort. Read the following opinion to find out what the elements are of the tort of intentional infliction of emotional distress. These elements will provide the organizational framework for the analysis of this claim.

Davis v. Finance Co.

Luella Davis (Davis) sued Finance Company (Finance) seeking to recover on the theory of intentional infliction of emotional distress.

In this jurisdiction, the courts have adopted the definition of intentional infliction of emotional distress provided in the Restatement (Second) of Torts. First, the defendant's conduct must be extreme and outrageous. Liability will be found only where the conduct has been so outrageous in character, and so extreme in degree, as to go beyond all possible bounds of decency.

Second, the plaintiff's emotional distress must be severe. Mental conditions such as fright, horror, grief, shame, humiliation, or worry are not actionable. The distress inflicted must be so severe that no reasonable person could be expected to endure it.

Third, the conduct must be intentional, or at least reckless. If reckless, the conduct must be such that there is a high degree of probability that severe emotional distress will follow and the actor goes ahead in disregard of it.

In this case Finance's conduct was not so extreme and outrageous as to constitute a basis for recovery under this tort. Davis claims that agents of Finance called her several times weekly, that they went to her home one or more times a week, and that they twice called her at a hospital where she was visiting her sick daughter. She alleges that Finance continued its practices even after she told them she was on welfare and was unable to make any additional payments. Davis, however, was legally obligated to Finance and had defaulted in her payments. A creditor must have latitude to pursue reasonable methods of collecting debts. Finance was attempting to collect a legal obligation from Davis in a permissible though persistent and possibly annoying manner. Such conduct is not outrageous, and therefore, Davis does not state a cause of action for intentional infliction of emotional distress.[1]

----

1. This example is based on and uses language from the case of Public Fi- nance Corp. v. Davis, 360 N.E.2d 765 (Ill. 1976).

In the Davis case, the court identifies three elements to the tort. First, the defendant's conduct must be outrageous. Second, the plaintiff's distress must be severe. Third, the defendant's conduct must have been intentional or, at least, reckless. The plaintiff must prove each of these in order to succeed. Therefore, you would organize an analysis of a problem dealing with intentional infliction of emotional distress around the three elements of the tort, in the order they appear in the definition. They become the issues you would discuss.

You may find that some issues will require extensive analysis, and others need be discussed only briefly. For example, in Davis, the most difficult issue to resolve was whether the company's conduct was extreme and outrageous. Finding that it was not, the court did not need to discuss the other two issues, since all of the elements of the tort must be met for the claim to succeed. If your facts paralleled those in Davis, you would discuss all of the elements in writing a memorandum on this subject. But you would devote more space to your analysis of whether the defendant acted outrageously than to the other issues, because it was the most complex.

Sometimes, however, you may want to discuss the elements out of order, for example, because one of them is more important than the other, or, you may want to discuss the less controversial issues first in order to dismiss them quickly. Then you would go into detail on the most problematic issue. For example, in another case dealing with intentional infliction of emotional distress, the real controversy might be over whether the plaintiff's distress was severe. You might decide that the analysis of whether the defendant acted outrageously and intentionally was so clear-cut that it could be disposed of quickly. You would then discuss extensively the more complex issue of whether the plaintiff's distress was severe. The discussion might run several paragraphs and be organized this way:

Paragraph 1—The defendant's conduct was both outrageous and intentional.

Paragraph 2—The plaintiff's distress was not severe because X.

Paragraph 3—The plaintiff's distress was not severe because Y.

Paragraph 4—The plaintiff's distress was not severe because Z.

If you analyze the elements out of order, include a brief explanation of why you are doing so. Otherwise, your reader will expect you to analyze them as they appear in the definition.

A variant on this pattern occurs when you work with a rule that is followed by explicit exceptions. In this situation, your client may come within the rule, but the important analysis is whether your client comes within an exception to that rule.

Exercise 4–A

Read the following case and identify the three elements of the tort of false imprisonment. Each element will be an issue in the analysis of a false imprisonment claim. Does the court break down any of these issues into subissues?

East v. West

Carol West appeals from a judgment that she falsely imprisoned the three plaintiffs.

The plaintiffs were comparing voter registration lists with names on mailboxes in multi-unit dwellings. They intended to challenge the registration of people whose names were not on the mailboxes. Plaintiffs testified that they entered West's house through the outer door into a vestibule area which lies between the inner and outer doors to West's building. They were checking the names on the mailboxes when West entered and asked what they were doing. They replied that they were checking the voter lists. She first told them to leave and then changed her mind and asked if they would be willing to identify themselves to the police. Plaintiffs said they would. West then asked her husband to call the police. While they waited, she stood by the door, but neither threatened nor intimidated the plaintiffs. In addition, the plaintiffs did not try to get her to move out of the way. When the police came, they said the plaintiffs were not doing anything wrong and could continue to check the lists. Plaintiffs later sued West for false imprisonment.

An actor is liable for false imprisonment if he acts intending to confine the other or a third person within boundaries fixed by the actor; if his act directly or indirectly results in such a confinement of the other; and if the other is conscious of the confinement or is harmed by it.

The evidence here is not sufficient to support the conclusion that West's acts directly or indirectly resulted in the plaintiffs' confinement. Confinement may be brought about by actual physical barriers, by submission to physical force, or by threat of physical force. The question in this case is whether confinement was brought about by threat of physical force. We think it was not. Plaintiffs acknowledge that West did not verbally threaten them. Since none of the plaintiffs asked her to step aside, they could no more than speculate whether she would have refused their request, much less physically resisted. Moreover, the three of them are claiming confinement by a single person. Accordingly, the judgment below is reversed.[2]

––––––––––

2. This example is based on and uses language from the case of <u>Herbst v.</u> <u>Wuennenberg</u>, 266 N.W.2d 391 (Wis. 1978).

According to the East case, what are the three elements of the tort of false imprisonment? These are the three basic issues and provide the organizational structure for your discussion. Of the three elements, on which does the court focus its discussion? As to this element, what are the different ways in which it can be met? These different ways suggest subissues that you must also consider in organizing your analysis of a false imprisonment problem.

Make an outline of how you would organize a false imprisonment problem. First, list the three elements of the tort—the basic issues that you must consider. Then look at the opinion and see how each of these elements is met. If any element can be met in different ways, list those ways beside the element. These are the subissues in the problem. This list provides the basic organizational structure for your analysis. Remember that subissues may also merit different degrees of analysis, depending on their applicability to the facts of your case, their intrinsic complexity, and the other subissues involved.

———

Sometimes the court defines the claim, but does not clearly outline the elements. Then you must identify and outline them yourself. Suppose your client, Mr. Smith, wishes to hire a new employee. He wants the employee to sign a restrictive covenant that he will not compete with him if the employee decides to leave Smith's employment in the future. In a restrictive covenant, the employee agrees not to engage in certain conduct that competes with the employer after she leaves employment with the employer. Read the following case. What does the court in this case consider necessary to determine whether a covenant not to compete will be enforced?

Columbia Ribbon v. Trecker

We are required to determine whether a covenant made by a salesman not to compete with his employer after the termination of employment is enforceable in whole or in part.

Defendant Trecker was employed by Columbia Ribbon as a salesman for several years. He signed an employment contract with the following restrictive covenant:

1. The employee will not disclose to any person or firm the names or addresses of any customers or prospective customers of the company.

2. The employee will not, for a period of twenty-four months after the termination of his employment, sell or deliver any goods of the kind sold by the company within any territory to which he was assigned during the last twenty-four months prior to termination.

After Trecker was demoted, he terminated his employment with Columbia Ribbon and took a job with a competitor, A–1–A Corporation. Columbia then sued to enforce the terms of the covenant.

Restrictive covenants are disfavored in the law. On the other hand, courts must also recognize the employer's legitimate interest in safeguarding its business. Enforceability, therefore, depends on the reasonableness of the terms of the covenant. In this case, the terms of the covenant are broad and sweeping. The affidavits do not suggest that Trecker was privy to any trade secrets which he would then use or disclose. Nor are there any confidential customer lists; the employer's past or prospective customer names are readily ascertainable from sources outside its business. Trecker was a good salesman, but he did not possess any unique or extraordinary abilities or skills.

Since there are no factors present indicating unfair competition, there is no need to consider whether the time and geographic restrictions are reasonable.

Accordingly, Columbia's motion for summary judgment is dismissed.[3]

In the Columbia Ribbon case, the court tells you it will enforce covenants that protect the employer's interests only under certain circumstances. A court will enforce a covenant if the employer can show that the employee had access to trade secrets or confidential customer lists or that the employee's services are unique. The court, however, tells you at the end of the decision that it considers these factors to prevent the employee from engaging in unfair competition. And then, even if the circumstances indicate unfair competition, the covenant's time and geographic restrictions must be reasonable. These elements, like those of a tort or crime, provide the organizational structure for the analysis of the problem.

An analysis of whether a covenant not to compete is enforceable could use this organizational structure.

1. The contract does not involve unfair competition

   a. no trade secrets

   or

   b. no confidential customer lists

   or

   c. no unique employee's services

   and

2. The contract terms are reasonable

3. This example is based on and uses language from the case of Columbia Rib- bon & Carbon Manufacturing Co. v. A– 1–A Corp., 369 N.E.2d 4 (N.Y. 1977).

    a.   reasonable time restrictions

and

    b.   reasonable geographic limitations

Notice the order of the issues in this problem. Reasonable terms are relevant only if unfair competition is involved. Thus section 1 must be discussed before section 2.

Exercise 4–B

1.   Read the following summary of a case involving the issue of whether the defendant breached a restrictive covenant in an employment agreement. In this segment of the case, the court explains the common law requirements for a restrictive covenant. If you were analyzing a restrictive covenant, outline how you would organize your analysis of this topic. The citations in the court's decision are omitted.

Woodbrook v. Donna

    A post–employment restrictive covenant will be enforced if its terms are reasonable. It must be reasonable in geographical and temporal scope, and necessary to protect a legitimate business interest of the employer. Prior to analyzing the reasonableness of a covenant not to compete, the court must make two determinations: (1) the covenant must be ancillary to a valid contract, that is, it must be subordinate to the contract's main purpose; and (2) there must be adequate consideration to support the covenant. A restrictive covenant agreement can be ancillary to either a valid employment contract or to a valid employment relationship if there is no written contract.

2. *The Terms of a Statute Identify the Elements*

    If you are analyzing a problem which is governed by a statute, the terms of the statute itself may identify the major issues you must analyze. These are the requirements for the statutory claim. The language will tell you to whom the statute applies and the kind of conduct it governs.

    Consider the following statute, also discussed in Chapter Three.

§ 140.20 Burglary in the third degree.

    1. A person is guilty of burglary in the third degree if he knowingly and unlawfully either enters or remains in a building, and

       2. does so with the intent to commit a crime.

    Most criminal statutes are composed of elements of a crime, each of which must be proved at trial. As with the elements of a tort, the elements of a statute become the issues that you will discuss. The elements in this statute provide the organizational structure for an analysis of the crime of burglary.

To determine those elements, first consider the overall structure of the statute. If any parts of the statute are given in the alternative, only one element need be satisfied, but you may have to analyze each. If parts of a statute are connected by the word "and," both parts must be considered.

Once you have a sense of the overall structure of a statute, you can go on to identify its elements. You identify the elements of the crime by looking at the terms of the statute. Each term may be significant and require some discussion. However, as with a tort, some elements will require detailed analysis, while others need be analyzed only briefly.

The statute defining burglary in the third degree is short and fairly simple. However, even this short statute includes a number of terms which identify the elements of the crime that must be analyzed.

According to the statute, guilt of burglary in the third degree is established if:

1) [a] person

2) (a) knowingly enters unlawfully [in a]

or

(b) knowingly remains unlawfully [in a]

3) building

4) [with] intent

5) [to commit a] crime

You might organize your analysis by disposing of some elements, such as whether the defendant entered a "building" in a sentence or two, and analyzing others in a paragraph or series of paragraphs. Some elements may be so obvious, i.e., that the defendant is a person, that they need not be mentioned at all. As with the elements of a tort, your treatment of each statutory element depends on its complexity in relation to the facts of your case.

Exercise 4–C

Consider what issues are raised by the following statute, a section of the Uniform Commercial Code.

§ 2–315. Implied Warranty: Fitness for Particular Purpose

Where the seller at the time of contracting has reason to know any particular purpose for which the goods are required and that the buyer is relying on the seller's skill or judgment to select or furnish suitable goods, there is, unless excluded or modified under the next section, an implied warranty that the goods shall be fit for such purpose.

According to the statute, to whom does the statute apply? What time period is relevant? What type of warranty is created? What must the seller know for the warranty to arise? How may the warranty be excluded or modified?

Make an outline showing the organizational structure of an analysis of implied warranty of fitness for a particular purpose.

Exercise 4–D

According to the following statute, what are the elements of burglary in the second degree? Notice that the structure of this statute is more complex than burglary in the third degree.

§ 140.25 Burglary in the second degree

A person is guilty of burglary in the second degree when he knowingly enters or remains unlawfully in a building with intent to commit a crime therein, and when:

1. In effecting entry or while in the building or in immediate flight therefrom, he or another participant in the crime:

    a) is armed with explosives or a deadly weapon; or

    b) causes physical injury to any person who is not a participant in the crime; or

    c) uses or threatens the immediate use of a dangerous instrument; or

    d) displays what appears to be a pistol, revolver, rifle, shotgun, machine gun or other firearm; or

2. The building is a dwelling.

———

To identify the elements of this crime, you must first examine the overall structure of the statute. Look for the relationships among the words connected by "and" and "or." Notice that the statute contains two sections that follow the introductory section. You must determine how sections 1 and 2 relate to each other and to the introductory section. By considering questions like these, you will be able to identify the essential elements of the crime.

In a discussion analyzing whether someone had committed burglary in the second degree, you would have to decide which, if any, of the subsections of section 1 you could prove. You might decide that of the subsections of the statute, subsection (b), was totally irrelevant to your case, and that three subsections (a), (c), and (d) might be relevant. You might decide to briefly dispose of the irrelevant section, and then fully discuss those subsections that seem to be relevant to your case.

Make an outline showing the organizational structure of an analysis of burglary in the second degree assuming that subsection (b) is not relevant to your problem.

3. A Rule Evolves Over a Series of Cases

Organizing an analysis is more difficult when the elements of a claim are not found in a single case, but emerge from a series of cases. One case may provide the basic standard without identifying all of the elements eventually required. Thus you must read all the relevant cases on the general topic to identify the elements of the claim and the ways those elements can be proven.

Read the following summaries of cases about the tort of negligent infliction of emotional distress. All of them are from the same jurisdiction and all are relevant to this topic.[4]

Sinn v. Burd

The plaintiff, Robert Sinn, sued to recover damages for the emotional injuries he suffered when he saw his minor daughter struck and killed by a car. Mr. Sinn became hysterical and then lapsed into a depression, sustaining severe emotional distress and repeated nightmares. He has had to spend considerable amounts of money for medical care. Mr. Sinn was not in any personal danger of physical impact when he saw the accident from the front door of his home.

Under the traditional rule, bystanders could not recover for mental injury unless they also suffered physical injury or were within the zone of danger, that is, they were in personal danger of physical impact. This rule, however, is unreasonably restrictive in cases where a parent views the death of a child, a situation which would cause at least as much emotional distress as being within the zone of danger. Here the injury was foreseeable since the plaintiff was the child's father, the plaintiff was near the scene of the accident, and the shock resulted from his sensory and contemporaneous observance of the accident. Therefore, the court below incorrectly dismissed the claim.

Kratzer v. Unger

The plaintiff sued the driver of a car, which struck and seriously injured her foster child, for negligent infliction of emotional distress. The child had lived with the plaintiff for over eight years. The plaintiff may bring a claim for negligent infliction of emotional distress.

Cathcart v. Keene

Ms. Cathcart sued her husband's employer for negligent infliction of emotional distress. She alleged that he had contracted asbestosis on the job and that she suffered emotional distress in witnessing his continual deterioration and death. Although the plaintiff did have a close relationship with the victim, this court must dismiss her claim since her injuries did not arise from the shock of viewing a single, identifiable traumatic event.

---

4. Case summaries in this example are based on Sinn v. Burd, 404 A.2d 672 (Pa. 1979); Kratzer v. Unger, 17 Pa. D. & C.3d 771 (Bucks Co. 1981); and Cathcart v. Keene Indus. Insulation, 471 A.2d 493 (Pa. Super. 1984).

Long v. Tobin

Ms. Long sued the driver of a car for negligent infliction of emotional distress caused by her viewing her neighbor's child being struck by a negligently driven automobile. She alleged that she became nervous and upset as a result of seeing the accident, since she has a child of the same age.

This court will grant the defendant's motion to dismiss the claim. Ms. Long does not have the requisite close personal relationship with the victim. Moreover, the mental distress she alleges is not sufficiently severe to warrant recovery. The type of stress required is that which no normally constituted reasonable person could endure.

———

In reading through the case summaries, you will have noticed that the most extensive discussion of this tort is given in Sinn v. Burd. Sinn is the leading case in the jurisdiction on the claim of negligent infliction of emotional distress. It sets out the basic standard for recovery: a person may recover for negligent infliction of emotional distress if the emotional distress is foreseeable. Distress is foreseeable when the plaintiff was the parent of the victim, when the plaintiff was near the scene of the accident, and when the distress resulted from a sensory and contemporaneous observance of the accident.

The other cases either elaborate on the elements raised in Sinn or introduce new elements. For example, the decision in Kratzer indicates that relationships other than parent and child can qualify, and thus elaborates on this prong of the test. Ms. Kratzer was not a parent, but a foster parent. The Cathcart decision elaborates on the relationship between plaintiff and victim by extending the coverage of the tort to spouses. In addition, the court in Cathcart establishes a new element. To be actionable, the distress must arise from a single, identifiable traumatic event. The court in Long also establishes a new element. To be actionable, the plaintiff's distress must be severe.

If you had identified the elements the courts address in determining whether a plaintiff states a claim for negligent infliction of emotional distress and made a list, the list would look something like this:

1. whether the plaintiff was closely related to the victim

2. whether the plaintiff was near to the scene of the accident and whether the plaintiff's shock resulted from a sensory and contemporaneous observance of the accident

3. whether the shock resulted from a single, identifiable traumatic event

    4.   whether the plaintiff's distress was severe.

Each of these elements becomes an issue that you would discuss in analyzing the tort.

Exercise 4–E

Read the following case summaries and determine which factors a court will consider in analyzing whether to grant a motion to quash service of process.

Finch v. Crusco

    The question before this court is whether a Delaware resident who brought a contract claim in Pennsylvania is immune from service of process in an unrelated action, if he was served in Pennsylvania while attending court proceedings in his contract claim. Philip Crusco was in Pennsylvania to testify in his breach of contract claim. When he came out of the courthouse, he was served in an unrelated tort action.

    The courts in this state have long provided that non-resident parties and witnesses in civil actions are immune from service of process. The purpose of this grant of immunity is not to protect the individual, but to assure that the courts' business is expedited and that justice is duly administered. The rule provides an incentive to those who might not otherwise appear whose attendance is necessary to a full and fair trial.

    However, courts should deny immunity where it is not necessary to provide this incentive. Where both cases arise out of the same transaction, the courts should not grant immunity. Under this circumstance, the reason for granting immunity would be outweighed by the importance of fairly resolving the full dispute between the parties. Nor will the courts grant immunity to a party or witness who is in the jurisdiction to serve his own interest, since he does not need an incentive to appear.

    Mr. Crusco falls into the second category. He did not require an incentive to appear in the state court since he had brought the suit himself and was personally benefitting from the court hearing. Therefore, his motion to quash service of process is denied.

Dulles v. Dulles

    Mr. Dulles was given a grant of immunity as a condition of his appearing and giving testimony in a matter relating to the Girard Trust Company. He remained in the jurisdiction for nineteen days after the matter regarding the Trust Company was resolved. On the nineteenth day, he was served with process in an action for support by his former wife.

    Mr. Dulles had immunity for a reasonable time before and after his testimony. But there was no need for him to remain in the jurisdiction for such a lengthy period of time after the testimony. Therefore, at the time he was served, he was no longer immune from service of process.

Cowperthwait v. Lamb

    Mr. Lamb was served with process in a tort action as he was leaving a proceeding before the Secretary of Revenue regarding the suspension of his motor vehicle license. He argues that he was immune from process because he was summoned to testify before this administrative tribunal.

The rule granting immunity should be applied when a party is testifying before a tribunal which is judicial in nature, whether the hearing takes place in a court or not. This proceeding was judicial in nature. The Secretary may suspend the license only after a finding of sufficient evidence. He passes on the credibility of witnesses and applies law to the facts. The purpose of the rule, to have a full and fair hearing unhampered by the deterrence of the important witnesses, is just as important in proceedings of an administrative nature as before a court.

State v. Johnson

The defendant was charged with the criminal acts of fraud and obtaining money by false pretenses. Moments after appearing before a magistrate and being freed on bail, Johnson was served with process in a civil matter. His motion to dismiss the complaint on grounds that he was immune from service of process is denied. Immunity from service of process is granted to a defendant in a civil action as an inducement to appear and defend. But a criminal defendant has no choice but to appear. Therefore, there is no need to extend the rule to provide such inducement.[5]

4. *The Rule Is Vague and You Must Extract the Factors From an Opinion or a Series of Opinions and Balance Them*

When a court explicitly identifies the elements of a common law claim for you, or when the language of a statute supplies the elements, you will not find it too difficult to know which issues to analyze or how to organize them. Often, however, a particular common law or statutory claim is defined more vaguely. Then the courts will frequently flesh out the requirements by identifying facts that are particularly relevant to deciding whether the rule is satisfied. In this situation, you must identify as factors the types of facts important to a court and organize around those factors.

Suppose you want to bring a negligence suit in federal court but there is a question about whether the plaintiff, a minor, could sustain a motion to dismiss for lack of diversity jurisdiction. The child's mother is a widow who has been in a one-year job training program in Massachusetts, where she intends to accept a job. While the mother was in this program, the child lived with her grandparents in New York, where she has always lived. Read the following case to determine what factors the court considers relevant in deciding whether the child has the domicile of the mother in Massachusetts, or the domicile of the grandparents in New York.

5. Case summaries in this example are based on, and use language from, Cowperthwait v. Lamb, 95 A.2d 510 (Pa. 1953); Crusco v. Strunk Steel Co., 74 A.2d 142 (Pa. 1950); Commonwealth v. Dulles, 124 A.2d 128 (Pa. Super. 1956).

These factors will form the organizational structure of your analysis.

Elliott v. Krear

It is alleged that on August 21, 1976, the defendant, 9–year-old Michael Krear, approached 10–year-old Keith Michael Elliott in a backyard in Virginia and, with a slingshot, shot a gumball at Keith causing an injury. Plaintiff's complaint alleges diversity jurisdiction under 28 U.S.C. § 1332. There is no question about the Virginia citizenship of the defendants. On the eve of trial, however, the court became aware that the plaintiff may have been a citizen of the Commonwealth of Virginia on the day this suit was filed. Accordingly, a hearing was held. The question of the court's jurisdiction is now ripe for disposition.

The court finds the facts to be as follows. Plaintiff is the son of divorced parents. His mother has custody. After the divorce, plaintiff continued to live in Virginia with his mother until early 1976, when his mother went to California to study law. The plaintiff was left in the custody of his maternal grandparents, who were citizens of Virginia. While in California, the plaintiff's mother formed an intent to remain indefinitely in California. The plaintiff's mother was residing in California when the gumball incident occurred. Though the incident occurred in August, the plaintiff's grandparents, who were caring for the plaintiff and paying for all of his support, did not inform plaintiff's mother of the incident until she returned to Virginia at Christmas time, 1976. Complete medical treatment and legal advice and services were sought and obtained by the grandparents without reference to plaintiff's mother. In the spring of 1977, the plaintiff went to California to live with his mother. In the spring of 1978, the plaintiff moved back to Virginia. In the fall of 1978, the plaintiff's mother decided to return to Virginia.

The applicable date for determining the citizenship of the plaintiff is the day on which the law suit was filed, August 21, 1978. The elements necessary to establish citizenship are the same as those to establish domicile: residence combined with an intention to remain indefinitely. An infant's citizenship must be determined by reference to the citizenship of some other person, because an unemancipated infant is not capable of forming the requisite intent to establish independent citizenship.

The domicile of an infant whose parents are divorced is, for federal diversity jurisdictional purposes, the domicile of the parent to whom custody has been given. However, strict adherence to this rule is appropriate only if the result obtained comports with the underlying policies.

The principal purpose of diversity jurisdiction was to give a citizen of one state access to an unbiased court to protect him from parochialism if he was forced into litigation in another state in which he was a stranger and of which his opponent was a citizen. Strict adherence in the present case does not comport with this policy.

Neither the plaintiff in this case, his grandparents, or his mother is a stranger to Virginia. Plaintiff was born in Virginia and has spent all of his life in this Commonwealth except for a one-year stay in California. Plaintiff's mother has returned to Virginia. Moreover, although plaintiff's mother was apparently awarded custody of plaintiff, it is clear that plaintiff's mother was not exercising control and did not have actual custody of the plaintiff at the time this suit was filed. Plaintiff's grandparents were and had been acting *in loco parentis* in providing for plaintiff's support, maintenance, protection and guidance at the time this suit was filed. Plaintiff's grandparents made all the important decisions affecting plaintiff's medical care, legal services, and education.

These considerations lead us to hold that the courts of Virginia would not view plaintiff in this matter or view any person who could conceivably be considered his custodian as a stranger. Thus, the policy that underlies diversity jurisdiction will not support jurisdiction in this case. Accordingly, the Court holds that plaintiff had the citizenship of his grandparents when suit was filed and there is no diversity of citizenship between the parties to this law suit. Thus the Court lacks subject-matter jurisdiction over this action.[6]

————

In Elliot v. Krear, the court tells us that an adult's citizenship is determined by residence and intent to remain in a state for an indefinite time, but that a child's citizenship must be determined by reference to the citizenship of an adult because an unemancipated child is not capable of forming the requisite intent to establish independent citizenship. Generally, a child has the citizenship of the parents or of the divorced parent to whom custody has been given. Sometimes, however, the child has the citizenship of the adult acting in *loco parentis*. To determine whether a child has the citizenship of the parent or of the adult acting in *loco parentis*, the court considers a number of factors.

—duration in a state

—intent of the adult to stay in a state

—actual custody and control of child

who supports the child?

who provides guidance?

who protects the child?

who is the decision-maker about medical treatment, education, legal advice?

When courts consider and balance a series of factors like these, they are engaged in what is called a totality of circumstances analysis. In a totality of circumstances analysis, you typically do not have to prove or disprove each factor. Instead you identify the most

6. This example is based on and uses language from Elliott v. Krear, 466 F. Supp. 444 (E.D. Va. 1979).

important factors in your case and decide, for example, whether on balance they establish citizenship in Virginia or in California.

Sometimes a vague rule is clarified in a series of opinions. For example, all states have adopted the Uniform Commercial Code § 2–302, which permits a court to refuse to enforce an unconscionable contract. The statute does not define unconscionable. The courts, however, typically require two types of unconscionability, procedural and substantive. Moreover, over time, courts have identified factors that can show that a contract is substantively or procedurally unconscionable. For example, one court held that a contract was procedurally unconscionable because of unequal bargaining power. Another court held a contract was procedurally unconscionable because one party had no meaningful choice. Finally, a third court held that hidden terms rendered the contract unconscionable. These factors must be synthesized to form an organizational structure for your paper.

You would start with the statutory language of § 2–302: "If the court as a matter of law finds the contract . . . to have been unconscionable at the time it was made, the court may refuse to enforce the contract. . . . " Then analyze procedural and substantive unconscionability separately, breaking each type of unconscionability into the factors that courts have identified. For example, because procedural unconscionability can result from unequal bargaining power, absence of meaningful choice, or hidden terms, you would analyze each relevant factor in relation to the contract in your case.

To prove this claim, like many totality of circumstances claims, you usually do not have to prove each of the factors you have identified, although the more factors you can prove, the stronger the claim. Thus, a contract may be procedurally unconscionable although it does not have hidden terms, if the parties were in unequal bargaining positions and the plaintiff lacked meaningful choice of terms. These factors could weigh strongly in the plaintiff's favor. (For more on the organization of this analysis, see Chapter Eight).

You may organize a totality of circumstances discussion in several ways. You may decide to analyze each factor separately. Then you should determine whether all the factors must be proven, and if not, how important the factors are relative to each other.

At other times, however, it may make more sense to organize a totality of circumstances problem around the principles the court has articulated for weighing the factors, if a court has done so. In other words, instead of taking each factor separately, use the court's guidelines for assessing the factors to organize your discussion. For example, suppose the court has said, as it did in Elliott, that diversity jurisdiction is appropriate only to give a stranger to the state access to an unbiased court. A good way to organize your assessment of the factors is to group those that show plaintiff is not a stranger to Virginia, and then to weigh those against factors that show plaintiff is a stranger. You then determine which set of facts is stronger.

An alternative organization is by the parties. Group the factors that favor one party, then the factors that favor another party. Then evaluate the strength of each party's case. This might be the best way to analyze a statute that requires the courts to consider seven factors to determine the best interests of a child in a custody dispute:

1. the wishes of the child's parent or parents as to custody;

2. the wishes of the child as to his custodian;

3. the interaction and interrelationship of the child with his parent or parents, his siblings, and any other person who may significantly affect the child's best interest;

4. the child's adjustment to his home, school, and community;

5. the mental and physical health of all individuals involved;

6. the physical violence or threat of physical violence by the child's potential custodian, whether directed against the child or directed against another person; and

7. the willingness and ability of each parent to facilitate and encourage a close and continuing relationship between the other parent and the child.

In a custody dispute, each parent may be requesting custody of the child, and the court will evaluate the strength of their requests. The child may wish to remain with her mother, but may interact well with both parents and both sets of grandparents; the child would remain in her current school if she lived with her mother, but not with her father; the fifth and sixth factors may not be relevant; and the mother may be less willing than the father to encourage the child to retain a close relationship with the other parent. The court will then have to weigh the child's wish to stay with her mother and the importance of remaining in the same school against the father's greater willingness to continue the child's relationship with the other parent.

Exercise 4–F

The Illinois Marriage and Dissolution of Marriage Act § 601 regarding proceedings to determine child custody permits a person other than a parent to petition for custody "but only if [the child] is not in the physical custody of one of [the child's] parents." Read these case synopses to determine what "physical custody" means. Then outline the factors involved and write a paragraph explaining the balance that is required.

a.   James and Joyce Peters had one child, Lynn. At their divorce, the court awarded custody of Lynn to Joyce and visitation rights to James. Joyce and Lynn moved in with Joyce's parents. Joyce contracted a fatal and disabling disease, during which her parents cared for her and for Lynn at their home. James exercised his weekly visitation rights during this time. After Joyce died, James asked for the child, but was refused, and James and Joyce's parents then filed petitions to modify custody. The court dismissed the grandparents' petition. It held that the grandparents did not have physical custody of Lynn but only possession. Joyce had physical custody until her death and Lynn was then in her father's physical custody. It would not have occurred to James that the grandparents were developing a position of physical custody by which they could deprive him of custody of the child. To hold otherwise would encourage the parties to engage in child abduction in order to remove the child from the parents, which was against the policy of the Act.

b.   After her divorce, Barbara turned over her younger daughter to the temporary care of Barbara's older adult daughter. This daughter then turned over the child to a friend who frequently had taken the child for overnight stays. The friend filed for custody. The court held that Barbara had never relinquished physical custody of her child and dismissed the friend's petition.

c.   Mennan left his child with his parents when his wife died. The grandparents kept the child for 7 years during which time they had almost no communication from Mennan. When Mennan returned, he took the child from them by force. The court held that the grandparents could petition because Mennan had voluntarily relinquished physical custody to them. Allowing the petition would promote the policy of the Act to foster stability in the child's home environment.

———

Exercise 4–G

Read the following cases, all of which deal with the question of a hospital's liability for the suicide of one of its patients. Ask yourself what the basic rule is regarding the standard of care and what factors the courts will consider in determining a hospital's liability.

Ross v. Brown Hospital

The plaintiff's wife committed suicide four days after she was admitted to the defendant mental hospital. The patient had twice tried to commit suicide before her admission to the hospital. The last time was the day before she was admitted.

The court denied the defendant's motion to dismiss and stated that the hospital owed the plaintiff a duty of exercising reasonable care to protect her from injuring herself. That duty was proportionate to her needs and constituted such reasonable care as her known mental condition required.

Smith v. Stevens Hospital

An acutely depressed patient was left unobserved in his hospital room by his nurses for successive periods of two hours each during the night and early morning. During the last of these periods, he hung himself with a bed sheet. The court held that the hospital did not exercise reasonable care in supervising the patient and was liable.

Moore v. United States

The patient voluntarily admitted himself to a hospital. His preadmittance diagnosis was arteriosclerosis. His examination revealed no signs of suicidal tendencies or any psychiatric disorder. He had no history of mental illness. The doctors accordingly placed him in an open ward.

Four days later, the patient's behavior changed. He became paranoid and in fear for his life. The doctors then transferred him to a closed ward. The doors were kept locked and heavy screens were placed over the windows. The attendants routinely counted the silverware on his meal tray. There was a high number of personnel per patient in this ward. Nurses observed the patient several times and saw no unusual behavior. One night the patient pried open the screen in front of a window and jumped out. The court held that the hospital had used reasonable care in diagnosing the patient in light of his history and in treating him.

Brown v. General Hospital

The plaintiff's wife had attempted suicide and had voluntarily admitted herself to the psychiatric department at General Hospital. For five months she was in a closed ward and received electroshock treatment. When her condition improved, her doctor transferred her to an open ward.

Under modern psychiatric theory, allowing patients as much freedom as possible is consistent with reasonable care. Doctors believe that an open ward is more conducive to the establishment of a therapeutic atmosphere in which the patient comes to trust the doctor than is a closed ward. Ms. Brown's doctor recommended a program of drug treatment and occupational therapy. For six months, Ms. Brown remained in the open ward and her condition continued to improve. She then took her life. The court held that the hospital had used reasonable care in supervising her and was not liable for negligence.[7]

———————

What is the basic standard that the courts use in determining whether a hospital is liable for the suicide of one of its patients? Make a list of the factors the courts consider in analyzing this standard. These factors are the issues that you would discuss in analyzing the hospital's liability. They form the organizational structure of your analysis.

7. Case summaries in the example are based on Stallman v. Robinson, 260 S.W.2d 743 (Mo. 1953); Smith v. Simpson, 288 S.W. 69 (Mo. App. 1926); Moore v. United States, 222 F. Supp. 87 (E.D. Mo. 1963); Gregory v. Robinson, 338 S.W.2d 88 (Mo. 1960).

Chapter Five

Organization of a Legal Discussion: Small–Scale Organization

I. Introduction

In Chapter Four, we discussed the need to organize a legal analysis around the legal issues of each claim for relief. In this chapter, we focus on the organization of a discussion of a single legal issue and suggest an organizational pattern that will enable you to write a clear analysis of that issue. The pattern presented here is a fairly standard format for fact-based legal problems because it logically orders the steps necessary in this type of legal reasoning. We focus here on fact-based problems because these are common assignments in both legal practice and first-year legal writing courses. Be aware, however, that a different kind of legal problem—one involving the meaning or the validity of a law, for example—will require you to adapt this pattern so that your focus is on statutory construction, weight of authority, judicial reasoning, or underlying policies rather than on factual comparison (see Chapter Eleven).

With this caveat in mind, a useful pattern for analyzing a single legal issue often has the following structure.

1. Explanation of the applicable rule of law

2. Examination of how the rule is applied in the relevant precedents

3. Application of the law to the facts of your case and comparison with the precedents

4.   Presentation and evaluation of counterarguments

5.   Conclusion

In other words, begin by explaining the controlling rule in the jurisdiction in which your problem is located. If there is no controlling rule in that jurisdiction, then discuss what the rule should be by looking at rules in other jurisdictions. The general rule comes from the elements of a statute or statutes or from a common law claim, and from the holding of a previous case or from a synthesis of holdings from more than one case on a topic. Summarize the explanations of a rule that have been offered by those authorities that have established and applied it. Explain the relevant facts of those cases. Then apply that rule to the facts of your case, and compare and contrast the facts of those precedents to the facts of your problem. Discuss the counterarguments and the exceptions that may apply. Finally, evaluate the arguments and counterarguments to reach a conclusion as to the outcome of your problem.

Adherence to this pattern ensures that the reader gets necessary information in an order which is readily understandable. You should not begin the discussion with a summary of the facts of your case, for example, because the reader cannot assess the legal significance of those facts without your having first explained the controlling rules and examined the relevant case law and the kinds of facts courts have previously decided were legally significant. Therefore, you usually examine relevant case law before you discuss how the law applies to the facts of your own case. Similarly, you should raise and answer counterarguments before you reach a conclusion because the success with which you handle a counterargument should be reflected in your final conclusion.

Sometimes the analysis of an issue is so clear cut that you can include all five analytic steps in a single paragraph. For example, if the case law in your jurisdiction on false imprisonment requires that a plaintiff be aware that he was confined and the plaintiff in your problem was clearly aware of his confinement, you can treat that requirement quickly. For most issues, however, you will need to break your analysis into parts. You can subdivide your discussion without sacrificing its logical structure if your paragraphs reflect those steps. You should also use topic and transition sentences to remind the reader what you have covered and to indicate where the discussion is going.

II.   *Steps and Organization of a Legal Analysis on a Single Legal Issue Using a Single Case*

The following pages attempt to illustrate the development of a discussion of one element in an action for intentional infliction of emotional distress. The client, plaintiff Livia Augusta, wants to sue Olympia Department Store for emotional distress suffered while the store attempted to collect payment for a debt she never incurred. The discussion is based on one primary authority, a case from the same jurisdiction as the problem, Davis v. Household Finance, and on one secondary source (full citations are omitted).

A.   *Paragraph or Paragraphs on the Rule of Law*

The discussion of a particular legal issue should begin with a sentence or one or more paragraphs that set forth and explain the governing rule of law. When the rule of law appears to be both straightforward and clearly articulated, a complete paragraph explaining it may be unnecessary. In these instances, you would still need to begin with a topic sentence informing the reader of the governing rule, but you could follow this sentence with a discussion of its application in decided cases. When the intent and the scope of the law is more complicated, however, you may need to write a much longer explanation clarifying its meaning or components. These explanations may require you either to analyze the language of a constitution or a statute, to set out the tests governing a law's application or the competing explanations, or to summarize a court's discussion of that rule or a pertinent discussion in a secondary authority, which has, perhaps, been adopted in that jurisdiction.

A paragraph that explains the applicable law governing a defendant's outrageous conduct might look as follows (the marginal comments refer to the paragraph's mode of construction).

Topic Sentence Announcing Element

Explication of Rule

> The first element for intentional infliction of emotional distress is whether the defendant's conduct was extreme and outrageous. Davis v. Household Finance. Outrageous conduct is distinguishable from minor insults, threats, or annoyances. Id. A defendant has engaged in outrageous conduct only if he has engaged in a "prolonged course of hounding by a variety of extreme methods." W. Prosser, Law of Torts 57 (4th ed. 1971). Such methods include abusive language, shouting, repeated threats of arrest, withdrawal of credit, and appeals to the debtor's employer. Davis.

B.   *Paragraph or Paragraphs on Case Law*

After analyzing the governing rule of law, your next step is to examine the relevant case law from which that rule came or in which it has been applied. In a fact-based problem, you should recount the relevant facts of the precedents because it is by identifying how the rules of law were applied to the facts of those cases that you give the rules meaning. Then by identifying similarities and differences between the facts of the precedents and those of your client's case, you predict the outcome of an action. It is also necessary to give the court's holding since, under stare decisis, it is the holding for each important case which establishes how the facts are to be interpreted. Finally, you should summarize for the reader the reasons and policies behind a court's determination of an issue. This type of analysis provides a basis for generating arguments about whether the legal requirements of that claim will be satisfied in your case. We illustrate this step with one paragraph because this discussion is based on only one precedent. A more complex discussion might require more than one paragraph.

It is important to remember that you are examining these cases to shed light on the legal principle you introduced in the opening paragraph. You must, therefore, connect the case discussion to that principle. If you fail to show how the precedent illustrates, limits, expands, or explains the law, the discussion falters. One general rule of thumb here is to avoid beginning this paragraph with a sentence giving the facts of a case, as "In East v. West, where a defendant stood in front of a door to prevent three men from exiting, the court found no basis for recovery." Rather, start either with a topic sentence setting forth the legal principle that case shows or with a transition sentence that makes it clear you are continuing the same topic.

Topic Sentence on Legal Principle

Holding

Reasoning

Pertinent Facts

When the defendant is a creditor, it may use reasonable if somewhat embarrassing and annoying methods to collect legitimate debts. Davis. In Davis, the court held that Finance Corp.'s conduct was not outrageous when it made numerous phone calls and visits to Mrs. Davis at her home and at the hospital where she visited her ailing daughter. Id. Finance Corp. made these phone calls for seven months. The Davis court reasoned that a creditor must be given some latitude in collecting a past due obligation and that Finance Corp.'s conduct fell within reasonable limits. Indeed, Mrs. Davis herself did not allege that Finance Corp.'s agents used abusive, threatening, or profane language. Id. Although the court said that Finance Corp. acted wrongly when it induced Davis to write a bad check, it found that one isolated act was inadequate to show the prolonged course of harassment that is required for a showing of outrageous conduct. The court permitted the creditor reasonable latitude to collect its debt, which it had a legal right to do. Id.

C. *Paragraph or Paragraphs on Application of Precedents*

The next step in a legal analysis involves applying the facts, policies, and reasons of decided cases to your case. In a memorandum, you should set out and evaluate the similarities and differences between the precedent and your case and determine their importance. The central job in this stage of analysis is to compare each relevant fact in the decided cases to those in your own case and to evaluate the strength of the claim you wish to make in light of these comparisons. You also apply the reasoning or policies of a decided case to your own case.

It is helpful to begin this step with a transition sentence which weighs the merits of the client's case in light of established precedent.

<table>
<tr><td>

Transition
Sentence
Distinguishing
Cases

Distinguishing
Facts

</td><td>

Augusta's situation is distinguishable from that of Ms. Davis in two ways. First, Augusta does not owe a debt to Olympia. Thus the reasoning in <u>Davis</u>—namely, giving a creditor latitude to collect debts—does not apply to Olympia. Olympia was not doing what it had a legal right to do. Second, Olympia's conduct was more extreme than that of Finance Corp. For example, the language of Finance Corp.'s personnel was neither abusive nor vituperative. Olympia's language, however, became increasingly abusive and vituperative—an employee called her "a welsher and a four flushing bastard." Thus, Olympia engaged in a type of conduct that the court said was not present in <u>Davis</u>. In addition, Olympia's wrongful conduct was not an isolated act, like inducing a plaintiff to write a bad check, but occurred over a period of many months. The billing department sent daily letters that demanded payment and that threatened to cancel her charge account and to report her delinquent account to the Credit Rating Bureau.

</td></tr>
</table>

When you believe your adversary has no authentic counterargument on this issue, do not feel compelled to create one. Instead, end your discussion with a conclusory sentence, for example, "Since these letters continued arriving for three months, Olympia engaged in a prolonged course of harassment." Normally, however, your adversary will have a valid argument which you must assess before coming to a conclusion, as discussed below.

D & E. *Paragraph or Paragraphs on Presentation and Evaluation of Counterarguments and Legal Conclusion*

A thorough discussion requires you to present and evaluate counterarguments. Evaluation of a counterargument is usually the last step before the conclusion in a legal analysis. When the evaluation is complex, it may require an extended analysis of one or more paragraphs.

Discuss those precedents and those facts from your problem that your opponent is going to rely on. Opposing counsel will highlight facts which are clearly unfavorable to your client or which can be interpreted differently by the parties. In an objective analysis, it is important to raise all reasonable interpretations of the issues. When issues are complex, the application of law to fact is rarely clear-cut and will often support more than one interpretation. Your job is to evaluate the strength of these interpretations.

When a legal memo is written analyzing a client's case, you will want to consider whether you can meet a counterargument by showing 1) that it is based on legally insignificant or incomplete facts or on a misapplication of the law to the facts, or 2) that it relies on inapplicable reasons or policy arguments. On the other hand, your analysis of the opposing argument might convince you that your client cannot prevail on this issue. If this is the case, you should say so. An office memorandum is an objective exploration of your client's legal situation and the basis for legal advice. (See Chapter Seven.) You do not want to be misleading in a document of this nature.

The final sentence should be the legal conclusion, a conclusion grounded in the prior analysis of the law, precedent, and facts. This conclusion differs from the one given in the thesis paragraph that begins the Discussion section of the memorandum. (See Chapter Six.) That conclusion offers an assessment of a client's overall chance of winning a suit or defending himself against a charge. Here, the conclusion refers only to the issue that has been under discussion.

Topic Sentence: Counterargument

Opponent's Facts & Reasoning

Opponent's Conclusion

Arguably, Olympia has not done anything as extreme as Finance Corp. Whereas Finance Corp. induced Davis to write a bad check and then phoned an acquaintance of Davis to inform her that Davis wrote bad checks, Olympia did nothing so publicly humiliating. Whereas Finance Corp. called Davis several times a week, frequently more than once a day, for a period of seven months, Olympia sent out daily letters and made daily phone calls only over a three month period. The court in Davis found that Finance Corp.'s numerous phone calls did not establish a prolonged course of hounding because there was no indication that the agents of Finance conducted themselves other than in a permissible manner during those calls. Thus, even if less extreme conduct is actionable when the plaintiff is not a debtor, Augusta may not be able to establish a prolonged course of harassment involving more than minor insults and threats.

Transition Sentence: Rebuttal

Facts & Reasoning Supporting Rebuttal

Legal Conclusion

This argument should not prevail, however. Even if Olympia did not commit so extreme an action as inducing Augusta to write a bad check, and even if its course of harassment was four months shy of Finance's, Olympia's abusive language and threats of ruination of credit are not permissible conduct under Davis. Had Augusta actually been a debtor, Olympia's conduct in comparison to that of Finance Corp. might nonetheless have stated a claim. Given that Augusta was not a debtor, and that the reasoning of Davis is therefore inapplicable, Augusta will satisfy the element of outrageous conduct in an action for intentional infliction of emotional distress.

Although you can handle counterarguments in separate paragraphs, it is possible, if also more difficult, to weave rebuttal into your analysis and application of the case law. (In the fact application paragraph of step three, for example, the writer begins to rebut potential opposing arguments by distinguishing the facts of the cases.) When the counterargument or the rebuttal is complex, however, or when the counterargument is based on policy or reasoning rather than precedent, it may be preferable to handle the rebuttal separately, as in the paragraphs above.

Exercise 5–A

In order to win a suit against Olympia Department Store on the grounds of intentional infliction of emotional distress, Livia Augusta must show that the conduct of the store was intentional or reckless. Read the following summary of Davis v. Finance Corp. on the requirement of reckless conduct. Then read Augusta's account of Olympia's reckless conduct. List the points you will make to show Olympia was reckless. Then list the points that show Olympia was not reckless. After this, write a discussion on whether Augusta can show Olympia acted recklessly.

Davis v. Finance Corp.

Defendant's conduct must be intentional or at least reckless to be actionable. If reckless, the conduct must be such that there is a high degree of probability that the plaintiff will suffer severe emotional distress and the actor goes ahead in conscious disregard of it.

Mrs. Davis told Finance Corp. that its visits to her at the hospital where she visited her ailing daughter were upsetting her daughter so much that her recovery was being impeded. Davis added that she herself was becoming extremely anxious, worried, and angry that Finance was dragging a patient into a dispute that "was none of the patient's doing." Upon hearing this, Finance Corp. suspended its visits to the hospital. At a later date, Davis informed Finance that "its harassment was driving her nuts."

The court held that the conduct of Finance Corp. was not reckless because it suspended its visits to the hospital when it became apparent that there was a high degree of probability that severe emotional distress would follow from those visits. It also stated that Davis's warning that Finance was "driving her nuts" did not sufficiently establish reckless conduct leading to severe distress since the phrase is routinely used to describe such trivial reactions as a parent's irritation at a child's misbehavior.

———

Livia Augusta told her attorney that she began informing Olympia personnel that its harassment was causing her insomnia, nightmares and weight loss after three weeks of abusive phone calls. After four weeks, Livia wrote the following letter to the president of Olympia.

The conduct of your personnel in pursuing payment for a purchase I never made is having a horrendous impact on my health and emotional stability. My physician is giving me tranquilizers around the clock to control the acute anxiety I have been experiencing. This situation is intolerable, and I expect you, as president of the store, to clear this matter up before I become a complete wreck.

The president wrote back to Augusta promising that he would resolve the matter, but telling her it might take a week or so to clear up the confusion. Two weeks after this response, Augusta received a letter from Olympia saying it had reported her delinquent account to the Credit Rating Bureau.

III. Case Synthesis in a Legal Analysis of a Single Legal Issue

Occasionally, one case like <u>Davis</u> will provide all of the authority you need to resolve a legal question. More frequently, however, you will need to use more than one case to analyze that question. The following example is an analysis of one part of a false imprisonment case brought by Alma Kingsford against her former employers. Alma Kingsford claims that her employers summoned her to an office where one of them blocked the exit by standing in front of the door. They then proceeded to threaten and shout at her in an effort to force her to resign from their firm and forgo severance pay. The requirements of this tort are that the defendant must actually have confined the plaintiff, that the defendant intended to confine the plaintiff, and that the plaintiff was aware of or harmed by the confinement. This part of the discussion is an analysis of the first element: actual confinement. In researching this problem, you will have found a number of cases dealing with the elements of a false imprisonment action. For the moment, set aside all of the cases that decided elements other than actual confinement. You will address those cases later.

In examining your cases on the element of confinement, you will discover that confinement can be brought about in several different ways. Kingsford's argument is that the defendant confined her in a room to question her by threatening to use physical force if she left the room. Your focus should therefore be on those cases that show confinement by threat of physical force.

Your discussion of confinement by threat of physical force must make sense of all the different factual situations which courts have held establish that requirement. In other words, you must synthesize the cases your research has turned up by articulating the factors that make analytic sense of decisions involving diverse fact patterns. In this false imprisonment problem, your case synthesis will reveal that a threat of physical force can be established by a defendant's actions, tone of voice, or size advantage. These are factors that have proven confinement in other cases. The cases also reveal two other factors necessary to a finding of confinement by threat of physical force, namely, that the defendant had the ability to carry out the threat and that the confinement was against the plaintiff's will. You should discuss each of these factors separately, and you should begin each discussion with a topic sentence that states how those factors can be established.

When you synthesize cases in your discussion, do not feel compelled to give all cases equal treatment. First, always give more weight to and begin with precedents from the jurisdiction of your problem than to precedents from other jurisdictions. Second, let your treatment of a case depend on its relevance to your client's situation. Some cases, for example, may not provide useful facts for comparison but may provide a rule of law or relevant policy. In this situation, a one sentence summary of the rule or policy may be all you need to use. Where, however, a case is especially relevant to your problem—either for the facts or for its discussion of the rule—your discussion of the precedent should be more extensive. In reading through the sample discussion that follows, notice when a one-sentence summary is used to state a rule or to characterize a set of facts and when a case is more thoroughly treated.

Notice also that the sample discussion begins with an introductory paragraph, the first sentence of which introduces the element of whether the plaintiff had been confined. The paragraph then identifies the factors that prove confinement and concludes with a statement about whether the element can be satisfied in the problem case.

The rest of the discussion demonstrates how the basic technique for organizing a discussion of an issue when working with a group of cases is similar to that used when working with one case—the rule is presented, the precedent or precedents are discussed, the facts of your case are compared, opposing arguments are raised and evaluated, and finally, a conclusion regarding that issue is stated. Notice in the sample discussion that when a requirement can be easily established, all the analytic steps described above are covered in a single paragraph. When the discussion is complex or case law abundant, however, the discussion is subdivided into paragraphs indicative of the steps in a legal analysis. Also notice that counter-arguments are not always raised. When counterarguments seem insubstantial, this step can be omitted or incorporated into the fact application paragraph. Note, all cases are from the jurisdiction of the problem, but full citations have been omitted.

Pattern of an Analysis Involving Case Synthesis

Topic Sentence:
Confinement

Case Used for
General Rule

The first element of false imprisonment requires that the defendant confine the plaintiff. In Kent, a defendant can confine a plaintiff by physical barriers, overpowering physical force, threats to apply physical force if the victim goes outside the boundary fixed by the defendants, submission to other types of duress, and submission to an asserted legal authority. <u>Johnson v. White</u> (adopting Restatement (Second) of Torts). Kingsford's chances of establishing confinement depend on her showing that the defendants threatened physical force. A plaintiff may be confined through threat of physical force by a defendant's action, see Atkins v. Barton, or by a defendant's tone, see Tyler v. Jones. Under any of these circumstances, the defendant must also have the ability to apply force. East v. West. Finally, the restraint must be against the plaintiff's will. Id. If the plaintiff voluntarily agrees to stay, he or she has not been falsely imprisoned. Lopez v. Winchell. Kingsford was confined because Peterson and Smith were able to carry out the threat they made and she submitted to them against her will.

An action so intimidating that its effect is to confine the plaintiff by threat of physical force may result from the defendant's movement and gestures and from the plaintiff's perception of the defendant's size advantage. Atkins v. Barton. In Atkins, the plaintiff successfully sued a deprogrammer, Barton, for false imprisonment. Barton was 6'2" and 225 pounds. When he stepped in front of the door to the plaintiff's bedroom, blocking her exit, she reasonably believed that she was confined by threat of physical force even though he did not say a word. Id. Similarly, Ms. Kingsford may have been confined by the threatening gestures of her supervisors. Smith moved to the door and leaned against it when Kingsford rose from her chair as if to leave. In addition, Smith has a size advantage. At 5'6" Smith is five inches taller than Ms. Kingsford. She is also athletic and works out at a health club several times a week.

Nonetheless, because Smith is significantly smaller and lighter than the defendant in Atkins, defendants will doubtlessly argue that Kingsford's reliance on Atkins is misplaced. In addition, whereas the female plaintiff in Atkins perceived the male defendant as having an unfair physical advantage because of his gender, there is no gender disparity between Kingsford and Smith. Yet these differences are probably not significant. Courts have consistently regarded the comparative sizes of the parties as more important for establishing intimidation than size or gender alone. See Cane v. Downs (defendant was six inches taller and fifty pounds heavier than plaintiff); Carey v. Robier (although defendant was only 5'5", plaintiff was four inches smaller). See also Mussel v. Wimple (defendant was a 5'11" male, plaintiff a 5'6" male). Thus, based on their gestures and size advantage, the defendants threatened physical force.

If the defendant does speak, his tone may be sufficient to establish a threat of physical force, even if he made no explicit threat. In Tyler v. Jones, the defendant accused the plaintiff of stealing money from his car. The defendant demanded that plaintiff be searched in front of his fellow workers. The defendant's confrontational manner and his belligerent tone of voice made it clear that there would be serious trouble if the plaintiff did not allow himself to be searched. Id. In calling his friends over to witness the "frisk," the defendant created a threatening atmosphere. Id. In Ms. Kingsford's case, threats of physical

---

Margin notes (left column):

Cases Provide Rule For 1st Subissue: Threat For 2nd Subissue: Ability

For 3rd Subissue: Involuntariness

Legal Conclusion

Topic Sentence: 1st Subissue

Case on 2 Ways Threat Can Be Made

Comparison with Problem Case

Transition Sentence on Counter- argument

Pertinent Facts

Parentheticals Support Rebuttal

Legal Conclusion

Topic Sentence On 3rd Way to Show Threat

Case Provides Example

Comparison with
Problem Case

Conclusion

Topic Sentence
On 2nd Subissue:
Ability

Precedent
Facts
Comparison

Topic Sentence
on 3rd Subissue:
Involuntariness

Case Analysis

Transition
Sentence
Suggests
Counter-
argument

Pertinent Facts

Transition
Sentence:
Rebuttal

Case Supports
Rebuttal

Distinguishing
Adverse Decision

Restatement of
Legal Conclusion

force, if not actually articulated, were at least implicit in Peterson's tone of voice, which Kingsford described as "loud" and "harsh." She also referred to a lot of "screaming and shouting." Thus, the defendants' actions and tone established a threat of physical force.

The ability to carry out a threat can be established if defendants outnumber the plaintiff. See Appley v. Owens (two defendants confined plaintiff); Atkins (parents and deprogrammer confined a single woman). Like the defendants in these cases, Peterson and Smith outnumbered the plaintiff. As Kingsford said, "there were two against one."

Finally, there is no confinement unless the plaintiff remains involuntarily. East v. West. The plaintiffs in East remained voluntarily. When told the police had been called, they agreed to wait. Id. In Lopez v. Winchell, the plaintiff, who was accused of stealing money from her employer, remained voluntarily. She decided to remain in the store with her employers so that she could clear her name.

Like Lopez, Kingsford agreed to remain in Peterson's office. Peterson and Smith had initially summoned Kingsford to the office to fire her. They also wanted her to agree to leave their firm without receiving severance pay. When Kingsford said that she would never agree to such a condition and that she would not hang around to be bullied into submission, Peterson told her that if she left, he would not only refuse to give her a reference but would actively spread the word that she was a sullen, incompetent, and lazy employee. Threatened by the prospect of both present and future unemployment if Peterson did as he said, Kingsford agreed to remain in the office to discuss the matter further, as Lopez did to clear her good name.

Yet this similarity between Lopez's situation and Kingsford's is probably not dispositive. A submission which is procured by an act or threat to take something of value from the plaintiff is not voluntary. Goodhart v. Butcher Restaurant. In Goodhart, a restaurant owner took and held onto a patron's wallet until he could determine if the patron had paid his bill. During this time, the patron remained because he did not want to lose the wallet's valuable contents. The court held that the plaintiff had not remained voluntarily when the defendant took something of value from the plaintiff in order to ensure the plaintiff remained. Id. Although Peterson did not take a tangible object like a wallet, he did have control over Kingsford's professional reputation, which is a thing of value. In contrast, although the plaintiff in Lopez was worried about her "good name," her employer did not threaten to give Lopez a bad reference if she left. Thus, Goodhart is the controlling case here, and Kingsford should be able to show that she was confined against her will. All three requirements for confinement by threat of physical force can, therefore, be established.

Two important writing techniques for handling case synthesis have been used in this discussion. First, the paragraphs often begin with topic sentences that state in general terms the principles that have been extracted from the precedents. Thus, the fact that the plaintiffs in Appley v. Owens and Atkins v. Barton were outnumbered is the basis of the author's general claim, made in the topic sentence of paragraph four, that "the ability to carry out a threat is established when defendants outnumber the plaintiff." Similarly, the defendants' overbearing size and movements in Atkins v. Barton, Cane v. Downs, and Carey v. Robier give rise to the topic sentence in paragraph two that "an action so intimidating that its effect is to confine by threat of physical force may result from the defendant's movements and gestures and from the plaintiff's perception of the defendant's size advantage." Constructing such general statements is one important way of bringing to your reader the results of your analysis. The topic sentences also promote clear organization by orienting the reader to the paragraph's place in the analysis.

The second important writing technique used in this discussion is the writer's considered use of parenthetical discussion. Because the deprogrammer Barton is such a clear and dramatic example of size advantage, the author discusses Atkins thoroughly in order to establish the main point. The references to Cane v. Downs and Carey v. Robier are necessary because they refine the point that size advantage can be relative, but the facts can be parenthetical because these cases are used to supply details and general support of Atkins. By using these parentheticals, the author keeps the text free from the specific factual details of these cases.

Exercise 5–B

To win a suit against Olympia Department Store, Livia Augusta needs to establish not only that Olympia used outrageous collection tactics, but that her distress was severe. Read Augusta's account of her emotional state and the following summaries of controlling precedents. Then write a discussion on the issue of whether Augusta can show her emotional distress was severe.

––––––

Augusta reports a variety of reactions to Olympia's tactics, including insomnia, nightmares, and weight loss (15 lbs.). When she began hyperventilating after each phone call from Olympia, Augusta became worried about her health. She went to see her doctor, who diagnosed her as suffering from acute anxiety. He gave her a prescription for 10 mg. valium and told her to take one tablet four times a day. Although Augusta has been following this regimen, she complains the medication has been interfering with her job performance and social life. She has trouble concentrating, dozed off during an important meeting, and feels too lethargic to go out in the evenings. Her employer has told her to "shape up." The tranquilizers have helped to control her anxiety and sleeplessness, but Livia is worried about their long term effect on her physical health.

Davis v. Finance Corp.

The tort of intentional infliction of emotional distress requires a showing that the distress is severe. Mental conditions such as fright, horror, grief, shame, humiliation, or worry may fall within the ambit of the term emotional distress. However, these mental conditions alone are not actionable. The distress inflicted must be so severe that no reasonable person could be expected to endure it. The court decided that Davis's distress was severe because she suffered shame and anxiety and required medical attention, but it dismissed the case because Davis was unable to establish the separate element of outrageous and reckless conduct.

Marlboro v. First Bank of Gilford

June Marlboro, a fifty-five-year-old widowed schoolteacher, was diagnosed as suffering major depression in June 1987. Four months prior to this diagnosis, Marlboro had defaulted on a home improvement loan from the First Bank of Gilford because she had lent her retired brother money to purchase a new car. In the month following the default, Marlboro received daily threatening letters. Later, the bank's collection agent began making nightly, obscene phone calls. June found herself going on eating binges after these calls. After the bank called the principal of her school to inform him of her default, June's symptoms of depression became more pronounced. She was often fatigued and began taking naps during the day and oversleeping in the mornings. She experienced a loss of self-esteem. She was unable to make decisions. She gained twenty pounds. She went to her physician, who found that her weight increase had raised her blood pressure. He put her on a salt-free diet and told her that she had to lose weight. He also referred her to a psychiatrist. The psychiatrist testified that June's mental health has been seriously threatened. The court found Marlboro's distress so severe no reasonable person could be expected to endure it.

Dale v. New City Hospital

Jim Dale lost his job when his employer went bankrupt. In the months that followed, money became increasingly tight. Then, Mrs. Dale was hospitalized with leukemia. Dale, who had never bought medical insurance to replace his old employee coverage, was unable to pay the hospital bills. The hospital turned his account over to a collection agency, which began hounding him for payment. Shortly thereafter, Dale sank into a serious depression. He suffered from an emotional paralysis so severe that he was unable to leave his apartment. He refused to visit his wife in the hospital and missed several job interviews. His physician placed him on anti-depressants. Although the court found Dale's distress so severe as to interfere with normal functioning, it concluded that his distress was not the result of the defendant's actions, but of his wife's diagnosis and his unemployment.

Histrionic v. Credit Inc.

Histrionic, a seasoned actor in rehearsal for an off-broadway musical, defaulted on his payments to Credit Inc. When Credit Inc. attempted to collect the debt, Histrionic reacted emotionally. He broke down several times during rehearsal, ranting about Credit Inc.'s persecution of him and weeping that he was misunderstood. On more than one occasion, he threw himself down on the stage, pounding the floor and moaning that he was ruined. His doctor testified that Histrionic's response to Credit's collection methods was extreme and that he had prescribed a mild sedative for Histrionic. Although Histrionic tended to forget his lines while on this medication, the musical, when it opened, was a smashing success. Histrionic was singled out for his excellent performance. The court found Histrionic's emotional distress not actionable. It said that Histrionic's feelings of hysteria and anxiety had not grossly impeded his functioning and that his behavior was in some measure consistent with his prior character and professional training.

Chapter Six
The Thesis Paragraph

A legal discussion should begin with a paragraph that introduces the reader to your client's claim for relief, to the legal issues it involves, and to your reasoned conclusions about their probable resolution in your client's situation. This paragraph is frequently called a thesis paragraph because it states your thesis, that is, your position on the outcome of a client's prospective case. One benefit of providing this kind of introduction early in the discussion is that it makes it easier for your reader to evaluate the analysis as it is being built. Another benefit is that it sets out the organization of the discussion.

One logical way of arranging relevant introductory material in a thesis paragraph is to

1. Identify the claim or defense in your problem;

2. Set out the rules that govern that claim in the order you intend to discuss them and explain how those rules relate to each other;

3. If length permits, or complexity requires, briefly apply those rules to your facts;

4. State the thesis (your legal conclusion).

If your memo is fairly simple, however, or if your professor or firm requires a Conclusion section rather than a Short Answer section (See Chapter Seven), you may want to shorten your thesis paragraph by eliminating or abbreviating some of the steps outlined above. One thing you can do is to eliminate step 3, the application of the law to the facts. You can also combine steps 1 and 4 and begin with a thesis sentence that introduces the topic of the discussion and gives your conclusion as to the claim or defense in your problem. After this, you could still indicate the organization of your discussion by introducing the rules that govern that claim in the relevant jurisdiction or, in a case of first impression, in other jurisdictions.

———

Assume you are writing about a due process problem based on the following facts.

Alice Doone, mother of three minor children, receives payments under the Aid to Families with Dependent Children program (AFDC), a federal program administered by the state. Her payments were reduced when she enrolled in a work-training program which paid her a stipend. Having unsuccessfully challenged the reductions at an administrative hearing of the state Social Services Department, Doone sought to appeal to the State of Kent Court of Appeals. Such appeals are authorized by state law. However, under state law, the filing of a civil appeal requires a $40 filing fee. Ms. Doone claimed she was unable to pay the fee and sought leave to proceed in forma pauperis (permission to proceed without liability for court fees); leave was denied without an opinion. Alice Doone would now like to file suit in the United States District Court for the Western District of Kent, claiming that application of a fee to indigent appellants violates the due process clause of the fourteenth amendment.

You might begin your discussion with a thesis paragraph like the one below.

Topic Sentence on Claim	To proceed with her claim against AFDC, Ms. Doone needs to show that the statutory $40 filing fee, as applied to her, violates the due process clause of the fourteenth amendment to the United States Constitution. Due process demands that an indigent person not be denied access to the courts for failure to pay a fee when
Applicable Rules	(1) the court is the only forum for resolving the dispute, (2) the underlying subject matter is itself of constitutional significance, and (3) the constitutional interest overrides a countervailing state interest. Boddie v. Connecticut, 401 U.S. 371 (1971). In this case, the court is the only forum in which Ms. Doone can challenge the Department's reduction of her benefits. However, the underlying subject matter, an increase in welfare payments for family
Application	support, is not constitutionally significant. Thus, the state's interest in defraying the costs of the judicial system will override Ms. Doone's interest. The filing fee will, therefore, probably be
Legal Conclusion	found constitutionally permissible under the due process clause.

This paragraph is an effective introduction in that it clearly states the legal question, the relevant legal tests and their applicability to the client, and the author's conclusion. A lot of this information is in the next sample thesis paragraph but in a less explicit manner.

> In <u>Boddie v. Connecticut</u>, 401 U.S. 371 (1971), the Court held that requiring a filing fee from an indigent seeking access to a state court for dissolution of a marriage was unconstitutional. Ms. Doone's situation is similar to that of the <u>Boddie</u> plaintiffs. Therefore, a court will probably find the fee must yield to Ms. Doone's right to have an opportunity to be heard in court regarding her challenge to the reduction of her AFDC payments. The court is the only forum for resolution of a dispute involving Ms. Doone's ability to provide basic necessities.

There are a number of problems with this thesis paragraph, foremost of which is the absence of a topic sentence which clearly sets forth the legal claim. By introducing the topic in terms of the <u>Boddie</u> holding, the sentence incorrectly identifies the paragraph as being only about <u>Boddie</u>. The first sentence also introduces the discussion too narrowly. It is unclear if the <u>Boddie</u> ruling on the constitutionality of filing fees extends to an indigent's appeal on grounds other than divorce. In order to avoid this kind of confusion, it is a good idea to begin a thesis paragraph with a topic sentence that sets out the legal claim in general terms, or in terms of your client, instead of tying it to the facts of a particular case.

Another shortcoming of this paragraph is that it does not make it clear that <u>Boddie</u> created standards for determining the constitutionality of filing fees. In the last sentence, two of the three <u>Boddie</u> standards are referred to in passing, but we are not specifically told that they are the tests announced in <u>Boddie</u>—nor is it clear that the statement about Ms. Doone's ability to provide basic necessities is the writer's attempt to establish the required presence of a fundamental, constitutionally protected interest. Thus, as readers, we are uncertain of the legal issues and legal principles involved and unclear about where the discussion is heading.

Because a legal analysis is supposed to include a fully developed discussion of the thesis, it is important to delineate the legal issues and conclusions carefully. A weak discussion is frequently one which begins with a vague introductory paragraph that leaves the reader unclear about which issues need to be discussed, how they relate, and how they will be resolved.

Although you want to provide an introduction that orients your reader to the analysis that follows it, be careful that the length of your thesis paragraph is proportionate to the length of your discussion. Although you must introduce the reader to a synthesized statement of what you will analyze, the thesis paragraph is not the place to offer an elaborate explanation or application of a rule. If your problem involves many rules of law and intricate facts, shorten or eliminate your application of the rules to the facts of your case. After listing the prongs of the controlling test, for example, you could conclude by saying, "Because Ms. Doone cannot satisfy all three prongs, it is unlikely the court will allow her to proceed in forma pauperis." Another way to keep your thesis paragraph to a manageable length is to begin with a thesis sentence that presents both the claim and your conclusion about that claim, as in, "Jane Simon will not be convicted of assault in the second degree for failing to act to prevent the injury of a minor whom she had taken care of for five years."

The Doone problem involved only one claim and thus it was possible to announce and apply all three legal requirements. When several claims are involved, however, each of which has several elements requiring discussion, you may need to rethink your strategy in order to prevent your thesis paragraph from becoming too long. One helpful tactic is to write a thesis paragraph that sets out all the claims and that explains how they relate and how they will be resolved. Then write separate introductory paragraphs which set out the elements of each claim, placing each introductory paragraph at the beginning of your discussion of that claim.

Assume, for example, that your client is embroiled in a dispute arising out of a contract within which there is a mandatory forum selection clause. Your client wants to know if that clause is enforceable. You might begin your discussion with the following thesis paragraph (citations are omitted).

Topic Sentence on Claim

First Issue

Second Issue

Conclusions

In deciding whether paragraph thirteen of the contract between Alta and MMI ousts it of jurisdiction over a dispute arising from the contract, the Southern District of New York must first decide whether the paragraph should be interpreted as a mandatory forum selection clause conferring exclusive jurisdiction on the courts of Milan, Italy for any dispute arising out of the contract, or simply as consent to Milan jurisdiction should a related action be brought there. Even if it finds that the Milan court has exclusive jurisdiction, however, the court may in its discretion decline to enforce the provision if it finds that to do so would be unjust and unfair under the circumstances. On the first issue, the court is likely to find that the language of paragraph thirteen unambiguously provides Milan with exclusive jurisdiction. In addition, it will probably find that it is reasonable to enforce the forum selection clause in this case.

This thesis paragraph, which bridges the issues and synthesizes the analysis, might then be followed by a more detailed introduction to the rules governing the first issue.

Topic Sentence
on Rule
Governing
First Issue
Factors

> To determine whether the language of a forum selection clause is mandatory or permissive, New York courts generally examine whether the language is clearly mandatory and all-encompassing, or whether there are two opposing, yet reasonable, interpretations of the clause. In particular, courts look for words like "shall" or "must" since these words commonly signify a command. If they fail to find that language, they will usually apply the traditional contract rule of interpreting ambiguous language against the drafter.

After this introduction to the factors involved in construing the language of a forum selection clause, the writer would analyze this issue in depth. Upon finishing that analysis, the writer would then write an introduction to the second issue, listing the five factors courts use to determine the reasonableness of enforcing a forum selection clause.

Of course, not all problems involving multiple issues or claims are necessarily complex. When you have a problem involving a couple of relatively uncomplicated issues or claims, you may still use one thesis paragraph to introduce all the issues, their relation to each other, their governing rules and their disposition. This is the situation in the following problem where Paul Hart is contesting his late father's will.

Topic Sentence
on Claim

First Issue

Application &
Conclusion

Second Issue

Application &
Conclusion

> Paul Hart has two different grounds upon which to challenge his father's will disinheriting him. The first ground is that the will is invalid because his father, who had been adjudicated insane, lacked the capacity to execute a will. An insane person can execute a valid will, however, if he is lucid at the time he executes it. Arnold v. Brown, 200 Kent 50 (1962). Because the evidence shows Mr. Hart was lucid when he executed the will, Paul's first challenge should fail. The second ground is that even if the will is valid, his father's will did not effectively disinherit him under Kent Rev. Code § 100 (1975), which requires a parent's will to show an intent to disinherit a child. Mr. Hart's will does not do so. Thus, Paul Hart's second challenge should be successful. Under Kent Rev. Code § 150 (1975), he will be entitled to a one-third share of his deceased father's estate.

If you wanted to shorten this thesis paragraph, you could rewrite as follows:

Topic Sentence
on Claim

First Issue

Second Issue

> Paul Hart has two different grounds upon which to challenge his father's will disinheriting him. The first ground is that the will is invalid because his father, who had been adjudicated insane, lacked the capacity to execute a will. The second ground is that even if the will is valid because his father was lucid when he executed it, his father's will did not effectively disinherit him

Conclusion

under Kent Rev. Code § 100 (1975). This section requires a parent's will to show an intent to disinherit a child. This second challenge should be successful, and under Kent Rev. Code § 150, Paul Hart will be entitled to a one-third share of his deceased father's estate.

After either of these two introductions, you would discuss each ground separately.

Exercise 6–A

1. Your client, John Wheeler, wants to sue Donald Lindhorst in a federal district court in Connecticut for negligence. There is a threshold question, however, as to whether the district court would have the power to hear this case. Lindhorst is a citizen of Arkansas. Wheeler lived in Arkansas until he was sent to serve a prison sentence in Connecticut, where he is still an inmate. If Wheeler is still a citizen of Arkansas, the federal court will lack diversity jurisdiction. Which thesis paragraph for this problem is better and why?

Thesis A

Wheeler is a citizen of Connecticut based on the decision in Ferrara v. Ibach. In Ferrara, the court ruled that serviceman Ibach was a citizen of South Carolina because of his physical presence there and his intention not to return to his former domicile in Pennsylvania. He established domicile by moving his family to South Carolina, renting a house there, enrolling his children in public school there, and maintaining a bank account there.

Thesis B

John Wheeler, a domiciliary of Arkansas before his incarceration in a Connecticut prison, would like to bring suit for negligence against Donald Lindhorst, an Arkansas domiciliary. In order to sue in federal court, however, Wheeler must be a domiciliary of Connecticut for the purposes of establishing diversity jurisdiction under 28 U.S.C. § 1332 (1994). In cases involving a person's involuntary relocation, there is a presumption in favor of an original domicile over an acquired one. Nonetheless, this presumption can be overcome by showing that the person clearly and unequivocally intended to make the new domicile home. Jones v. Hadican. The Wheeler family's actions and Wheeler's statements demonstrate such clear intent to make Connecticut the Wheelers' new home that diversity jurisdiction can be satisfied.

2. Livia Augusta wants to sue Olympia Department Store for emotional distress suffered while the store attempted to collect payment for a debt she never incurred. Which thesis paragraph is a clearer introduction to the problem and why?

Thesis A

Ms. Augusta's claim for damages rests on Olympia Department Store's negligence in billing procedures. The claim for damages from severe emotional distress depends on the store's intentional employment of outrageous collection methods which Ms. Augusta asserts precipitated her severe emotional distress.   Also Olympia's collection department was harassing Ms. Augusta without right since she was not indebted to them.

Thesis B

Olympia's liability to Livia depends on her satisfying the three standards that establish intentional infliction of emotional distress in the state of Kent.   First, the defendant's conduct, which gives rise to the distress, must be extreme and outrageous.   Second, the plaintiff's distress must be severe.   Third, the defendant's conduct must have been intentional or reckless.   Davis v. Finance Corp.   The Kent courts have extended considerable latitude in interpreting these standards in favor of creditors pursuing legal debts.   In this case, there was no legal debt, so Olympia's actions will not be granted that latitude.   Livia Augusta will be able to satisfy the tests for this tort because Olympia threatened Livia for over six months, her distress required medical attention, and Olympia knew that its harassment would cause such distress.

3.   Read the following facts and rules of law and then write a thesis paragraph on whether John Starr and Alice Doe can recover for negligent infliction of emotional distress as a result of Pennsylvania Deluxe Hotel's negligence in hiring and supervising the security guard who fired at Jane Starr (you can assume the negligence for the purpose of this exercise).

———————

On Election Day, John Starr, the husband of candidate Jane Starr, and Alice Doe, Jane's great aunt and former guardian, decided to watch the television election coverage at campaign headquarters at Pennsylvania Deluxe Hotel.   They were waiting for Jane to return to the hotel after visiting her supporters at local campaign offices.   The campaign had been marred by numerous threats of violence against the candidate and her family.

At 9:30 p.m., Jane and several staff members arrived at the hotel, and Jane began walking to the hotel's entrance.   Halfway there, a psychotic hotel security guard pulled out a pistol and shot at Jane.   The television cameras picked up the guard pointing and shooting his pistol in Jane's direction.   The shot was heard on the T.V.   The cameras did not actually show Jane being hit and falling, but they did immediately show her lying on the sidewalk, unconscious, in a pool of blood.

John and Alice were watching the T.V. as the entire scene unfolded.   They say they realized immediately after the shot was fired that Jane was seriously hurt.   John immediately collapsed, and Alice became hysterical.

Although Jane's injuries were not fatal, both John and Alice were extremely depressed in the months following the incident.   Alice was put into a sanitarium to recover from a breakdown.   John was too shaken to work for three months.   John and Jane's marriage suffered as John insisted that Jane resign the post she had just recently won. Neither John nor Alice has any physical ailment associated with their emotional problems.

————

As you may recall from Chapter Four, case law establishes the legal requirements of this tort as follows:

1. The plaintiff must be closely related to the victim, as opposed to being distantly related or unrelated;

2. The plaintiff must have been near enough to the scene of the accident that the ensuing shock was the direct result of the impact of a sensory and contemporaneous observance of the accident, as opposed to shock which results from learning about the accident from others after its occurrence;

3. The shock must have resulted from a single, identifiable traumatic event; it cannot be the result of a condition that occurs over time;

4. The plaintiff's distress must be severe, although there need not be a physical manifestation of a psychic injury.

Chapter Seven

Writing a Legal Document: The Legal Memorandum

I. Introduction

In the previous chapters we have discussed how to analyze and apply legal authority. We have also discussed how to write a case brief, which law students usually write for their own use. Most legal writing, however, is done to communicate with others. As a first-year law student, you will receive legal problems and will be asked to analyze the problem and write up the results of that analysis. The typical vehicle that lawyers use to do this is the legal memorandum. When you write a memorandum, you will make use of the several analytical skills you have been developing. This chapter explains the form and content of a legal memorandum.

A. Purpose of a Memorandum

A legal memorandum is a document written to convey information within a law firm or other organization. It is a written analysis of a legal problem. The memorandum is usually prepared by a junior attorney or by a law clerk for a more senior attorney early in the firm's handling of a legal dispute. The writer analyzes the legal rules that govern the issues raised by that problem and applies those rules to the facts of the case. The attorneys will then use the memo to understand the issues that the case raises, to advise the client, and to prepare later documents for the case.

The memorandum should be an objective, exploratory document. It is a discussion in which you explore the problem, evaluate the strengths and weaknesses of each party's arguments, and reach a conclusion based on that analysis. It is not an advocacy paper in which you argue only for your client's side of the case. The memorandum should be persuasive only in the sense that you convince your reader that your analysis of the problem is correct.

B. *Audience*

When you write a memorandum, you should be aware of your reading audience and its needs and expectations. The hypothetical audience for a student memorandum assignment is usually an attorney who is not a specialist in the field. Most attorneys for whom you write will be very busy and will have certain expectations that you must fulfill. For example, they will expect to receive a core of information about the controlling law and its application to the facts of the problem, but will not expect to be given a lesson in fundamental legal procedure. Because the reader is an attorney, you will not have to explain the legal process steps of the sort that you have been learning the first weeks of law school. You need not explain, for example, "This case is from the highest court of this state and so is binding in this dispute." You may wish to give this information to a lay reader, but a lawyer knows that a case decided by the jurisdiction's highest court is binding. On the other hand, the lawyer probably does not know the facts, holding, and reasoning of that case and does expect that you will supply that information.

C. *Writing Techniques*

Your reader will also have expectations about how the memorandum should be written. The legal profession is dependent on language. However unfamiliar you are with legal analysis and its presentation in a professional document, you are still writing English and you should continue to follow the principles of good written English. The general characteristics of good writing need to be cultivated because legal analysis can be complicated and involve difficult ideas. In order to communicate these ideas clearly to your reader, you need a firm control over language. Chapters Nine and Ten and Appendix A explain the principles for clear writing.

The memorandum is a formal document in that it is a professional piece of writing. Thus, you should use standard written English and avoid slang, other kinds of informal speech, and overuse of contractions. For example, you should not write, "for starters, we have to decide if John Doe's parents are immune from suit." Say instead, "the first issue is whether John Doe's parents are immune from suit." On the other hand, you should not be pompous and stuffy. Use simple, direct words and sentence structures. You do not have to say, "one can conjure multiple scenarios for fulfillment of these objectives." Say instead, "the agency can fulfill its goals in several ways." In addition, you should not write a verbose sentence like, "in applying the above precedent, it is clear that the lack of action by the school implies that the incident was not considered to be unlawful." Just say, "the school's inaction implies that school officials did not consider the incident unlawful." Since the revised sentence is of reasonable length and contains no empty phrases, it is easier to understand. Moreover, since the sentence is written in the active voice, there is no ambiguity about who considered the incident lawful.

Another aspect of presenting yourself as a legal professional is that you are writing as the client's attorney. Many students forget that role, and, for example, may write, "John Doe's attorney moved for a continuance." Remember that you are John Doe's attorney, or part of a team of attorneys, and instead should write, "we filed for a continuance." You should not, however, inject yourself into your legal analysis by using the first person pronoun. The purpose of the memorandum, and of many other legal documents, is to analyze the law and facts. You want to communicate that analysis persuasively and convincingly, not present it as your opinion only. For example, you should say "in Doe v. Doe the court held ...," not "I believe [or I think] that in Doe v. Doe the court held...."

One problem of legal writing that deserves particular attention is the problem of legalese. Lawyers frequently are criticized for using archaic terms and incomprehensible sentence constructions in legal documents. This criticism is especially aimed at the form documents that many attorneys use. An example is a form that begins "whereas the party of the first part," and uses expressions like "herein" and "hereinbefore." This type of legalese usually does not afflict law students, and we hope it will not afflict you. In the end, you will sound more professional and more in control if you use a vocabulary and syntax with which you feel comfortable.

Some legal terms are substantive, however, and you should use them. For example, you should use the operative language of a statute or of a judge's formulation of a rule when that language controls the analysis of a problem on which you are working. Although that language may not strike you as admirable, it supplies the general principle of law to which you must give meaning. Your reader should be told what that language is and will expect you to repeat those operative terms.

Your language should also be responsive to your audience. You will be writing for several different audiences during your legal career and you will have to adjust your prose accordingly. Not all of your readers will be lawyers. For example, often you will write to your clients, to administrative personnel, and to other government officeholders. Although you should write accurately about the law, you should also explain your message in good written English, using terms that a non-lawyer can understand. When you write to lawyers, you should also use good written English, although you may use legal terms without as much explanation. Keep in mind that each audience has a different need, but that all audiences need and appreciate good writing.

Nonetheless, if as a law student you face the particular challenge of navigating between legalese and terms of art, in most respects, legal writing requires only what any thoughtfully written paper requires. As long as your prose adheres to the rules of standard written English and composition and respects legal terms, you will fulfill your reader's expectations for memorandum style.

II. *Format*

Most office memoranda are divided into sections that are assembled in a logical order.

There is no required format that all lawyers use or that all law schools use for a legal memorandum. Most memoranda, however, are divided into from three to six sections, each of which performs a particular function within the memo and conveys a necessary core of information: the Statement of Facts, the Question Presented, the Short Answer or Conclusion, the Applicable Statutes, the Discussion, and perhaps a final Conclusion. Under some formats, the Question Presented may come before the Statement of Facts.

You do not need to write the memorandum in the order you assemble it, however. Instead, you may first want to write tentative formulations of certain sections (such as the Question Presented) and then rewrite those sections when you have a final draft of the part of the memo that is pivotal to your writing process, usually the Discussion. After that pivotal section is written, you should rewrite the sections you wrote earlier to ensure they are in accordance with the finished section. This type of writing process requires drafts and revisions before you reach your final copy.

The memorandum usually begins with a heading with the following information:

To: Name of the person for whom the memo is written
From: Name of the writer
Re: Short identification of the matter for which the memo was prepared
Date:

Then the body of the memo may be divided into the sections described below.

A. *Statement of Facts*

Because the heart of legal analysis is in applying the law to the facts, the facts of the problem can be the most important determinant of the outcome of a case. Each case begins because something happened to someone or to some thing.[1] The Statement of Facts introduces the legal problem by telling what happened.

The purpose of this section is to state the facts and narrate what happened. Therefore, use only facts in this section; do not use conclusions, legal principles, or citations to authorities. This section should include all legally relevant facts, all facts that you mention in the other sections of the memo, and any other facts that give necessary background information. If the problem for your memo is already in litigation, you should include its procedural history.

Facts are relevant or irrelevant in relation to the legal rules at issue. In order to know which facts are relevant, you will need to know what the issue in the problem is. If the issue is whether the client committed a crime, then you must know the elements of that crime from the statute. The relevant facts are those that are used to prove or disprove those elements.

Do not omit facts that are unfavorable to your client. The attorney for whom you are writing the memo may rely on the Statement of Facts to advise the client, for negotiations with other attorneys, and to prepare other documents for the case. Without the complete facts, the attorney for whom you are writing will be surprised and unprepared while handling the case.

Be careful to use objective language. The facts should not be slanted, subtly or not so subtly, toward either party. Sentence one of each of the following sets describes facts using partisan language inappropriate for a memorandum. Sentence two of each set uses language more appropriate for a memorandum.

1. John Smith endured three hours of his family's presence.

2. John Smith remained with his family for three hours.

1. Because Ms. Jones deserted her husband, he was left the unenviable task of raising three children.

---

1. You may be assigned to write a memorandum that involves a legal issue only, such as how a new statute has changed the common law. Then, you may wish to omit a Statement of Facts, and perhaps substitute a short Introduction.

2. After Ms. Jones left her husband, he raised his three children by himself.

Whether you are given the facts with your assignment or you gather them yourself, you should sort them out and organize them rather than repeat them as the information came to you. Put the crucial information first. Generally, in the first paragraph, you should tell who your client is and what your client wants, or what the problem is about. By doing so, you provide a framework for the problem. The reader then can more easily evaluate the rest of the facts within that framework. For example, compare these two paragraphs, each of which was written as the first paragraph of a Statement of Facts for the same problem.

1. John Davis is a high school graduate who has been unable to keep a job. He first worked as a machinist's apprentice, but after two years he was asked to leave. Since then he has worked at various trades, including carpentry and plumbing, in retail stores, and at McDonald's. None of these jobs lasted more than a year.

2. Our client, William Mathews, has been sued by John Davis for fraud. The charge stems from statements that Mathews made to Davis in the course of a stock investment proposal.

Example 2 is better because it tells the reader the context of the problem. The reader of the first paragraph does not know what the problem is about. Is it an employment contract case? An unemployment compensation application problem? The reader of the second example knows that she should read the rest of the facts with an eye toward a fraud suit.

Use the rest of this section to develop the facts. Explain who the parties are and give any other descriptions that are necessary. Always group like facts together. For example, if your memo topic is a false imprisonment topic about a person confined in a room, you may want to present in one paragraph or series of paragraphs all the facts that describe the physical appearance of the room.

For many of the assignments you receive, the best and easiest way to develop the events is chronologically, that is, in the order in which the events occurred. For some problems, however, a topical organization in which you structure the facts in terms of the elements you need to establish or by the parties involved, if there are many parties, may work better.

You also may want to include what relief your client wants, or what you have been asked to analyze in the memo. This information often provides a natural ending to the section.

Exercise 7–A

Which Statement of Facts about a prisoner's domicile for a memo about a diversity jurisdiction issue is best? Why?

1. Mr. Fred Wheeler is a prisoner in the federal prison in Danbury, Connecticut. Wheeler was convicted of bank robbery in Arkansas, which was his domicile at the time of the robbery. He has asked us to sue his attorney in that case for malpractice. The attorney, Donald Lindhorst, is a domiciliary of Arkansas. We would like to sue in the United States District Court if we can establish diversity jurisdiction.

Wheeler is in the second year of a five-to-seven year prison term. His wife and son moved to Danbury four months ago, and his wife is now working here. His son is enrolled in the Danbury public school. Mrs. Wheeler has registered to vote in Danbury and has opened an account at a bank there. The Wheelers have no financial interests in Arkansas. His wife's sister, who is her only family member still alive, lives in nearby Bethel, Connecticut. Wheeler's brother-in-law has offered Wheeler a job there after Wheeler's release from prison. Wheeler has said he will not return to Arkansas, and that he wants to "start fresh in Connecticut."

This memo analyzes whether Wheeler is a citizen of Connecticut for purposes of federal diversity jurisdiction.

2. Donald Lindhorst is a lawyer in Little Rock who unsuccessfully defended Fred Wheeler against a bank robbery charge in Arkansas. Wheeler is now in federal prison here in Danbury and wants to sue Lindhorst for malpractice. Wheeler has called Lindhorst a "rotten lawyer" and "a crook," who was only interested in getting his legal fee from him.

Wheeler is serving his second year of a five-to-seven year prison term. He hates the prison because of the food and lack of recreational facilities. His wife has moved to Danbury with their son and visits him often. Wheeler wants to remain in Connecticut when he gets out of prison and take a job offered him by his brother-in-law in nearby Bethel. His wife is working in Danbury and his child is in school here.

Lindhorst had been recommended to Wheeler by a mutual friend in Arkansas, and now Wheeler is sorry he hired him. He says that Lindhorst spoke to him only once, and did not interview any witnesses before the trial. He has asked us to handle his malpractice case. We would like to sue in the United States District Court in Hartford if we can establish diversity jurisdiction.

3. On March 4, 1986, Fred Wheeler was convicted of bank robbery in the federal district court in Arkansas. At his sentencing hearing in May 1986, he was sentenced to a five-to-seven year term in federal prison in Danbury, Connecticut. Wheeler was represented by a Mr. Donald Lindhorst, an Arkansas attorney, in the bank robbery case.

Wheeler now wants to sue Lindhorst for malpractice, and wrote us on March 10, 1988, asking us to represent him in this suit. We want to sue in the federal district court in Hartford. When I interviewed him last month, Wheeler told me that he does not intend to return to Arkansas and wants "to start fresh in Connecticut."

Mrs. Wheeler moved to Danbury in January, 1987. That month she enrolled their son in the public school and opened a bank account. In February, she started work in Danbury, and has remained with that job.

Mrs. Wheeler visits her husband frequently. Her brother-in-law has offered Wheeler a job in Connecticut when he gets out of prison.

B. *Question Presented*

The most important inquiry for the memo writer, as it is in other legal inquiries, is "what is the legal issue in this problem?" The Question Presented is a sentence that poses the precise legal issue in dispute that the problem turns on. There are two ways to formulate the questions for a memorandum. The first, and easier way, is to be very specific to the problem and identify people by name and identify events by reference to them. This type of question works if the reader already knows the facts of the problem. For example, suppose you have a contract problem and the fact statement includes the facts that Mr. Smith is mentally incompetent and Mr. Jones is Smith's guardian. If the issue is written as "is the contract between Mr. Smith and Mr. Jones valid?" the reader who has read the facts will probably understand that the problem in the case is whether a contract between a mentally incompetent person and his guardian is valid. Many law firms require only this type of specific identification in the Question Presented of a memorandum. If you write a very specific question, the important things are to be sure that the reader knows the facts already and that you identify the issue correctly.

The other way of formulating issues is to write them so that they can be understood by a reader who does not know the facts of the problem. It is usually necessary to write the Question this way if the Question Presented precedes the Statement of Facts. Then the Question Presented should be written to include not only the legal principle that controls the claim, but the key facts that raise the issue. A Question written this way does not describe people or events specifically by name, however, because the reader does not know who or what they are. Instead, the issue must be written more generally by describing the relevant characteristics or relationships of people and events. This type of question is written to apply to anyone in the position of the person described in the question. For example, the contract question would be written, "Is a contract between a mentally incompetent adult and his guardian valid?" This question does not name the parties to the contract but describes their relationship and the relevant characteristics that raise the contract issue. It is a good idea to identify people by relationships appropriate to the cause of action. For an adverse possession problem, for example, you could identify the parties as a "possessor of land" and a "title holder."

You can write the Question Presented either in the form of a question as in sentence one below, or as a statement beginning with the word "whether," as in sentence two. Issues written as questions usually begin with a word such as "does" or "is."

1. Does a prisoner's domicile change to that of the state in which he is incarcerated for purposes of satisfying federal diversity jurisdiction?

2. Whether a prisoner's domicile changes to that of the state in which he is incarcerated for purposes of satisfying federal diversity jurisdiction.

You may find it helpful at first when you begin research for the problem to isolate the issue in specific terms (Is the Smith–Jones contract valid?), but then after you begin writing the memorandum, you should rewrite that specific question into more general terms.

Typically, the question should identify the cause of action, either a common law cause of action or the statutory or constitutional provision that the plaintiff is suing under or the state is prosecuting, the key relevant facts, and the people involved described in general terms.

An exception to this pattern exists, however, if the problem involves a question of law only rather than a question of law applied to facts. For example, the issue may be whether a jurisdiction will adopt a new cause of action, or an element of an established cause of action. Then, the question may not require specific facts of the problem. In the following set of questions for a memo, the first issue is a question of law. The second issue asks how the law (assuming the new rule is adopted) applies to the facts. The second question thus includes specific facts of the problem, and is logically linked to the first question.

1. In Illinois, must a plaintiff in a false imprisonment claim be aware of the confinement?

2. If so, is a plaintiff who believes a door will not open because it is stuck, when it has been locked by the defendant, aware of his confinement?

If the problem contains more than one issue, such as an assault and a battery, then set each out as a separately numbered question. If the problem has one issue, but two or more sub-issues, you may consider using an inclusive introduction and then sub-parts. For example, a wills issue could be written as follows:

Is a handwritten will valid under the Wills Act if

a. the will is dated with the month and year but not the day, and

b. the will is written on stationery that contains a printed letterhead?

———

One important decision you must make is the level of generality to use for your description of facts. To identify parties, we have suggested that you not name the parties specifically, but, instead describe them more generally in relation to the claim at issue. "Mr. Smith" then becomes "a mentally incompetent person" and Mr. Jones is "his guardian." But do not generalize the category so much that you obscure the issue in the problem. For example, if the case involves the duties of a school district to provide services, then "an arm of the county government" is not specific enough. The proper level of generality here is probably just "a local school district".

The facts other than the identities of the parties should be described specifically enough to be understood. The issue in a problem involves how the law applies to those particular facts. If a contract is at issue between Smith and Jones, call it a contract, not a business relationship. If the school district is being sued for not providing a sign language interpreter to a hearing impaired student, do not write "appropriate instructional aids" instead. If the defendant is sued for building a one-car garage that intrudes over a property line, do not write "a small structure." One benefit of using specific facts is that you will avoid inappropriately inserting judgments into the Questions. For example, if you called a garage a "small structure," you have made a judgment about the size of the structure that intrudes over the property line. If you said a "one-car garage," you avoided that judgment.

Consider these other suggestions for a good Question Presented.

1. Isolate the specific issue. The issue should not be so broadly stated as to encompass many possible issues under the cause of action. For example, "Was Carey denied due process?" is a poorly conceived question because due process refers to many different legal issues and the question does not specify the relevant one. A question that adequately isolates the issue is, "Is a juvenile denied due process because he is not represented by counsel at a delinquency hearing?"

2. Do not make conclusions. The Question should pose the inquiry of the memorandum, not answer it. You will avoid making conclusions if you use facts and legal principles. For example, if the case law in a jurisdiction establishes that a person can be guilty of criminal contempt if he disobeys a court order intentionally or recklessly, the following question contains a conclusion: "Is a person guilty of criminal contempt if he recklessly does not read a court order and disobeys it?" The inquiry in this case is whether the person acted recklessly. By concluding that the defendant acted recklessly, the writer has concluded that the defendant is guilty.

The writer should have asked whether the defendant is guilty under these facts, as in the question, "Is a person guilty of criminal contempt if he disobeys a court order because he did not listen to or read the order?"

3. Keep the question to a readable length. You should not include all the relevant facts in the question, just the key ones that raise the issue. The following question includes too many facts: "Is a person guilty of criminal contempt if he disobeys a court order that he never read because he left the country for several weeks, his attorney's letter was lost while he was gone, his seven-year-old daughter forgot to write down the telephone messages she took, and his cat shredded the messages from his wife?"

4. If the question does become complicated, keep it readable by moving from the general to the specific. One way of doing that is to first identify the claim and then move toward the specific facts, as in these examples.

> Did a person commit theft of lost or mislaid property when he pocketed a locket that he had found on a baseball field just after the conclusion of a YWCA team practice, and that locket was stolen from him as he walked away from the field?

> Whether a prisoner's domicile changes for purposes of federal diversity jurisdiction when he is incarcerated in another state, the prisoner's family moves to the state of incarceration, and the prisoner has secured employment there upon his release from the penitentiary.

5. Questions are less ambiguous and are easier to understand on a first reading if they begin with a short concrete subject that is quickly followed by an active verb, rather than if they begin with a long abstract subject. For example, for these questions, the writers have used abstract nouns (the failure, the entrance) as the subjects of their sentences.

> Whether the failure to appear in court for a scheduled trial by an attorney is contempt of court if he was notified of the date of the trial but never wrote it in his calendar.

> Does entrance into a tent pitched in a park constitute entering a building for purposes of burglary?

The subjects of these questions are nominalizations, that is, they are nouns or noun phrases that have been constructed from verbs. Sentences that begin with nominalizations are often difficult to understand because the reader has to unpack the event described in the nominalization (the failure to appear in court ... by an attorney) and then fit that event into the question.

Another type of abstract subject that can be difficult to understand on first reading is a subject that is a gerund. A gerund is a present participle of a verb that is used as a noun. Because a gerund is a form of a verb, it may be ambiguous whether the word is the subject or the verb of the sentence. In the following question, "refusing" is a gerund.

> Did refusing to give an entrapment instruction by the trial court because the defendant pleaded not guilty constitute error?

In this question, "refusing" is the subject. But the sentence is about the trial court. "Refusing" is what the trial judge did.

These questions should be rewritten so that they use short concrete subjects that name who the sentence is about, followed quickly by the verb.

> Did an attorney commit contempt of court when he failed to appear for a scheduled trial if he was notified of the trial date but never wrote it in his calendar?

> For purposes of burglary, does a person "enter a building" if he enters a tent pitched in a park?

See Chapter Ten for more information about nominalizations and concrete subjects.

C.   *The Short Answer or Conclusion*

The function of this section is to answer the Question Presented and to summarize the reasons for that answer. This section can be written in either of two ways. One way is to write a short answer of one or two sentences, such as "Yes, a juvenile is denied due process if he is not represented at a delinquency hearing. Due process does not require that the juvenile be represented by an attorney, however." To write this form of Answer, you answer the Question Presented and add a sentence that summarizes the reason for your conclusion or adds a necessary qualification to the answer. Some lawyers write only one or two sentence answers to the Question. For your assignments, the Short Answer may be more appropriate for a short memorandum, such as one of three or four pages.

The alternative form is a section, here called a Conclusion rather than a Short Answer, that answers the Question and then summarizes the reasons for that answer from the Discussion section of the memo. A Conclusion should be longer than the Short Answer, but it still should be a summary only, and it should answer the Question. Depending upon the complexity of the problem and the length of the memorandum, the Conclusion may be one or two paragraphs or, for a long memorandum, it may require a few paragraphs. You should have a Short Answer or Conclusion for each Question Presented and number each to correspond to the number of the Question it answers.

Sometimes you cannot confidently reach a conclusion because the law is too uncertain or you need more facts. In that situation, explain briefly why your conclusions are tentative, or what the alternatives are, or which additional facts you need.

The following are suggestions for writing this section.

1. Be conclusory. A Short Answer or Conclusion should be an assertion of your answer to the issue you have posed. But it is not a discussion of how you evaluated strengths and weaknesses of alternate arguments in order to reach that conclusion. That evaluation and a full discussion of your reasons for the conclusion belong in the Discussion. Which of these examples is conclusory?

> 1. Jones was falsely imprisoned because he reasonably believed that he was confined by Smith's dog. Jones's belief was reasonable because the dog growled at him and Jones knew that the dog had bitten other people in the past.

> 2. Jones may have been falsely imprisoned depending upon whether he reasonably believed that Smith's dog would bite him if he moved. Several facts show that Jones could have reasonably believed he was in danger because the dog had bitten other people before. But some facts do not. For instance, the dog had been sent to obedience school after those incidents. The issue depends on the importance of these latter facts.

Example one is conclusory. The writer has reached an answer to the Question Presented. The writer of example two is discussing and weighing alternate arguments.

2. Do not include discussions of authority. Although your answer to the question will necessarily come from your analysis of the relevant primary and secondary authorities, your discussion of those authorities belongs in the Discussion section. In the Conclusion or Short Answer, you need not discuss or name particular cases or other authorities you rely on.

Which of the following examples is better?

> 1. The Popes adversely possessed the strip of land between their lot and Smith's. Although they occupied the land mistakenly believing it was theirs, their mistaken possession should be considered hostile as to Smith's ownership.

> 2. Whether the Popes adversely possessed the strip of land between their lot and Smith's if they mistakenly believed that the strip is theirs depends upon whether the Oz court relies upon old decisions that a claimant's mistaken possession cannot be hostile to the title holder. Several courts in other jurisdictions recently have decided that a person who possesses land mistakenly thinking it is his own can still possess the land hostilely to the true owner. The Oz court has strongly indicated that it may adopt those rulings.

Example two is a discussion of authority but not a conclusion about the adverse possession problem. Example one is an answer to the problem.

One exception to this rule arises when the problem is a statutory issue, in which case you should refer to the statute and include the essential information about the statutory requirements.

> Smith did not violate the Theft of Lost or Mislaid Property Act, 12 Oz Rev. Stat. § 2 (1960). The statute applies only if a person "obtains control over lost or mislaid property." Because Lyons robbed Smith of the locket almost immediately after Smith found it, Smith never obtained control over the property.

Another exception occurs if one case is so crucial to deciding the issue that it controls the analysis and cannot be omitted. In this situation, you should also include the citation.

> The defendant attorney should be liable for malpractice even if the plaintiff is not in privity of contract with him. The Oz Supreme Court has held that a notary public who practiced law without a license by writing a decedent's will was liable to the decedent's intended beneficiary for his negligence. Copper v. Brass, 10 Oz 200 (1965). This decision should apply to attorneys as well as to notary publics. If so, the defendant will be liable to Jones for negligently drafting the Jones will.

Exercise 7–B

Evaluate the following pairs of Question Presented and Conclusion. Which pair is best? Why? What is wrong with the others?

1. QP: Whether an attorney should have been convicted of criminal contempt of court for negligently failing to appear at a scheduled trial and not representing his client if he was told the date, had cases in other courts that same day, and had already failed to appear in court once before.

Conclusion: The attorney should not have been convicted. Applying the precedents to this case, his failure to record the trial date and his failure to appear will not be criminal contempt.

2. QP: What shall determine if an attorney's failure to appear in court for his client's trial constitutes criminal contempt?

Conclusion: In Oz, whether an attorney is in criminal contempt for failure to appear at trial depends on the attorney's intent. If the attorney shows that the failure to appear was not willful disregard of duty, then there is no contempt. Mr. Bass should be able to show that.

3. QP: Is an attorney who does not appear in court for his client's trial guilty of criminal contempt if he was notified of the trial date but did not record it, and on the day of the trial, had the case file in his briefcase along with files of cases for which he did appear?

Conclusion: The attorney should not be held guilty of criminal contempt. In Oz, the attorney's failure to appear must have been willful, deliberate, or reckless. Mr. Bass did not act with the intent required.

Instead, he inadvertently did not appear in court because he forgot to write down the court date and never took the case file from his briefcase in the rush of his other court appearances.

   4.   <u>QP</u>: Does an attorney who fails to appear at his client's trial commit criminal contempt of court under Oz law?

   <u>Conclusion</u>: In Oz, an attorney is in criminal contempt of court if he acts willfully, deliberately, or recklessly in disregarding a court order.   The court will have to decide.   If the court can be persuaded that Mr. Bass did not so act when he did not appear for his client's trial, then Bass will not be in contempt.

D.   Applicable Statutes

   If your problem involves the application of a statute, a section of a constitution, or an administrative regulation, set out the exact language of the pertinent parts in block quote form.   Include the citation.

   A block quote is indented, single spaced, and does not include quotation marks.

E.   Discussion

   Up to this point, the memorandum contains the facts of your problem, poses the specific legal question that those facts raise, briefly answers that question, and sets out the relevant enacted law.   In the Discussion, you will analyze the question by applying the relevant legal rules and their policies to the facts of the case. The process of analyzing is a process of breaking down a subject into its component parts.   To analyze a legal subject, you break it down into its issues and then break each issue down into subissues. You give content to the legal rules you have found by examining the facts of the cases from which the rules came and in which the statutes were applied.   You also examine the reasons for the rules and compare those cases to your problem.   Only then can you determine what those rules mean.   The purpose of this inquiry is to reach a conclusion and predict the outcome of the problem, that is, to determine whether the requirements for that claim are satisfied by the facts of your problem.   This analysis provides the reasons for your conclusion about the outcome.

   Because a memorandum is used to advise a client or prepare for further steps in litigation, the reader is looking in this section for a thorough analysis of the present state of the law.   Thus, the Discussion should not just be a historical narrative of the relevant case law and statutes or a general discussion of that area of the law. Instead, you should discuss the law specifically as it controls your problem.

The Discussion provides an objective evaluation of the issues. Thus, you should evaluate all the interpretations possible from applying the law to the facts, not just the interpretations that favor your client. Analyze as many arguments for your client that you can think of, but also analyze those arguments against your client. In addition, evaluate which ones are most persuasive. Do not predict an unrealistic outcome only because that outcome favors your client. If you will need more facts than you have been given in order to reach a conclusion, then explain which facts you need and why they are relevant.

A legal discussion is written according to certain patterns of analysis. These patterns were discussed in chapters Four, Five, and Six.

F. *Conclusion*

In some formats, where the memorandum includes a Short Answer of one or two sentences after the Question Presented, the memorandum ends with a Conclusion section that summarizes the Discussion. We have explained this type of Conclusion in Part C above.

Editing Checklist: Memoranda

A.   Statement of Facts

    1.   Did you provide an introduction that sets out the context of the problem?

    2.   Did you then arrange the facts in an organization that is easy to understand, such as chronologically, topically, or chronologically within a topical organization?

    3.   Have you included all the facts that bear upon the analysis of the problem and are necessary to understand the problem?

    4.   Have you omitted distracting and irrelevant facts?

    5.   Does this section include only facts and not analysis or argument?

    6.   Did you include procedural facts, if any?

B.   Question Presented

    1.   Have you identified the correct and the specific issue and referred to the common law, statutory, or constitutional claim?

    2.   Unless the issue is solely a question of law, have you incorporated the facts that raise the issue?

    3.   Have you identified the facts as specifically as appropriate, rather than use an overly generalized description?

4. If there is more than one issue, have you organized the issues in a logical order, which you will adhere to through the memo?

5. Is the Question readable?

C. Conclusion or Short Answer

1. If you use a Short Answer, have you accurately and clearly answered the Question Presented?

2. If you use a Conclusion,

a) have you accurately and clearly answered the Question Presented, and

b) have you summarized the analysis in the Discussion and briefly applied the controlling law to the facts of your problem?

D. Discussion (See Chapters 4–6)

1. Did you begin with a thesis paragraph, the length of which is appropriate to the length and complexity of the discussion?

2. Have you organized your discussion logically?

a) Is the discussion organized into separate claims that are presented in a logical order?

b) Is each claim broken down into the issues and sub-issues by which the claim is analyzed?

3. For each issue and sub-issue, do you

a) analyze the controlling rules drawn from the jurisdiction's statutes and case law and then the persuasive authorities,

b) apply the legal rules from those statutes and cases to the facts of your problem,

c) draw analogies and distinctions to the precedents, and

d) objectively evaluate and explore all credible interpretations?

4. Does your analysis reflect an accurate synthesis of the authorities so that you explore all the ramifications of a topic as a related analysis?

5. Have you kept firmly to what is relevant for the claim or defense you are analyzing?

6. Have you explained and supported your conclusions with adequate reasons? Do you analyze all interpretations before coming to an unqualified conclusion?

7. Are you creative in using facts and analogizing to similar issues?

8. Have you supplied citations to authority and are they accurate?

E.   Writing Style (See Chapters 9–10 and Appendix A)
    1.   Are your paragraphs unified around a topic and is that topic clear?
    2.   Do you use transitions to show the logical relationships between sentences and between paragraphs?
    3.   Do your sentences carry the reader forward rather than bog the reader down?
        a) Are your sentences a readable length without too many interrupting phrases and clauses?
        b) Do the verbs of your sentences carry the action or have you nominalized the verbs?
        c) Do you use concrete nouns as subjects rather than abstract ones?
        d) Are most of your sentences in the active voice?
        e) Did you edit out unnecessary throat clearing words and phrases?
    4.   Have you checked for correct grammar and punctuation?
    5.   Do you use past tense for events that already occurred?
    6.   Do you use quotations only when necessary, and do you fit them into your text?

Chapter Eight
The Writing Process

I. Introduction

The first time you are asked to prepare an inter-office memorandum is often the first time you have to integrate many of the concepts being taught in your legal writing course: identification of rules, statement of holdings, application of law to fact, issue organization, citation, and memorandum format. Many first-year law students become frustrated as they try to work with all these pieces and put a memorandum together. In an effort to alleviate that frustration, this chapter focuses on the process of writing that memo and tries to break the process down into smaller, less overwhelming pieces. The chapter deals only with the process of analyzing and writing about the materials. It assumes that your research is complete or, as is common in many first memorandum assignments, that your teacher provided copies of or cites to relevant cases and statutes. This chapter also assumes that your first memo requires you to apply established rules to facts, rather than to predict new rules of law. (For more complex issues of law, see Chapter Eleven.)

The suggestions offered here have helped many students to break through writers' block and move onto the next step. Still, there are other effective methods of writing. If you have done a lot of writing and have a process that works well in helping you organize your thoughts and put them on paper, you may want to continue to use that process. But if you have not done a lot of writing, or if you have had difficulty getting started, these suggestions may help you avoid hours of staring at blank sheets of paper or empty computer screens.

Even if you have done a lot of writing, you may want to read these suggestions with an open mind. Legal writing is different from a lot of college and graduate writing in that it does not build to a crescendo; it starts with its conclusion and moves on to justify it. This structure is as much a part of the "convention" of legal writing as a newspaper lead consisting of "who," "what," "when," "where," and "why" is a convention of journalism. Thus, even if you have a successful method of writing, you may want to adopt some of the suggestions here in order to smooth the transition from writing in other fields to writing legal documents.

We suggest a four-step process to get ready to write.

- Read the problem to understand your assignment.
- Read the cases and statutes (and other materials) to see what they are about.
- Read the materials again and take notes.
- Transform your notes into a topical outline.

When you write, we suggest you do the following.

- Write a first draft.
- Revise for organization and analysis.
- Revise for fluidity and clarity.

The suggestions below are linear in that they suggest a series of steps from beginning to end. The writing process, however, is recursive, and at any point along the way, you may find you have to go back, either to reassess some of your primary authorities to take account of new insights, or to add or omit something from an earlier discussion.

II. Beginning Your Assignment

Our first recommendation is that you start to work on your assignment as soon as possible, preferably immediately after you receive it. Your writing assignments will take more time than you think. Even if you have a successful track record writing papers as an undergraduate or graduate student, or in a business or professional career, your legal writing assignments involve many new skills. Until you have had more practice and some of the work, such as citation form, becomes more automatic, even short assignments will take a lot of time. Do not expect to hand in a successful paper if you begin only the day before the memorandum is due. Even if you are willing to pull an all-nighter, legal writing requires more time for reflection than you will have if you start at the last minute.

Once you are ready to begin, make sure you understand the problem you have been assigned. Read the facts carefully, and look for the issue that you are to write about. In your first assignments, the issue is probably identified for you. Carefully read the question you have been asked to address and be sure you respond to that question. For example, if you have been asked whether the facts alleged by the plaintiff state a cause of action for negligence, do not write a memo analyzing whether the defendant was in fact negligent. That is a different issue. In addition, be sure to note any assumptions your assignment tells you to make, as well as any instructions to ignore certain other issues that may be presented by the materials. Sometimes legal writing teachers include this type of information to help you stay focused on the issue assigned.

The next step is to start researching the problem. Once you have most of the relevant materials, either through your own research, or because they were provided to you, read them through once. The purpose of this first reading is simply to help you familiarize yourself with the issue and with the language the courts use in addressing it. When you are given the cases and statutes, you can assume that they were chosen because they are about the issue/s in your assignment. When you do your own research, an additional goal of your first reading should be to ensure you have found relevant law.

After you have read the materials once to familiarize yourself with the issue, you should begin to re-read them to learn precisely what the law is and how that law applies to different facts. You are now ready to move from the relatively "passive" stage of simply reading statutes and cases to the more "active" and difficult stage of working with those materials to organize and analyze your problem.

Think about what you need from a case: issue, facts, holding, and reasoning (see Chapter Two). Then concentrate on how the issue is raised by the facts of the case and on the rule that the court applies to resolve the issue. Sometimes, different courts use different language but they are really using the same rule. For example, some courts in false imprisonment cases talk about "restraint," while others talk about "confinement." (If the rule is different, then your assignment may involve a question of law, that of choosing the best rule.) Ask how that case applies to your assignment. Your goal is to use these materials, first to identify the rule that controls your issue, and then to analyze separately each of the elements of that rule.

Thus when you re-read the cases and statute(s), start taking notes so that you can understand precisely what the law is and how the law applies to different facts. Keep in mind your two slightly different but related purposes. First, use the cases and statutes to identify the controlling rule. Second, regardless of whether the issue is resolved by a common law rule or by a statute, use the cases to flesh out the meaning of the elements of the controlling rule.

III. *From Research to Outline*

Once you have briefed your cases and thought about how they apply to your problem, you need to organize your notes into an outline. Rewrite your case summaries so that they are organized around the elements of the rule that govern your problem. This outline of the rule is the large-scale organization of your memorandum discussion. Then flesh out that outline using the analytic steps that comprise the small-scale organization of a memorandum discussion.

The next pages use several examples to illustrate how to organize your notes into an outline. First, take your case briefs or summaries and rewrite them so they are organized by issues. For example, suppose you had written the four case summaries for the parental immunity synthesis in Chapter Two, Part IV. When you reread these case briefs, you notice that in each case the court mentions the child's age. In Case One, the child was a minor and the parent was immune from suit. In Case Two, however, the child was a minor but the parent was not immune from suit. In seeking an explanation for this difference, you notice that a second requirement is involved, the type of tort, whether an intentional tort or negligence. In Case Four, the parent was negligent, but the child was not a minor and the parent was not immune from suit. These two requirements now become the building blocks of your notes: 1) the child must be a minor, and 2) the child must sue for negligence.

Instead of organizing your notes by each case you read, organize instead by these two topics. If you take notes on index cards, then head each card by one topic: child's age or type of tort. Write on each card the information from one case relevant to that topic. Include citation and page numbers so that you do not have to go back later. If you take notes on a word processor, use these same topics for your entries. The important point is to organize by topics or issues, not by cases.

Your next step is to change your note cards into an outline. As explained in Chapter Four, your outline is dictated by the structure of the claim. You would outline the parental immunity topic into the two primary divisions.

If your assignment involves the intentional tort of battery, the cases will tell you that battery is usually defined by a three-part test:

1) whether the defendant causes an unconsented contact with the plaintiff,

2) whether the contact is harmful or offensive, and

3) whether the defendant intended the contact.

Organize your outline by those three parts. This is your large-scale organization. Lawyers, that is, your readers, expect this kind of structure.

If the common law or statutory claim does not have a fixed definition, then read the cases to find out the factors that the courts use. For example, the Uniform Commercial Code § 2–302, which permits a court to not enforce an unconscionable contract, does not define the term unconscionable. However, the cases tell you that the courts break down unconscionability into procedural and substantive unconscionability. Those two requirements will form the large-scale organization of your outline.

Once you have outlined the requirements for each issue, you are ready to analyze what each requirement means. For this step, you must find the types of facts that satisfy or do not satisfy the requirements. These become the next subdivisions of your outline. By pulling out these facts and categorizing them, you create the subissues by which to analyze the meaning of each requirement in order to determine whether the claims will be successful. For example, if you are outlining the issue of procedural unconscionability, you will find that procedural unconscionability is an abuse of the bargaining process. Often this abuse arises because the purchaser did not understand the contract terms. There may be several reasons why he or she did not: perhaps the purchaser did not understand English well, or the contract was written in legalese, or printed in small type. You may find that another important factor is whether the agreement was voluntary; contracts may be procedurally unconscionable if the terms were not negotiable or if there was unfair disparity in bargaining power. These factors become subissues in the outline of procedural unconscionability cases that follows.

I. Procedural Unconscionability: Abuse of the bargaining process produces "absence of meaningful choice" on the part of one party to a contract. Williams v. Walker–Thomas

    A. Purchaser Did Not Understand Contract Terms.

        1. Lack of Education/Understanding

            a. Zabel v. Circleville Enterprises: Door-to-door salesman's specifically drafted contract clause requiring new customer to purchase over 150 compact disks within the next two years held procedurally unconscionable because salesman's continued "badgering" during sale combined with plaintiff's second grade education level indicated he did not understand the clause and thus had no meaningful choice.

b. Wunsch v. Big Truck: Hispanic lawyer's assent to contract clause requiring 150% interest on loan for new Toyota 4–Runner held not procedurally unconscionable although clause in small type on back. Plaintiff's education and occupation indicated he understood the terms of the contract, even though English not first language.

2. Clause "Hidden" or "Unreadable"

a. Kelsh v. Airless Tire Co.: Clause in fine print in corner of reverse side of contract that limited defendant's liability for defective motorcycle tires held procedurally unconscionable because purchaser unaware of the clause due to manufacturer's deceptive trade practices.

b. Essig v. Fast Go–Carts, Inc.: Clause numbered No. 20 in contract containing 53 listed clauses all in readable size type held not "hidden" despite fact plaintiff never actually read the clause, which indicated the go-cart would be sold without an engine. Plaintiff had done other shopping.

B. Agreement not Voluntary: Lack of Bargaining Power/Grossly Unequal Bargaining Power.

1. Henningsen v. Bloomfield Motors: Car manufacturer's limitations of warranty to "repair or replacement" of defective part(s) held procedurally unconscionable because purchaser, average middle class U.S. buyer, had no power to negotiate for alteration of warranty in "take it or leave it" contract that all car manufacturers offered.

2. Shmikler v. Rip–Off, Ltd.: Department store's exorbitantly high credit terms and sales contract clause allowing repossession of all purchased items for default upon one item held not to be procedurally unconscionable because plaintiff travelled to particular store and store across the street had much more favorable credit terms. Purchaser had a meaningful choice.

3. Kelsh v. Airless Tire Co.: Purchaser under time pressure. Needed motorcycle quickly for job. Plaintiff's job put him at low economic level. Thus, lack of bargaining power.

After outlining procedural unconscionability, you would go on to outline substantive unconscionability.

Many people turn their first case outlines into more detailed outlines that reflect the five-step analysis discussed in Chapter Five on small-scale organization. To fill in your outline of each factor, supply both information from the cases about that point, and information about how the law and precedents apply to your case. By this point you should not be parroting language, but you should be asking questions about the cases' relevance to your problem.

You will probably be listing cases in more than one place. Remember to include cites and specific page numbers.

It is especially important to be open-minded and thoughtful about different ways to interpret the facts and to draw inferences from them. Usually not all the factors you identify for your small-scale organization must be present in any one case. Thus, you must evaluate their importance. Remember also that in writing a memorandum, you want not only to analyze the reasons that lead to one set of conclusions, but also the reasons for the opposite conclusions. The cases should give you ideas about what kinds of arguments to raise for both sides of the issue. For example, if, in the precedents, the defendants who had incurred liability all acted in bad faith, can you discern any facts by which to characterize the defendant's conduct as bad faith in your case, or to characterize the conduct as good faith? Is there any way that the facts you characterize as showing bad faith can be explained differently? The last entry on your outline for each issue should summarize how the point applies to your assignment. You may want to use two columns here: one for cases and analysis that lead to one conclusion, the second column for those that lead to the opposite conclusion.

What follows is an example of a more complete outline for an assignment involving a battery. The parties were arguing while riding together in Fleming's car. The day was hot, the windows were up, and the car air conditioning was on. Rondo said something that angered Fleming while Fleming was driving past a house where the water sprinkler was on in the front yard. The water reached to the street. Fleming used the power button to lower Rondo's window. The water from the sprinkler came in the car and splashed on Rondo's seat. Rondo sued Fleming for battery.

The outline here includes the first part of the "contact" element of battery, namely, whether there was a contact at all. A complete outline of this element would have two other subissues (numbered 2 and 3), discussing whether the contact was caused by the defendant and whether the plaintiff consented to it. The other elements of battery (intent and harmfulness of contact) would be outlined as parts B and C. Any second claim would be Part II of the outline.

I. Battery

    A. Defendant Caused an Unconsented Contact with Plaintiff

        1. <u>Contact with Plaintiff</u>:

        a. <u>Rule</u>:

The contact need not be directly with the plaintiff's body. "Actual physical contact with the plaintiff's body is not necessary to constitute a battery so long as there is contact with the clothing or an object closely identified with the body or attached to it, for example, an object plaintiff holds in his hand." Carousel v. Manager, 35 Kent 69, 72 (1984).

b. Cases:

Carousel: defendant pulled plaintiff's lunch plate from his hands, insulting plaintiff as he did so. A contact.

Rogers v. Evans, 40 Kent 105 (1987): plaintiff was riding a horse. Defendant hit the horse on the saddle and the horse galloped off. A contact.

Daley v. Ryan, 43 Kent 170 (1989): defendant pulled chair away as plaintiff was about to sit down and plaintiff hit the ground. A contact.

Helmut v. Chapeau, 5 Kent 47 (1902): defendant used his cane and knocked plaintiff's hat off his head. A contact.

c. Application to Problem:

Although water from sprinkler hit on the seat of the car where Rondo was sitting and didn't touch Rondo, direct contact with plaintiff's body not necessary. Though Fleming didn't touch Rondo's clothing (Helmut), or an object Rondo held in his hand (Carousel), or anything physically attached to plaintiff, contact can be with the surface plaintiff sitting on. In Daley, plaintiff's contact was direct with the ground, but in Rogers, contact was with saddle that plaintiff sat on, and was indirect.

d. Counter–Analysis:

Plaintiff wasn't "identified" with the vinyl car seat in Fleming's car. In Rogers, the saddle belonged to plaintiff and plaintiff used it often so could have been an object more "identified with the body" than is a vinyl car seat. In Daley, Plaintiff hit the ground, a direct contact. This is indirect: water on car seat—car seat with plaintiff.

e. Conclusion:

Contact with seat on which plaintiff sitting is too indirect.

Some students find it difficult to develop this kind of issue outline. They find it hard to move from a case-by-case survey to an issue analysis. Often students have read so much and become so bogged in specifics that they lose the big picture and overlook patterns and trends. Some students find graphic representations of their research help them obtain the perspective they need to develop an outline. If you have a visual imagination, you might want to try diagramming your cases. List the cases down the margin. Write the issues across the top and then fill in the boxes.

PROCEDURAL UNCONSCIONABILITY

Case	Plaintiff did not Understand K Terms		Unequal Bargaining Power or Duress	Proven
	Lack Ed./English	K Difficult to read		
Zabel v. Circleville	Yes—2nd grade		Yes—salesman badgering	Yes
Wunsch v. Big Truck	No—professional degree, high economic status	Yes		No
Kelsh v. Airless Tire		Yes	Yes—duress	Yes
Essig. v. Fast Go Cart		No—but many clauses	No—did other shopping for Go Cart	No
Henningsen v. Bloomfield Motors	No—middle-class		Yes—important case —K of adhesion	Yes
Shmikler v. Rip off			No—other terms available elsewhere	No

You can use this chart to develop the kind of outline that has been illustrated in this section.

IV. *The First Draft: Putting It Down on Paper*

After developing an outline, you are ready to begin writing your first draft of the memo. Before actually putting pen to paper, however, remember that a legal memorandum has several sections; you need to review the format and decide where to start. Each part of the memo has its own purpose, and each part should be written with that purpose in mind. The purpose of the Question Presented, for example, is to raise the issue in the case, not to conclude on the issue. Answering the Question Presented is the purpose of the Conclusion section. The Conclusion also summarizes your analysis, so it should not include material that is not in the Analysis section. The Facts section is supposed to include the "relevant" facts. To determine the relevant facts, you must know how you are going to analyze the issues in the Discussion section.

Thus, you probably do not want to write the memorandum in the order you present the sections. Instead, you may want to write a rough statement of the Question and either an outline or a rough draft of the relevant facts. Then concentrate on writing the Discussion. When you complete your Discussion, you will be able to cross-check that your Question isolates the issue you wrote about, and that you selected facts for the Question and the Fact section that actually are relevant to the issue. Similarly, once you have completed the Discussion, you can ask yourself what the essential elements are and summarize each for the Conclusion. The important point in approaching each section is to remember its purpose and the type of information it includes.

Sometimes, despite all the above advice on how to get started, you may experience a paralyzing uncertainty about where and how to begin your memorandum. Almost all authors confront writers' block at one time or another. Fortunately, there are a couple of techniques that may help you get started.

Writers frequently have trouble getting started because they find introductory or thesis paragraphs hard to write. Until the analysis has been completed, for example, you may be unsure of your thesis or conclusion. Thus, it may come as a relief to know that you do not need to write your thesis paragraph first. In fact, you do not need to write up your issues in the order you finally present them. If one issue is easier to analyze than other issues, write the easier one first. Then go on to the next easiest. Not only does your confidence grow as the document grows, but the sorting and thinking that occurs as you write the easier sections may equip you to handle the difficult issues. You then have to rearrange the sections in the right order.

Although writing in the order-of-ease often makes a lot of sense, you must be careful to review your organization once you have put all the sections together. Do you address threshold issues first? Does your thesis paragraph reflect your final structure? Do you provide transition sentences? It is important to make sure your final draft is consistent and has smooth logical connections.

If you are the kind of writer who finds it either difficult to outline or difficult to flesh out an outline, you might find "freewriting" is a helpful technique to get started or to break a writer's block. Freewriting is stream-of-consciousness writing. When you freewrite, you dump every idea you have about your topic on paper without regard for logical sequence, grammar, or spelling. You simply put your pen on the pad, or fingers on the keyboard, and record all your passing thoughts. If you are unable to think of anything to say, that is what you type until you have a breakthrough.

> I can't think of anything to say. I still can't think of anything. Still not. Not. Not. Still no thoughts. This is boring . . . it's also making me feel silly. Guess I'd better focus harder on covenants not to compete. What should I say? Did I mention geography seems to be a big factor? It comes up in quite a few cases. Let's see. One case says. . . .

As the example suggests, freewriting often begins as a rambling, even banal, muttering. But after a paragraph or page of private inanity, valuable thoughts usually begin to emerge. For a while, therefore, just go with the flow. Then, when some useful thoughts have been committed to paper, stop writing and reread your musings to determine what they amount to. Do certain points crop up more than others? Why? Do some facts loom large? Why? Do some points seem related? Try some provisional re-ordering: group related paragraphs and points, separate primary and secondary ideas, try to articulate headings or categories that encompass details.

This sorting, grouping, and categorizing may enable you to undertake a more focused type of freewriting. Summarize in a sentence or two one of the main ideas in your initial freewriting. Then embark on further free association just on that topic. Make lists of every aspect of that topic, focus on what confuses you, role play—explore your case as if you were your opponent. Once some profitable thoughts emerge, stop and assess your work again. Perhaps your role playing has led to a viable counter-analysis. Perhaps your confusion stems from an ambiguity or gap in the law. Does this ambiguity or gap help you or harm you? As your freewritings become more directed you may find that you are able to work some of these more focused meditations into your actual first draft with only minor revision.

Sometimes you may get bogged down in the middle rather than at the beginning of a draft. You may find you have gotten stuck on a particular point and keep writing and rewriting that section. If this rewriting is unproductive, generating more frustration than insight, abandon that section temporarily. Some distance on the topic may help you gain perspective. You may have gotten so bogged down in detail that you lose the forest for the trees. There is often a tension between picking up the important details in the cases and losing track of the main points.

Sometimes writers bog down because they become confused about terms, defenses, or exceptions as they probe a problem. When this happens, you must go back to your cases and rethink them. For example, if you are working on a battery problem, you may realize that you no longer understand what is required for a contact. You may have to go through the materials again to build up the meaning of those terms. For example, can contact be indirect as well as direct? Ask yourself at what point the contact is too indirect. When you have reclaimed the meaning of these terms, return to thinking about how they apply to your assignment.

Sometimes writers use rewriting as an evasive maneuver designed to postpone confrontation with a thorny issue. If you find yourself doing this, try "invisible" writing. Turn off your computer screen to end your tinkering and forge ahead. As soon as you are immersed in your next analysis, turn the screen back on. Rewriting is an important step in the writing process, especially when it is done to clarify your thoughts. But you should not become so focused on finding the exact words that you become distracted from your primary task, which is to get all your ideas out on paper.

V. *Rewriting*

Even though your first task is to get your ideas down, most people will do some revision from the beginning. This is especially so if you use a word processor. In the process of writing a first draft, you may find yourself moving whole sections, omitting paragraphs, and even altering your conclusion. This occurs because the first draft is typically the place where you clarify your ideas as you struggle through the analysis. The process of writing is a means for thinking through the problem, learning where you need more information, and arriving at a conclusion which you may not even have been aware of when you started the writing process.

Once you have written the first draft, however, it is very important to put the work aside for a day, or at least a few hours, so that when you come back to it, you can view it from a different perspective. (Few people have any perspective on their writing at three a.m., let alone a different perspective.) To revise your draft, you need to think about your work in a somewhat different way. You need to consider whether the document answers the question that you have been asked, and whether the reader, who does not have your familiarity with the issues, can understand your analysis. The first is easier to determine. Go back to the original question in your assignment and make sure that your analysis responds to that question. It is more difficult, however, to take a hard look at your own work to see whether you have presented your analysis to the reader in a logical, coherent manner.

You will probably find it easier to revise your work if you do the revision in stages instead of trying to do everything at once. The most important and most difficult revision is in checking the organization and analysis (see Chapters Four, Five, and Six). When you are reasonably satisfied with that, you can next focus on paragraph unity and coherence (see Chapter Nine) and sentence level changes (see Chapter Ten and Appendix A). The final step, and one which should not be forgotten, is proofreading. You do not want to create a bad impression and detract from the substance of your work with spelling errors, typos, and incorrect citation form.

A. *Revising Your Organization and Analysis*

The most important part of a legal document is the section in which you present your analysis of the problem. Throughout the writing of the first draft, you have attempted to identify the issues, put them in logical order, and analyze them fully, relating the law to your particular problem. But it is hard to assess your work from a reader's perspective. A number of different techniques are available to help you do this.

First, try to put yourself in the position of the person you are writing the document for. Ask yourself whether that person, who does not have your familiarity with the research and analysis that you have just done, would be able to follow your analysis. A second technique in revising is to use the Editing Checklist for Memoranda on pages 87–89. A third method is to use the thesis paragraphs as a check. See if you have started each major section with a thesis paragraph that states the issues, identifies the basic legal context, and concludes, applying the law to the facts of your case. If so, then check to see whether you in fact have analyzed the issues that you identified in the thesis paragraph, generally in the order in which you raised them.

Another technique is to make a topic sentence outline. If you are using a word processor, you can block and then print all of the headings, sub-headings, and topic sentences in your analysis. Or you can take a copy of your draft and, with a colored marker, either underline or highlight the headings, sub-headings, and topic sentences. As you read this outline, ask yourself whether the topic sentences accurately identify the material in the paragraph, whether the topic sentences in the outline seem to be in logical order, and whether each step in the analysis is included. Where there is ambiguity, the idea in the paragraph may be appropriate but the topic sentence may not identify the idea. So write a new topic sentence. Or the topic sentence may be the correct next step, but the paragraph is about something else. Then revise the paragraph. Or the problem may be that a step in the analysis has been omitted (See Chapter Six). You have gone from A to D assuming the reader understood B and C. In this case, supply B and C. Or the problem may be that the issues are not in the logical order. In this case, revise the order of the paragraphs. After you make these changes, make sure that you have included transitions that clarify the relation between paragraphs.

B. *Revising Sentences*

Some sentence level problems will disappear once your analysis is effectively organized. However, you still need to look at the sentences you have written and make sure that you have presented your ideas grammatically, clearly, and concisely (See Chapter Ten and Appendix A). Avoid long, complicated sentences. A sentence that runs more than four lines in the text should be scrutinized. Omit wordy, unnecessary phrases ("It is established that," "It is clear that," "It must be shown that"). Omit legalese. Put the action of the sentence into the verb. In general, use the active voice. Keep your language simple and straightforward. If you have been told that you have a particular sentence level problem—like faulty parallelism or misplaced modifiers—try editing your work just looking for that one thing. Another helpful technique is to read the document aloud. A sentence that does not work when you read it aloud probably does not work in writing either. Finally, check and correct your punctuation.

C. Proofreading

Nothing detracts as much from a document as spelling errors, typos, or omitted words or phrases. If you have a program on your computer which checks spelling, use that first. Do not, however, rely solely on spell-check. Such programs do not pick up on errors like typing "statue" for "statute" or "the" for "they," nor do they detect omitted words, or an incorrect homonym like "their" for "there." Thus you must read the document aloud to yourself, or even better, read it line by line, using a ruler to help your eye focus on one sentence at a time. Then, proofread your citation form. Finally, make sure that you have not exceeded the page limitation of the assignment, and that your pages are in the right order and numbered.

Chapter Nine
Effective Paragraphs

I. Introduction

A paragraph is often described as a group of sentences developing a dominant idea that is usually expressed in a topic sentence. A paragraph should have both unity and coherence. It has unity when every sentence relates to the topic. It has coherence when there is a smooth and logical flow between sentences and a clear and explicit connection between any one sentence and the topic of the paragraph.

While unity and coherence are essential for any effective paragraph, well written paragraphs in a lengthy discussion have an additional function. They must not only be understandable internally, but they must also indicate their place in the overall argument. Clear writing depends on providing the reader with signals so that the direction and point of an analysis are always apparent. The most common way of achieving continuity and logical progression is to begin paragraphs with topic and transition sentences. Topic sentences introduce new issues and sub-issues and show their connection with the thesis presented in the thesis paragraph. Transitional sentences bridge subjects or connect the steps within an analysis.

II. Topic Sentences and Paragraph Unity

A paragraph is a subdivision of a text indicating that the sentences within the subdivision develop one idea. That idea is usually expressed in a topic sentence which pulls the lines of a paragraph together by summarizing the basic idea developed in that paragraph. Without this summarizing sentence, the reader may have difficulty understanding the paragraph and its place in the analysis. Thus, the topic sentence expresses the writer's intention for the paragraph the way a thesis paragraph expresses the writer's intention for a paper. And just as a thesis paragraph ought to be the first paragraph in your discussion, so a topic sentence should generally be the first sentence of a paragraph.

Topic sentences can unify ideas which might appear unrelated by establishing a context which makes their relation and the point of a paragraph clear. Consider this paragraph.

> In Red v. Black, five-year-old Johnny Black broke a windshield while throwing rocks. The court held him to the standard of conduct of a reasonable person of like age, intelligence, and experience under like circumstances. Id. Similarly, a twelve-year-old was held to a child's standard of care for his negligence in swinging a badminton racquet and hitting a teammate. Nickelby v. Pauling. However, the same court held an eight-year-old to an adult standard of care when the infant defendant injured a spectator while driving a go cart on a golf course. Delican v. Cane. That decision was affirmed two years later when an adult standard was applied to an eleven-year-old girl who shot another child with an arrow during archery practice. Marion v. Hood.

Although each sentence seems vaguely connected to the others, the reader does not understand their precise relation. The discussion suffers from the vagueness that often occurs when a paragraph begins with the facts of a case rather than with a topic sentence. A topic sentence eliminates this vagueness or confusion by establishing a context for understanding the cases. For example,

> Infants are held to a child's standard of care for damages occasioned by their tortious acts, except when those infants engage in adult activities involving dangerous instruments for which adult skills are required. Delican v. Cane.

Thus, topic sentences play a key role in ensuring paragraph unity by forcing the writer to articulate the point and the function of the paragraph. If the topic sentence given above was added to the sample paragraph, the author would have at least presented the principle explaining how these cases fit together instead of having offered a mere summary of her research. In fact, if the author had written that topic sentence, the substance of the rest of the paragraph might have improved. The writer would probably have realized the relevance of the courts' explanations of why archery and go cart driving are adult activities, and would have included those discussions in her paragraph.

Not only do you need topic sentences to present your analysis of a case or group of cases, but you need topic sentences to introduce legal issues and subissues. In a problem involving the admissibility of expert testimony on the Battered Wife Syndrome, for example, you would need a topic sentence to introduce each prong of a test that is often used to determine admissibility. For example,

> To determine the admissibility of expert testimony, many courts first decide if the subject matter is so distinctly related to some science, profession, or occupation that it is beyond the ken of the average juror.

Because the first sentence in a paragraph plays a crucial role in informing the reader of the point of the paragraph, it should not be wasted on a citation. Citations often distract the reader from the point you mean to stress. The following sentence should have introduced the claim, not the facts behind a precedent which recognized that claim.

> In Apple v. Baker, 688 N.E.2d 600 (1988), the plaintiff brought an action for breach of warranty based on the blighted quality of 20% of the wheat delivered to him.

It would have been preferable to use the first sentence to introduce the basic idea of the paragraph. Then, if appropriate, follow with a citation that shows your authority. After this, you can use the case as an illustration of the basic idea.

> An implied warranty of merchantability is breached when the goods are not fit for their ordinary purposes. See Apple v. Baker, 688 N.E.2d 600 (1988). In Apple, the plaintiff brought an action for breach of warranty based on the blighted quality of 20% of the wheat delivered to him.

In addition, you do not want to waste your opening statement on a sentence that merely "treads water," that is, one that does not go anywhere and that immediately needs to be explained.

> The court has had to deal with the issue of a child's suit for loss of parental consortium. In a recent case, the court has held that the child has no cause of action.

The paragraph should immediately say that the court has held against the claim, not that the court "dealt" with it.

Although topic sentences play a major role in orienting your reader to your organization, not every paragraph requires a topic sentence. A complicated topic will require several paragraphs to explain, and thus a new paragraph may just be continuing the topic of the preceding paragraph. For this series of paragraphs, you would use a topic sentence in the first paragraph, and then use transitional words or sentences to begin the next paragraphs. Transitions are discussed in section III of this chapter.

After you have written a first draft, you can focus on your topic sentences as a method of editing your work. Topic sentences, or the lack of them, can help you to assess paragraph unity. You can check the body of a paragraph against the topic sentence to see if the paragraph contains more than one topic, wanders into an irrelevant digression, or lacks development. If so, you should divide, edit, or develop the paragraph to achieve unity. If you find yourself unable to state the topic in a sentence, your paragraph needs to be sharpened, focused, or omitted.

Evaluate the following two paragraphs for unity.

Example 1: In determining whether an infant will be held to an adult standard of care, courts first examine the infant's activity to see if that activity involves a dangerous instrument which requires adult skills. In Marion v. Hood, archery was considered an adult activity because of the intrinsic danger of arrows and the skill required in operating a bow and arrow. See also Delican v. Cane (go carts are intrinsically dangerous and require skill in handling). In contrast, in Nickelby v. Pauling, a badminton racquet was found so lightweight as not to constitute an intrinsic danger.

Example 2: An infant will be held to an adult standard of care if the infant was engaged in an activity involving a dangerous instrument for which adult skills are required. Marion v. Hood. Because of the intrinsic danger of arrows and the skill required in using a bow and arrow, archery was found to be an adult activity in Marion v. Hood. In Delican v. Cane, an infant driving a go cart was held to an adult standard of care because of the intrinsic danger of go carts and the skill required in their handling. Although the court in Ashley v. Connor did not scrutinize a squash racquet for its intrinsic danger, it found squash to be an adult activity because knowledge of the game's traditions and customs is required to mitigate the potential risks of the game. In squash, it is customary for a player to yell "clear" before taking a shot directed at the partner in order to avoid striking that player.

Example one has a clear topic sentence supported by the succeeding sentences. The paragraph exhibits direction and unity. Each sentence develops the general principle articulated in the topic sentence by setting forth authority for that principle.

Example two lacks unity because it introduces a factor not announced in the topic sentence. The paragraph begins well. It initially focuses on one factor the courts examine to determine whether a game is an adult activity: whether the instrument used in the activity is so inherently dangerous as to require adult skill. Yet the writer gets sidetracked in the last two sentences. The Ashley court's silence on the first factor leads the author to a second: whether traditions and customs have evolved to mitigate the risks of the game. This is an important factor and deserves discussion. But the discussion should begin in the next paragraph and should be announced in a separate topic sentence. Having written a topic sentence that refers to the first factor only, the author should be guided by it.

Attention to paragraph unity and topic sentences may help with paragraph length also. Long paragraphs—paragraphs the length of a page or more than 250 words—should send you looking for logical subdivisions which are often natural places for paragraph division. In contrast, a very short paragraph, when used other than for emphasis, is often part of a larger discussion and should, therefore, be combined with another paragraph. A one sentence paragraph, for example, is frequently the conclusion of a prior paragraph or an introduction to the next. If it is not, a short paragraph should be examined for lack of development.

Examine the following paragraph for a logical subdivision.

A landlord's duty to maintain the premises in safe and sanitary condition does not require the landlord to provide protection from criminal activities directed against persons lawfully on the premises. Pippin v. Chicago Housing Authority. Pippin was a wrongful death action against the landlord concerning not so much the conditions, but the policing, of the premises. Pippin had been an acquaintance of one of the tenants in the building. During an argument with the tenant, Pippin was fatally stabbed. The Pippin decision was a simple restatement of the common law in Illinois: a landlord does not have the duty to protect a tenant from criminal acts nor does it have a duty to protect a third party lawfully on the premises from criminal activities. Nonetheless, a landlord who has provided part-time guard service may have a duty to make security provisions for the hours when the guards are not on duty. In Cross v. Wells Fargo Alarm Services, the court held the landlord responsible for the safety of the building during those hours for which it had not provided guard service. The court relied on the theory that the provision of part-time guard service had the effect of increasing the incidence of crime when the guards were not there. The plaintiff had been injured by several unknown men at a time when the guards were not on duty.

The paragraph breaks naturally after the fifth sentence when the writer begins explaining an exception to the common law rule that a landlord has no duty to provide protection from criminal activity. The writer should indent and begin a new paragraph there.

Decide which of the following paragraphs can be logically combined with another.

In Holley, the plaintiff paid $5.00 a month as a security fee, aside from the regular rent. The court stated that this fee created a contractual duty on the landlord to provide protection to the tenants. Ms. Parsons was charged a $10.00 a year security fee. This fee, like the one in Holley, was for the purpose of maintaining a security system. Although Ms. Parsons paid $50 a year less than the plaintiff in Holley, the $10 fee could establish a contractual duty for Fly-by-

Night to provide the plaintiff with protection against third party crimes occurring on the defendant's premises.

If the duty is not contractually established, Fly–by–Night may still be under a duty to protect the tenant from the results of reasonably foreseeable criminal conduct. See Ten Associates v. McCutchen.

For example, in Stribling v. Chicago Housing Authority, the plaintiff was a tenant whose apartment was burglarized on three separate occasions. On each occasion, the thief entered the plaintiff's apartment through a wall shared with a vacant adjacent apartment. The landlord negligently failed to secure the apartment after the first burglary, despite many demands by the plaintiff. The court held that the landlord was liable because the second and third burglaries were reasonably foreseeable.

The second paragraph should be combined with the third. That sentence provides a transition from the first paragraph and introduces the issue illustrated by the third.

III. *Paragraph Transitions*

Transitional phrases or sentences are often used to show the relationships between an individual paragraph and the preceding and succeeding ones. They tend to appear either at the end or at the beginning of paragraphs and are used to summarize what has been covered and introduce what is to come. They are particularly important in long or complex discussions to prevent a reader from feeling lost. Although you can expect your reader to read carefully, you should not expect that reader to do your work, to provide the clarity, structure and development which are not in the paper itself. You can avoid overreliance on your reader if you use transitional phrases or words to show how a paragraph advances your discussion.

Sometimes transitions announce a change in subject. Thus they can underscore a shift in topic which might otherwise be announced in a heading or topic sentence. Sometimes transitions track the steps in an argument, informing the reader, for example, that a case just described is now going to be distinguished or that a rule just discussed will now be applied. There are numerous ways to effect these transitions.

1. You may want to raise a new point with a sentence that summarizes a completed discussion while relating it to the upcoming issue.

    Although the prosecution will have little difficulty showing assault, it may have trouble proving battery.

2. You may want to keep track of the issues with enumeration.

    The second exception to the employee-at-will rule arises when there are implied contractual provisions such as terms in an employee handbook.

3. You may want to show the relation between paragraphs by showing a substantive connection.

    A. There is no causal connection offered to link Joan's prior passivity with her present aggressive activity.

        A similar causal element was missing in the expert testimony on the battered wife syndrome offered in Buhrle v. Wyoming.

or

    B. The Tarasoff holding has been applied in this jurisdiction.

4. You may want to link paragraphs with a simple transitional word or phrase showing the logical connection one paragraph has with another.

    Therefore, although a court will not enforce that part of the contract which is unconscionable, it will generally refuse to award punitive damages.

    In Frostifresh, however, the court awarded the seller not only the net cost but also a reasonable profit.

    Since transitions play so central a role in showing the reader how you are building the argument, it is especially important that your transitions be thoughtful. You should not mechanically insert transitional words or phrases between your paragraphs without thinking about the relationship you wish to establish. Imprecise, erroneous, or ambiguous transitions can be misleading because they point the reader in the wrong rather than the right direction. The list of transitional expressions provided below, therefore, should be used cautiously. Although it supplies some of the phrases that establish particular kinds of logical relationships, you must still check that the transition you have selected is the one most appropriate for the connection you wish to establish. You should also be sure that you are entitled to use the transition. For example, the word "therefore" signifies a conclusion. Yet, before you can persuasively signal your conclusion with "therefore," you must be sure that you have provided supporting reasons.

Transitional Expressions

1. To signal an amplification or addition:

    and, also, moreover, in other words, furthermore, in addition, equally important, next, finally, besides, similarly, another reason, likewise.

2. To signal an analogy:

similarly, analogously, likewise, again, also.

3. To signal an alternative:

    in contrast, but, still, however, contrary to, though, although, yet, nevertheless, conversely, alternatively, on the other hand.

4. To signal a conclusion:

    therefore, thus, hence, as a result, accordingly, in short, consequently, finally, to summarize.

5. To establish a causal consequence or result:

    because, since, therefore, thus, consequently, then, as a result, it follows, so.

6. To introduce an example:

    for example, for instance, specifically, as an illustration, namely, that is, particularly, in particular.

7. To establish temporal relationships:

    next, then, as soon as, until, last, later, earlier, before, afterward, after, when, recently, eventually, subsequently, simultaneously, at the same time, thereafter, since.

8. To signal a concession:

    granted that, no doubt, to be sure, it is true, although.

Exercise 9–A

1. Reread Exercise 5–B. Write a topic sentence synthesizing the holdings in Dale v. New City Hospital and Histrionic v. Credit Inc.

2. Reread Exercise 2–I. Write a topic sentence synthesizing the holdings in cases 5, 6 and 7.

3. Read the following discussion. Then provide topic and transition sentences where appropriate.

Ellen Warren must show that Diethylstilbestrol (DES) was more than a merely possible cause of her various injuries in order to present her negligence claim against the manufacturers to the jury. Since statistics show that DES is a probable cause of adenosis, distortion of the uterus, and cervical cancer, the question of the defendant's liability for Ellen Warren's injuries should be presented to the jury. However, Ellen Warren will have a harder time showing that DES is more than a merely possible cause of her infertility, although she can probably establish this also.

In Kramer Service Inc. v. Wilkins, the defendant negligently cut the plaintiff's skin. Two years later a skin cancer developed at the spot. Two medical experts testified. One said the cancer was not caused by the cut; the other said it was possible that the cut caused the cancer, but the chances were only one out of one hundred. The court ruled that this evidence was not sufficient to permit the jury to find the defendant liable for the cancer. The court held that a plaintiff must show more than a merely possible connection between the defendant's negligence and the plaintiff's injury to permit a jury to consider whether the negligence caused the injury.

Ellen Warren's evidence includes the FDA decision to ban DES for use during pregnancy; the statistics that a substantial percentage of women exposed to DES develop cancer; and her doctors' diagnoses that adenosis, distortion of the uterus, and cervical cancer are characteristic of DES exposure. These facts demonstrate that DES is more than merely a possible cause of those injuries.

Ellen Warren's family has a hereditary history of cancer. Because heredity does not seem a more likely cause than DES, particularly in light of Warren's combination of DES-related disorders, this argument does not negate the evidence that DES is a probable cause of her cancer.

While DES causes or contributes to infertility in a substantial percentage of exposed women, many women are infertile without exposure. Moreover, Warren has suffered some other reproductive disorders that may be to blame. Nevertheless, given her combination of DES-related symptoms and the statistical evidence the DES contributes to infertility, Warren still has more evidence of causation than Wilkins did and should be able to present the issue to the jury.

IV. *Paragraph Coherence*

A paragraph has coherence if it promotes continuity of thought. Even a unified paragraph—that is, a paragraph with a single topic—can seem choppy and disconnected if the sentences are not in a logical order or are not clearly related to each other.

Paragraph coherence depends in part on clear paragraph organization; you must arrange your sentences in a logical order. If the final sentence of a paragraph contains information that the reader needs in order to understand the first sentence, then the paragraph will be hard to understand, regardless of the clarity of these sentences.

Although logical sequence promotes easy comprehension, it alone does not ensure paragraph coherence. Smooth progression from one sentence to the next often requires you to use connectors or transitions, just as you use transition sentences to get from one paragraph to the next. Sometimes, of course, you can juxtapose two ideas and feel confident the reader can infer their logical connection. For example, a reader can probably infer the connection between the following sentences: "You said you put the check in the mail a week ago. I have not received it." The discrepancy between these two events alerts the reader to the writer's skepticism about the first assertion, even without a connector like "but." Sometimes, however, the specific relation of one sentence to the next is not obvious. In this situation, part of your second sentence must be devoted to giving directions which enable your reader to perceive an otherwise buried connection. One way writers do this is by repeating key words or by using transition words and connectors. Another way writers promote continuity of thought is to overlap their sentences so that a new sentence begins with a brief summary of an idea in the prior sentence. By moving from old, known information to new information, the writer links the sentences together and moves the reader forward.

Of course, coherence on the paragraph level cannot be achieved without sentence coherence, that is, there must be clear and logical connections between the parts, even the words, of a single sentence. See Chapter Ten for suggestions on how to achieve sentence coherence.

A. *Paragraph Coherence: Organization*

The sense of a paragraph becomes clearer when ideas are put in a logical order. What is logical depends, of course, on the purpose of a paragraph. If, for example, you are trying to narrate events, such as in a Statement of Facts, you would probably use a chronological order. If you are developing an analysis, however, the order of ideas will probably follow either a deductive or inductive pattern of reasoning. Although thought processes are frequently inductive—that is, an examination of particulars enables you to formulate a generalization—most written arguments benefit from a deductive presentation—that is, the argument opens with a generalization which is then supported by particulars.

When ideas are not in a logical order, as in the following paragraph, the sense of that paragraph is hard to understand.

> A mental hospital has a duty to provide its patients with such care as would be reasonable to prevent self-injury given their individual mental problems. Stallman. Ms. Brown was a nonviolent suicidal patient whose cure had been progressing steadily during her sixteen month hospital stay. The standard of care is based upon the reasonable anticipation of the probability of self-inflicted harm. Gregory. In Stallman, the court found the duty breached when a violently suicidal woman was left unattended for 30 minutes. Based on Ms. Brown's progress, the doctors would not have reasonably anticipated her suicide.

If the writer had discussed the test defining a hospital's duty of care before launching into the facts of Brown, i.e., if the ideas had been organized deductively, this paragraph would have been easier to understand.

> A mental hospital has a duty to provide its patients with such care as would be reasonable to prevent self-injury given their individual mental problems. Stallman. The standard of care is based upon the reasonable anticipation of the probability of self-inflicted harm. Gregory. In Stallman, the court found the duty breached when a violently suicidal woman was left unattended for thirty minutes. Ms. Brown was a nonviolent, suicidal patient whose cure had been progressing steadily during her sixteen

month hospital stay. Based on Ms. Brown's progress, the doctors would not have reasonably anticipated her suicide.

B. *Paragraph Coherence: Sentence Transitions*

1. *Transition Words and Coherence*

For a reader to follow your thought processes, you must provide transitions that signal where you are taking your analysis next. After finishing a discussion of a general rule, you must clearly indicate to the reader that you now want to explain an exception. If you have just described two requirements for a cause of action, announce that you are now going on to the third. Transitions (perhaps "nevertheless" in the first instance, "in addition" or just "third" in the second) will tell the reader what you are doing.

The following passage is an example of a paragraph which lacks coherence because the sentences are not explicitly connected to each other.

> Express oral contracts between unmarried, cohabiting couples are enforceable. Implied contracts in these situations are unenforceable. Vague terms render a contract unenforceable. Jessica Stone and Michael Asch expressly agreed that Mr. Asch would repay his share of their living expenses once he began practicing law in exchange for Ms. Stone's support for three years. They entered into an enforceable contract. Ms. Stone may bring an action for its breach. Ms. Stone's understanding that Mr. Asch would support her during graduate school is unenforceable since it is an implied agreement. Mr. Asch's boast to "take care of" Ms. Stone forever is too vague to be enforced.

The sense of this passage would be clearer if more transitional expressions were used to establish the logical relationship one sentence has with another.

> <u>Although</u> express oral contracts between unmarried, cohabiting couples are enforceable, implied contracts in these situations are unenforceable. Vague terms <u>also</u> render a contract unenforceable. <u>Because</u> Jessica Stone and Michael Asch expressly agreed that Mr. Asch would repay his share of their living expenses once he began practicing law in exchange for Ms. Stone's support for three years, they entered into an enforceable contract. Ms. Stone may, <u>therefore</u>, bring an action for its breach. Ms. Stone's understanding that Mr. Asch would support her during graduate school is unenforceable, <u>however</u>, since it is an implied agreement. <u>Similarly</u>, Mr. Asch's boast to "take care of" Ms. Stone forever is too vague to be enforced.

2. *Other Connectors*

Transition words are used to show the reader the logical connection between sentences. Other kinds of connectors orient your reader in time or place or inform your reader that you are looking at the material from a particular point of view or perspective. The underlined phrases in the following passages illustrate the use of these kinds of connectors.

> During Mardi Gras week 1989, Jeffrey Bond boarded a trolley in New Orleans and sat down in the rear of the car. At a later stop, three teenage boys, Joseph Claiborne, Robert Landry, and Thomas Vallee, boarded the trolley. The four boys wore stockings over their heads and streamers around their necks. They were obnoxiously loud and drunk. At one point, Claiborne, who was 6′7″ tall, turned to Bond and demanded, "What are you looking at?" The two other boys gathered in behind Claiborne, blocking Bond's exit through the aisle. Given these circumstances, Bond thought it best not to antagonize this group of teenagers; thus he averted his eyes and kept quiet. From a tactical point of view, however, this proved to be a mistake. Claiborne started screaming, "Answer me when I speak to you!" Then he stood up, drew a gun, and shot Bond in the leg.

3.   Overlapping Sentences

Cohesion is often achieved when a new sentence opens with a brief reference to all or part of the prior sentence. In other words, you begin a sentence with old information and then move on to new information. This overlapping of sentences leads your reader gently into the new idea. The underlined phrases in the following passage illustrate overlapping.

> Ms. Moultry has been addicted to crack for the past two years. During this time, she gave birth to a son, a baby born with a positive toxicology. After his birth, Ms. Moultry placed her child into temporary foster care so that she could enter an in-patient drug rehabilitation program. While there, she repeatedly said that her resolve to come "clean" would weaken if she was denied visitation with her infant. To prevent such a relapse, Ms. Moultry's foster care worker sanctioned visitation. The initial visits went smoothly; the foster parents were supportive of Ms. Moultry and Ms. Moultry felt good about the care her baby was receiving. Then Ms. Moultry learned she tested positive for the AIDS virus. When the foster parents learned she was HIV positive, they refused to admit her into their home. Ms. Moultry disappeared three days later.

4.   Coherence and Complex Sentences

Complex sentences—sentences with a dependent and independent clause—often establish relationships more economically than do compound sentences—sentences consisting of two independent clauses joined by a coordinating conjunction. Dependent clauses begin with subordinating conjunctions which establish that clause's temporal or logical connection with the main sentence. Therefore, complex sentences clarify relationships between ideas within a sentence. There are many subordinating conjunctions, but some key ones are *because, since, if, when, while, although.*

In contrast, independent clauses joined by the coordinating conjunction "and" are clauses which are juxtaposed but not related. "And" is a vague connector; it joins sentences without establishing a logical connection between them.

> **Example:** Richard began suffering from arthritis in 1981, and he stopped working.

> **Rewrite:** Because Richard began suffering from arthritis in 1981, he stopped working.

5. *Coherence and the Repetition of Key Words*

Continuity is better served by the repetition of key words than by elegant variation. For example, transitions and key words effectively bridge these paragraphs.

> Thus the only factual distinction between Hughes and this case seems to be the emotional nature of Mr. Jackson's response.

> Emotions, however, are at the core of many family matters, especially those involving finances.

It is also important to use consistent terminology when referring to the parties to a suit. In the following sentence, it is unclear whether the court is referring to one person or two persons. It is also unclear whether the court is referring to the particular defendant before it or is stating a principle of law:

> In Windley, the court stated that if a person has any personal or financial interest in bringing trade to the seller, then the defendant was not acting solely as an agent for the buyer.

Some of the ambiguity in this sentence also comes from the change in verb tense. Propositions of law should be stated in the present tense while the facts of a case should be described in the past tense. Thus, the sentence should be rewritten in one of the following two ways.

> In Windley, the court stated that if a person has any personal or financial interest in bringing trade to the seller, then that person is not acting solely as an agent for the buyer.

or

> In Windley, the court stated that if the defendant had any personal or financial interest in bringing trade to the seller, then the defendant was not acting solely as an agent for the buyer.

Exercise 9–B

1. Reorder the sentences in the following paragraph to improve organization.

> In Kelly, the court found that the defendant, who had demonstrated a long and broad experience with the legal process, had knowingly and intelligently waived counsel, although the trial judge made no detailed inquiry. Kelly v. State, 663 P.2d 967, 969 (Alaska Ct. App.

1983). In some cases, a defendant may be permitted to waive his right without detailed inquiry. Id. Furthermore, unlike Miller, Kelly availed himself of some of the services of court appointed counsel while defending himself. Id. Here, although Miller stated that his mother had married an attorney after his father's death, this cannot be construed as meaningful legal experience. Because a waiver of the right to counsel may not be lightly inferred, Ledbetter v. State, 581 P.2d 1129, 1131 (Alaska 1978), the degree of the court's inquiry must be tailored to the particular characteristics of the accused. O'Dell v. Anchorage, 576 P.2d 104, 108 (Alaska 1978).

2. Add transition words to improve the coherence of the following passage.

The degree of judicial inquiry will also depend on the complexities and gravity of the legal issues raised by the charge against the defendant. O'Dell v. Anchorage, 576 P.2d 104, 108 (Alaska 1978). Traffic misdemeanor cases are easily understood by lay persons and the consequences are usually not severe. Id. The inquiry in such cases need not be extensive. Id. Miller, if convicted, faces a mandatory jail term and not a simple parking fine. The severity of the charges mandated a more extensive inquiry by the judge.

3. Rewrite to improve the coherence of this paragraph. Use transition words, connectors, subordinate clauses, and sentence overlapping.

The state's suppression of evidence in a criminal prosecution may constitute a violation of the defendant's due process rights. Whether the defendant's rights were in fact violated depends on four conditions. The state must be responsible for the loss of the evidence. The evidence must have had exculpatory value that was apparent before it was lost. Then the defendant must show that he would be unable to obtain comparable evidence by any other reasonable means. If the evidence was only potentially exculpatory, the defendant must demonstrate that it was lost due to bad faith on the part of the state. Roger Keith can show that the state was responsible for the loss of the alleged murder weapon, the car. The car disappeared from the police garage before it was examined. Its exculpatory value was never demonstrated. It would be difficult to determine what comparable evidence might consist of. The record offers little to prove that the loss of the potentially exculpatory car was due to bad faith on the part of the police. Keith cannot meet the conditions for determining violation of his due process rights because of state suppression. The court will most likely deny the motion for dismissal.

4. Rewrite the following paragraph to improve its organization and coherence.

The parties agree that First Sergeant Valiant of C. Company first picked up the phone to learn who was being called. During the first few seconds after picking up the phone, Valiant overheard a conversation between members of His Company that began "Do you have any of the good stuff?" He recognized the speakers, who were later court martialed on drug charges. Valiant had not "intercepted" the conversation. The sergeant's act in picking up the phone must be considered in the ordinary course of business. When the use of an extension comes within the ordinary course of business, no unlawful interception of the defendants' communication occurs. When there are several extension phones, as there are in the orderly room, it is not unusual that when a call comes in, a person will pick up the receiver to see who the call is for.

V. *Paragraph Development*

You cannot write clearly if you assume too much knowledge on your reader's part. Your papers must be self-explanatory; they must follow through on an idea, consider its meaning and significance, and come to a logical conclusion. Do not cut your discussions short; develop them. It is only in the development that the meaning of a paragraph becomes apparent.

The principal methods of development include A) comparison, B) illustration, C) classification, D) definition, E) cause and effect, and F) description and chronological narration. Frequently, these methods of development occur in tandem. If you are defining prosecutorial misconduct, for example, you might define it by offering illustrations of what constitutes misconduct and what does not.

A. *Comparison*

Paragraphs developed by comparison are common in legal writing since the principle of stare decisis requires factually similar cases to be decided by application of the same rule of law and to result in the same decision. By comparing and contrasting the facts of your problem with those of the precedents, you will be able to show how the rules of those cases fit your case.

For a comparison to be fruitful, you must compare things which are not only alike, but which are relevant and significant. For example, in a claim involving a hospital's negligent failure to prevent a mentally ill patient's suicide, a central issue is whether the patient received reasonable supervision given that patient's medical history. Thus, it might be fruitful to contrast the care of a patient who had attempted suicide twice to the care of a mentally ill patient who had no history of self-inflicted injury, as the difference is germane to the issue of supervision. On the other hand, it would be fruitless to spend time establishing that one patient did watercolors as occupational therapy and the other did weaving because the difference is irrelevant to the issue of reasonable supervision in light of the medical history. A comparison is useful, therefore, only if you are comparing relevant and significant things.

You must also take care to compare like things. It would be meaningless to compare the supervision of an acutely depressed patient with the supervision of a patient with chronic back pain because one condition involves a patient's psychiatric history and the other involves a patient's medical history. You must, therefore, compare similar things for a comparison to be illuminating.

It is generally easier to avoid the impact of a previous decision by distinguishing your facts from the precedent facts than by asking a court to overrule its previous decision. Thus, comparisons are as central a device in writing a persuasive argument as they are in predicting the outcome of a suit in a memorandum. In the following example, the author distinguishes Carol Smith's situation from that of the victim in a decided case in order to overcome that adverse decision.

Example: Comparison

The right of confrontation includes the literal right to confront adverse witnesses face-to-face when they testify. Dowdell v. United States; Mattox v. United States. Thus, lower courts have repeatedly held that procedures which prohibit face-to-face confrontation violate the defendant's constitutional right of confrontation. In Powell v. Texas and Long v. Texas, the defendants' confrontational rights were held to be violated where children who were victims of sexual abuse testified on videotape without having to hear or see the defendants. However, in State v. Sheppard, the court permitted testimony without face-to-face confrontation because the crime involved was incest and the witness was a child testifying against her father.

Carol Smith's situation is distinguishable from that of the victim in Sheppard. Not only had the defendant in Sheppard lost his confrontation rights because he had physically threatened and abused his child, but the crime was more serious than that charged in the present case. Williams is charged with lewd conduct, not incest. In addition, he did not physically threaten or abuse Carol Smith. Thus Carol's situation is more akin to that of the victims of sexual abuse in Powell and Long. Although the trial court permitted Carol to testify without being able to see or hear Williams, the Court of Appeals will probably find the defendant's confrontation right was abridged.

B. *Illustration*

Paragraphs may be developed by illustration. A general principle, the meaning of which is abstract, can be made concrete, and thereby clarified, by examples. In the following passage, two illustrations clarify when a party owes a duty to an incidental beneficiary of a contract.

Example: Illustration

A putative wrongdoer may be liable to one with whom he or she does not have a contractual relation if by acting or failing to act, the wrongdoer works an injury to the non-contracting party. The court in Rensselaer offers two examples of a putative wrongdoer's liability to a third party. An auto manufacturer may be liable to third parties who are injured as the result of its failure to inspect. Similarly, an engineer is liable to a casual bystander who receives burns as a result of that engineer's failure to shut off the steam. See H.R. Moch Co. v. Rensselaer Water Co.

C. Classification

Classification is a process which involves locating the class to which an object belongs in order to gain greater understanding of that object. Classifying requires you to identify the common characteristics of that category or class. After identifying the class by articulating the significant property shared by all the members of that class, you may want to divide that class into subclasses. In subdividing, the relationships between classes become sharper because division clarifies which classes are subordinate to others and which are coordinate with others.

In law, classifying is routinely done. Lawyers classify factual situations as particular causes of action. They also develop legal arguments by classifying their clients' facts as falling or failing to fall under the categories established in a decision or a statute. When courts interpret law, they do it by formulating their holdings in such a way that the classifications involved have either a broad or narrow reach. When courts make law, they erect new categories. Thus, classification is an essential part of legal analysis and legal writing.

Classifying is often crucial in attempting to clarify and establish a legal conclusion, as in the following example.

Example: Classification

The issue is whether Pappagano is violating the state's Wild Animal Act by keeping birds in his aviary. The statute prohibits the capture or restraint of wild animals and applies only to animals known in the common law as *ferae naturae*. This classification consists of animals usually found at liberty. J.W. Blackstone, Commentaries 349 (1845). The statute does not apply to domesticated animals, which are those that are accustomed to living in association with humans and that are not disposed to escape. Id. Pappagano keeps birds such as robins, blue jays, and sparrows in his aviary. Because the birds are usually found at liberty, flying freely, and migrating with the seasons, they are *ferae naturae*, and Pappagano is violating the statute.

D. Definition

Definition provides the meaning of a term by establishing its borders, that is, by announcing what it does and does not refer to. In clarifying what is and is not distinctive about a term or concept, definition further refines classification and strengthens it as an analytical tool. A formal definition begins by placing the term within a class and then differentiating it from other members of that class. Sometimes a term requires an entire paragraph before it is adequately defined. Such extended definitions are developed or built by example, comparison, analysis, stipulation, or function (defining what something is by describing what it does).

Example 1: Definition

A wrongful threat exists when one party to a contract threatens to breach the contract by withholding goods unless the other party agrees to a further demand. The court in Austin found a wrongful threat when a subcontractor would not deliver on a first subcontract unless it got a second contract. It is, however, not wrong to threaten if there is a legitimate contract dispute. In Muller, a delay in construction increased the costs of construction. The builder said the defendant must pay those costs or face a slowdown. Defendant then served notice to terminate the construction contract. The court found there was no wrongful threat since the threat to terminate the contract was related to a relevant dispute about the contract.

Definition can be a method of persuasion in legal writing. Although the meaning of a rule is partially fixed by its wording or its application, there is frequently room for maneuver, room for your own explanation of what is or is not meant by the term. In the following paragraph, the author argues that under even a broad definition of delivery, Davis was improperly served with a summons.

Example 2: Definition

Generally, service under C.P.L.R. § 308[1] is accomplished by delivering the summons within the state to the person to be served. However, a line of cases has interpreted "delivery" more broadly and upheld service under C.P.L.R. § 308[1] even if the summons was not handed to the person to be served. Thus, in Daniels v. Eastman, the court upheld service although the process server erroneously handed the envelope to Dr. Zippen instead of Dr. Lutker when the two were sitting together. The court ruled that the erroneous delivery and the subsequent redelivery to the intended recipient were "so close in time and space that [they] can be classified as part of the same act." Id. The delivery to Ms. Jones, however, was not so close in time and space to the redelivery to Mr. Davis as to constitute one act. Whereas, in Daniels, Dr. Lutker was sitting with Dr. Zippen at the time of delivery, Davis was not even present when the process server delivered the summons to Ms. Jones. Moreover, Ms. Jones did not redeliver to him until later in the day.

E.   *Cause and Effect*

A cause and effect analysis requires a writer to explain the reasons for an occurrence. Because one frequently engages in causal analysis of facts, it is important to be alert to the complexity and subtlety of establishing and developing causal connections.

Although a cause must precede an event, you cannot assume that whatever precedes an event causes it. Even if event X precedes event Y, X may be entirely unrelated to Y. You should not confuse seriality and causality, i.e., the temporal and the logical orders. To do so is to commit the fallacy of *post hoc ergo propter hoc* (after this therefore because of this). It is also important not to be too superficial or simplistic about identifying causes. A cause can be either necessary, contributory, or sufficient. A necessary cause is one which must be present for an effect to occur but which cannot alone produce that effect. A contributory cause is one that may produce an effect but cannot produce it alone. A sufficient cause is one that alone produces the effect. Do not, therefore, identify one cause but ignore others of equal significance. Many events involve multiple causes.

Example: Cause & Effect

Not only was Bob's failure to repair his refrigerator a breach of his duty to protect a business invitee against dangers he knew or should have known about, but that breach was the proximate cause of Bull's injury. When the refrigerator tray broke, frozen hamburgers spilled onto the counter, knocking the mugs that were there onto the floor. Bull slipped on the spilt liquid and fell onto the shards of the broken mugs. As a result of this fall, he broke his ankle and cut his hands. Therefore, there was a reasonably close causal connection between the duty breached and the resulting injury. Bob's failure to have the refrigerator unit inspected and repaired was the proximate cause of the accident from which Bull suffered injuries.

F. *Narration and Chronology*

For a paragraph concerned with narration—as in the Statement of Facts—you will probably want to develop events in clear chronological order, that is, the order of their occurrence. You would also follow chronology to describe a process; for example, you would relate the steps necessary for filing a suit in small claims court in the order required by the court. When writing a chronological narrative, be careful not to confuse the reader by changing the sequence of events or by omitting important events.

In a descriptive paragraph, you may need to convey to your reader the setting in which some event occurred by establishing the location of persons or objects in a scene. Although there is no one way to describe a person, a place, or the location of persons or things in a scene, you will need to supply such spatial directions as "to the right," "in the foreground," or "five yards from the fire hydrant."

In the heat of creation, you may not be aware of how you developed a paragraph. At the less frenzied stage of rewriting, however, you may become aware that an idea needs explication and that one of these methods of development would clarify and strengthen your argument.

Exercise 9–C

The following exercise is a review exercise of some of the principles covered in earlier chapters and in Appendix A. Reread Exercise 2–H1; then read and edit the following sample answer to the Peterson exercise in Chapter Two. Consider the following questions:

1. Does the statement of the issue include enough information about the rule of law and relevant facts?

2. Does the "thesis" or introductory paragraph end with a conclusion that relates the law to the facts of the case? If not, write one.

3. Can you eliminate wordiness and improve sentence coherence?

4. Do the topic sentences effectively introduce the point of each paragraph?

5. Does the writer include the relevant law and facts from the precedent in the second paragraph?

6. What problems with paragraph unity does the third paragraph have?

―――――

The issue that we must explore in this case is the question whether the father is responsible for the injuries resulting from his son's misuse of a hammer. The applicable rule would be that a person has a duty to protect another against <u>unreasonable</u> risks. A person who breaches this duty is negligent and liable for injuries resulting from his negligence. It must be shown that leaving the tools in the basement was an unreasonable risk.

In the present case, the father left his tools in the basement. Tools are not "obviously and intrinsically dangerous." The case must be discussed in light of relevant precedent. The <u>Smith</u> case clearly applies to the case herein. In <u>Smith</u>, the court sustained defendant's demurrer to the complaint, challenging the sufficiency of the complaint. In <u>Smith</u>, the children were playing with a golf club. Many similarities obviously can be pointed out between <u>Smith</u> and the present case. The children were identical in age. The instruments were left in an area played in by children; the accidents occurred without warning the victims.

Plaintiff herein may claim that the tools should not have been left where children could reach them. Defendant may state that in <u>Smith</u>, the golf club was left in the backyard, also a play area for children. The golf club was not held to be intrinsically dangerous. We must also be concerned with whether tools, although not inherently dangerous, can be considered more dangerous in the hands of a child than a golf club. Tools are like a golf club because they are not weapons; however, they may be misused by a child.

Chapter Ten

Sentence Structure

As discussed in the chapter on paragraphs, the flow of a discussion depends on the effective use of topic and transition sentences, paragraph organization, and transition words. But coherence on the paragraph level cannot be achieved unless there is coherence on the sentence level as well. Poor diction, punctuation, and sentence construction break a chain of thought by forcing readers to stop to decipher the meaning of a particular sentence. Thus, even if law students and lawyers do everything else right (display deft organization and incisive analogies), they are not communicating effectively if their sentences need translation.

It is surprising—but true—how many lawyers have sentence level problems, a phenomenon caused in part by the complex ideas that are the core of many legal documents. To write about these complex matters clearly, to communicate effectively with such diverse audiences as law professors, clients, colleagues, judges, witnesses, and juries, law students and lawyers need to pay special attention to syntax: they must make clear and logical connections between the parts, even the words, of a single sentence. The bulk of this chapter is, therefore, devoted to giving you specific suggestions that will help you avoid common sentence level problems. Before enumerating these "do's and don'ts," however, it might be fruitful to reflect a little on what a sentence actually is.

A sentence is traditionally defined as a set of words that expresses a complete thought and that contains, at the very least, a subject (a noun) and a predicate (a verb). Yet this is a somewhat

bloodless definition that directs a writer to grammatical requirements of a sentence at the expense of giving a writer a "feel" for
readable sentence structures.

It takes only a moment's reflection to realize that many sentences are narratives about real characters who perform real acts.
Less apparent is the impact this realization should have on sentence structure. Yet the fact that sentences are often narratives
about characters and their actions should lead you to write sentences that follow the action of the narrative rather than sentences
that bury the characters and their actions in passive voice constructions or that begin with abstract nouns. Sentences are clearest
when the character in the sentence is the subject of the sentence
and when the verb in the sentence describes what the character
did, does, or should do.[1]

In this regard, you should be aware that many sentences about
abstract ideas—principles of law, for example—are nonetheless also
sentences with characters who perform actions. Sometimes these
characters are mistakenly concealed:

> Contractual choice-of-forum clauses are "prima facie valid" and should
> be enforced unless it can be shown that enforcement would be unrea-
> sonable or that the clause was affected by fraud or overreaching.

The characters in this sentence go unidentified, although a reader
could guess at their identities. The character who should enforce a
choice of forum clause is the court, and the character who must
show unreasonableness or fraud is the resisting party to the suit.

Because your reader probably needs information about each
party's responsibilities, the sentence should chart those parties and
their obligations, as in the following rewrite:

> Because a contractual choice-of-forum clause is "prima facie valid," a
> court will enforce it unless the resisting party can show that enforce-
> ment would be unreasonable or that the other party to the suit
> procured the clause through fraud or overreaching.

Of course, not all sentences are about actions. Some describe
people, things or conditions. Others are about ideas and concepts.
Sentences about ideas often have abstract nouns as their subjects
and frequently define or comment on that subject, as in, "Truth is
Beauty," or "The necessity of protecting the first amendment
rights of the press from the chilling effects of defamation actions
makes summary judgment an appropriate procedure." In most
analytic writing, some sentences will inevitably begin with abstract
subjects. Yet abstract subjects, or long subjects which present a lot
of new and complex information, tend to strain the reader's concentration. To alleviate that strain, you should begin as many of these

---

1. See Joseph M. Williams, Style:
Ten Lessons in Clarity and Grace, (4th
ed. 1994) for a fuller discussion of some
of the ideas in this chapter.

sentences as possible with easily comprehensible, short, and specific subjects: "Summary judgment is an appropriate procedure for protecting the first amendment rights of the press from the chilling effects of defamation actions."

A first-year law student might worry that short, specific subjects and simple active voice sentences will fail to impress professors, associates, clients, and courts. Yet legal writing is often a lawyer's single opportunity to tell a client's story and to reveal its legal significance to audiences that are pressed for time and unwilling to translate archaic diction and contorted sentence constructions. Thus, simple and direct sentences are more effective than convoluted sentences. In fact, the ability to write about complicated matters in a straightforward manner is the art of lawyering.

The following suggestions will help you write clear and persuasive sentences.

1. *Whenever Possible, Use Short, Concrete Subjects*

A subject is that part of a sentence about which something is being said. It may consist of a single word or of many words (a simple subject and all its attendant modifiers). The easiest sentences to read, however, have short subjects that use concrete rather than abstract nouns. No reader wants to wade through a fifteen word subject, comprised in the following sentence of "use" and its modifiers.

> Defense counsel's use of racially discriminatory peremptory challenges arising out of a state-created statutory privilege deprives excluded jurors of their equal protection rights.

Your reader would much prefer you to start with a short, concrete noun.

> Jurors are deprived of their equal protection rights by defense counsel's use of racially discriminatory peremptory challenges arising out of a state-created statutory privilege.

2. *Use Short, Active Predicates—Not Nominalizations*

The predicate is that part of a sentence that says something about what the subject is or is doing. Sentences are more dynamic and more concise when you use short verbs that express actions rather than states of existence.

> **Not:** The actions of the transit authority in firing appellants for criticizing fare increases were a violation of the appellants' first and fourteenth amendment rights.

> **But:** The transit authority violated the appellants' first and fourteenth amendment rights when it fired them for criticizing fare increases.

Sentences are more forceful if they focus on a verb rather than on a noun. Yet many writers convert verbs into cumbersome nouns called nominalizations. Instead of writing "the judge decided to continue the trial," they write "the judge made a decision to continue the trial." Instead of writing "the defendant knew injury could result from his negligence," they will write "the defendant had knowledge that injury could result from his negligence." The latter sentence, with the nominalization "had knowledge," dissipates the energy of the verb.

3.   *Whenever Possible, Use Active Rather Than Passive Voice*

In the introduction to this chapter, we suggested that sentences focus on characters and actions. To achieve such a focus, you should write most of your sentences in the active voice, that is, you should follow a subject-verb-object sequence (actor—action—object of action). Active voice sentences are easier to read because they begin with a short specific subject who then explicitly does something to someone. They have the additional virtue of being somewhat shorter than passive voice sentences.

A passive construction follows an object-verb-subject sequence (object of action-action-actor). It is constructed from forms of the verb "be" and the past participle of the main verb. In passive construction, you do not have to include the actor to have a grammatical sentence, although you risk obscuring the narrative if you end the sentence without identifying the actor.

Passive voice may be appropriate, however, if you do not know or do not want to emphasize the actor or subject, if the object of the sentence is more important than the actor, or if the actor is obvious, as in "a new mayor was elected." Finally, passive voice sentences are appropriate when they promote paragraph coherence. Beginning a new sentence with the object of the prior sentence is one way of overlapping and connecting sentences.

a.   Unclear Use of Passive Voice

Example: In balancing the interests, full factual development is needed in order to ensure the fair administration of justice. (Who needs full factual development? Who is balancing?)

Rewrite: To balance the interests, the court needs full factual development in order to ensure the fair administration of justice.

Or

Rewrite: In order for the courts to balance the interests, the parties should fully develop the facts.

b. Wordy Passive Voice

>**Example:** A duty of care to the plaintiff was breached by the defendant when the slippery floor was left unmopped by the defendant.

>**Rewrite:** When the defendant failed to mop the slippery floor, she breached her duty of care to the plaintiff.

c. Appropriate Use of Passive Voice

>**Example:** Under Rule 11 of the Federal Rules of Procedure, factual errors alone are not enough to justify sanctions. Sanctions would be granted, however, if the attorney knew there was no factual basis for the complaint. (Here, passive voice promotes paragraph coherence in that the second sentence picks up where the first left off and focuses the reader on what is really at issue: grounds for sanctions.)

4. *To Promote the Main Idea of the Sentence, Do Not Separate the Subject From the Verb With Intruding Phrases and Clauses*

A sentence does not begin to become an intelligible thought until the reader knows its subject and verb. When you separate the subject and the verb with a series of interrupting phrases and clauses, you leave the reader in limbo. To be reader-friendly, keep the subject of the sentence near the verb and the verb near the object. You can move interrupting phrases and clauses either to the beginning or the end of a sentence. You can also break the sentence in two.

>**Example:** In 1987, the patients of Kent Family Planning Center, 50,000 in number, 35% of whom were adolescents, 50% of whom were at or below the poverty level, received in the mail a sex education manual published by the Center.

>**Rewrite:** In 1987, Kent Family Planning Center published and mailed a sex education manual to its 50,000 patients, 35% of whom were adolescents, 50% of whom were at or below the poverty level.

Or

In 1987, Kent Family Planning Center published and mailed a sex education manual to its 50,000 patients. Thirty-five percent of these patients were adolescents, and fifty percent were at or below the poverty level.

>**Example:** Officer Miller, who at the preliminary hearing on August 8 had said the car did not look like it had been in an accident, fell ill just before the trial was due to begin and never testified.

>**Rewrite:** Although Officer Miller had said at the preliminary hearing on August 8 that the car did not look like it had been in an accident, he fell ill just before the trial was due to begin and never testified.

5. *Keep Your Sentences Relatively Short (under 25 words)*

Although varying the length of your sentences makes your writing less monotonous and more interesting, it is not a good idea to pack several ideas into one unreadably long sentence. If you have written a long and involved sentence, consider dividing it into shorter ones.

It is easy to split apart a compound sentence (two independent sentences joined by a coordinating conjunction). Instead of joining those sentences with a coordinating conjunction (and, but, or, nor, for, so, yet), put a period between them. You can also divide a long complex sentence (a sentence that has a dependent and independent clause). To do so, you must make the dependent clause independent by deleting the word that makes the clause dependent. These words are called subordinating conjunctions and include, among others, such often used words as *because, since, while, when,* and *although*. You can also shorten a sentence that ends with a long modifier tacked on to the end by converting that modifier into an independent sentence.

When you break long sentences into shorter ones, link your ideas with transition words that carry a preceding idea into the next sentence. Put these transition words early in the sentence so that the specific relation between the sentences is quickly apparent.

Example: Although the Kent statute authorizes a court to sentence a defendant for criminal contempt, the statute does not define contempt, and the Kent courts have been left with the task of defining contempt, which they have interpreted as requiring intent to disobey the orders of a court, a requirement similar to those in other jurisdictions.

Rewrite: Although the Kent statute authorizes a court to sentence a defendant for criminal contempt, the statute does not define contempt. The Kent courts have, <u>therefore</u>, been left with the task of defining contempt, which they have interpreted as requiring an intent to disobey the order of a court. This requirement is similar to those in other jurisdictions.

6. *Maintain Parallel Sentence Structure (Parallelism)*

Repeating a grammatical pattern is a good way of coordinating ideas in a sentence and maintaining control over complicated sentences. By making phrases or clauses syntactically similar, you are emphasizing that each element in a series is expressing a relation similar to that of the other elements in the series. Such coordination promotes clarity and continuity.

To maintain parallelism, nouns should be paired with nouns, infinitives with infinitives, noun clauses with noun clauses, etc. Faulty parallelism results when the second or third element breaks the anticipated pattern. "Hypocritical and a fraud" shows faulty parallelism, for instance, because an adjective is paired with a

noun. Parallelism can be restored either by changing "hypocritical" to the noun "hypocrite" or "fraud" to the adjective "fraudulent."

> **Example:** She also served on the Board of the Fresh Air Fund, as a
> participant in the YMCA programs, and she worked for
> Planned Parenthood.
>
> **Rewrite:** She also served on the Board of the Fresh Air Fund,
> participated in the YMCA programs, and worked for
> Planned Parenthood.
>
> **Example:** An agency defense depends upon whether the agent was
> acting as an extension of the buyer and not for himself, if
> the agent was motivated by compensation, and finally,
> was salesman-like behavior exhibited.
>
> **Rewrite:** An agency defense depends upon whether the agent was
> acting as an extension of the buyer and not for himself,
> whether the agent was motivated by compensation, and
> finally, whether the agent acted like a salesman.

When you are coordinating ideas in a sentence, you normally
begin your coordination after the subject, that is, with the verb (as
in the first example above) or with the complement (as in the
second example). A complement is that part of the sentence which
completes the meaning of the subject and predicate. For example,
if you said only, "They made," your thought is unfinished. You
must add a complement to complete the idea: "They made a last
effort to settle out of court." If you have a series of parallel
complements or verbs + complements, a good idea is to build your
sentences so that the shortest unit of the series comes first and the
longest comes last, unless logical order dictates otherwise.

> **Example:** Some of the factors a court considers in determining the
> reasonableness of enforcing a forum selection clause are the residence
> and citizenship of the parties, the proximity of the contractual forum
> to probable witnesses, and the comparative convenience for the parties
> of litigating in each forum.

Here, the parallelism begins with the complements and the complements are arranged in order of length.

7. Avoid Misplaced and Dangling Modifiers

Aside from the primary parts of a sentence (the subject, predicate, and complement), sentences have secondary parts called modifiers. Modifiers are words, phrases, or clauses that describe or
define one of the primary parts or that further describe or qualify
one of the modifiers (as in, "a court may impose sanctions upon an
attorney who solicits clients that are still hospitalized").

Modifiers must be placed so that there is no uncertainty about
the word or phrase they modify. A modifier should, in general,
stand as close as possible to the word it modifies.

a. A modifier is *misplaced* if it modifies or refers to the wrong word or phrase. You can correct this situation by shifting the modifier closer to the word being modified. If this is not possible, rewrite the whole sentence.

> **Example:** The court reached these conclusions by applying the "general acceptance" test for the admission of evidence resulting from the use of novel scientific procedures first articulated over sixty years ago. (The test was first articulated over sixty years ago, not the use of novel scientific procedures.)

> **Rewrite:** The court reached these conclusions by applying the general acceptance test, which was first articulated over sixty years ago, for the admission of evidence resulting from the use of novel scientific procedures.

Or

The court reached these conclusions by applying the general acceptance test for the admission of evidence resulting from the use of novel scientific procedures. The test was first articulated over sixty years ago.

> **Example:** Undercover agent Jones walked up to a group of teenagers standing in front of a store with the intention of buying some cocaine. (Did Jones intend to buy cocaine or did the teenagers?)

> **Rewrite:** Intending to buy cocaine, undercover agent Jones walked up to a group of teenagers standing in front of a store.

b. A *dangling modifier* points to a word that is not in the sentence. Revise by inserting the word which is being modified.

> **Example:** In Kent, a plaintiff whose spouse has been wrongfully killed has no cause of action for loss of consortium, denying, in effect, recovery for the destruction of the marital relationship.

> **Rewrite:** In Kent, a plaintiff whose spouse has been wrongfully killed has no cause of action for loss of consortium. This ruling denies, in effect, recovery for the destruction of the marital relationship.

> **Example:** After dismissing the claim, the attorney was chastised.

> **Rewrite:** After dismissing the claim, the court chastised the attorney.

8. *Identify and Punctuate Restrictive and Nonrestrictive Modifiers Correctly*

There are two kinds of modifiers, restrictive and nonrestrictive. Restrictive modifiers are those that narrow the denotation of a word, that is, they narrow the class of things or persons covered.

> Example: Courts that recognize loss of parental consortium as a cause of action emphasize the child's best interest.

Here, the modifier—"that recognize loss of parental consortium as a cause of action"—is restrictive because it limits the number of courts under discussion.

A nonrestrictive modifier adds information about a primary element in the sentence but does not define that element.

> **Example:** Trial courts, unless faced with a case of first impression, tend not to make policy decisions but rather follow precedent.

In punctuating your modifiers, notice that nonrestrictive modifiers are surrounded by commas while restrictive modifiers are not. It is important to recognize the difference between restrictive and nonrestrictive modifiers, and to punctuate accordingly, because of the impact they have on the meaning of a sentence. If you write, "the court is opposed to loss of consortium damages that are speculative," you have limited the number of consortium damages to which the court is opposed. If you write, "the court is opposed to loss of consortium damages, which are speculative," you imply the court opposes <u>all</u> consortium damages because they are speculative in nature. Far too often litigation arises because of disputes over whether a modifier is restrictive or nonrestrictive, as in "the employee will not disclose to a competitor the names on the customer list which are not publicly known." Is the employee prohibited from revealing all names or only those names not publicly known?

Besides using commas to indicate restrictive and nonrestrictive meaning, you should be aware that the relative pronoun "that" is properly used when it introduces restrictive modifiers. "Who" and "which," however, are used to introduce both restrictive or nonrestrictive modifiers. Conventional usage also requires you to use "who" or "that" when referring to specific individuals, "that" when referring to a class composed of persons, and "which" or "that" when referring to things or ideas.

9. *Eliminate Unnecessary Words*

Aim for economy and simplicity of phrasing.

a. Substitute Simple Words for Cumbersome Words.

> **Example:** By reason of the fact that the witness was out of the country, the trial was postponed.

> **Rewrite:** The trial was postponed because the witness was out of the country.

b. Avoid "Throat–Clearing" Introductions to Sentences

Start right away with an argument. If you make the argument well, you do not have to tell the reader that you are about to do so. Most "throat-clearing" introductions are padding. They can usually be replaced with a word or omitted entirely.

Example: After discussing this question, it is important to consider the possibility that Michael's "acceptance" may have been a counter-offer.

Rewrite: A second question is whether Michael accepted the offer or, instead, counter-offered.

10.   *Use Quotations Sparingly*

In using quotations, be selective, grammatical, and accurate. Quotations should be used selectively for two main reasons. First, a heavy reliance on quotations is frequently a signal of adequate research but inadequate analysis. Second, a paper littered with quotations is often disjointed; differences in style may jar your reader. Before you use a quotation then, think about whether the quote is necessary or whether it can be eliminated from your paper. You may be able to put the idea into your own words more efficiently and effectively. Whether you quote or you paraphrase, make sure that you then cite to the source of the idea.

It is sometimes appropriate to quote the holding of a case, and you should quote language that supplies the controlling standard for a particular area of the law. When you quote the controlling language of a statute, it is important to repeat the exact wording of the statute as you apply it to your problem. Besides using necessary quotes from the language of precedents, you might want to quote some judges for their particularly eloquent or apt language.

Generally, you should not quote a court's description of the facts. However, you should quote, rather than paraphrase, the words of a party or a witness if they are important to your case.

Example: The witness said, "I killed him and I'm glad."

Not

The witness dramatically confessed.

A quotation that is embedded in a longer sentence must fit into that sentence grammatically and logically. This sometimes takes some juggling. It is frequently easier to recast that part of the sentence which is not a quotation than to alter the quotation. The following sentence needs to be revised because the possessive pronoun "its" in the quotation wrongly refers to the parent company. "Its" is meant to refer to subsidiaries.

Example: The court found it decisive that the parent company, through its American subsidiaries, had "continued to engage in the market penetration and expansion that are its raison d'etre...."

Rewrite: The court found it decisive that the American subsidiaries of the parent company had "continued to engage in the market penetration and expansion that are its raison d'etre...."

Keep quotes short. But if you do use a long passage of fifty words or more, you must set out the quote in block form, that is, indented and single spaced. You do not use quotation marks when you set out a quote in block form. Put the citation as the first nonindented text after the quotation.

11. *Use the Appropriate Tense*

English is a language that has many tenses; this characteristic is a sign of the importance we place on accurately reporting the sequence of events and conveying the relation of one event to another. In legal writing, it is particularly important to pay attention to tenses when narrating facts and discussing case law. You should use the past tense to state all facts that have already occurred. Thus, you should use the past tense to discuss precedents. However, use the present tense to state a proposition of law.

> **Example**: The court held [past tense] that due process requires [present tense] court-appointed counsel.

When discussing two events both of which occurred in the past, use the past perfect tense ("had" plus the past participle) to describe the earlier of two past actions.

> **Example:** The defense objected, arguing that the court **had** already **overruled** that line of questioning.

12. *Make Your Comparisons Complete and Logical*

A comparative sentence must have two terms. Do not say "Jones has a stronger case." Finish the comparison by adding the second term: "Jones has a stronger case than you." In addition, make sure you are comparing like or comparable things. Do not compare, for example, your facts to a case. Compare your facts to the facts in a case. Do not say "Smith's fraudulent statements are like John v. Doe." The proper comparison is "Smith's fraudulent statements are similar to those of the defendant in John v. Doe."

13. *Check That the Words in Your Sentence Have a Rational Relationship*

The subject of your sentence should be able to perform the action expressed by the verb; if the subject cannot, your sentence lacks coherence. A court, for example, does not *contend* or *argue* that a defendant is negligent. It "holds" the defendant negligent. A court is not an advocate in the litigation; the attorneys are the advocates. Nor do courts *feel* or *believe;* their decisions are presumably based on reasons, not emotions or beliefs. What then might a court do? The court may have said something, or decided, stated, concluded, held (for propositions of law), found [that] (for facts), weighed, reasoned, indicated, implied, considered, stressed, noted, compared, added, analyzed.

A court, for example, might "apply" a balancing test or might "balance" the state's interest against a private interest. It would be incorrect, however, to write that a "test" balances those interests. A "requirement" does not "show" a "foreseeable injury," although a test might "require" a plaintiff to "show" the defendant could have foreseen injury. In other words, make sure the subject, predicate, and object of a sentence rationally relate to each other.

14. Select Concrete, Familiar, and Specific Words: Avoid Vagueness and Imprecision

We have already recommended that you use concrete words as subjects instead of abstract nouns. You should also use concrete facts in your descriptions rather than words that characterize. Instead of saying, "The defendant drove several miles over the speed limit," report that the defendant drove sixty miles per hour in a fifty mile zone. If you say, "After a period of time, Roche purchased the drugs," we do not know whether minutes elapsed or years.

Do not be afraid to use a familiar vocabulary, one you feel comfortable with. To sound professional, you do not need to inflate or strain your diction. You need not say, "The car accident victim expired." Simply tell us that he died. You run far more risk using a word the meaning of which you are uncertain than you do using a familiar vocabulary.

15. Avoid Jargon, Informal, and Esoteric Language

As an attorney, you will be writing mostly formal documents. Informal expressions in these documents jar the reader because of their inappropriate tone. Do not say, "the car's rear end abutted the public road." Say, "the rear of the car abutted the public road."

You need not be a slave to jargon or legalese, however. Delete expressions like "hereinafter" and "cease and desist" (unless the phrase describes the remedy that is being asked for). Moreover, although courts sometimes employ an esoteric vocabulary, you need not parrot that language. If a court says, "the statute does not pass constitutional muster," you can paraphrase that statement in a more contemporary idiom. For example, you could simply say that "the statute is unconstitutional."

On the other hand, you should use the wording of a court when applying a particular test that a court uses to evaluate claims and use the exact statutory language that you are applying.

16. *Avoid Qualifiers and Intensifiers; Do Not Overuse Adjectives and Adverbs*

It is better to demonstrate the clarity of an idea by supplying supporting arguments than to insist on it with adverbs like "clearly" or "certainly." Do not overuse adjectives and adverbs. One apt adverb is more effective than many.

17. *Avoid Sexist Language* [2]

The legal profession has become increasingly sensitive to the use of sexist language. To avoid antagonizing colleagues and clients, it is important to use gender neutral language when you write.

    a.   The generic use of the pronoun "he" should be avoided.

— Use plural nouns and plural pronouns.

> **Example:** The attorney must represent his client to the best of his ability.
>
> **Rewrite:** Attorneys must use their best abilities in representing their clients.

— Substitute articles for pronouns or use "who" instead of he.

> **Example:** The judge handed down his opinion on June 1st.
>
> **Rewrite:** The judge handed down the opinion on June 1st.

> **Example:** If an attorney solicits a client, he may be disciplined.
>
> **Rewrite:** An attorney who solicits a client may be disciplined.

— Substitute one, you or we for "he" or delete pronouns altogether.

> **Example:** The litigator must exercise his judgment in selecting issues.
>
> **Rewrite:** The litigator must exercise judgment in selecting issues.

— When all else fails, try the passive voice.

2. The recommendations made in this section are adapted from the "Guidelines for the Nonsexist Use of Language" written for the American Philosophical Association by Virginia L. Warren. They were published in PROCEEDINGS AND ADDRESSES OF AMERICAN PHILOSOPHICAL ASSOCIATION, vol. 59, no. 3 (Feb.1988), at 471–84. Copyright © 1988 by the American Philosophical Association; reprinted by permission.

Example: The judge handed down his opinion on June 1st.
Rewrite: The opinion was handed down on June 1st.

— If you know that the judge is a man or a woman, use the correct pronoun.

b. The generic use of "man" and other gender specific nouns should be avoided.

— Use person, individual, human, people.

— Use spouse instead of wife or husband, sibling instead of sister or brother

c. Address people by their titles whenever possible.

— Use Dr., Prof., Ms., Editor, Colleague, Chair or Chairperson.

Exercise 10–A: Sentence Structure

Diagnose error and correct.

1. In calculating damages, the salary of a full-time companion was considered to be the greatest expense.

2. The drug companies can either insure themselves against liability, absorb the damage awards, or the costs can be passed along to the consumer.

3. Canon 9, which prohibits both impropriety and the mere appearance of impropriety, and which alone is a basis for a disqualification motion, reflects the Bar's concern with protecting the integrity of the legal system.

4. Heated arguments had often occurred over technicalities in the middle of negotiation.

5. A trial by jury was requested by defendant.

6. Keith Johnson's case is more factually similar to Ziady v. Curley.

7. The court admitted into evidence the decedent's letter charging her husband with cruelty, indifference, and failure to support, emphasizing that admitting the letter did not violate the statute.

8. A determination of the awarding of consequential damages is done largely on a case-by-case basis.

9. The state interest in setting a filing fee relates to revenue raising and arguably to act as a deterrent to unmeritorious use of judicial time.

10. Unlike Elliot, Keith's mother had never relinquished her custody.

11. In order for the plaintiff to state a claim, it must be shown that he suffered severe emotional distress.

12. Any instrument, article, or substance which, under the circumstances in which it was used, is capable of causing death or serious injury is a dangerous instrument.

13. The jury, knowing the prosecutor has the authority of the government behind her, and aware of her access to the files, gave her words great weight.

14. The proscription against a prosecutor expressing his personal opinion goes to the heart of a fair trial.

15. The McCaren–Ferguson Act makes an exemption for the business of insurance.

16. Breach of the implied warranty of habitability can occur even without a landlord's violation of city building and housing codes.

17. Turn the material below into a sentence with parallel structure.

    The landlord agrees to

    - Provide heat
    - All utilities will be paid for
    - Premises to be in good order
    - He will keep the air-conditioning system maintained

Exercise 10–B: Sentence Structure

Diagnose error and correct.

1. A social host may be liable for the consequences of a guest's drunken driving if the host directly serves the alcohol, continues serving after the guest is visibly drunk, and knowing that the guest will soon be driving home.

2. Her innovative programming drastically increased attendance at the youth programs.

3. The firm entered into a two year contract with Ms. Taylor, who introduced several new products which increased sales and earned her an "employee of the year" award.

4. By silencing you, I believe your teacher violated your First Amendment rights.

5. The trial court, in dismissing Mann's complaint under Rule 12(b)(6) of the federal Rules of Civil Procedure, stated that it was not necessary to decide the merits of defendant's argument.

6. The defendant's acting with deliberate indifference is the second requirement.

7. Robertson granted visitation rights to Ms. Cavallo after she had abandoned Julia, abused another child, and she had committed heinous acts of abuse against Julia.

8. Although settlement will probably not result in the compensation of your damages to the same extent as that which would occur if you prevail at a formal hearing, it is a much quicker and more flexible process.

9. Only when the court would be interfering in inherently ecclesiastical matters and the court would be excessively entangled in Church matters will a church be able to avoid state laws.

10. By firing you, your contract was violated.

11. Such neutrality on the part of Utopia's School District cannot be compared to cases such as <u>Lee</u>, <u>Engel</u>, and <u>Abington</u>.

12. Julia was born prematurely and shortly thereafter began suffering withdrawal symptoms associated with drug addiction on August 3.

13. Should these matters go to trial, the Board will be exposed to the possibility of having to pay compensatory and punitive damages.

Chapter Eleven

Types of Legal Arguments in Resolving Questions of Law

I. Introduction

The first half of this book focuses on the relatively straightforward application of settled legal rules to the facts of a case. Not all legal disputes stem from disagreement about the appropriate application of a rule, however. Some disputes concern the rule itself. Disputes about rules, called doctrinal questions or "questions of law," arise when (1) it is unclear what a rule means; (2) there is a gap in the rules, perhaps because an issue has not been litigated in your jurisdiction; (3) there are conflicting rules because of a split among the courts; or (4) changes in law and society suggest a rule is no longer practical or equitable. In these situations, lawyers must either (1) interpret the rule before applying it, (2) extend a rule or create a new rule to fill the gap, (3) explain why one rule is better than another, or (4) explain why a rule needs to be refined or overruled. Only after the law has been thus clarified, can it be applied. Many disputes require both a decision about the law and its application to the facts.

The types of arguments lawyers make about questions of law can be helpfully, if not exhaustively, catalogued, for many legal arguments are standard and therefore predictable. Indeed, not only are legal arguments often predictable, but so are their counterarguments: legal reasoning tends to fall into dualistic patterns that reflect law's adversarial nature.[1] If there is a sound analogy, there is likely a sound distinction. If a flexible rule ensures equity, a fixed rule provides notice and stability. Thus, up to a point, arguments and responses can be matched. Finally, lawyers tend to support their conclusions with multiple arguments (including arguments in the alternative), and these arguments often appear in predictable sequences: arguments based on authority generally precede arguments based on policy; plain meaning analyses precede legislative history. Nonetheless, not all arguments are equally relevant or equally strong. The choice and order of legal arguments are strategic decisions, especially in briefs, and require thought.

This chapter looks first at the types of arguments lawyers make about legal authority—precedents and statutes. It then describes the kinds of policy arguments that are prominent in legal discourse.

II. *Authority Arguments Based on Precedent*

Stare decisis makes precedent binding authority within a jurisdiction. Precedent functions in two ways: courts create common law rules and they also create binding interpretations of enacted law. Yet, under either of these two situations, *stare decisis* does not necessarily result in a rigid and mechanical application of law because there are often debates about what the precedent means. These debates tend to fall within four categories mentioned above and discussed in more detail here.

A. *Broad and Narrow Interpretation*

Arguments founded in precedent state, in effect, that prior decisions compel a particular outcome because the precedents and the instant case are analogous or distinguishable. Yet courts and practitioners rarely find the matter so simple. First, it can be difficult to determine exactly what the precedents require. Then, for courts, fairness to the parties and social goals also influence their formulation of holdings, requiring them to frame holdings either broadly or narrowly depending on the results they seek.

Assume a rent control law fails to define "family," and a court needs to decide if unmarried domestic partners are included in that term. One court might conclude that a domestic partner is not included in the term "family" because he or she is not a legal spouse by virtue of marriage, an institution supported by the state. In addition, this court might fear the difficult problem of defining unmarried domestic partners or of predicting the economic and

---

1. For more detailed discussions, *see* James Boyle, "The Anatomy of a Torts Class," 34 Am. U. L. Rev. 1003 (1985); Duncan Kennedy, "A Semiotics of Legal Argument," 42 Syracuse L .Rev. 75 (1991).

social consequences of a broad definition. In contrast, another court might define the term "family" in a noneviction provision to include adult partners unrelated by blood or law whose relationship is long-term and characterized by emotional and financial commitment and interdependence. The court might define family this way both because of the changing configuration of domestic nuclear units and to avoid the health and welfare catastrophes that could result from evicting large numbers of people from their homes upon the death of the tenant-of-record.[2]

A good practitioner will similarly manipulate the scope of a holding to serve a client's interests. The decision to interpret law broadly or narrowly is shaped by an attorney's persuasive purposes. If a precedent is favorable, it may have to be interpreted broadly and analogized as similar to the instant case. A broad interpretation is one that characterizes facts, reasoning, and holding in general or abstract terms. Thus a lesbian ex-partner might argue that the changing notions of family that prompted one court to define that term broadly in the rent control case are equally applicable in a child visitation case and support her visitation rights as the non-biological parent of a child jointly reared.

Conversely, if the precedent is unfavorable, it is often easier to argue that it is inapplicable to your case than it is to convince a court to overrule it. To convince a court to overrule, you must convince the judges that the court's own precedent is wrong. Thus, the first tactic where unfavorable precedent is involved is usually to distinguish the cases by interpreting the decision narrowly. Thus the biological mother fighting visitation by her ex-partner might argue that the health and welfare concerns that justify a broad definition of family in an eviction situation do not apply in a visitation situation,and that visitation should be awarded to biological or adoptive parents only.

B. *Extending Precedents to Cover a Gap*

Sometimes the facts of a precedent are significantly different from the facts in a case on which you are engaged, but the underlying rationale of the precedent seems applicable to your case. In this situation, you might want to argue that the precedent is sufficiently analogous that it should be extended to the new situation.

Assume, for example, that the courts in your jurisdiction recognize a discovery rule exception to the statute of limitations for negligence suits. The statute requires the plaintiff to file an action

---

2. As the court did in Braschi v. Stahl Assocs., 543 N.E.2d 49 (N.Y. 1989).

within two years of the accrual of the claim, but it is unclear when a claim begins to accrue. Generally, claims have been held to accrue at the time of injury. However, where the plaintiff learns of his or her injury only after the two-year limit has expired—as is often in the case in toxic torts, for instance—the claim accrues not at the time of injury, but at the time the injury is discovered. The courts recognized this discovery rule exception because of the unfairness to plaintiffs who, through no fault of their own, would be denied an opportunity to litigate if the claim began to accrue at the time of injury, instead of at the time the injury was discovered.

Your case is somewhat different. Your client knew about her injury before the statute expired, but she did not know its cause. She had undergone radiation therapy for breast cancer. Her reaction to this course of therapy was poor. She suffered burns, nausea and pain. Within two years of the radiation therapy, necrotic ulcers appeared, requiring surgery. During a follow-up visit six months after the surgery, your client overheard her surgeon saying to colleagues, "And there you see, my friends, what happens when the radiologist puts a patient on the table, and goes out and has a cup of coffee."[3] Here the patient knew of radiation burns and ulcers within the two year limitations period, but she did not know that the injury was caused by her radiologist's negligence until after the limitations period had expired.

As plaintiff's attorney, you would argue that the situation is analogous to hidden injury, and as with hidden injury, so here justice demands the client be afforded a day in court. The discovery rule is a rule of equity, developed to mitigate the harsh and unjust results that flow from a rigid adherence to a strict rule of law. In this case, the strict rule should not apply because the passage of time does not make it unduly difficult to present a defense and the claim is not false, frivolous or speculative. Thus you would argue that the discovery rule should be extended to include the delayed discovery of negligence as well as the delayed discovery of injury because the rationale for each exception is the same.

C. Conflicting Lines of Authority

Sometimes there are two equally valid lines of authority that point in opposite directions. In cases of first impression, for example, a court may look to other jurisdictions for guidance and find that there are two or more dominant trends. These alternatives require courts and counsel to explain why one line of authority is preferable to another. Among the reasons an attorney might offer is that one line of authority is easier to apply than the other or that one trend reflects a sounder social policy. Often advocates make a

---

3. Based on *Lopez v. Swyer*, 300 A.2d 563 (N.J. 1973).

"weight of authority" argument to support their positions, arguing that more courts have adopted one position than another. But numbers do not always prevail, and this type of argument must be supported by other reasons.

For instance, until resolved by the Supreme Court, there was a split among the federal courts about what "use" meant in a federal statute that enhanced the prison sentence for anyone who "uses" or "carries" a firearm during a drug transaction. One line of cases distinguished "active" from "passive or potential" employment of a firearm and held that active employment is required because such an interpretation is consistent with the ordinary meaning of "use." The other line of cases suggests that if a firearm in any way facilitates a drug transaction, it has been "used." Under this definition, a gun left on a table that is visible through a doorway may be "use" of a firearm. The Supreme Court eventually settled this split by adopting the narrow definition of use, requiring "active employment" of a weapon.[4]

D. *Overruling Precedent*

Sometimes precedents need to be overruled because they are outdated and no longer reflect good policy. An increase in teenage drunk driving, for example, has led a number of courts to overturn precedents prohibiting "social host" liability; the new rule renders hosts negligent when they serve liquor to teenage guests who then drive and injure a person. The old rule of nonliability simply did not work well under modern conditions.

Even if a rule is not an old one, another reason to overrule a precedent is that important new decisions in other jurisdictions have held the other way based on better reasoning. For example, many state courts have held that a defendant who raises an entrapment defense cannot also deny the crime by pleading not guilty.[5] Entrapment presupposes the defendant committed the crime. Thus many states do not permit a defendant who pleads not guilty to use an entrapment defense because the defenses of not guilty and entrapment are thought to be inconsistent.

The Supreme Court has held, however, that a criminal defendant could plead not guilty and still enter an entrapment defense if

---

4. Bailey v. United States, 516 U.S. 137 (1995).

5. Entrapment is a defense based on the claim that the government "set up" the defendant. In the Supreme Court case cited most often as authority for this defense, the Court explained that entrapment occurs "when the criminal design originates with the officials of the Government, and they implant in the mind of an innocent person the disposition to commit the alleged offense." Sorrells v. United States, 287 U.S. 435,442 (1932). Entrapment is thus interpreted as a two-part test: The criminal design must originate with the government and the defendant must not be predisposed to commit the crime.

the defendant denies an element of the crime.[6] The Mathews defendant had pleaded not guilty because he denied the intent element of the crime. The Court acknowledged that inconsistent defenses ("I didn't do it; I did it but was entrapped") could be seen as encouraging perjury. Nonetheless, the Supreme Court said other more beneficial consequences outweighed the perjury concern. The legitimate purpose of entrapment in a sting operation is to take a dangerous criminal out of circulation: this purpose is thwarted if entrapment leads an otherwise law abiding citizen into unintentionally committing a crime. Permitting the defense in this situation is a way to discourage the abusive use of sting operations. Moreover, the Court stated that the risk of perjury is actually minimal because a defendant who offered conflicting testimony would significantly reduce his credibility before the judge and jury, and thus reduce the chance of acquittal.

The Mathews case does not bind the states because it is based on federal criminal law, not on a state criminal statute. Thus, to state courts, it is only persuasive authority. Nonetheless, in a state criminal trial, defense counsel could argue that the superior reasoning in Mathews should persuade a state court to overrule precedents that held the defenses of not guilty and entrapment inconsistent.

III. *Authority Arguments Based on Statutes*

Additional layers of complexity are added with statutory interpretation. As we mentioned in Chapter Three, statutory interpretation begins with the "plain meaning" rule. To determine legislative intent, you look first at the statutory language to determine whether the words have a commonly accepted meaning that render the statute unambiguous. If not (and many times, even if so), you then analyze what the legislature intended the statute to mean by using the materials that were generated during the legislative process leading to enactment of that particular statute. You might also look at the larger legislative history—at predecessor statutes, amendments, and even similar statutes in other jurisdictions. Another technique of statutory interpretation explained in Chapter Three is the use of canons of construction, which interpret statutory language according to types of statutes or general principles of grammar and usage.

Both courts and advocates use these interpretative techniques to explain and justify their positions. Advocates are, of course, bound by the interpretative analyses of the courts in their jurisdiction. However, since these techniques do not always yield clear answers, arguments about interpretation are the basis of many

6. Mathews v. United States, 485 U.S. 58 (1988).

briefs. And there, as with a case law analysis, you must marshal as many arguments as are relevant to support your conclusion about the statute's meaning.

A. *Plain Meaning Analysis*

The plain meaning rule dictates that where the language of a statute is clear, other evidence of legislative intent is unnecessary. Only when the meaning is ambiguous should extrinsic sources be consulted. Frequently, the plain meaning of a rule can be inferred because language is rule-governed and therefore predictable. The rules of grammar govern the structure of a sentence, that is, the order and relationship of words within a sentence. Thus, for example, when Section 12102(2) of the Americans with Disabilities Act [ADA] defines disability as *"a physical or mental impairment that substantially limits one or more of the major life activities,"* we know from the rules governing adverb and adjective placement that "physical" and "mental" modify impairment, not activities, and "substantially" modifies "limits." Dictionaries, stipulative definitions,[7] and common and technical usage also govern the meanings of words. Thus, for example, when Congress defines "public entity" in the ADA as "any department, agency, . . . or other instrumentality of a state ... or local government," an entity like a state department of welfare falls squarely within the plain meaning of the statutory definition.

Nonetheless, plain meaning analyses are often less definitive than they might first appear. The plain meaning of a statute is often threatened by syntactic ambiguity (uncertainty that results from the arrangement and relationship of words in a sentence) and semantic uncertainty (uncertainty that results from confusion about a word's meaning or its range of meanings).

1. *Syntactic Ambiguity*

Syntactic ambiguity is the ambiguity that results from confusion about how the parts of a sentence fit together. One of the most common syntactic problem results from the careless use of conjunctions and disjunctives: "It is a crime to solicit funds and to loiter while on public transit." Must a person both solicit and loiter to be guilty of a crime? Although the drafter probably wanted to forbid each activity independently, the use of "and" instead of "or" undermines this intention.

Another common problem is caused by the unclear placement of modifiers, especially modifiers that are positioned at the begin-

---

7. Stipulative definitions are defini- regulation.
tions created for use in just that one

ning or end of a series. Consider the provision, "No one may transport wholesale or retail vegetables, dairy, fruit, or other perishable products without a certificate of conveyance." It is syntactically unclear whether the modifier "without a certificate of conveyance" is confined to "other perishable products" or whether it also applies to "vegetables, dairy, and fruit" since end modifiers can describe all the items in a list or only the item closest to it. Moreover, an adjective or adverb preceding a series can be interpreted to modify the first or all the elements of the series. Thus it is ambiguous whether the adjectives "wholesale and retail" modify only vegetables or all the items in the list.

Dangling modifiers also create confusion. Justice Scalia criticized this provision in a statute controlling the National Endowment for the Arts: "Artistic excellence and artistic merit are the criteria by which applications are judged, taking into consideration general standards for decency and respect for the diverse beliefs and values of the American public." There is no subject to which the modifier "taking into consideration" is attached. When syntax is ambiguous, context should direct our choice.

Yet another ambiguity that bedevils legal prose is the common failure to distinguish between restrictive and nonrestrictive modifiers. If a provision requires "two day delivery of all produce which is quickly perishable," it is unclear whether all produce is being regulated or only that which is quickly perishable. If the clause had used "that," the modifier would be restrictive. It would limit the kind of produce regulated to that which perishes quickly. If the drafter had preceded the "which" with a comma, the modifier would be nonrestrictive and mean that all produce is regulated because all produce perishes quickly. Without the comma, however, it is unclear whether the modifier is restrictive or nonrestrictive, and thus the scope of the provision is ambiguous. (See Chapter 10, Section 8.)

Finally ambiguous pronoun reference causes syntactic ambiguity: "After a plaintiff makes a prima facie case and the defendant articulates a legitimate reason for the discharge, he resumes that burden of proof." It is unclear whether "he" refers to the plaintiff or the defendant. When syntactic ambiguity exists, you must seek clarification from other sources.

2. *Semantic Uncertainty*

One common semantic problem is atypical usage. Words have a range of meanings—some of which are more typical than others. When the Supreme Court in Smith v. United States[8] held that trading a machine gun for drugs is active employment of a firearm

---

8.   508 U.S. 223 (1993).

and thus one way of "using" a firearm in violation of a statute, it was not wrong. Nonetheless, it was not employing the ordinary meaning of "use" of a firearm either. When most people think about using firearms, they think about using them as weapons, not as commodities of exchange. Thus practitioners and courts sometimes stretch words in ways that generate heated debate about their meanings and that require looking at other sources to determine intent.

There are two other frequent causes of semantic uncertainty: ambiguity and vagueness. Semantic ambiguity exists when words have two or more meanings. The meaning of "no drinking in the pool room" is ambiguous because we cannot determine on the basis of the word alone whether a "pool room" is a room with billiard tables or a room with a swimming pool, or whether "drinking" refers to the consumption of any beverage or only alcoholic beverages. Although context could possibly remove some of our uncertainty, language alone cannot.

Vagueness is uncertainty that results when the boundaries of a word are fluid. Consider the ordinance "No Parking Near Hydrant." It is unclear whether "near" means 5 inches, 3 feet, or fifteen feet. Or, to take a more complicated example, consider the American Disabilities Act's definition of disability as an impairment that "substantially limits one or more of the major life activities." The federal agency charged with enforcing Title III of the ADA recognized that "substantially limits" is a vague term and thus defined it further, explaining that a person is "substantially limited" if he or she is "unable to perform" a major life activity or is "significantly restricted" in performing an activity. But this clarification is itself vague: what is the difference between being restricted in performance and being significantly restricted? The uncertainty remains and recourse to other interpretative techniques is required.

To cover unanticipated situations, legislatures sometimes purposely use vague or general language, as in "unfair competition." In these situations, the legislatures expect courts to decide on a case-by-case basis what conduct falls within the category and what falls outside it. On the other hand, some statutes are so hopelessly vague that courts hold them "void for vagueness."

———

In deciding that a person who has asymptomatic HIV infection is protected by § 12102(2)(A) of the Americans with Disabilities Act,[9] the Supreme Court began its opinion with a plain meaning

9. Bragdon v. Abbott, 118 S.Ct. 2196 (1998).

analysis of whether asymptomatic HIV infection met the definition of disability, that is, whether it is a "physical . . . impairment that substantially limits one or more of the major life activities of such individual." The lower courts had split on two issues: first, whether asymptomatic HIV was a physical impairment, and second, whether it substantially limited a major life activity, reproduction.

Major life activities are defined in the regulation as activities like "caring for one's self, performing manual tasks, walking, seeing, hearing, speaking, breathing, learning, and working."[10] Many people with HIV refrain from a major life activity, namely, reproduction. Yet some courts said reproduction is not as fundamental as the listed activities of breathing and speaking, nor is an HIV–positive person unable to perform these activities, though he might chose not to engage in them. Other courts said procreation is as fundamental as "working" and "learning."

The Supreme Court held that reproduction falls within the phrase "major life activities," agreeing with the court below that "[t]he plain meaning of the word 'major' denotes comparative importance" and "suggest[s] that the touchstone for determining an activity's inclusion under the statutory rubric is its significance."[11]

The Supreme Court also decided that asymptomatic HIV infection is a physical impairment, but not primarily on plain meaning grounds. Some of the lower courts had decided that the dictionary definition of "impairment" as "lessening" and "weakening" suggests a person who is asymptomatic is not impaired under a plain meaning analysis since there is no weakening. Others said asymptomatic HIV is a physical impairment because it attacks the immune, the hemic, and the lymphatic systems immediately. These courts were influenced by the Justice Department's definition of "physical impairment" as a disorder that detrimentally affects the hemic and lymphatic systems, among others.[12] Although the Supreme Court gave weight to the regulatory definitions of physical impairment, the Court focused on medical journals and reports when it determined that asymptomatic HIV infection is a disability.

B. *Other Sources of Legislative Intent*

When there is no commonly accepted judicial interpretation of statutory language, as in the lower courts' split over the meaning of physical impairment, it is necessary to consider other evidence of legislative intent. Sometimes an ambiguous term or provision can

---

10. 28 C.F.R. § 41.31(b)(2).

11. Bragdon, 118 S.Ct. at 2205, citing 107 F.3d at 939–940.

12. 28 C.F.R. & 41.31(a)(1). The Justice Department was charged with enforcing Titles II and III under the ADA.

be clarified by examining the statutory context, since the language in one part of a statute may help in determining the meaning of ambiguous language in a different part of the same statute. Preambles or Statements of Purpose are another important source. Evidence of legislative intent also comes from extrinsic evidence, especially from a bill's legislative history. Intent is often inferred from the paper trail that tracks a statute's process through the legislature—from its introduction as a bill, to its deliberation in committee, to the vote on the floor. Each stage produces documentation that provides evidence of intent. Committee reports are important sources of legislative intent. Legislative activity and inactivity is yet another useful type of analysis: a statute's relation to predecessor statutes as well as its history of amendment, whether the amendments are rejected or adopted, all provide clues to legislative intent. Sometimes lawyers go even further afield to determine intent: they examine similar statutes in other jurisdictions to see what light they may shed on the statute in question.

1. Statutory Context

Sometimes statutory context can resolve questions about the meaning of terms within that statute. Statutes should be interpreted to promote coherence among the parts of the statute itself. If the exact language of one provision is used elsewhere in the statute, that initial use may give clues to the intended meaning of the words when they are used later. If similar but not identical language is used elsewhere in the statute, the difference in the wording may help you interpret the different meanings. Thus, the context of the statute as a whole and the language in other parts of the statute may help you interpret the scope of the disputed language. It also follows that language should be interpreted in the spirit of a statute's preamble or statement of purpose.

The introductory language of the ADA could also be interpreted to indicate its broad remedial purpose. The introduction states "the nation's proper goals regarding individuals with disabilities are to assume equality of opportunity, full participation, independent living, and economic self-sufficiency for such individuals" 42 U.S.C. § 12101(a)(8). The Act aspires to give "people with disabilities the opportunity to compete on an equal basis and to pursue those opportunities for which our society is justifiably famous." 42 U.S.C. § 12101(a)(9). A plaintiff may argue that this broad statement of purpose supports an inclusive rather than exclusive interpretation of disability: it weakens the argument that asymptomatic HIV is not a disability. A defendant, however, would interpret that language to mean only that the ADA should be interpreted to end discrimination toward disabled people, not to interpret the term "disability."

Some might interpret the broad remedial purpose of the ADA to also be embodied in the third prong of the disability definition,[13] which includes those persons who are not in fact disabled, but who are "regarded as" disabled, 42 U.S.C. § 121202(2)(c). Here Congress was implementing a policy of broad protection by recognizing that a discriminator's actions and beliefs toward an individual are as handicapping as the physical limitations of the impairment itself.

2. *Legislative History*

When Congress enacted the Americans with Disabilities Act in 1990, it left a well documented record of its deliberations. The ADA is therefore a good illustration of the uses of legislative documents. Indeed, the United States Congress often produces a voluminous legislative history, whereas state legislatures tend to have insubstantial records. Where the record is insubstantial or where it reveals ambivalence and conflict, courts have to extrapolate purposes from evidence other than legislative documents.

In the case of the ADA, both House and Senate Committee Reports as well as statements from the Congressional Record demonstrate the consensus within Congress that AIDS, as well as asymptomatic HIV, was intended to be a protected disability. The Supreme Court relied on these reports in Bragdon.

> All indications are that Congress was well aware of the position taken by the Office of Legal Counsel [of the Justice Department] when enacting the ADA and intended to give that position [asymptomatic HIV infection is a disability] its active endorsement. H.R.Rep. No.101–485, pt.2, p.52 (1990)(endorsing the analysis and conclusion of the OLC Opinion); id., pt. 3, at 28, n. 18 (same); S. Rep. No. 101–116, pp.21,22 (1989) (same). . . . Again the legislative record indicates that Congress intended to ratify HUD's interpretation [disability includes infection with HIV] when it reiterated the same definition in the ADA. H.R. Rep. No. 101–485, pt. 2, at 50; id., pt.3, at 27; id., pt. 4, at 36; S. Rep. No. 101–116, at 21.

3. *Predecessor and Similar Statutes*

It is often helpful to look at predecessor statutes when interpreting a current statute, since continuity and change are both equally significant.

The Supreme Court in Bragdon relied especially on the fact that the ADA incorporated almost verbatim the definition of disability used in the Rehabilitation Act of 1973,[14] and that Congress

---

13. This was not an issue in the Bragdon decision.

14. The Rehabilitation Act applied to government employers and employees.

included a provision directing the courts to construe the ADA as granting at least as much protection as that provided by the regulations implementing the Rehabilitation Act. Thus the precedents that arose under the Rehabilitation Act apply to the ADA. The Rehabilitation Act cases have consistently held that both AIDS and asymptomatic HIV infection constitute disabilities, and the Supreme Court took account of those cases.

Statutes that adopt rather than reject provisions of predecessor statutes should be interpreted consistently, as should other statutes relevant to the same area of law, in order to keep the body of the law coherent. This is the policy behind the in *pari materia* canon discussed in Chapter Three.

4. *Regulatory Agencies*

If the administrative agency charged with enforcing a statute offers a construction that is reasonable and that does not conflict with the statute, courts defer to that agency's construction. In the context of the ADA, the Justice Department is the agency charged with enforcing Title III of the ADA. Its regulations specifically define the phrase "physical impairment" by a list of diseases that includes HIV disease, whether symptomatic or asymptomatic.[15] Although a court is the final arbiter of statutory construction, it will not substitute a different reading for that of a reasonable agency interpretation unless that interpretation is capricious or manifestly contrary to the statute.

5. *Legislative Activity*

A sometimes useful, but often inconclusive, type of analysis is one that examines related legislative action or inaction. If language was changed by amendment or changed in a related statute, the change may clarify and make explicit the legislature's intent. If it remains the same, the continuity may be an indication that the language as currently interpreted comports with legislative intent.

The 1990 ADA broadened the protection against discrimination that disabled persons received under the Rehabilitation Act of 1973 and the National Fair Housing Act Amendments of 1988. The Rehab Act protected disabled government employees from discrimination. The Fair Housing amendments barred housing discrimination. The ADA extends that protection in employment and places of accommodation. In adopting the same definition of disability in each of these statutes, one that encompasses HIV infection, Congress indicates no change in interpretation is intended.

The ADA extended the scope of the Rehab Act.

15. 28 C.F.R. § 36–104(1)(iii).

It is also important to note regulatory action and inaction. For example, the Justice Department originally took the position that decisions about whether asymptomatic HIV-positive persons were disabled should be made on a case-by-case basis rather than by a *per se* rule. It later reversed its position on the physiological impact of HIV infection, reasoning that the overwhelming majority of infected persons exhibit abnormalities of the immune system and are therefore disabled as a matter of law. Its new provision eliminates one of the previous possible outcomes. Such changes need to be tracked for your analysis to be complete and accurate.

C.   Canons of Construction

As discussed in Chapter Three, the canons of construction provide guidelines for interpreting statutes when meaning is ambiguous. To the discussion in Chapter Three, we add here a word of warning: just as there are arguments and counter-arguments, so are there canons and, so to speak, "counter-canons."[16] Thus, if one canon says courts must give effect to unambiguous statutory language, another says plain language need not be given effect when doing so would defeat legislative intent or have absurd or unjust results.

The dissent in <u>Bragdon v. Abbott</u> conceded an *expressio unius, exclusio unius* argument (the expression of one thing excludes another) when it agreed that the list of activities that follows "major life activities" in the ADA is illustrative, not exhaustive. The list does not include reproduction. Nonetheless, Chief Justice Rehnquist's dissent argued that reproduction is not "major" in the sense that it is not performed as often or to the same extent as the listed activities of "caring for one's self, performing manual tasks, walking, seeing, hearing, speaking, breathing, learning, and working." Thus the Chief Justice made an *ejusdem generis* argument (of the same genus or class) that reproduction does not fall into the same class as the activities mentioned. The majority disagreed, interpreting "major" as meaning important.

IV.   Policy Arguments

Policy arguments will often decide a case, especially when each party offers plausible interpretations of the law. In this situation, the judge may then decide the case on the basis of the social goals that the decision will promote, and the purposes behind the particular rules.

16. For a more complete listing of opposing canons, *see* Carl Llewellyn, "Remarks on the Theory of Appellate Decisions and the Rules or Canons about How Statutes are to be Construed," 3 Vand. L. Rev. 395, 401–06 (1950).

Policy arguments can be categorized in many ways, but one useful system is to divide them into four basic groups: normative arguments, that is, arguments about shared values and goals that a law should promote; economic arguments, which look at the economic consequences of a rule; institutional competence arguments, that is, structural arguments about the proper relationship of courts to other courts and courts to other branches of government; and judicial administration arguments, arguments about the practical effects of a ruling on the administration of justice. These categories are not, of course, mutually exclusive.

A. *Normative Arguments*

Normative arguments fall into at least three types. There are moral arguments, which are arguments about whether a rule advances or offends moral principles; there are social policy arguments, which involve a discussion of whether a rule advances or harms a social goal; and there are corrective justice arguments, which revolve around whether the application of a rule is just in a particular case. Moral and social policy arguments are not always easily separable because they both debate the greater good, but the following example illustrates the difference: draft evasion should not be a crime because the taking of life is morally reprehensible, or draft evasion should be a crime because it is a threat to national security. Some rules of equity are derived from moral principles and social policy, for example, a person may not profit from his own wrong, and a plaintiff must come into equity with "clean hands." Corrective justice arguments focus on the actual parties before the court and are traditionally, but arguably, both the basis of our legal system and the province, in particular, of every trial court.

Assume you are involved in a case that asks the court to recognize for the first time a claim for damages for loss of parental consortium. Your clients are children whose mother suffered injuries when an intoxicated driver went through a red light and struck her. The mother now suffers from permanent spinal paralysis, brain damage, and impaired speech. She is confined to bed and requires constant custodial care. She no longer recognizes her children.

Plaintiffs here can make corrective justice and social policy arguments. They can argue that a small but steadily increasing number of jurisdictions permit loss of parental consortium claims because compensation comports with notions of public policy and fairness. Between the two parties, corrective justice demands that the tortfeasor compensates the children for their tragic loss of parental guidance, services, love, and companionship. Providing them with the resources to obtain live-in help or to receive psychiatric assistance can help the children make a permanent adjustment to their loss. Recognition of the claim also serves two important social policies: it preserves the deterrent function of tort law and compensates for real losses.

Some normative arguments are vulnerable to the accusation that they are political. Judges may be therefore reluctant to base, or to admit basing, decisions upon their moral and political views. Yet, as one judge has written, cases that break new ground[17] are often decided on "moral, social, or economic, *i.e.*, political reasons."[18]

B. *Economic Arguments*

Economic arguments have assumed an increasingly important role in legal decisionmaking. Economic arguments are concerned with efficient allocation of resources. One economic approach to the law asks, for example, whether a particular decision is preferable because it spreads the losses among larger segments of the population. Other economic arguments focus on whether a rule ensures optimal efficiency.[19] For those who subscribe to this approach, an efficient outcome is the preferred outcome regardless of fairness between the parties.

The defendant in the loss of parental consortium problem may have trouble countering the plaintiffs' normative arguments, but he has some reasonable economic ones. First, he may argue that permitting these claims could effectively result in a double recovery since a jury may, as a practical matter, compensate a child by means of an award to the surviving parent, if there is one. Moreover, double recovery costs will ultimately be borne by the public generally through increased insurance costs.

C. *Institutional Competence Arguments*

Institutional competence involves an examination of the proper role of each branch of government. For example, courts may defer to the legislature to create or to repeal a cause of action if they believe that the legislature, as the popularly elected branch of government, is the more appropriate forum to change the law. Lower courts will defer to the binding power of higher appellate courts' rules. Another aspect of institutional competence that

---

17. Consider, for example, Brown v. Board of Educ., 347 U.S. 483 (1954); Roe v. Wade, 410 U.S. 113 (1973); Meritor v. Vinson, 477 U.S. 57 (1986).

18. Robert A. Leflar, "Honest Judicial Opinions" 74 Nw. U. L. Rev. 721, 741 (1979). See also Judith S. Kaye, "[A] court must resolve every dispute before it. The court has to go one way or another, and either result necessarily involves a judge's choice, sometimes a judge's social policy choice." Things Judges Do: State Statutory Interpretation, 13 Touro L. Rev. 595, 610–11 (1997).

19. For an explanation of the application of basic economic analysis to law, see Shapo and Shapo, Law School without Fear (1996).

courts consider is whether a particular decision will interfere with the work of administrative agencies.

Both parties in the loss of parental consortium hypothetical have strong institutional competence arguments. The defendant will argue that any change in the law on an issue of public policy should be made by the elected members of the legislature and not the courts. As an institution, the legislature, unlike a court, can gather information on a number of relevant questions, such as:

> 1) whether there is any practical necessity for creating a separate cause of action for a child whose parent has been negligently injured;

> 2) what limiting principles—for example, the age of the child—should circumscribe such a cause of action;

> 3) what impact such a cause of action would have on insurance rates and other costs to the general public;

> 4) what, if any, limit on allowable damages should be imposed as a matter of social policy.

Accordingly, the defendant will contend it is for the members of the legislature to debate and decide this issue.

Plaintiffs will respond that loss of consortium is an item of damages that was initially created by the courts. Changes in the law of consortium have been made by the courts, for example, in permitting wives as well as husbands damages for loss of consortium. Moreover, it is not a highly complex doctrine. Therefore, it is wholly appropriate for the courts to decide this issue and not defer to the legislature. In fact, the plaintiff will argue the courts would be abdicating their responsibility if they did not reform the common law to meet the evolving standards of justice.

D. *Judicial Administration Arguments*

Judicial administration arguments are arguments about the practicality or impracticality of applying a rule. One typical administration of justice argument analyzes the merit of a "bright line" rule versus a flexible rule. Precise, narrow rules provide clear notice and consistency and are easy to administer. They leave little to judicial discretion. In contrast, flexible rules are more responsive to individual circumstances and more likely to promote fairness to the parties. Because flexible rules involve judicial discretion, however, they are less predictable and relatively prone to judicial abuse. Other judicial administration arguments include "slippery slope" and "floodgate" arguments respectively, that the rule is so broad it will be applied in inappropriate circumstances or inundate the courts with suits. Such suits waste judicial resources, as do rules that open the door to speculative, frivolous, or false claims. Finally, if a rule is so complex that it will be difficult to administer, practitioners might make arguments about conserving judicial resources.

The defendant in the loss of parental consortium suit will argue that since each injury would lead to an increased number of law suits, the liability of an individual tortfeasor to a single family based on a single event would become unreasonable and oppressive. Moreover, recognition of the claim will create a slippery slope. It could become unclear how to measure damages and whether to draw the line at children or to include grandparents, or aunts and uncles. Plaintiffs will counter that where children's welfare is at stake, administrative concerns, like the possibility of increased litigation, should be secondary. Moreover, damages are no more uncertain in this type of claim than they are for pain and suffering in personal injury and wrongful death actions, or in the spouse's claim for loss of consortium. Thus this claim is no harder to handle than those, especially since the possibility of double recovery can be avoided by careful jury instructions.

———

As the issue of loss of parental consortium illustrates, policy arguments often compete against each other. Sometimes one party will directly refute the logic of another's argument: although children whose parents have suffered a severe injury have themselves suffered a severe loss, an action for loss of parental consortium is simply unnecessary since compensation for emotional loss and lost economic support can be factored into an uninjured parent's award. Sometimes, one policy argument is countered by shifting the context. If one party argues fairness to the individual, the other stresses the needs of the community or efficiency. If one party focuses on freedom of action (the right to drive), the other focuses on the right to be secure (the right to be protected from drunk drivers). In the consortium case, competing policies need to be balanced: the negative effects of an increased burden on judicial resources and increased insurance costs must be weighed against fair compensation for children and society's interest in deterring negligent conduct. A court might decide, for example, that, in the context of single-parent families, the possibility of parental injury compels recognition of the cause of action because a child of a single parent cannot receive compensation through an uninjured parent's cause of action. This interest outweighs concerns over economic and judicial resources. Thus you must assess competing policies by testing their logic or by deciding that although a number of policies have merit, some policy interests are weightier than others.

V. *Organizing Levels of Argument in Questions of Law*

When you write about questions of law, there are four primary analytic strategies.

- Statutory interpretation focusing on the language of a statute.

- Statutory interpretation focusing on the legislative history of a statute.

- Case law analysis focusing on which common law rule applies, how to frame a common law rule, or how courts have interpreted statutory language.

- Policy analysis focusing on the underlying reasons why a statute or common law rule should or should not control or be interpreted in a particular way.

The extent of these analyses depends on the strength of the arguments you want to make, although in statutory analysis you would always start with plain meaning, even if you can only say there is none or that it is ambiguous. Then go to legislative history. In the asymptomatic HIV problem, plaintiffs would start with a plain meaning analysis and move on to legislative history, since those arguments favored them. The defendants might open by arguing that the statutory language requires individualized inquiry, and then go to the cases that have adopted that statutory interpretation. Thus you must assess what types of argument you can make and their authority and strength.

In addition to making a variety of arguments in support of a contention, you will often need to make alternative arguments also. Alternative arguments are a staple of legal analysis. To argue in the alternative, you must concede your first theory in order to raise additional ones. In an entrapment case, for example, you might be defending a client who denied the intent element of a state charge of drug possession: he did not know that the pipe an undercover government agent handed him contained cocaine, although he admitted committing the act itself, that is, admitted smoking the pipe. As defense counsel, you would interpret the state precedents narrowly and try to distinguish them. Unlike your client, the defendants in the precedents had not denied intent; they denied committing the crime altogether. If the state court is not persuaded by this distinction, your alternative argument is that those precedents should be overruled. You would justify this argument by pointing to the important policy argument in Mathews that the government must be prevented from enticing innocents into a criminal act.

As the above example suggests, authority arguments often depend on or are supported by policy arguments. In assessing the merits of a broad versus a narrow interpretation of precedent or of one line of cases over another, policy plays a role. In deciding whether to extend a precedent or to overrule it, policy plays a role. Thus policy arguments are often raised in context, interwoven into the discussion of other points, rather than separated out. Sometimes, however, policy concerns are raised in a separate section. Here you could organize either around the types of policy arguments being made, describing and evaluating each party's argument on one policy concern. After discussing all the relevant policy issues, you would assess which party had the stronger overall position. Alternatively, you could organize around parties—making all the arguments of one party before moving to the next. Here too, you would need to conclude by weighing the overall merits of each position.

Thus, complex legal analysis often involves strategic thinking and several levels of argument. You will need to examine a variety of sources and their interrelationships, and to develop analytic strategies that will enable you to resolve a question in a logical and persuasive manner. Persuasion is especially important when you write a brief, but even in a memorandum you want to persuade your reader that your analysis is correct and complete.

Exercise 11–A

The defendant Smith was charged with burglary, which under the New York Penal Law § 140.20 requires the defendant to "enter . . . unlawfully in a building with intent to commit a crime." Smith had climbed on the roof of a one-story structure in order to pour oil on the building to set it on fire.

1.   Which statutory language is at issue in this prosecution?

2.   Below are two columns of arguments that can be made in this case. The left column lists arguments the defendant can make; the right column lists the state's answering arguments. The arguments are not listed in matching order.

Match the defendant's and the state's arguments and characterize them as to the type of argument each is. Then write an outline of the order in which you would analyze this issue

How would you decide this case if this were before you on the defendant's motion to dismiss the indictment?

Smith	State
a. The statute does not define "enter . . . in a building" and the plain meaning of the words requires some opening to the building large enough for the defen-	a. The scope of the common law of burglary and its purpose was expanded by the concept of the curtilage, which is the area in close proximity to the dwelling

<table>
<tr><td>Smith</td><td>State</td></tr>
</table>

Smith	State
dant's body to pass through.	house. Unlawful entry of an out-building within the curtilage is burglary. The crime is not re-stricted to maintaining security within the four walls.
b. In a recent case from the N.Y. Court of Appeals, *People v. King*, the court held that the defendant violated § 140.20 when he cut a small hole in a part of a metal security gate. Defendant attempt-ed to get into a store on the ground floor of a building. The metal gate covered the display windows and the vestibule area that led past the display windows into the interior of the store. Defendant cut the hole in the gate directly in front of the vesti-bule. The court held that the vestibule was functionally indis-tinguishable from the display window and store because it could be closed off from the pub-lic by the security gate. *King* requires that a defendant must intrude into an enclosed space in or connected to a build-ing.	b. Because the Penal Law does not define enter, the word retains its common law meaning which is that entry is accomplished when a person intrudes within a building no matter how slightly.
c. The purpose of burglary stat-utes is to preserve the internal security of a dwelling and the crime requires some breaking of the planes created by the thresh-old and walls of the structure.	c. *King* means that the element of entering is satisfied if the de-fendant goes into an area of a building or an area related to a building to which the public can be denied access.

Exercise 11–B

When John Trent was arrested for possession of a controlled sub-stance, he was in Illinois, and with his friend Timothy Lot who had given him the cocaine-filled pipe. Suppose that Lot was not a police informer, and indeed did not know that it was an undercover police officer who supplied him with cocaine. Suppose also that the undercover officer urged Lot to provide the drugs to his "special friends in government positions," and Trent was a local government official.

An Illinois statute, § 7–12, provides the entrapment defense for a person whose conduct "is incited or induced by a public officer or employ-ee, or agent of either." The statute does not define "agent."

The trial court denied Trent's request for an instruction on the ground that Lot was not an agent of a public officer because he did not knowingly act on the officer's behalf.

1. List the types of materials you would research to analyze whether an agent must be a knowing agent under the Illinois statute.

2. Which types of arguments would you want to use? How would you organize your analysis?

3. Read the arguments set out below. Which kinds of strategies are each of these writers using? Evaluate the strength of each. Which ones would you prefer to use? Which ones would you avoid? Organize the strategies you would use in a memorandum analysis as they pertain to 1) statutory arguments, 2) case analysis, and 3) policy analysis.

Arguments:

a. Section 7–12 does not define the term "agent." However, the Committee comment suggests that the legislature did not intend to require a knowing agent. The Comment provides:

> The defense has been recognized as proper not only when the person alleged to have incited the offense was a government officer or agent, but also when he was an investigator privately hired and acting without contact with law enforcement authorities. One case sometimes cited as an entrapment case involved a burglary of a private office, planned and executed by a detective with the knowledge of the owner of the office, to cause the arrest and prosecution of several men who were suspected of having perpetrated a series of burglaries. Although the Illinois Supreme Court referred to the entrapment situation, the basis for the reversal of the judgment was that the "victim" consented to the conduct, and since lack of consent is an element of the offense, no burglary was committed.

b. If the legislature intended to require a knowing agent, it would have said so. For example, § 4–3 of the Criminal code generally defines the mental state element for the entire Criminal code and says that "knowledge is not an element of an offense unless the statute clearly defines it as such."

c. Two Illinois appellate courts have reached opposite conclusions as to whether a defendant is entitled to an entrapment instruction where a private person unknowingly worked with an undercover policeman to buy drugs from the defendant.

In one case, in which the appellate court held that the trial court correctly rejected the instruction, the private party had initiated the contact with the police officer. He also had initiated the contacts with the defendant, and urged the defendant to sell the drugs. In the other case, the private party's only role was to communicate the government's inducements to the defendant directly. The appellate court held that the trial court should have instructed the jury on entrapment.

d. The lower federal courts are split as to whether the middleman must know he is acting for the government.

e. Recognition of entrapment where the police use an unknowing middleman is necessary to prevent the police from engaging in unchecked abuses. Otherwise, police will avail themselves of this technique and unfairly induce people to commit crimes.

f.   When the police instruct a middleman to target a particular person, all courts permit that person to raise the entrapment defense. In this case, the police did not name Trent as the target but described the target in a way that logically led Lot to Trent.

g.   If the legislature were opposed to police using middlemen, it would have legislated against it.

h.   Law enforcement agencies can best control abuses administratively by issuing clear guidelines to their personnel.

i.   Section 7–12 defines the terms "public officer" and "public employee" as well as several other terms. In light of this specificity, the fact that the section does not define "agent" implies that the legislature intended not to restrict its meaning.

j.   Black's Law Dictionary defines agent as "one who represents and acts for another under the contract or relation of agency."

k.   If a police officer is not present during the transaction between a defendant and a middleman, an entrapment defense would present the danger of collusion between the defendant and middleman and would encourage false statements at trial.

Exercise 11–C

1.   Title 18 U.S.C. § 2511(1)(a) of the Omnibus Crime Control and Safe Streets Act makes it unlawful for "any person . . . [to] intentionally intercept . . . any wire . . . communication" without a court order. Edna Mack was charged with a violation of this section for installing a tape recording device on her home telephone and taping her husband John's conversations with a woman with whom he was having an extra-marital affair. Her husband had not consented to the wiretap and Ms. Mack had not gotten a court order. John Mack sued his wife (from whom he then separated) under the statute, which permits civil damages suits for violation of the statute. This suit raised two issues: Does the statute apply to Ms. Mack, and if so, was her husband entitled to damages.

For the first issue, organize the following into arguments for each party, and explain what type of argument each is.

a.   The statute apples to "any person." Section 2510 defines "person" to include "any individual." Therefore, Ms. Mack is a person within the meaning of the statute.

b.   The statute implicitly excepts from its coverage interspousal wiretapping. The purpose of the statute is to regulate the law enforcement personnel and prevent them from invasion of privacy of citizens by wiretapping without court order. Congress would not have intended to interfere with domestic relations and household use of the telephone.

c.   The legislative history concerns only law enforcement personnel and crime control. The only mention of other uses of wiretapping concerned testimony of matrimonial lawyers who used recording devices for divorcing spouses.

2.   If the court holds that this statute applies to interspousal wiretapping, is Mr. Mack entitled to damages?

Section 2520(c)(2) provides that "the court may assess as damages" the plaintiff's actual damages, or statutory damages of $100 a day up to $10,000, whichever is greater. John Mack had no actual damages, and his wife violated the Act on two days.

At issue is whether the court has discretion to award damages or whether it must award Mr. Mack $200. Consider this information.

— In 1986, Congress amended the damages section, increasing maximum statutory damages to $10,000 from $1,000. The amendment also changed the language from "the court shall assess as damages" to the current "the court may assess.... "

— Section 2500(c)(1) assesses damages in cases involving interception of private satellite video communication. That section's language is "the court shall assess.... "

— The legislative history does not contain an explanation of why Congress changed "shall" to "may," or whether Congress intended damages as discretionary or mandatory.

— Besides increasing the maximum statutory damages and changing "shall" to "may" in § 2520(c)(2), the 1986 amendments changed the damages for intercepting private video satellites, and the legislative history documents contain information only about the penalty structure for this violation.

— The only precedent on this issue held that the statute does not give a court discretion to withhold damages. The court said that to adopt a literal application of the word "may" would lead to results at odds with the purpose of the statute, which is to protect privacy.

Evaluate these possible conclusions. Which is best supported by the previous information?

— Congress apparently intended to give the courts discretion in order to ameliorate the possible harshness of the increased statutory damages amount.

— The wiretap provisions were designed to protect the privacy of wire and oral communication and to set out uniform standards for courts to authorize wiretaps. To accomplish these goals, the statute does not permit the court to exercise discretion, but requires the court to assess damages for violation of the act.

— In the absence of a legislative record explaining why Congress changed "shall" to "may," the court should hesitate to read a grant of discretion where none had been permitted in the past, especially when the language is somewhat ambiguous.

3.   If the court decides that the Crime Control Act applies to spousal wiretapping, in that jurisdiction does the statute give a cause of action to a minor child against his custodial mother, when the mother recorded the child's conversations with his father from their home telephone, and the parents are divorced?

Chapter Twelve
Research Strategies

I. Introduction

When you work on a problem, your research goal is to find the relevant binding and persuasive primary authorities of law. However, a law library contains many other materials that will not only help you find the primary authorities, but also will help you analyze the issues you are researching. This chapter will not explain the basic bibliographic information about those resources. Instead, it gives advice for using them for different types of research projects that you may encounter as a law student.

A client will come to you with a story, not an identified claim or defense. To determine how to proceed, you should gather all the facts that you can. You need a complete account of what happened, of the problems your client currently faces, and of the result the client seeks[1]. As a lawyer, your goal is often to convert the facts from your client's story into a legal claim that states a cause of action, into a viable defense to a legal claim, or into the terms of a transaction. If you are an experienced attorney, the client's information may suggest to you a claim or defense and the issues that are involved, without your having to do research to identify them. If you are an inexperienced attorney or a law student, however, you may have to do research first to identify the relevant claims and then to diagnose the problem and find an appropriate solution.

---

1. *See* David A. Binder & Susan C. Price, Legal Interviewing and Counseling: A Client–Centered Approach 2 (1977) and Chapter Thirteen on Interviewing the Client.

The facts of your client's problem are important at all stages of your work. Initially, you want to identify the important facts and use them both to determine which legal claims or defenses will be involved and to provide search terms with which to begin your research. After you have begun your research and have read some of the primary and secondary authorities, you will be able to make a more sophisticated identification of the legally relevant facts. Then you can use those facts not only as search terms for your research, but also analytically to help you prove or disprove the elements of the cause of action and to provide analogies to the important precedents.

In your legal writing assignments, you may be told the nature of the claims and the particular issues to research and write about. If not, then first you should determine the general body of law that is involved. For example, the facts and the relief your client wants may bring your client's problem within the body of contract law because the problem involves a written or oral exchange of promises.

After making this general classification, try to identify the more specific problem within that body of law. If you identify the cause of action as a tort, for example, determine which particular tort or torts are involved. If you face a property law problem because your client is a tenant who has a disagreement with his landlord about terms in a lease, then you probably are concerned only with landlord-tenant law. Or the problem may be a statutory one in which a governmental agency is requiring your client to comply with a statute or with the agency's regulations.

Your research methodology depends on the nature of the problem and the knowledge you have to begin with. If you are not familiar with the cause of action and do not know, for example, which particular torts the client's facts suggest, then you need to begin differently from the way you would if you had previously done research in that area of law and knew relevant cases and statutes. The scope of your research will also depend on other factors, most importantly, the jurisdiction of the problem. Because the law of that jurisdiction governs, you should examine the jurisdiction's law first. Other factors that affect your research are whether you need state or federal materials or both, whether the problem involves statutes or common law or both, and whether it involves a new cause of action or statute or a well-settled body of law. When you are in practice, the scope of your research will also be influenced by the time and financial resources you have to expend on the case.

II. *Practical Considerations*

By the time you graduate from law school and pass the bar exam, you will be much more experienced in doing research than you are as a first-year law student. Your goal in doing research will always be the same: to get an understanding of the relevant area of law so that you can determine how it relates to your client's problem. However, the cost of the time you spend doing research will not be the same. As a student, you have a limited amount of time to do research because you have other academic obligations in addition to your writing and research course. And although your law school will probably be paying a significant amount for its package of computer services (LEXIS and WESTLAW), your personal use of computer-assisted legal research (CALR) is free. When you are an attorney, you will be busier than you are in law school, and time is money—yours and your client's. Your research must not only be effective, it must also be cost-efficient. For attorneys, computer time is not free; it must be paid for by someone, either the client, or as some clients are demanding, by the lawyers as overhead.

Therefore, to be an effective researcher in practice, learn how to develop appropriate research strategies while you are a student. First, do not assume you can always do research better and faster on a computer. A section in a good treatise can, in a short period of time, give you an enormous amount of information about an area of law and important cases. And computer time on LEXIS and WEST-LAW can be expensive. Second, become proficient in using all of the research sources lawyers now use in practice (books, LEXIS, WESTLAW, CD–ROM, the Internet). Finally, learn the advantages and limitations of each, so that you can research a problem both fully and cost-effectively.

In addition to LEXIS and WESTLAW, two other technologies are having a significant impact on how some lawyers are doing research: CD–ROM (compact disc-read only memory) and the Internet. The CD–ROM disc has become very useful as a source of material for attorneys working in specialized areas like tax and bankruptcy, and attorneys in smaller law offices whose practice is largely based on local law. The CD–ROM disc stores large amounts of information (including historical information) and is updated usually through the issuance of a new disc on a monthly or quarterly basis. LEXIS and WESTLAW, in contrast, have extraordinary storage capacity, access to thousands of databases, and are constantly updated. However, the CD–ROM is a less expensive way than the online services for an attorney to maintain a "library." And it offers space-saving advantages over a traditional library. A great variety of material is now available on CD–ROM, including case law and statutes from many states, and such titles as, for example, the United States Supreme Court on CD–ROM, the Occupational Safety and Health Administration Compliance Encyclopedia, the New York Times Ondisc, and the Federal Register on CD–

ROM. When using a CD–ROM, you must be aware of the scope of the disc and of the need to update its contents.

As for the Internet, it is not possible to discuss in detail all of the legal and legally-related information available on the Internet or to describe the impact that the Internet will ultimately have on research techniques. However, some significant changes have already occurred. First, both LEXIS and WESTLAW are now available on the Internet and at some point will be available only on the Internet. Second, the Internet, at minimal or no cost, provides some material for which otherwise lawyers would have to pay. For example, government and law school web sites provide primary materials such as New York Court of Appeals decisions and Second Circuit decisions. Third, the Internet provides access to documents that are not easily available from other sources, such as current information from federal agencies. Finally, the Internet is a source of important non-legal information through the world wide web directories.

The Internet, however, has its own disadvantages. First, the Internet response time can be slow, especially compared to the speed of LEXIS and WESTLAW on proprietary software. Second, and more important, the reliability of web sites varies greatly. When using material on the Internet, you have to ask whether the source is authoritative, accurate, and current.[2] Ask yourself who the sponsoring institution is, who the author is, who posted the material, and how current it is (see "last updated on . . . . ") Despite these concerns, however, the potential of the Internet is enormous.

The research sources you will use when working in a law office will depend on that office's needs and resources. But today, even a sole practitioner has far more options than before. One option is to rely solely on books. Another option is to use a customized form of LEXIS or WESTLAW that would focus on the law of one jurisdiction, for example, the Massachusetts Reports and cases from the First Circuit Court of Appeals. A third option is to subscribe to a set of CD–ROM discs covering Massachusetts state law updated by quarterly discs and weekly advance sheets. Other general updating options are legal newspapers, online services, or Internet sites of state and federal court opinions.

Whatever research tools you have available, to be an effective researcher, you should always begin by developing a research plan for the particular problem you are dealing with. Although the process is not linear, usually you start by getting an understanding of the general area of law before you focus on case-finding tools. This will also give you some familiarity with the particular vocabulary used in that area of law. The next step is to find, read, and

---

2.   Jean Davis et al., Using the Internet for Legal Research 2–3 (1998).

analyze cases and statutes. Finally, you need to update your research and make sure it is current. Throughout, you must make the best possible use of all of the research tools relevant to your problem, going back and forth from one tool to the other as your research progresses.

III.   Types of Research Materials

The traditional classification of legal research materials includes three types: primary materials (cases, statutes), secondary materials (texts that analyze legal topics), and search materials (indexes, digests). But these classifications have become somewhat blurred. Some materials, such as the annotated American Law Reports (A.L.R.) series, combine features of primary and secondary sources. Computers are search tools, and also sources of primary and secondary authority.

A.   Primary Materials

Primary materials consist of cases, statutes, constitutions, and administrative regulations. One kind of primary materials, reported cases, is reported in print form by jurisdiction and in a roughly chronological order, rather than by topic. In order to find cases about a particular topic, you will need to use the secondary and search materials published for this purpose that classify materials by topic.

Statutes, another kind of primary materials, are published in a variety of sources. A jurisdiction's statutes are first compiled and published as session laws, which are the statutes passed during each session of the legislature. Because the session laws are published in chronological order and not by subject matter, they too are difficult to use for research. Instead of using session laws to find statutory materials, a researcher uses the statutory publication called a code in which the jurisdiction's statutes are arranged by subject matter and indexed. In a code, all statutes pertaining to a topic are grouped together (for example, the criminal laws) in numbered chapters or titles.

The commercial publishers' unofficial editions of each jurisdiction's code are especially valuable for research because they are annotated and provide you with citations to the cases that have applied each statute, or part of it. The codes also contain other information about the statutes, such as historical information that can help you begin a legislative history.

Each jurisdiction also publishes its constitution and court rules of procedure. Administrative regulations, the regulations of government agencies, usually are published in official publications (the

Code of Federal Regulations and the Federal Register)and in publications by commercial publishers.

B. Secondary Materials

Most of the other research materials that you will use, such as treatises, legal periodicals, and legal encyclopedias, fall into the next category of materials—secondary sources. They provide text that explains and analyzes legal topics. Secondary sources also provide citations to primary sources of law and to other secondary materials. Unlike primary authority, however, the secondary sources do not supply binding law; they are persuasive authority only.

C. Search Materials

Search materials, the third category, are tools that help you find the other materials. A familiar example is an index. The most specialized search tools are the West Group digests and the Shepard's and KeyCite citators. These search materials contain no original text of their own, and you never cite them in your written work. LEXIS and WESTLAW are both search tools and sources of primary materials. You may cite to LEXIS or WESTLAW for primary authority if the primary authority has not yet been published, but is available on a computer.

D. The Weight of Authority

As you do your research and writing, you should become aware of the differences among these materials, not only as to the information they provide, but also as to their value as authorities. Primary sources are always the most important legal authorities. Primary sources do not all have the same weight, however; among primary authorities, always look first for the binding authority in the jurisdiction of your problem, and then look for sources from other jurisdictions and from analogous areas of the law.

Secondary materials are generally of less weight than persuasive primary authorities. However, not all secondary materials have the same weight. For example, a well-written treatise by a named author who specializes in that field is far more authoritative than an encyclopedia article about that topic. Certain treatises and law review articles may even be more authoritative to some judges than some case law. Many non-legal research materials, such as statistical or sociological studies, are also secondary materials and can prove very useful to your research.

Whichever sources you use to find primary authority, be sure that you yourself read the relevant primary sources. It is not acceptable research to rely on the descriptions of those sources in the secondary materials.

IV. Beginning Your Research

A. Statutory Research

When you begin your research for a problem, you should determine if there is a statute that governs. Even if no state statute applies, a federal statute may, or both federal and state statutes may apply.

1. Starting With Known Relevant Citations

If you know statutes relevant to the subject matter of your problem, you can begin your research differently from the way you begin if you do not know of relevant materials. When you know the citations to relevant statutes, read the statutes immediately, and then expand your search as described below in Part A(2). If your client is being sued for violation of a statute, for example, then the litigation has already identified the statute by citation. You could find the statute in that jurisdiction's code either by using the printed version of the code or by using the FIND command in WESTLAW or the LEXSTAT service on LEXIS. (As of the fall of 1998, annotated codes for all jurisdictions are not available on CD–ROM or the Internet.) Although proper citation form is to the official code, for research purposes you probably will want to read the statute in the unofficial code because of its annotations. Then, proceed with your research as explained below.

2. Starting With No Research Information

If, as you begin your research, you do not have citations to relevant statutes, then you have to search for them yourself. Unless you are very familiar with the structure of the jurisdiction's code and can go directly to the title that includes the subject matter of your problem, start by using the index volume of the code to find whether there are statutes related to your topic. Indexing techniques and problems associated with indexing are discussed below in Part B(2). You can also find statutes by using one of the computer services, but statutory research on computer may be more difficult. It is harder to formulate a search request that anticipates the language of a statute. Statutes are generally not written using ordinary speech patterns. The language may be stilted and the structure of statutes—definitions, headings, sections and sub-sections—may undermine precise and complete retrieval. Moreover, in books, indexes to codes are easy to use and provide cross-references, and case annotations are easy to browse through. So if a statute and its annotations are merely replicated on the computer screen, it would make more sense to simply pick up the book and read the material there.

If you cannot find an index entry, you may be using the wrong search terms. If there are treatises available, or other secondary sources about that area of law, look through the information to pick up the correct terms. For example, it is a crime for a person with knowledge that someone has committed a crime not to report it. This crime is called misprision of justice and is indexed under that term. If you knew nothing about this area of law, you would not likely know that term and would not find this statute in the index.

If there are statutes that appear relevant to your problem, read them to determine whether they apply to your case. Then use the statutory annotations or the computer services to find the cases applying that statute.

You must update the statute in the code by using the pocket parts to the statutory index and to the code volume, and also by using the interim annotation services that accompany codes. Besides providing citations to more recently decided cases applying the statute, these sources tell you whether the statute has been amended or repealed, or whether a new statute has been passed. You may also have to update the statute on the computer's database.

Other reference sources besides the code volumes and computer services supply information about statutes. For example, you can use a Shepard's statutory citators for information about the legislative changes in the statute, such as amendments, and for cases that cite the statute. Also use the indexes to legal periodicals, which include tables of statutes with citations to articles about them. Loose-leaf services, either of national or state-wide scope, are especially helpful for specialized statutory subject matter like labor law or securities law. Law review articles may lead you to a specific statute. But you usually would not use an encyclopedia for research on statutory issues.

B. Case Law Research

1. Starting With Known Relevant Citations

If you already know an important case and know its citation, either from an annotated code or another source, and you want to limit your research to finding other relevant cases, one way to begin is by reading that case.

A quick way to retrieve a case when you know the citation is to use the FIND feature on WESTLAW or the LEXSEE service on LEXIS. Or you may read the case in a regional reporter and use the West Group headnotes to work from the case to the most relevant topics and key numbers. Then use the key number to look through the relevant digests or do a key number search on WESTLAW to find more cases on the point of that key number. Or, using the parties' names, you can find the case by doing a field search (WESTLAW) or segment search (LEXIS) to retrieve the case with its citation.

You can find more cases using the case citation by using Shepard's in print, the citator functions in LEXIS or WESTLAW, or Shepard's on CD–ROM. WESTLAW has its own online service called KeyCite, which gives the direct and indirect history of cases and analyzes their treatment. You can then find more recent cases citing your original case that are likely to be relevant to your topic. Moreover, the case itself will give you citations to earlier cases that the court regarded as relevant. The context of the opinion should help you to determine which cases you should track down and read. Finding new cases and updating are immensely easier on a computer. Citations to a case are collected in one place and given at the touch of a key.

2. Starting With No Research Information

If your problem is a common law problem, and you start with no citations to cases, then you should first get relevant background information by using secondary sources. You can then use digests or computers to find relevant cases. In general, use the facts of your problem to provide words for your search.

a. Using Secondary Sources

If you are unfamiliar with an area of law, you would be wise to begin with a secondary source. These materials provide background information and citations to relevant cases. If you have identified the general area of law in which the problem belongs, such as tort or contract, then a good place to start your research may be a treatise in that field, or an A.L.R. annotation. Then look for articles in law reviews and other periodicals. For many conventional legal problems, however, articles in periodicals may be too specialized to use at the beginning of your research. But if your problem involves a fairly new claim, then a periodical article may be a useful place to begin. You probably would not use a computer at this point because you would not be able to formulate accurate search terms. However, some people use a computer to begin if the problem involves very distinctive concepts that provide accurate search terms, like surrogate motherhood.

Use the indexes for these sources by identifying and searching under key words or ideas you have developed from the facts of the problem. Concentrate on the relationships among the parties, the underlying events, and their chronology. These concepts will describe people, relationships, places, things, and events that supply search terms.

For example, your client may be a person who is legally a minor and seeks to disaffirm a contract he made for a used car. However, when buying the car, he misrepresented himself as an adult to induce the salesperson to contract with him. He asks whether he can disaffirm the contract.

To find out you would research the problem using such words as:

- minor
- child
- infant
- contract
- disaffirm
- age
- misrepresentation
- voidable

Remember also the legal theory that appears to be involved and the relief your client is asking for. If your client wants someone to stop doing something, for example, then your research should concentrate on the requirements for injunctive relief, not for civil damages.

Many of the secondary sources provide cross-references to other materials published by that same publisher, thereby saving search time. Remember also to use looseleaf services. If there is a service for that particular area of law, it will include the most current information available (except for that in computer databases).

b.   Using Digests to Find Relevant Cases

If you are familiar with the broad area of law and do not need explanatory or analytical text from a secondary source but immediately want to find relevant cases, then you may want to start your research with a digest. Although other publishers publish digests, the most extensive digest system is that of West Group, which digests every case it publishes in its case reporters. To use the digest system, you must identify the topic and the key number for the specific legal point you are researching. A useful place to start is with the Descriptive Word Index.

Using a general index such as a Descriptive Word Index to a digest sometimes is a simple task, but also can be a frustrating one, and one that requires creativity. For certain problems, it is easy to formulate index search terms, but finding the proper entries in a general index may be more difficult. Even a relatively straightforward topic requires perseverance and willingness to search under a variety of words that describe the problem when the first attempts fail. Be prepared to use synonyms for your original search terms. For example, try the words "counsel" and "lawyer" as well as "attorney." If your problem involved a doctor, you could look under "physician" or "surgeon" as well as doctor; if your problem involved a car, you could look up "automobile."

You should also be ready to formulate broader categories, using more general terms, such as "motor vehicle" instead of automobile. Remember, however, that the more specific the term is to your problem, the more relevant the materials your research turns up should be. Thus, start with the specific term. Also remember that at a certain point, categories can become too broad to be accurate. Although "litigation" instead of "trial" may not go far afield from your needs, the term "professional" instead of "attorney" would. You also must be prepared to use terms describing other aspects of the problem. Finally, you need the patience to look line-by-line through an index entry that is long and contains many subdivisions. Once you have found the most relevant topic and key number, you can use them to look through the entire West Group digest system to find cases for your problem.

Remember that the digest entry for each case is not necessarily the holding of the case. Rather, the digests are statements about a point of law mentioned in the case, not all of which will be relevant to your problem. You must read the case yourself before you cite it for the point of law at issue. Moreover, even if a case is in the digest, you must check to see that the case is still good law.

C. Using Computer–Assisted Legal Research (CALR)

To use the computer for your research, instead of looking words up in an index as you would using books, you formulate your own search request or query. Before you can use CALR effectively, however, you should read enough background materials to find the words that describe your problem.

Computers are most successful in searches involving unique terms and somewhat narrow topics. To use CALR to retrieve cases, you can either formulate a query of your own or use a natural language feature. Because of the cost of using computers, you need to develop a plan before you turn the computer on. That means determining how computers fit into your overall research plan, thinking about the relevant jurisdiction so you know which database to use, and writing out a query. You formulate a query using terms and connectors by identifying the words that courts are likely to use in writing an opinion about the topic you are researching, and by determining how those words are likely to appear in relation to each other.

If, for example, you are doing research on whether a mother who saw her child killed by a negligent driver can recover for the tort of negligent infliction of emotional distress, you would first identify words like:

- mother
- child
- see
- negligence
- death
- emotional distress

Since computers are literal, they retrieve only what has been requested. Thus, you need to identify appropriate synonyms, like "parent" for mother and "watch" or "witness" for see. Finally, you need to picture how the words are likely to appear in relation to each other in courts' opinions, and use appropriate connectors.

To broaden your search, include synonyms connected by the word OR. Where you want to retrieve documents that contain two or more of your words, link them with the AND connector. Or you could use a numerical proximity connector when you want to narrow your search by retrieving only those documents in which words appear in a specific relation to each other. With a numerical connector, w/n or /n, the words must appear within the specified number of each other. For example, "emotional /5 distress" indicates that the words "emotional" and "distress" must appear within 5 words of each other for the document to be retrieved. The number will differ depending on whether you are using LEXIS or WESTLAW. Each system considers some words to be non-searchable (for example articles), but WESTLAW counts them with a numerical connector and LEXIS does not.

The exclamation mark (!) at the end of the word instructs the computer to retrieve the root word with various endings. The emotional distress search might ultimately be:

"Mother or father or parent and child or daughter or son and saw or witness! and negligen! /5 inflict! and emotion! /5 distress and death."

In addition to the terms and connectors method of case finding, both WESTLAW and LEXIS have a retrieval mechanism in which the computer formulates the query for you after you type in a statement of the issue in your problem. WESTLAW calls its program WIN (WESTLAW is Natural) and LEXIS calls its program

FREESTYLE. For example, if you type "Can a mother who saw her child killed by a negligent driver recover for negligent infliction of emotional distress?", the computer will 'translate' that to "mother saw child killed negligent driver recover 'negligent infliction of emotional distress'." The computer will retrieve the cases which have the highest statistical probability of matching the words in the query. (Usually the program is set at 20 or 25 words, but it can be set to retrieve more.) To do this, however, the computer ignores the date of decision and level of court, two very important factors in determining the weight of authority.

Natural searching language is not intended to provide complete information. Query formulation is necessary when you want to limit your search to documents which contain every concept in the search request or when you want to specify the relationship between words. And even the computer companies do not suggest that you use only natural language searching. Rather, they suggest that terms and connector formulation and natural language searching supplement each other.

Computers can perform specialized functions like finding the opinions of a judge on a particular topic or giving you the citation to a recent case not yet reported in print. Computers also make updating easier, give with remarkable speed the text of opinions from some courts, and provide the text online of a number of background sources, like law reviews and A.L.R. However, computers are less useful in getting an overview of a topic, or in searches involving broad issues, complex concepts, procedural questions, or common terms. In these contexts, books are much more useful and can save considerable time and money.

> **Example 1:** Your client has been charged with unlawful possession of cocaine with intent to distribute in violation of 21 U.S.C. § 841 (a)(1) (1994). You want to bring a motion to suppress evidence of drugs seized in his apartment on the ground that his fourth amendment right to be free from unreasonable searches and seizures under the United States Constitution was violated after the police entered his apartment building and had a dog sniff outside his apartment door. The question is whether the dog sniff is a search within the meaning of the fourth amendment and so requires a warrant. The only thing that you know is that there is no law directly on point in your federal circuit. And you believe that there have been a lot of cases involving dog sniffs. You, therefore, need to research how the Supreme Court and the federal circuit courts have dealt with this or similar questions. Because constitutional issues are so broad and because there are so many cases, you begin by getting background information.
>
> A good place to begin is a well-respected treatise, so you find Wayne R. LaFave's multi-volume treatise on Search and Seizure. You look up dog sniff in the Index. There is a reference to "Dog's nose, use of;" you turn to a 16–page section which discusses the issue of dog sniffs under

federal law. It analyzes the two governing Supreme Court cases, discusses several circuit court cases in the text and footnotes, and in the pocket part, identifies United States v. Thomas, a case in which the Second Circuit held that a dog sniff outside an apartment door was a search within the meaning of the fourth amendment, since the defendant had a heightened expectation of privacy inside his home. Although this case is very useful persuasive authority, you can also tell from the section in LaFave that the federal courts, in general, give the prosecutors a lot of leeway on this question, so your argument will not be easy.

Another place to get background information on this question is A.L.R. Federal, which also has a very useful article on dog sniffs. Or there may be some law review articles dealing precisely with this point. However, if you were to begin with a query on the computer in the West ALLFEDS database or the Lexis COURTS file of the GENFED library, such as "Dog or canine w/5 sniff or smell and apartment or house or home and door and search and fourth w/5 amendment," you would retrieve almost a hundred and fifty cases. This is too many to read and analyze efficiently. (The first case alone is 99 pages long on the computer.) And if you limit the number of cases by doing a natural language search of 20 cases, you will retrieve United States v. Thomas and some other useful cases, but you will not get either of the Supreme Court cases, or a helpful explanation by an expert in that area of law.

Example 2: You are representing a woman in New Jersey who wishes to have a child, but is unable to for medical reasons. She and her husband are thinking about having someone act as a surrogate mother, but they are worried about what the surrogate's rights would be and whether she could change her mind and refuse to give up the child. This is the type of question for which CALR will be quite effective since the terms are unique[3]. Moreover, this is a state law question so you can limit your research to the laws of one state. If you use the search request "surrogate /5 mother!" in the New Jersey database, you will retrieve 12 cases. If you browse through them, you will soon view the Matter of Baby M case, the decision by the New Jersey Supreme Court on surrogate motherhood. You could then either continue to browse through the cases, or print a list of the cases. In any event, you will probably want to turn off the computer and read the cases in full in the reporters. You could then go back to the computer to update them.

V. *Tailoring Your Research*

A. *Researching Federal Law*

When you are doing research on a problem governed by a federal statute, your approach will frequently be different from the approach you would use in doing common law research or even

---

3. Even a term as unique as surrogate motherhood may not give you all of the relevant cases. A few courts in the country have started using the term "surrogate parenthood."

researching a state statute. The digest approach in books or the query formulation approach in computers will not give you an overview of the problem. Moreover, reading the annotations to the statute may not be an effective way to begin if the statute is complex and has hundreds of annotations.

You may find it more helpful to begin this type of problem by reading about the issue in a law review article. Law reviews can give you an overview of the problem, identify the major issues, and provide references to other materials analyzing the problem. Since even the best law reviews cannot tell you about cases decided after their publication, however, you may also find looseleaf services helpful. You could use either a general looseleaf service, like United States Law Week, which can identify recent cases on a variety of topics, or a specialized looseleaf service that deals with a particular subject area, like employment discrimination law or securities law.

If you are doing research on a federal constitutional issue, you might begin with a treatise, and then go on to law reviews for a more detailed analysis. Some looseleaf services are also very important when researching constitutional issues. The Supreme Court edition of Law Week will tell you whether and how the Supreme Court has dealt with an issue; the general edition of Law Week will provide the lower courts' treatments of important issues. A looseleaf service for a specific subject area, like criminal law or first amendment law, should also be consulted.

If your case involves issues of federal law only, then you will use some different sources from the ones you would use for issues of state law.[4] If your research concerned only a federal statute imposing penalties for criminal contempt, you would find that legislation in the United States Code. Federal administrative regulations, such as those by the Equal Employment Opportunity Commission on employment discrimination, are published in the Code of Federal Regulations and the Federal Register. Federal administrative decisions on this topic may be found in looseleaf services, such as CCH Employment Practice Decisions. In addition, some research tools publish separate volumes for federal law. For example, you could use the federal law digests to find cases from the federal courts only. You could also look for annotations in the A.L.R. Federal. Moreover, various treatises discuss federal law topics such as civil procedure or securities law.

You can limit your search for federal law on a computer by choosing the database: federal law in general; the decisions of a particular court, like the Supreme Court or the Second Circuit; or even the decisions of a particular judge. You can also make excellent use of the Internet for certain problems relating to federal law.

---

4. Of course, some problems involve research into both federal and state law.

If you know the address of a web site that is likely to have the information you want, you can go there directly. You may have found this information from a text that lists web sites or from previous research. If you do not know the address of a web site, you can find it in different ways. If, for example, you want the web site of a federal agency, you can go to a web site designed for locating agencies, like *www.cilp.org/Fed–Agency/* or to a law school web site which has links to federal agencies, like *www.law.vill.edu* or to a legal directory like *www.FindLaw.com*. If you were researching a problem relating to AIDS, for example, you could go to the web site of the Centers for Disease Control or the Department of Health and Human Services resources (AIDS related information).

You can also use the Internet to do related nonlegal research. In 1998, for example, the Supreme Court interpreted the term "disability" in the Americans with Disabilities Act to cover a person who was HIV positive, but asymptomatic. One issue that arose in the HIV case is whether reproduction is a major life activity, since one method of defining "disability" is through a physical impairment that substantially limits a major life activity. If you were representing a male client who said he would not attempt to father a child because of his HIV infection, you might want information about the likelihood of a male's transmitting the HIV virus to a fetus. Since this issue is not discussed in any of the court opinions, a possible source of information would be the many web sites dealing with AIDS and HIV.

B. Researching the Law of One State

You can also narrow your research if your case involves the law of only one state. If, from your own experience, or from the instructions with your assignment, you limit your research to one state's law, then you can use sources limited to that state's law. Start with the state code to see if there are any relevant statutes. Use the state's annotated code not only for citations to cases applying the statute, but also for its cross references and for citations to such sources as law review articles about state law. See if there is an encyclopedia of that state's law. Use the digest or digests that are limited to that state. An assignment limited to one state's law permits you to limit your citator search to a state citator, where you will also find references to state law materials, such as the attorney general's opinions.

You can limit your search in LEXIS and WESTLAW by selecting a data base limited to the local scope of your problem, like a single state. In addition, you can use a CD–ROM for that state's law.

VI. *Doing Your Research*

Before you begin your research, develop a plan. Make sure that you understand your problem and its issues. If the problem is from a class assignment, read it carefully to determine exactly what you have been asked to do. Try not to waste your time by going off on tangents. Make preliminary identifications of the jurisdiction of the problem, the claim involved, the issues within that claim, and the most relevant facts. Identify statutes that may apply and other relevant reference materials. Reserve computer time if your library provides sign-up reservations.

When you begin your research, take steps that will save you time later. Do not print a case identified from your computer search until you have at least skimmed the case to find out if it is relevant. If you read the cases to determine their relevance before you photocopy, you may save time and money. Even if you photocopy and highlight information on your copies, you should read the cases as you go along and take notes about what you are reading. Your notes should identify your emerging analysis of the issues and facts and which cases are relevant to them. In that way you are not faced with a mass of undifferentiated highlighted copies when it is time to analyze the problem and write. You may want to start an outline right away. The outline should identify the issues and break them down into their component parts. Then preliminarily fill in the cases and statutes you need for each part. (See Chapter Eight.)

Copy important information so you will not have to retrieve it later on. Be careful to put quotation marks around all exact quotes so that if you use a quotation in your written work, you will identify it as such. Write down the page numbers of the text you are quoting or paraphrasing to use in the citation. Remember that you must attribute paraphrases and ideas from the texts with citations to their sources, including the pages on which they are found.

Take down full citation information of all authorities when you read them, including parallel citations if needed, the courts and dates of the cases, and the edition numbers of books such as treatises. If you read a case in which more than one issue was decided, write down the headnote numbers for those issues relevant to your research. You will shorten your search in citators and eliminate the reading of cases cited for statements about issues different from yours if you search with the relevant headnote numbers.

One of your most difficult judgments will be to decide when to stop your research. On the one hand, a little more digging may turn up the perfect case. On the other hand, that time, for which you will be charging your client, may yield nothing that you have not seen, perhaps many times. When you already have found and read the cases and secondary sources that are cited in the new materials you are turning up, then you probably have done enough research.

Often, you will find deficiencies in your research when you outline or begin to write. You may not have thought through every relevant line of analysis, or you may not have enough support for a particular conclusion. Once you start writing and thus must commit your reasoning to paper, you should confront these flaws in research or analysis. If you begin writing early enough, you leave time to evaluate your progress and your understanding of the problem. Then you can continue research in those areas in which you are not satisfied with your work.

For all research, remember: (1) learn which sources are most useful and efficient for particular research; (2) be resourceful when you use indexes; (3) update all printed sources by using pocket parts and supplements, and then updating materials since the cut-off date; (4) eliminate sources that merely duplicate what you already have done; (5) update with a citator all primary authorities you rely on; (6) evaluate the authoritative value of the sources and the quality of their analyses.

Exercise 12–A

For each of these problems, write out a research plan:

1.   In the newspaper, you read about a case that the Supreme Court of the United States decided the day before, June 26, 1998. You want to read the case. You know that the names of the parties are Beth Faragher and the City of Boca Raton.

2.   You are representing Betty Abbott. She tells you that her supervisor at work has been continually upsetting her. It started a few months ago. He began making lewd remarks about her figure. She told him that she did not think the comments were funny or flattering, but he told her he was just a friendly guy. Lately he has been putting his arm around her shoulder when he comes by her desk and squeezing her shoulder. Two days ago, he suggested that if she slept with him, her career would take off, but if she did not, she would find herself getting poor evaluations.

You believe her supervisor's conduct is sexual harassment and is a form of sex discrimination.

Ms. Abbott works in Philadelphia, Pennsylvania, in an office with 35 employees. Philadelphia is in the Third Circuit.

3.   Your client has been charged under 18 U.S.C. § 1111 (1994) with the second degree murder of his doctor. He was not charged with first degree murder because his act was not premeditated. Based on your conversations with him, you believe that at the time he stabbed the victim, he was suffering from Post Traumatic Stress Disorder, a result of his wartime experience in Vietnam. You want to research whether his mental condition would be a defense to the crime, either because he could not formulate the

necessary mens rea (intent) or because he was not guilty by reason of insanity. The crime took place in a federal veterans' hospital in Boston, Massachusetts. Massachusetts is in the First Circuit.

4.   An attorney in your law office is going to be arguing a case before the Supreme Court of the United States. She wants you to find all of Justice Scalia's opinions on the confrontation clause.

Chapter Thirteen
Interviewing the Client

I. Introduction

In your first few weeks of law school, you may have been assigned a legal office memorandum, a document containing a section called the Statement of Facts. But you may not have thought about the process by which a lawyer gathers the facts that appear in that section. You may have assumed that the client would provide all of the relevant facts and that the lawyer would easily know what facts are relevant to the client's problem. But you may not have considered how often in describing a problem, people are likely to omit critical facts, to characterize facts in a way that puts them in the best light, to misstate facts, and to give facts in an idiosyncratic order. You may also have assumed that a lawyer would know which facts to probe. However, if a lawyer is not familiar with all of the issues relating to a legal theory, a lawyer is not likely to initially ask about all relevant facts. Moreover, a lawyer's ability to help the client may depend on whether the client trusts and has confidence in the lawyer. A client who does not trust a lawyer will probably not be forthcoming about providing facts or even revealing objectives.

Thus, effective interviewing involves skills in listening, in questioning, and in understanding the full dimensions of a client's problem. At your initial interview with the client, you will have your first opportunity of what will probably be an ongoing process of both gathering facts related to a client's problem and establishing a relationship of trust with the client.

228

To understand how a client may feel when meeting a lawyer for the first time, imagine that you are a college senior on your way to see a doctor. You have had recurrent headaches and blurred vision for the previous two months and have decided to do something about the problem. Although you assume that nothing terrible is happening to you, you are uneasy about what the doctor may conclude. In fact, this has not been an easy year for you. You have done well academically, but have developed major doubts about a career in law, although this had been your goal since high school. Ultimately, you decided not to apply to law school. Your parents were surprised, then concerned, then anxious about why you changed your mind and about what you are going to do with your life. They have said that they cannot support you indefinitely. You do not want to cause them economic or personal anxiety, particularly since your father is not well. Moreover, the person you have been dating seems to have lost interest in you now that your career plans have changed.

How would you want the doctor to deal with your situation? First, you would want the doctor to be skilled in diagnosing and treating the medical issues relating to the headaches and blurred vision. But you might also want to doctor to be interested in some of the other problems that you have been having, both because they are troubling you and because they may be related to the medical issues. What would make you likely to discuss these other problems with the doctor? The doctor would have to be someone who listened carefully to what you are saying, who seemed both to understand what your concerns are and to care about them, and who believed you could decide better than anyone else what the right career choice was for you.

Like patients seeking medical advice, clients come to lawyers first for legal advice and help. Foremost, the client wants a competent lawyer. In fact, the first rule in the ABA Model Rules of Professional Conduct deals with competence.

> A lawyer shall provide competent representation to a client. Competent representation requires the legal knowledge, skill, thoroughness and preparation reasonably necessary for the representation. Rule 1.1.[1]

But your ability to help your client also requires your understanding that the "legal" problem may not be the whole problem.[2] Thus

---

1. Model Rules of Professional Conduct.

2. Throughout this chapter, the authors have drawn on material from the following very helpful texts: David A. Binder et al., Lawyers as Counselors: A Client–Centered Approach (1991); Robert M. Bastress and Joseph Harbaugh, Interviewing, Counseling and Negotiation: Skills for Effective Representation (1990); Marilyn J. Berger et al., Pretrial Advocacy: Planning, Analysis & Strategy your interpersonal skills are as important as your research and analytic skills. Clients' legal problems often relate to other nonlegal concerns that the client has, just as medical problems may relate to non-medical concerns. For example, the college senior who has decided not to go to law school might be wondering if the headaches are related to the other concerns which may be psychological (where do I go from here?), interpersonal (I am causing my parents a lot of worry by changing my mind about law school), economic (I have to go out and get a job now), or moral (I should not be a burden to my parents at their age).

Finally, your ability to help your client may depend on your understanding the lawyer-client relationship. You may have thought that your role as a lawyer means that based on your legal expertise, you tell the client how to solve the client's legal problem. After all, what did you go to law school for if not to dispense legal advice?

Yet Rule 1.2(a) of the Model Rules of Professional Conduct[3] on the Scope of Representation states:

> A lawyer shall abide by a client's decisions concerning the objectives of representation. . . .

Comment 1 on the Scope of Representation states:

> Both lawyer and client have authority and responsibility in the objectives and means of representation. The client has ultimate authority to determine the purposes to be achieved by legal representation, within the limits of the law and the lawyer's professional obligation.

Your role, then, is not simply that of the technical expert and adviser. Although you must be knowledgeable about the law (just as a doctor must be knowledgeable about medical issues), you also need to understand that the person in the best position to make the decision about a legal problem is the client. After all the client, not you, is the person who must live with that decision. Your role is to help the client find the best solution to the client's problem. To do this, you need to understand the problem as the client perceives it, and to discover what is most important to the client.

Every client is different. So your approach to each client will vary depending on the client's basic situation. Is the client meeting with a lawyer for the first time? Does the client want to bring a lawsuit? Is the client a defendant in a civil lawsuit? Has the client been charged with a crime? Is the client a sophisticated business person who wants to set up a new company and who has had significant contact with lawyers? Is the client someone who has no

(1988); and Thomas L. Shaffer and James R. Elkins, Legal Interviewing and Counseling in a Nutshell (2d ed. 1987).

3. Model Rules of Professional Conduct.

knowledge of the law? Is the client dealing with painful personal issues like divorce or a relationship with estranged children? Is the client worried about the cost and stress of litigation? Just as you consider your audience when you write, you should consider each client individually when you meet with that client.

II. *Goals of the Interview*

A client may come to discuss a matter relating to litigation (suing a hotel for negligent infliction of emotional distress, defending an adverse possession claim, defending a charge of armed robbery) or relating to a transaction (buying a house, negotiating a commercial lease, signing an employment contract). Consider then what you want to achieve in an initial interview with the client. You may think it is obvious–you want to find out what the client's legal problem is. You can then research the problem to find out if the client has a good case, or if the client should renew the commercial lease under the terms offered, and then tell the client what you know.

Certainly, one of the major goals of the interview is to get the facts that are relevant to the client's problem and to understand what the client's goals are. However, if you focus your efforts in the interview on the facts relevant to the "legal" problem, you may discourage the client from providing other highly important information. For example, if a client describes a series of conflicts that have occurred between her and her spouse, you might assume that the client has come to get representation for a divorce. You may be tempted to tear yourself away from the interview so that you can immediately begin researching the state law on divorce. But the client may not consider divorce for religious or moral reasons. Rather, the client may be concerned about the escalating conflicts with her spouse and wants to know if there is a way in which she could get an order of protection or could force her spouse to vacate the premises. Or the client may ultimately want a referral to a marriage counselor. If you failed to elicit or develop this information, you would have completely misunderstood the client's objectives. So a more useful way of viewing the goals of the interview would be to try gather facts that relate to what brought the client to see you, to what the client would like to happen, and to how the client feels about the situation.

Gathering facts is not your only goal. The interview is also the critical first stage of your developing a lawyer-client relationship based on trust and mutual respect. The client will be revealing information about issues of importance and concern. The client will want to feel that you are an understanding and trustworthy professional, capable of effectively representing the client's interests.

Finally, assuming that the client agrees to hire you and you agree to represent the client, you and the client will be establishing a contractual relationship. That relationship entails your assuming obligations to the client under the Model Rules of Professional Conduct. Moreover, you will probably discuss your fee arrangement with the client at the end of the initial interview and indicate what tasks you will probably need to undertake in order to achieve the client's objectives. Accordingly, bear in mind your goals for the initial interview: to gather as many of the relevant facts as you can, to establish a relationship of trust with the client, to establish a contractual relationship (you may have the client sign an agreement), and to assign tasks to yourself and to the client in preparation for the next meeting.

III. *Preparation for the Interview*

Planning is important at every stage of your relationship with your client. Interviewing is a skill. You cannot expect to "wing it" and assume that you will intuitively know how to conduct an initial interview, even after you have gained some experience.

Even before you have met the client, you may be able to begin considering the client's situation. Often the client making the appointment over the telephone will have provided you or your assistant with some information about the problem, or the client may have dropped off some documents before the interview. In these situations, you may have learned some of the facts relating to the client's problem and some idea of what to expect. Thus you can think about the client's situation in advance, and even do some preliminary research on what the legal problem seems to be. Consider, also, if there are any documents you want to ask the client to bring (a notice from the landlord, a summons and complaint in a lawsuit filed against the client, a business contract which is about to expire).

For example, assume that a new client, John Starr, has made an appointment to meet with you in two days. Mr. Starr mentioned over the phone that his wife is Jane Starr, the newly elected city councillor. You remember that around three months ago, there was a terrible incident during the election in which Jane Starr was shot and wounded by a hotel security guard. Before meeting with John Starr, you looked up the newspaper account of the shooting. You consider whether Mr. Starr's visit relates to the shooting incident. Or since Mr. Starr, but not Mrs. Starr, is coming to talk with you, you wonder if the meeting deals with a totally different matter. So although you should consider the likely content of the interview and how you would generally like to structure it, you should keep an open mind and not prematurely diagnose the client's problem or prejudge the client personally.

IV.   *The Interview*

You will probably begin your interview of the client by meeting the client in your waiting room, introducing yourself, and bringing your client into your office. Once you sit down, spend some time chatting with the client about nonlegal issues to put the client at ease. This is not a waste of time. Remember, you are a stranger. The client has to feel comfortable about discussing all sorts of issues with you. In addition, the preliminary conversation may give you some insight into the client's personality and concerns.

> *Good morning Mr. Starr. My name is* _____ _____, *I'm pleased to meet you. Let's go into my office to talk. Would you like some coffee, or tea, or perhaps a cold drink?* [*Did you have any difficulty finding the office?*] OR [*I understand that Joe Black gave you my name. How is Joe doing? I haven't seen him in a while.*]

When you feel the time is right, begin with a general question to the client. [*Mr. Starr, what brings you here today?*] This will give you an idea of how the client characterizes the problem that brought him to see you. This is the best way to begin understanding the problem from the client's perspective. Asking an open-ended question and permitting the client an initial opportunity to talk without interruption will give you very important information and will also aid in putting the client at ease. If you take control of the conversation too early, you may inadvertently silence the client. You should also ask how the client would like to have the problem resolved. The client may have already considered some possible solutions or at least can give you a range of objectives. [*I want the hotel management to admit that they should never have hired that guard and to pay for the misery they caused.*] In telling the story, the client may also gradually feel unburdened and begin to feel a rapport with you. Finally, the client may reveal important nonlegal concerns that may bear upon the client's situation. [*I have to tell you that my wife thinks this is a bad idea. We have had a lot of arguments about it, and I don't know if I am doing the right thing or if a lawsuit would just make things worse between us.*]

While listening to the client's story you will probably begin thinking of potential legal theories which relate to the client's case. But before prematurely diagnosing the client's problem, ask the client for a chronology of the events (often called a time-line) which led to the client's coming to see you. [*Mr. Starr, could you give me a step by-step account of the events leading to the shooting of your wife, and of what has happened since.*] Remember that although you may ask the client to start at the beginning, do not expect a flawless narrative which proceeds from one legally relevant fact to another in perfect chronological order. Like all of us, clients are likely to include irrelevant facts, to omit important events assuming the other party is aware of them, to provide information out of order, and to be reluctant to provide certain information because it may be personal, embarrassing, or even incriminating. To get a reasonably complete time-line, you will have to ask different types of questions (open-ended, specific, leading, follow-up, yes/no) to try to get a step-by-step sense of what happened.

A broad, open-ended question will encourage the client to respond at length, focusing on the material that seems most important to the client. [*Mr. Starr, would you tell me about what happened the day you and your aunt were watching television coverage of your wife's campaign.*] A narrow, specific question or a yes/no question will elicit detail. [*Where were you and your aunt sitting in relation to the television set?*] A leading question will clarify or verify information or enable to client to respond to a difficult question. [*And you and your wife continue to disagree about whether you should sue the Hotel?*] You will likely use a combination of these types of questions. A general approach is using a "funnel" technique; that is, beginning with open-ended questions and then moving on to narrower, more specific questions.

Your skill as an interviewer depends on your ability both to listen and to ask questions. Of course, you need to listen carefully to the client's account of the events in order to learn the details that relate to the client's case. This is particularly important at the beginning of the interview when you have asked the client a general question about why the client came to see you. However, you are listening not only for an understanding of the client's legal problem, but also for the client's concerns. You need to understand what the client wants, as well as what the client needs. You may sometimes become aware of the client's attitude and concerns by observing the client as he or she is telling the story. Non-verbal cues like facial expressions and hand gestures can help you understand the client's concerns. Finally, you want to establish a rapport with the client, and to do that you have to give your full attention.

You can encourage the client to talk using two different listening techniques (sometimes described as "passive" and "active" listening). When your client is responding to an open-ended question and you want to promote the free flow of information, you can encourage him or her by using short phrases [*I see. Really? And then what happened?*] and by nodding or maintaining eye contact. Even "passive" listening requires that you remain involved and attentive. A more difficult technique but one which demonstrates empathy with the client's situation, is to respond to a statement by summarizing the content of the statement and the client's feelings about it. [*So you are furious at how the Hotel's carelessness disrupted your life?*] If a client can respond to your summary by saying "Yes, that's what I meant", then you have been successful in using that technique.

As you listen to the client's account and record the events, you may at the same time be considering the legal theories that the account suggests. At some point, though, you need to consider elements of the potential legal theories and ask questions eliciting facts that relate to those elements. Here you are seeking detail, wanting to verify certain facts and clarify others. To get these details, you will probably have to ask specific questions and be a more active questioner than you were in the initial part of the interview when the client was doing more of the talking.

At the end of the interview, the client will probably ask you for a legal opinion. If you are sufficiently familiar with the law, you may want to give a tentative assessment of the client's situation. But as a new associate, it is likely that you would need to do some further research into the client's case before you can provide a final assessment. Moreover, you may not have gotten all of the relevant factual information in the initial interview. Accordingly, a useful way to end the interview is to tell the client what you are prepared to do and tell the client what you would like the client to do. [*Mr. Starr, I am going to* .... *I would like you to* ....] You should also indicate a future date at which you will meet again or at which some event will take place. Finally, if the client wishes your representation and you wish to represent the client, you need to formalize an attorney-client relationship. That means you have the authority to act on the client's behalf and have reached an understanding as to fees.

V. *The Memo to the File*

After a client interview, lawyers often write a Memo to the File. This is different from the legal office memo described in Chapter Seven. The Memo to the File summarizes:

- who the client is

- the nature of the client's problem as the client perceives it

- the client's goals

- the factual information the client gave

- what the lawyer told the client

- how things were left:

     the lawyer's tasks

     the client's tasks

     the next steps

- the lawyer's preliminary case theory assessment

Here is an example of a Memo to the File written by an attorney who just completed an initial interview of John Starr, a new client.

Memo to the File: First Interview of JOHN STARR

Attorney Work Product

July 1, 1999

I met a new client, JOHN STARR, this morning. John is a 38–year old computer programmer who is married to Jane Starr, a newly-elected member of the city council. John has recently returned to work after a three-month absence. He said he was unable to work during that period because of depression and nerves stemming from an incident before the election involving the shooting of his wife by a Hotel security guard at the Pennsylvania Deluxe Hotel. John spoke at length about the problems he and his wife have been having, focusing on a major disagreement over her continuing as a city council member. John believes the position is too public and that Jane could be in more danger. I remembered the incident when he called to make an appointment, and re-read the newspaper account before our interview. I was not sure for the first half of the interview whether John was coming to me because he wanted to institute divorce proceedings. But he says he loves his wife and is just concerned about her safety.

John came to see me because he is furious at the managers of the Pennsylvania Deluxe Hotel. He wants to sue them because they hired the security guard who wounded Jane. Jane's campaign headquarters was at the Hotel. John believes the Hotel did not adequately check the references of the security guard, and if they had, they would have discovered that Raymond Acker, the security guard, had a history of violent behavior. John seems less interested in the money he would get from the Hotel if he succeeds than in holding them accountable for the injury to Jane, for his shock, and for the continuing disruption of their normal lives.

As John described the facts, on election day, April 2, 1998, he and Alice Doe, Jane's great aunt and former guardian, were watching the television election coverage at campaign headquarters at the Hotel. They were waiting for Jane to return to the Hotel after visiting her supporters in local campaign offices. At 9:30 p.m., Jane and several staff members arrived at the Hotel and Jane began walking towards the Hotel's entrance. When she was halfway there, Acker pulled out a gun and shot at Jane. John and Alice heard the shot on the television. The cameras showed Jane lying on the sidewalk, unconscious, in a pool of blood. John said they realized immediately after the shot was fired that Jane was seriously hurt. John collapsed and Alice became hysterical.

Jane was elected, recovered from her injuries in a month, and according to John, wants to put the whole thing behind her. But both John and Alice became depressed and anxious after the incident; Alice is still under a doctor's care for her nerves. Neither of them has any physical problems resulting from the incident and its aftermath, but John has just now felt able to return to work.

John seems to be largely recovered from his depression. But he still seems agitated about the incident and it is not clear whether he will be able to resume his work without any psychological aftereffects. John and Jane also have a number of issues that they need to work out between them. Jane personally does not want to sue the Hotel. Acker has been charged with aggravated assault and will either be incarcerated or committed to an institution. That seems to give Jane a sense of closure.

I told John that, depending on the results of my research, I would represent him on a claim against the Hotel if he decided to sue them and told him my customary fee in cases like this. Since he personally was not injured by Acker, I told him he would not be able to sue the Hotel under general negligence theories. But one possible theory of recovery would be negligent infliction of emotional distress. I told John we would have to prove certain things to recover, and that we would have difficulty with some of them. First, we would have to prove that the Hotel was indeed negligent in hiring Acker. Then we would have to convince the court that seeing an event on television was the same as seeing it in person. I forgot to ask John if he and Alice actually saw Jane getting shot on television. It could make a difference if they heard the shot, but did not actually see her being shot. And I need to make sure that they saw live coverage as the event occurred, rather than a later taped version. Finally, since he did not suffer any physical injury, we would have to prove that his emotional distress from the incident was nonetheless severe.

I also strongly suggested to John that he and Jane should discuss his desire to sue the Hotel even though she opposed the idea. This conflict could create a major source of tension between them in addition to their already serious dispute about whether Jane should keep her seat on the city council. Their entire relationship could be at risk. Moreover, as a practical matter, if Jane refuses to cooperate, the success of the lawsuit would be unlikely.

We set up a second interview for July 14th. I said I would do some research on the cases in this state dealing with negligent infliction, and, in particular, how strict the courts have been in requiring that the plaintiff actually be present at the time of the injury. I also need to do some research on whether the plaintiff has to see the injury at the exact moment that it occurred. In addition, I would check the cases dealing with the severity of the psychological injury when there was no physical injury. I asked John to bring in his medical bills containing a diagnosis from the psychiatrist he has been seeing over the past three months. I asked him for the psychiatrist's name and phone number and got John's written permission to call him at a later time. In addition, I asked John if I could speak with Alice to get some additional information from her. He was not sure that she was in a strong enough condition to review the events, and also thought that Jane might have strong feelings about my speaking to Alice. John said he would get me a list of other people who worked in Jane's campaign headquarters and their phone numbers to see if they had any information about Acker.

John has a chance to succeed in his claim, but I will have a better sense of that after I do some research. He will be a credible witness and remembers many details of the shooting. I also need to get a clearer sense of Acker's history, and will try to find out if he has a conviction record. Finally, I think that John and Jane have a number of issues to work out which will bear upon whether John decides to go ahead with his suit.

Exercise 13–A

In this exercise, your teacher or one of your fellow-students is going to play the role of Anne Atkins who is coming to your law office to see you for the first time. You got very little information over the phone. You only know that she is furious about an incident in which her parents hired a "deprogrammer" in an effort to convince her not to live on a communal farm run by an organization called the "Family of Truth and Light."

The person acting as Ms. Atkins will be provided with the facts. Before you interview her, think about the likely content of the interview and how you would like to structure it. Consider what questions you would need to ask to determine her objectives and the facts of her case.

After the interview, write a Memo to the File on Ms. Atkins' case.

Chapter Fourteen
Counseling the Client

A lawyer often engages in an on-going relationship with a client that involves counseling, either in person or by letter. Because our focus in this text is on writing, we have concentrated on counseling by letter. (See Chapter Fifteen.) However, more often than not, a lawyer would not simply write a letter to a client without also counseling the client in person. An interpersonal meeting provides an opportunity for dialogue, client involvement, and client decision-making not possible in a letter, which is solely under the lawyer's control.

This brief chapter is not intended to deal with counseling in all its complexity. Rather, the chapter is intended to give you an introduction to the process of counseling.

I. Roles of the Lawyer and the Client

Both the lawyer and the client have significant roles in decision-making. We noted in Chapter Thirteen on Interviewing that the client is the ultimate decision-maker. About certain decisions, the Model Rules of Professional Conduct[1] are explicit. Rule 1.2 states:

> A lawyer shall abide by a client's decision whether to accept an offer of settlement of a matter. In a criminal case, the lawyer shall abide by the client's decision, after consultation with the lawyer, as to a plea to be entered, whether to waive jury trial and whether the client will testify.

---

1. Model Rules of Professional Conduct.

Moreover, according to the Model Rules, Rule 1.2, the lawyer must abide by the client's decisions concerning the objectives of the litigation, and must consult with the client as to the means by which they are pursued. The final decision is appropriately the client's, since the client is the one who has to live with the decision.

Yet lawyers also have a very important role in the process of decision-making. This role has been characterized in two ways: counseling and advice giving.[2] Counseling is primarily guidance and is part of virtually every lawyer-client interaction. A lawyer is counseling when the lawyer discusses with the client the client's objectives in light of the facts of the situation, suggests alternatives, identifies the pros and cons of each, helps the client evaluate the pros and cons of the alternatives, and finally, helps the client come to a decision which provides the best solution to the client's problem.

But clients may sometimes ask their lawyers for more. The client may want the lawyer's opinion about what the client should do. The client may simply say, "What would you do if you were me?" This is a question you may have asked a doctor at some point in your life. In responding to this question, lawyers must be aware both of their professional obligations and of the client's objectives and values, so as not to suggest a result based on the lawyer's own values, which could yield an unsatisfactory result for the client. On the other hand, this situation requires the lawyer to be a more complete counselor than one who only provides information about the law. On the lawyer's role as counselor, Rule 2.1 of Article II of the Model Rules states

> In representing a client, a lawyer shall exercise independent professional judgment and render candid advice. In rendering advice, a lawyer may refer not only to law but to other considerations such as moral, economic, social and political factors, that may be relevant to the client's situation.

The Comment to Rule 2.1 goes even further:

> [2] Advice couched in narrowly legal terms may be of little value to a client, especially where practical considerations, such as cost or effects on other people are predominant. Purely technical legal advice, therefore, can sometimes be inadequate.

Since nonlegal factors may be as important to the client's decision as legal factors, the lawyer must also make them a part of the counseling process and help the client give them appropriate

---

2. Throughout this chapter, the authors have drawn on material from the following very helpful texts: David A. Binder et al., Lawyers as Counselors: A Client–Centered Approach (1991); Robert M. Bastress and Joseph Harbaugh, Interviewing, Counseling and Negotiation: Skills for Effective Representation (1990); Marilyn J. Berger et al., Pretrial Advocacy: Planning, Analysis & Strategy (1988).

weight in the client's decision-making. And to encourage frankness, the lawyer must be both objective and nonjudgmental. In all of these ways, the lawyer can help the client make a decision, while giving the client a sense of support and confidence.

II. *Preparation for Counseling*

A lawyer may counsel a client at various points in their relationship. Certainly, the lawyer is likely to counsel the client soon after the initial interview. But since the lawyer-client relationship may be an ongoing one, a lawyer and client may discuss strategy many times during the course of litigation or a transaction, or the lawyer may be asked to deal with a legal question tangential to, or completely unrelated to, the original problem.

Moreover, preparing for and conducting a counseling session will be different where the matter deals not with litigation, but with a transaction, such as an employment contract. For that, the initial interview will likely focus on the client's objectives, any contractual terms upon which the parties may already have agreed, other potential terms of the contract, and any conflicts between the parties on the terms. The lawyer must become familiar with business practices in that area and the client's business situation in particular. The lawyer may then prepare a draft agreement, send it to the client for review, and discuss it more fully with the client at their next meeting. When the lawyer and the client have come up with a satisfactory revised draft, they will send that draft to the other party. Or the client may receive a draft agreement from the other party that would be the basis of a counseling session. Then the lawyer would negotiate with the other party, which may lead to further discussions with the client, further revisions, and, one hopes, a deal which meets the client's objectives.

To get a sense of how to prepare for a counseling meeting with a client in a litigation context, however, assume that you are representing John Starr whose problem was discussed in Chapter Thirteen. At the end of your interview with him, you indicated that you were going to research certain issues relating to negligent infliction of emotional distress, to speak with John's psychiatrist when John gave you permission, to speak with Alice Doe if you got John's permission, and to try to learn more about Raymond Acker's history. John, in turn, was going to provide you with copies of medical bills, his written consent to speak with his psychiatrist, and a list of people involved in the campaign of John's wife, Jane Starr. John also said he would discuss the whole question of a lawsuit against the Hotel with Jane. You and John agreed to meet in two weeks.

To be prepared, you should plan the counseling meeting in advance. This means focusing again on the client's problem, researching the law as it relates to the problem, and investigating the facts as much as you can. Begin by thinking about what the client said in the interview that relates to the problem as the client sees it, and what the client would like to happen. Then consider the results of your research. In researching John Starr's problem, you have come upon the question of whether the plaintiff has to be physically present to satisfy the requirement that the shock results from a sensory and contemporaneous observance of the act. You are not sure whether watching the shooting on television is enough. If Pennsylvania courts strictly enforce the requirement of physical presence, you then need to decide if there is a Rule 11 problem in bringing a suit on Starr's behalf. You may conclude from reading the precedents that extending the law to cover Starr's situation would not be frivolous and that there would be no impediments to suit on that account.

As to the facts, John told you over the telephone that he spoke to Alice Doe, Jane Starr's great aunt and former guardian. Alice said she does not want to talk about the incident anymore and refuses to meet with you. You did speak, however, with John's psychiatrist. She said that John was seriously depressed following the shooting. He was unable to work for more than three months, had difficulty sleeping, and when he did sleep, often had nightmares about the shooting. He lost weight and became withdrawn. Now, the psychiatrist said, she believes he has fully recovered. His spirits are good, he is looking forward to returning to work, and he has regained his equilibrium. Finally, you checked the Hall of Records, which contains records of criminal convictions for the city and surrounding counties. You learned there that Raymond Acker was convicted of assault three years ago.

Ultimately, your goal in a counseling meeting is to help the client reach a decision that best meets the client's objectives and solves the client's problem. You may find it helpful to write out a plan, so that you and the client are less likely to forget important issues. First, identify the client's objectives. Then list the alternative courses of action, both legal and nonlegal, that have been suggested by your research, your investigation of the facts, and by the client's statements to you. For each of the alternatives, write the pros and cons to clarify the probable legal and nonlegal consequences of each alternative in your own mind and in your client's. Then indicate the costs and the likelihood of success of each alternative. You may also want to make notes beside each alternative of questions for the client that can explore the client's feelings about the alternatives and consequences.

Before meeting with the client, think about how to present this material to the client and how the client is likely to respond. Try to anticipate problems. Finally, consider having either a written agenda or an outline to give the client near the start of the meeting. But make sure that you have significant room to add comments or responses from the client. You do not want to give the client the impression that you have already decided what is best. You have a lot to hear from the client about clarification of objectives and of the relative importance to the client of various consequences.

Exercise 14–A

Based on the information in the lawyer's Memo to the File in John Starr's case in Chapter Thirteen, write a plan for a counseling meeting with John Starr. This plan assumes that you have already developed you legal theory (you know what claims would be viable). Your plan could use the format below or another format that you find useful. For your guidance, one alternative has been completed.

JOHN STARR

Objectives: Possibly sue Pennsylvania Deluxe Hotel for negligent infliction of emotional distress based on Starr's TV viewing of his wife's being shot by Hotel security guard; hold Hotel accountable for pain, stress, disruption to his life (and his wife's life and great aunt's life?); get financial compensation (damages from Hotel); maintain strength of marriage to Jane Starr.

Alternatives:

COURSE OF ACTION #1—DO NOTHING FURTHER

    A. *Pros*

        — no future expenditure of time or money

        — alleviate stress on marriage due to different views on lawsuit between John and Jane

        — maybe put incident behind them and get on with their lives

        — no conflict with Alice [and therefore Jane]

    B. *Cons*

        — no resolution of John's anger at Hotel

        — no possibility of award of damages

    C. *To evaluation the pros and cons, what questions would you ask John?*

        — How strongly does he feel about compensation (financial? psychological?) from the Hotel?

— How strongly does Jane feel that she does not want him to file a lawsuit, that she wants to put the whole thing behind her?

— How strongly does Jane feel that Alice should not be further distressed? Would refraining from suit end the stress between John and Jane?

— How much of the stress is due to Jane's new position (exposure to danger; position of importance)? [be careful asking this]

COURSE OF ACTION #2—_____

    A. *Pros*

    B. *Cons*

    C. *Questions*

COURSE OF ACTION #3—_____

    A. *Pros*

    B. *Cons*

    C. *Questions*

III. *Structure of the Counseling Meeting*

Because a client is likely to want to quickly hear a lawyer's assessment of the situation, the lawyer should spend little time talking about general issues and begin the meeting by focusing directly on the client's major concerns. Remember the college senior who visited a doctor for recurrent headaches and blurred vision. The senior's first question to a doctor who had done some tests would probably be, "Am I all right?" The law client's equivalent is probably to ask for a single, bottom line answer. Often, there is no single answer. However, the lawyer can briefly summarize the alternatives at the start of the meeting (with an explanation of the legal basis for the suit), indicate the pros and cons of each alternative, and then discuss them with the client in what seems to be the order of importance to the client.

Before discussing the alternatives in detail, however, it would be useful for the lawyer to summarize the client's objectives as the lawyer understands them. In this way, if the lawyer is mistaken about what the client really wants, the client can clarify the situation at the start. And the lawyer does not waste time emphasizing what turns out to be of minor importance to the client.

The lawyer's goal in the counseling session is to help the client decide on a course of action that will best help the client achieve his objectives. Clients should be encouraged to take an active role in the process of considering alternatives. However, the meeting is not likely to follow the orderly format of the lawyer's plan. Rather, the client, like most people, is likely to bounce from one topic to another before exhausting all of the relevant considerations, go back and forth, and sometimes go in circles. The purpose of the lawyer's counseling plan is not to control the meeting, but to have a reminder of the major issues the lawyer and the client should discuss.

IV. *Techniques of Counseling*

All of the interpersonal skills important in interviewing the client are equally or even more important in counseling a client. The counseling meeting may very well be stressful for the client and the lawyer needs to be aware of the client's state of mind and concerns. The lawyer should also consider the particular client's level of sophistication and experience with similar problems, his aversion to risk, time pressures the client may be under, and financial concerns. Finally, throughout the meeting, the lawyer's attention should be undivided.

The lawyer is in the best position to predict the legal consequences of each of the alternatives. The lawyer has researched the law and can explain the legal context. This means telling the client how courts have decided similar cases, indicating what issues of law remain unresolved, and suggesting how a jury or a court is likely to view the case. In Mr. Starr's case, for example, the lawyer would need to explain the elements of the tort and, in particular, the element of a sensory and contemporaneous observance of the accident, which Mr. Starr may have difficulty proving because he did not see the shooting in person. The client, however, is the most important predictor of the nonlegal consequences of each alternative. And the client is the only source of the client's values. Mr. Starr may feel that he will not have closure if he does not get some sort of satisfaction from the Hotel.

Throughout the counseling meeting, the lawyer can use different types of questions to advantage. (See Chapter Thirteen.) Open-ended questions will enable the client to respond fully, to play an active role in the discussion and decision-making, and to encourage the client to explore a range of issues. Narrow questions can elicit specific information and clarification. A lawyer may help the client focus on certain issues by summarizing the client's responses in a way that gives the client an opportunity to confirm, clarify, or reject the summary. The lawyer may also need to point out to the client when the client's wishes are in conflict and help the client determine which objectives are paramount.

The client will want to know what the probability of success is for each alternative. Some lawyers suggest that stating the percentage likelihood of success is easier for a client to evaluate [*You have a 70% likelihood of success if you go to trial.*] than a general statement [*You have a pretty good chance to win if you go to trial.*] Another way to express the client's likelihood of success concretely is by stating the odds. For example, a lawyer might say that the client's likelihood of success at trial was 60–40 in favor. But above all, the lawyer must give candid advice. Although no one wishes to be the bearer of bad news, the client's best interest can only be served by the lawyer's honest assessment of the claim.[3]

Finally, a client may have difficulty making a decision and may ask the lawyer not for predictions about consequences, but what the lawyer would advise him to do. Under this circumstance, assuming the lawyer has had an opportunity to review the alternatives and consequences with the client and the client is still undecided, the lawyer should try to give an opinion based on the client's values. For example, the lawyer might say [*Since you feel strongly that the Hotel should have to admit its negligence in hiring the security guard and compensate you for the misery this has caused in your life, since your claim on the merits is fairly strong, and since your wife is willing to go along with your decision, then I think you should file a lawsuit against the Hotel.*] At a later stage in the proceedings of the same case, the lawyer might say [*Since you feel the Hotel has acknowledged its error by offering to settle the case and since you would now like to put an end to the whole incident, I think you should accept the Hotel's $30,000 offer of settlement even though you asked for a much higher amount in the complaint.*]

If the client then asks what you would personally do, you can give your opinion, indicating what the basis for that opinion is. For example, you could say [*Since I personally don't have any immediate financial need and since I don't mind taking a risk, I would wait before accepting the settlement offer.*] Where you feel you could not give a basis for an opinion, do not give one.

Exercise 14–B

All of the students in the class completed a counseling plan for John Starr in Exercise 14–A. However, for purposes of this exercise, half of you will play the role of John Starr and half of you will play the role of Mr. Starr's attorney in a 20-30 minute counseling session.

Those of you acting as Mr. Starr should try to put yourself in his position, thinking about his objectives and state of mind. Those of you who are acting as attorney should think about your plan and about counseling techniques in general.

---

3. Section 1 of the Comment to Rule 2.1 on Counseling states in part:

In presenting advice, a lawyer endeavors to sustain the client's morale and may put advice in as acceptable a form

as honesty permits. However, a lawyer should not be deterred from giving advice by the prospect that the advice should be unpalatable to the client.

Chapter Fifteen

Letter Writing

Letters may be the most frequent type of writing that lawyers do. Even lawyers whose practice does not require them to write interoffice memos or court documents write letters. In fact, Rule 1.4 of the Model Rules of Professional Conduct requires a lawyer to "keep a client reasonably informed about the status of a matter," and clients are quick to complain when their lawyers do not communicate with them enough.

Like office memoranda, the letters that a lawyer writes to or on behalf of a client often require total familiarity with the law, the facts, and their interaction. But letter writing is also the most personal kind of writing a lawyer does and the most stylistically varied because, in letters, analysis and tone must always be tailored to individual audiences and specific purposes. A lawyer who begins the letter-writing process by analyzing audience and purpose—the two primary elements of the rhetorical context—is thus in a good position to formulate effective writing strategies.

Given the importance of rhetorical context in letter writing, this chapter begins by discussing the elements that comprise it. Part II then examines four types of letters that lawyers commonly write: client opinion or advice letters, letters to adversaries, letters to third parties, that is, to parties indirectly but significantly involved in a legal dispute, and finally, transmittal letters, letters that accompany documents and provide instructions.

I. Analyzing the Rhetorical Context

A. Audience

Whether writing memoranda or letters, you must know your audience or you will be unable to develop effective strategies. But while the audience for law school memos is unvarying—legal practitioners with a generalist's knowledge of the subject matter—the audience for letters is varied and diverse. It is rarely adequate, therefore, to label your audience as "client" or "adversary." Rather you must analyze your reader in detail.

There are a number of factors you can consider in drawing a portrait of your reader. First, consider your reader's legal experience. Is she a general practitioner, specialist, business woman aware of the laws affecting her business, or lay person? Second, determine your reader's level of education. Is he a professor or a high-school dropout? Third, take into account your reader's physical, mental, and emotional condition. Is your reader emotionally fragile, hostile, or physically debilitated? Finally, note the age of reader. Are you communicating with a teenager or with a senior citizen?

Such an analysis will help you make a variety of rhetorical decisions. First, it will help you determine whether a letter is the most appropriate way to communicate with your client. In a number of situations, a phone call or a counseling session in your office may be preferable. Certainly if the client is distraught, personal communication is more suitable. If your client is uneducated, you would probably want to meet with the client in person to make sure that your client fully understood your analysis and his or her options. A stubborn or angry client would be better met in person. And under any circumstances, a personal meeting provides an opportunity for interaction, listening, and discussion that a letter cannot provide.

Nevertheless, there are a number of instances where lawyers would write letters to clients giving an opinion or advice. First, business clients often want letters giving legal advice regarding a transaction. Second, a client may be unable to come to the lawyer's office because of distance or the client's infirmity. Third, the lawyer may be unable to reach the client by phone. Fourth, a lawyer may want to write to a client in advance of a counseling meeting to set out some issues that will be the basis of his discussion. Finally, a client may find it helpful to receive a follow-up letter summarizing the options discussed at a counseling meeting so that the client can review the options at leisure.

If written communication is in order, an audience analysis will help you find the level of analysis and detail that is appropriate for your reader. It will also help you determine whether you can use terms of art or must stick to plain English. In addition, it will help you make decisions about the kind of personal interaction that is appropriate. Although young lawyers worry that the human touch might make them appear unprofessional, responding to a client's implicit or explicit worries is central to establishing rapport. Clients often need and appreciate a few words of sympathy, reassurance, and good humor and may be put off by a technocrat.

Of course, the business of audience analysis is complicated by the fact that lawyers often write for multiple audiences. For example, a letter from a defense attorney to an elderly witness to an accident might be read by the attorney's supervisor, the witness's family, the family's lawyer, the court, and even the public-at-large.

When you have multiple audiences, you probably want to target your strategies at your primary reader—or at the middle range of possible readers. When, however, your audiences have vastly different backgrounds, consider drafting different letters for each or, if appropriate, include your office memorandum for those who might need a more detailed understanding of the dispute. Finally, remember that some letters are read from the file long after they are written. Thus all your correspondence should be accurate and ethical. Although courts rarely review letters, it is wise to write letters as if review was inevitable.

B. *Purpose*

Decisions about content and tone do not depend solely on audience assessment. Equally important is the purpose of the letter. Indeed sometimes your letters to a single individual will differ in tone or content because the purpose of each letter is different. A short note informing a client about a meeting the attorney had with a witness may be, for example, more informal than a letter setting out the client's legal options.

Most letters have at least one of three primary purposes:

- to counsel a client about available options
- to persuade someone to a course of action, or
- to inform someone of something.

The "counseling" category includes letters advising clients about their best legal options. The "persuasive" category includes letters negotiating settlements or letters requesting favors or information. Within the "informative" category fall letters notifying a party of a legal development, letters describing an event, letters analyzing a legal problem, letters denying a request, or letters giving instructions.

Frequently, letters have more than one primary purpose. For example, one common client letter, the advice letter, offers both a general analysis of the client's legal problem and a description of the advantages and disadvantages of each of the client's legal alternatives.

In addition to these primary purposes, an advice letter may also have a host of secondary goals:

- to establish rapport
- to check facts
- to request directions as to how to proceed
- to establish a time-frame for response

Sometimes all these goals work in harmony. Your analysis of the client's problem informs your discussion of the client's alternatives. Sometimes, however, a letter has conflicting purposes. Although you think the claim is strong on the merits, you feel obligated to warn the client about the risk, stress, expense, and prolonged nature of a court trial. Prioritizing and balancing primary, secondary, and conflicting purposes are part of the art of letter writing. You need to organize your document so that your highest priorities receive the greatest stress.

C. *Writing Strategies*

Once you have examined your audience and purpose, you must think about what kind of approach would best achieve your purpose with that audience. In other words, you must develop a rhetorical strategy. There are four central elements to consider in developing a strategy.

1. *Writer's Persona*

Because readers form impressions of their lawyers largely on the basis of their letters, it is a good idea to think about how you want to appear to your reader—about what kind of persona, or image, you want to present in that document. Ideally, you want to adopt a persona that your reader will find appealing, or at least worthy of respect.

In legal writing, you are not likely to assume extreme voices or personalities. But not all legal correspondence should sound the same either. Within somewhat narrow boundaries, there is a range of personae you might want to adopt. For example, as a probate lawyer for a grieving widow, you might want to appear as a "family solicitor"—reliable, comforting, experienced. But when you are representing the state, which has charged a business partner with embezzlement, you would present yourself as a hard-nosed prosecutor—sharp, efficient, authoritative. In contrast, when you are drafting an informative rather than persuasive letter, you will probably don the persona of a neutral reporter. Since your only purpose is to convey data, you will offer an objective, impersonal perspective on the material.

2.   *Tone*

Tone is an extension of the writer's persona and is similarly limited by notions of professional decorum. Generally, lawyers' letters are courteous, cooperative, reasonable, straight-forward, clear, precise, and assured. They avoid invective, exaggeration, sarcasm: displays of anger, contempt, or boredom are unprofessional and counterproductive. Yet between the intemperate and the impersonal exists room for the human touch.

When writing to a colleague, a long-time client, or a young adult, you might wish to adopt a friendly, somewhat informal tone. Convention would still require grammatical correctness and educated diction, but your style could be more relaxed than in a memo. Contractions and personal pronouns, for example, would be permissible. You might decide to use first names in the salutation and signature.

In fact, personal pronouns are often used to establish solidarity and rapport with clients. Simply by using the first person plural, as in "we need to review your options here," you identify with your reader and establish rapport. Another popular technique is to use the second person singular, as in "you asked me to research possible claims against AC Company." By directly addressing the reader, you bring her into the flow of discourse.

Other letters might require greater distance and formality. A letter to a business client might resemble an office memorandum in format and tone. To an adversary, you might write a brisk, chilly letter. Such a letter might have a "bottom-line" attitude conveyed by short, to-the-point sentences and a no-nonsense, concrete vocabulary: "Your client cut the boy three times on his face and arms. He then left him to bleed in the alley." In contrast, to an elderly "old-world" client who needs assurances of your attention and good will, a discursive, leisurely letter might be the most effective. "I trust your recovery will proceed speedily as you continue in the care of your doctors and wife, and as we strive to reach a prompt and equitable resolution in your action against Kent City Taxis. Indeed, some progress has already been made."

As suggested by the above examples, variations in tone are determined in part by sentence length and diction. A discursive, leisurely letter like that above has a goodly share of long sentences with parallel, coordinate clauses—totally unlike that "bottom-line" letter, which has a blunt, businesslike effect. But even more important to tone than sentence length is diction. To motivate and persuade a reader, use vivid language. Vividness requires specificity and sensitivity to connotation. To bring home the heinous conduct of a defendant who knifed a child, you could write to the defendant's attorney about how the victim was "cut" or "slashed" or "slit." To distance yourself or your reader from the subject matter, however, use general language. If you were writing to the boy's mother and wished to spare her further distress, you might more generally refer to how the boy was "injured." Word choice reveals the author's attitude toward the reader and the subject matter.

Juxtaposition is another powerful way to communicate attitude. By yoking together two antithetical statements, for example, you can express incredulity without actually stating it: "You said the check was in the mail. I have not received it." Or, if you juxtapose bad news with an acceptable alternative, you demonstrate empathy and alleviate your client's disappointment.

No matter whom you are writing, however, remember that most attorney letters are courteous. Even with adversaries, diplomacy is often needed, especially when the relationship between attorneys is likely to be long term. Thus, lawyers must be able to confront each other as politely as they do forcefully if they are to serve their clients well. Framing requests or denials of requests indirectly is one important way attorneys can be both civil and effective. For instance, requests framed as imperatives are often perceived as threatening and hostile, and generate resistance rather than acquiescence: "Provide us with this information before our next meeting." If this directive is framed indirectly, as a question or declarative statement, it is more likely to achieve the results desired: "Can you provide us with this information in time for us to review it before our next meeting?" Or "We would welcome an opportunity to review this information before our next meeting."

Refusing a demand or request also requires tact. Avoid abruptness. Instead, give reasons why you cannot perform the requested act: "The pressure of work makes it unlikely we can compile the information you want in time for our next meeting."

3. *Treatment of Law and Facts*

A general desire to present a reader with a comprehensive legal analysis must be balanced against your audience and purpose. For example, in an advice letter, a detailed analysis of authority is probably appropriate if you are writing to a corporation's in-house counsel. Yet many lay clients would be confused by this kind of in-depth analysis and would profit more from a simple application of law to facts. Sometimes, even if your audience has the intellectual sophistication to understand a comprehensive analysis, you would nonetheless be wise to keep your analysis of the issues short. If your reader is suffering under time constraints, for example, an accurate but crisp summary of the issues might be better appreciated than a lengthy exposition. Finally, thoroughness must be informed by purpose as well as audience. When writing to an adversary, for instance, you must make a strategic decision about how much of your research you wish to share.

Purpose also governs your recitation of the facts. When you are checking facts for their accuracy, your summary should be exhaustive. When you are summarizing facts for an adversary, however, you might choose, within the bounds of professional responsibility, to be more selective.

4. *Organizational Concerns*

Up to a point, your organization of material in a letter is governed by the conventions of the genre. An opinion letter, for example, has a format somewhat similar to an office memorandum. Yet within these confines, there are many organizational decisions to make.

In letters, as in memos, introductory paragraphs usually define the issues and frequently provide a roadmap informing the reader of the document's organization. Yet many letter writers regard introductory paragraphs as an equally important opportunity to develop a relationship with the reader. Early rapport makes the reader more receptive to later more complicated matters. Thus, the opening sentences might inquire after an injured client's medical progress, acknowledge a harried reader's hectic schedule, or appeal to a hostile reader's sense of fair play. In taking the time to show your concern and good faith, you may be able to secure the cooperation of a depressed, impatient, or defiant audience.

Strategy is behind a number of other organizational decisions. Should you announce your conclusion up front or lay the groundwork for it first? Generally, readers are anxious to know your conclusion, and thus stating it early is advisable. Should you put your reader on the defensive by opening with a warning or threat, or should you begin with the events that underline the threat? An analysis of the rhetorical situation will help you answer these questions.

II.   Letters

A.   Opinion or Advice Letters

When a lawyer communicates her legal analysis and advice to a client, she is writing either a formal opinion letter or an advice letter. A written opinion letter is a formal expression of your belief that a specific course of action is legal, and it most typically involves financial transactions. It is not a guarantee of legal rights, however; it is restricted to its jurisdiction, to the law at the time the letter was written, and to its facts. Moreover, it usually contains a caveat testifying to these limitations. Nonetheless, because clients place great reliance on them, and because opinion letters are the grounds of malpractice actions when they fail to meet established standards, law firms often limit the number of attorneys who can issue opinions on their behalf.

In contrast, advice letters are written by most attorneys. These letters are informal evaluations of the relative merits of the client's case and of its probable outcome. They are meant to guide clients in decision-making. Indeed, Rule 1.4 of the Model Rules of Professional Conduct requires a lawyer to explain "a matter to the extent reasonably necessary to permit the client to make informed decisions regarding the representation."

Because advice letters are thus more frequently written than opinion letters, we focus on them here. Be aware, however, that advice letters also open an attorney to liability, as well as protect her from it. When the client's legal problem is carefully re-searched, analyzed, and communicated, they are proof of profes-sional conduct.

An advice letter opens with an introductory paragraph that states the issue and conclusion. Often it then summarizes the facts that gave rise to the dispute. The facts are followed by an explanation and application of the law, and this in turn leads to a discussion of the alternatives. Finally, the closing paragraph indi-cates the next step in the proceedings.

Some attorneys separate these sections with headings, especial-ly when the subject matter is complex, or the letter is long, or a business-like appearance is appropriate. Many times, however, section headings are unnecessary and off-putting, especially when you are writing to a lay client about a relatively uncomplicated matter. Topic sentences and unified paragraphs are good substi-tutes for section headings in this situation.

1.   *The Introductory Paragraph*

The introductory paragraph should, at a minimum, articulate the question that your client asked and that your letter analyzes and answers. Often the question is two-sided, involving first, an inquiry into the client's legal position, and second, an inquiry into the legal alternatives.

Frequently your introductory paragraph also answers the ques-tion you pose. Not only are many clients made anxious and annoyed by having to wait for a conclusion in which they have a stake, but many find they can concentrate on the analysis more easily when they know where the discussion is heading. Some few attorneys do defer the conclusion until after the analysis, especially when the legal outcome is unfavorable. They hope their discussion will make the disappointing conclusion understandable, if not entirely palatable. The general consensus seems to be, however, to summarize your conclusion early in the letter—but be careful to indicate your conclusion is an opinion, cogent and reasoned, but not definitive.

Above and beyond framing and answering the issue, most introductory paragraphs also try to set a tone conducive to a good working relationship. Sometimes this is achieved by explicitly sympathizing with your reader: "I know you've been anxious about finding grounds for an appeal." Often you can tie your legal conclusion to an expression of solidarity or sympathy: "I know this has been a difficult time for you, so I am pleased to report that your claim is strong." Occasionally, if you have gotten to know your reader well, you may address the reader by his first name: "Dear John" instead of "Dear Mr. Doe."

The paragraph below begins an attorney's advice letter about a widower's claim against a mental hospital for negligently failing to prevent his wife's suicide while she was a patient there. The widower is a thirty-five-year old architect who is still recovering from his wife's protracted mental illness and eventual suicide.

February 24, ___

Mr. John Braun
114 Garden Place
Heights City, Missouri 1230___

Re: Park Crest Hospital

Dear Mr. Braun,

I hope I will be relieving some of your distress by informing you that your claim against Park Crest Hospital for its negligent care of your wife seems to be well founded. You have, therefore, several available options, including a suit against Park Crest. Another option is to attempt to negotiate a settlement. I will suggest some of the advantages and disadvantages of these alternatives after reviewing both the facts of your case and the law that governs them.

2. *The Facts*

Most advice letters include a summary of the facts similar to that in an office memorandum. This account should be objective, narrated chronologically or topically, and concisely focused on the legally relevant facts. In addition, to protect yourself from liability in the event that other material facts become known at a later date, make it clear in your statement that your opinion is based on the facts stated and might change if other facts are disclosed. This disclaimer does not absolve you, however, of the responsibility of checking and rechecking the facts before you write your advice letter.

Before I summarize the tragic events that underlie this suit, however, please note that my opinion is based on the facts as stated and might change if others become known. I would therefore appreciate it if you read the following account for accuracy and completeness and report any mistakes or omissions.

On June 21, 1994, the day after her second attempt at suicide, your wife, Rachel Braun, voluntarily checked herself into Park Crest Hospital. Park Crest is a private hospital that specializes in the treatment of mental disorders. After she was admitted, Dr. Richmond, the attending physician, diagnosed Ms. Braun as severely depressed with suicidal tendencies. He ordered that she be monitored closely for any suicide attempt and prescribed a program of anti-depressants and psychotherapy.

For the first 18 days of her hospitalization, your wife was placed on accompany status in a ward for acutely ill patients. Access to this ward was restricted. Hospital personnel could enter and exit the ward only through locked elevator and stairway doors. Visitors could come only once every two weeks. Nurses checked on patients every 20 minutes.

At the end of this period, Dr. Richmond noted in your wife's chart that she showed good response to her treatment. Her mood was brighter, and she seemed less preoccupied and withdrawn. Because of her improved condition, he transferred her to an open ward. Patients on an open ward could leave their rooms and congregate in the halls and lounges. Nurses were present on the ward at all times. Twelve nurses worked 3 eight-hour shifts, taking care of a total of 23 patients.

For the next ten days, your wife continued to improve. She began and appeared to enjoy occupational therapy. She socialized with other patients. Dr. Richmond then told her she was well enough to go home. That night, two days before her scheduled release, Ms. Braun was agitated. The nurse noted in her chart that she found Ms. Braun weeping. When the nurse questioned her, Ms. Braun expressed worry about whether she could manage in the "real" world. In response, the nurse administered sleep medication, for which the doctor had left an "as needed" order. The nurse also noted that a visitor, the spouse of another patient, had reported seeing Ms. Braun earlier that day swallowing pills taken from her pocket.

There is nothing in Ms. Braun's chart indicating that any physician acknowledged or responded to these observations of your wife's increasingly disturbed condition. The release order was not rescinded. On her last night at the hospital, the nurses checked your wife every two hours, noting she was sleeping heavily and her breathing was depressed. At 6:30 A.M., your wife was found in her bed, dead of a self-administered overdose of sleeping pills. Ms. Braun had not been searched for contraband when she was first admitted to the hospital, or at any other time.

3. *Legal Analysis*

Like the discussion section in a memorandum, the analysis section of an advice letter should be organized around the issues. Where there are many issues or subissues, you may want to begin this section with a roadmap orienting your reader to your organization.

As discussed in Part I of this chapter, your analysis of each issue must be tailored to your audience. At a minimum, you want to apply the law to the facts and come to a conclusion. Occasionally, when your client has some legal background or special need for a full discussion, you might decide to provide a full review of legal authority (citing both statutes and cases). Never, however, go into an extensive analysis of a point just to show the research you have done if the bottom line is undisputed.

Although discussion of legal authority tends to be less extensive in letters than in memos, many lawyers do not stint their discussion of the relative merits of each party's claims and defenses. Your client will be especially interested in learning the legal arguments supporting his side and wiser for learning those of his opponent. Informed decisions cannot be made without this kind of full coverage.

> Park Crest's liability for the suicide of one of its patients depends on whether it used such reasonable care as the patient's known mental condition required. The hospital's duty is proportionate to the patient's needs. In examining a hospital's conduct, courts look at the propriety of the medical judgment and at the sufficiency of the nonmedical ministerial care. Park Crest probably breached both duties of care.

> The propriety of a medical judgment is measured against the skill and learning ordinarily used under the same or similar circumstances by members of the medical profession. Medical judgment includes determining the appropriate level of supervision. The hospital's initial care of Ms. Braun seems to meet this test. At in-take she was properly diagnosed and treated. It was appropriate to place her on a closed ward while she was acutely depressed and it was appropriate to move her to an open ward as she improved. Indeed modern psychiatric theory dictates that patients receive as much freedom as is consistent with their safety. Normal interaction is regarded as the best way of restoring the confidence necessary to mental health. Nonetheless, the hospital was negligent in failing to search for contraband at intake and for

failing to address, or even to acknowledge, the developing depression the R.N. noted in your wife's medical chart.

Park Crest will probably argue that a hospital is not an insurer of a patient's safety. Given that psychiatry is an inexact science and that treatment involves taking calculated risks in the hope that increasing freedom will cure the patient, it will claim it exercised reasonable care in gradually easing Ms. Braun's supervision. The absence of any notation that Ms. Braun's depression continued past the restless night supports its contention that it could not have reasonably anticipated Ms. Braun's suicide. However, given your wife's mental history, Park Crest's failure to follow up on the nurse's observations, especially when she noted that Ms. Braun might have been in possession of her own supply of drugs, is a breach of the hospital's duty to safeguard Ms. Braun.

In determining whether the nonmedical ministerial care was sufficient, courts apply the standard of ordinary care. Factors that determine what is ordinary include the regularity of observation, the number of nurses in attendance, and the safety of the premises. The hospital here cannot be faulted for insufficient staffing or dangerous conditions. The nursing staff could be faulted, however, for its failure to search and seize contraband from Ms. Braun. It might also be liable for failing to notify a physician of your wife's depressed breathing, since the nurses had not administered any sleeping medication and depressed breathing is often a symptom of over-medication.

4. *Recommendations*

Your legal analysis prepares for your recommendations. Begin by explaining the client's various alternatives—often to file a lawsuit, to begin negotiations, or to suggest defenses. Your job sometimes involves coming up with a plan to protect someone from liability. You may suggest to an employer, for example, that it implement procedures against sexual harassment to prevent future liability. After describing your proposals or a client's alternatives, outline the advantages and disadvantages of each suggestion. If the client has pressed you for an opinion on what he should do, indicate which you think is the best course of action in light of the client's objectives. Remember, however, that the decision about how to proceed is your client's, and it is inappropriate to push too hard for any particular course of action. Thus you should conclude this section by requesting instructions or suggesting that further discussion in person may be appropriate.

Under either test, therefore, a jury might well find Park Crest breached its duty of care. Were we to go to trial, it is possible you would win substantial monetary relief. However, trials are costly, time-consuming, and ultimately unpredictable. Thus I think you should also consider pursuing an out-of-court settlement with Park Crest. Although negotiations tend to result in lower awards, they have two primary advantages. First, they would save you from the continuing stress that will undoubtedly be encountered by litigating your claim. Second, negotiations are likely to succeed. It is in the hospital's interest to avoid the negative publicity that would accompany a trial, and additionally, a settlement is likely to cost both parties less in legal fees and damages than a lawsuit. Thus it is likely we can bring Park Crest to the bargaining table.

5. Closing Paragraph

Your closing paragraph provides you with a second opportunity to demonstrate your personal concern and goodwill. Reiterate, for example, your willingness to be of service. It is also the paragraph in which you inform the client of the next step in the proceedings. If the next step must be taken within a specified time period, be certain your reader is aware of it. "Very truly yours" or "Yours sincerely" are the traditional complimentary closings.

> I suggest we meet to discuss these options, their risks, and their advantages so that you can make a thoroughly informed decision. You also need to phone about any corrections or additions you think need to be made to the statement of facts. Once you have decided how to proceed, we can discuss the next step in the process of compensating you for your terrible loss.
>
> Very truly yours,
>
> Jane Turner

One final reminder: client letters almost always need to be rewritten. Even if you analyzed the rhetorical situation before you began your letter, writers tend to use first drafts to work through their own thinking. This is natural. Until the subject matter is clear to you, it is difficult to clarify it for another. By the second draft, however, you should be writing for the reader, looking for an organization and tone appropriate for just that audience.

B. Letters to an Adversary

Your first letter on behalf of a client may be one informing the opposing party of your client's claims. Frequently this letter explores the possibility of an out-of-court settlement.

The format of such letters may not differ radically from the client advice letter. They too might open with statements identifying the purpose or, in this case, the demands of the letter. They may then go on to summarize the facts and arguments that support the client's claim. Finally, they might close by reiterating the client's demands and the consequences of failing to meet them.

Yet each part of an advocacy letter is informed by your persuasive purpose. Thus your treatment of the subject matter may be quite different from that in an advice letter. In particular, the degree to which you expound on the facts and the law depends on the strategy you have devised for that case.

1. The Opening

It is common to begin a first advocacy letter by identifying yourself as your client's legal representative. After this sort of ritual recital, present your client's claims and demands. In presenting these demands, most lawyers adopt a courteous, reasonable tone. Certainly as long as a compromise is possible, you want to appear cooperative. If negotiation falters, you may decide to assume a firmer, more indignant, or more threatening tone. But at no time should you become so strident and angry that you put your client's case in jeopardy.

2. Factual and Legal Summary

When writing to the opposing party, strategy dictates your treatment of the factual and legal basis of your client's claim. Where your case is strong, a thorough and well-crafted presentation of facts and law may convince the opponent it is better to concede or to compromise than to persist in opposition, especially if you couple your analysis with explicit warnings about your other less pleasant, but legal, alternatives.

On the other hand, you might decide not to do your opponents' work for them, believing that they will see the strength of your position only if they do the research themselves. Within the bounds of professional responsibility, you might also decide to withhold facts or to remain silent about legal theories.

3. Closing

An effective way to close an advocacy letter is to suggest the parties will mutually benefit from a compromise. This conciliatory gesture might be followed by a reminder of the actions you will take if your letter fails to effect this desired resolution. To avoid uncertainty and needless delays, be sure to set a date by which the other party must respond and be prepared to act if the party does not.

What follows is the first letter Mr. Braun's attorney wrote to Braun's adversary, Park Crest Hospital. The letter is addressed to the president of the hospital, but an obvious second reader is the hospital's attorney.   Both these readers are likely to have fairly broad knowledge of the law governing medical malpractice.   The letter tries to convince Park Crest that settlement is its best option.

March 21, ___

James Jones
President
Park Crest Hospital
3405 South Main Street
Heights City, Missouri 1230___

Dear Mr. Jones,

I represent Mr. John Braun in his claim against Park Crest Hospital for breach of its duty to exercise reasonable care to prevent the suicide of his wife, Ms. Rachel Braun, while she was a patient at your hospital.   As you know, liability depends on the propriety of the medical judgment and the sufficiency of the nonmedical ministerial care.   Once you have reviewed the facts of this case, you will realize that Park Crest breached both duties.   Thus, it is in your own interest to agree to my client's offer to settle this case quietly, quickly, and equitably.

The facts that have led to this claim are unfortunate and painful.   On June 21, 199__, the day after her second attempt at suicide, Rachel Braun voluntarily checked herself into Park Crest Hospital.   Upon admission, Dr. Richmond, the attending physician, diagnosed Ms. Braun as severely depressed with suicidal tendencies.   He ordered that she be monitored closely for any suicide attempt and prescribed a program of antidepressants and psychotherapy.   He did not search her for contraband.

For the first 18 days of her hospitalization, Ms. Braun was placed on accompany status in a ward for acutely ill patients.   At the end of the period, Dr. Richmond transferred her to an open ward.

After ten days on the open ward, Dr. Richmond told her she was well enough to go home.   That night, two days before her scheduled release, Ms. Braun became agitated.   The nurse noted in Ms. Braun's chart that she found the patient weeping.   When the nurse questioned her, Ms. Braun expressed worry about whether she could manage in the "real" world.   In response, the nurse administered sleep medication, for which the doctor had left an "as needed" order.   The nurse also noted that a visitor, the spouse of another patient, had reported seeing Ms. Braun earlier that day swallowing pills taken from her pocket.   Regrettably, she took no action other than to record this report.   No one searched Ms. Braun for unauthorized drugs.   Nothing in Ms. Braun's chart indicates that any physician acknowledged or responded to your nurse's observation that Rachel Braun was becoming increasingly depressed.   Certainly, the release order was not countermanded.

On Ms. Braun's last night at the hospital, the nurses checked the patient every two hours, noting she was sleeping unusually heavily and her breathing was depressed. At 6:30 A.M., they found her in bed, dead of an overdose of sleeping pills.

You are well aware that a hospital's liability for the suicide of one of its patients depends on whether it used such reasonable care as the patient's known mental condition required. Courts have held that the determination of the proper degree of supervision is a medical judgment and that the propriety of that medical judgment is measured against the skill and learning ordinarily used under the same or similar circumstances by members of the medical profession. Your failure to search Ms. Braun's person and possessions when she was reported to have an unauthorized supply of drugs is, in light of Ms. Braun's medical history, a breach of your duty to safeguard her from harm. See Stuppy v. United States, 560 F.2d 373 (8th Cir. 1977). Equally reprehensible is your failure to reassess your medical diagnosis after receiving the nurse's report that Ms. Braun was becoming increasingly distressed about her release.

Park Crest was also negligent in its ministerial supervision. The nursing staff as well as the physicians can be faulted for their failure to search Ms. Braun. In addition, the nurses were negligent by failing to notify a physician of Ms. Braun's unusually deep sleep and depressed breathing, given that these are symptoms of overmedication and the staff had not administered sleeping medication to Ms. Braun that evening. See M.W. v. Jewish Hosp. Ass'n of St. Louis, 637 S.W.2d 74 (Mo. App. 1982).

In light of these instances of serious misconduct, I believe a trial court would award Mr. Braun the damages that he justly deserves. Nonetheless, I am concerned that protracted court procedures would only add to the suffering Mr. Braun has already endured. Since settlement would enable both parties to avoid the costs, publicity, and burdens of litigation, I suggest we meet in an effort to resolve this unfortunate dispute.

I welcome your serious consideration of this request and invite you to call my office as soon as possible to arrange a meeting. If I do not hear from you by April 18, ___, I will proceed to file Mr. Braun's claim.

Very truly yours,

Jane Turner

C. *Letters to Third Parties*

As an attorney, you will need to write to witnesses, experts, investigators, agencies, and numerous other parties. Sometimes you will be requesting information or favors from them. At other times, you will be informing them of some development. But whatever the occasion, your letters will be stronger if you consider your audience and purpose before drafting them. Keep the following general considerations in mind.

When you are asking the reader to do something for you, you may have to create a little incentive. If you acknowledge the burden you are imposing but then appeal to your reader's good will, you might secure the reader's cooperation: "I realize compiling this information will probably take more time than you can easily afford. Yet Mr. Doe's claim cannot proceed without it." If possible, offer any assistance that could ease the burden. When simple appreciation fails to create incentive, however, a warning might be in order: "I am sorry that I will have to inform your supervisor that my last three requests for copies of Mr. Doe's insurance claims have gone unnoticed."

When you are relaying neutral information, your task is simple. State your news quickly and clearly, and then explain why you are communicating it. Readers like to feel you value their understanding.

More difficult to write are letters conveying bad news, which is often best communicated on the phone or in person. But if you need to do it in writing, try to soften it by first extending one or two courtesies. "I appreciate your reluctance to get involved in a dispute between your employer and a co-worker. Regrettably, you are the only witness to the altercation that occurred on March 13th." After this, state your bad news clearly: "Thus I must inform you that a deposition has been set for...." The temptation to misunderstand is too great to permit even minor evasions. Nonetheless, where possible, look for options or ways to mitigate the effect and soften the blow.

The following is a letter to Ms. Diana Wells, who—while visiting her husband at Park Crest—had observed Rachel Braun taking unauthorized drugs.

September 30, ___

Ms. Diana Wells
123 First Street
Heights City, Missouri 1230__

Dear Ms. Wells,

I have just received your letter expressing your reluctance to testify about the events leading to Ms. Braun's tragic suicide.

Let me assure you that I appreciate the difficult position you are in. From your letter, I infer that, having entrusted Park Crest Hospital with the care of your husband, you feel it is imperative to maintain good relations with the hospital's administration and staff. Thus, although you empathize with Mr. Braun's bereavement, you wish to avoid becoming involved in a dispute between them.

If your testimony were not so vital, I would not press you on this matter. Unfortunately, you are an important link in establishing that Park Crest knew Ms. Braun had her own drug supply and failed nonetheless to take steps to prevent her from harming herself. I think you will agree with me that a jury ought to be allowed to determine Park Crest's liability not only because Mr. Braun deserves to be compensated for his painful loss, but because other patients, like your husband, may need to be protected from such fatally negligent conduct.

I suggest that we meet to review your potential testimony. Such a meeting would enable me to prepare you for the courtroom experience and thereby allay some of the natural anxiety you may feel about participating in this trial. I will call you in a few days time to arrange a meeting at your convenience. I would sincerely regret having to subpoena you to obtain testimony that I believe you would freely give in happier circumstances. Let me assure you I will do all I can to minimize the repercussions of your participation.

Very truly yours,

Jane Turner

D. *Transmittal Letters*

Transmittal letters are cover letters that usually accompany documents and provide instructions to the recipient. Transmittal letters are often quite short, yet it is surprising how badly written and organized many are. These letters should be written clearly and logically. They should not be written in old fashioned legalese, but neither should they be casually thrown together. For example, you need not write "Enclosed herewith please find as per your request two copies of the Anderson agreement. Said agreement should be kept by you in and only in your safety deposit box. I remain yours faithfully." But also, do not write "Here are the copies of the agreement you asked for. Keep them safe. Yours...." A middle ground is the simple, "I am enclosing two copies of the Anderson agreement that we discussed this morning. Please keep the copies in a secure place, preferably your safety deposit box. Let me know if you need any other documents. Yours truly...."

When you write instructions, make sure the recipient understands the purpose of the transaction, and explain the steps in the order that they should be done. For example, "Please read through this agreement to ensure that it is in the form we discussed. If the agreement is acceptable to you, bring it to a notary public. You should sign it in front of the notary at the line marked 'Signature.' Sign your name exactly as it is typed under the line. Write the full date on the line marked 'Date.' The notary will then sign and stamp the agreement. Bring the agreement with you to our next appointment on May 4th."

If the instructions involve several steps or several documents, number them. For example, "I am enclosing the forms you will need to probate your aunt's will:

1. Petition to Admit the Will to Probate and Appoint an Executor

2. Oath on the Bond

3. Waiver of Notice

4. Affidavit of Heirship

5. Petition for Independent Administration."

Then explain in turn your instructions for each document.

Exercise 15–A

Critique each of the following excerpts from letters to Mr. John Starr concerning possible action against the Pennsylvania Deluxe Hotel for negligent infliction of emotional distress.

1. Sample openings

Do the following introductory paragraphs effectively establish rapport, provide an organizational roadmap, and summarize options?

   a) Dear Mr. Starr,

   The decision to seek legal advice concerning your situation was intelligent, and one I commend you for, because the laws concerning the infliction of mental injuries are complex. You do have several options, both legal and otherwise, in attempting to obtain redress from the Pennsylvania Deluxe Hotel, and I will explain them to you.

   b) Dear Mr. Starr:

   After carefully scrutinizing the facts of your situation and the relevant laws and cases, there is no question that your reasons for wanting to sue Pennsylvania Deluxe Hotel are well founded. However, the courts take many things into consideration when making such decisions. The facts of your case are such that a jury could conceivably find either way on whether or not the Hotel negligently inflicted emotional distress. There are a number of courses of action we can take at this point, including taking your case to court or seeking a settlement. It is my opinion that we first try the latter, to resolve the situation privately by seeking from the Hotel a public acknowledgment of wrongdoing and an apology, and perhaps some compensatory damages. I will explain why I have come to this conclusion after I review the facts of your case and Pennsylvania law pertaining to your situation.

   c) Dear Mr. Starr:

   I would like for us to meet on April 30, at 4:00 p.m. in order to discuss your options in dealing with its matter. Before coming to the meeting, I would like you to have an understanding of how the law has treated situations similar to yours.

2. Sample Presentation of Law

Does this paragraph clearly communicate the law in terms that are ethical and accurate and that a lay person could understand? Does the attorney appropriately apply the law to the client's circumstances?

To recover for negligent infliction of emotional distress in this state, we have to prove that the plaintiff is closely related to the victim, that the plaintiff's distress was severe, that the shock resulted from a single identifiable traumatic event, and that the plaintiff was near the scene of the accident and that his or her shock resulted from a sensory and contemporaneous observance of the accident.

We will have no trouble proving the first three elements, although it would strengthen our case if you continued to refrain from working to underscore the severity of your injury. The last prong is problematic, however. We would have to convince the court that seeing a live action event on T.V. is the same as seeing it in person. In Trask v. Vincent, this prong was not satisfied when plaintiff was in a phone booth with her back to the sidewalk when her husband was floored by a falling window box. She emerged two minutes after the incident to find a crowd around her husband, who was lying on the pavement in a pool of blood. Since you were not even as near the scene as the Trask plaintiff, and similarly failed to witness the actual shooting, we may have trouble satisfying this test.

3. Sample Presentation of Options

Does the following paragraph effectively consider the non-legal implications of each option and convincingly communicate that the decision on how to proceed is the client's?

It may be in your best interest to try to talk with your wife and great aunt before you seek a legal remedy since your aunt's health and your marriage might suffer if you proceed against their wishes. Both parties seem to want to put the event behind them. Moreover, were you to litigate, there is a real chance you could lose since you were not at the scene of the shooting.

Another less stressful option is settlement talks. Since you seem most interested in holding the Hotel accountable for its negligence, we could seek a public statement of accountability and a public apology instead of compensatory damages, though we could ask for some out-of-pocket reimbursement if you wish it. Whatever course of action you decide upon, I will support absolutely.

The ultimate decision on how to proceed is yours and yours alone. Please do not hesitate to call me if you have any questions. When you've decided what to do, we can discuss the specifics of what the next steps will be.

Exercise 15–B

1. You are an attorney for Mr. Timothy S. Eliot. Read the following facts
and cases. Make an outline of the law relating to covenants not to
compete. Then edit the letter to Mr. Eliot that follows the case summaries.

Facts

Your client, Mr. Eliot, has been a salesperson for Kid–Vid
Corporation, which manufactures and sells electronic toys like
video games, robots, computers, etc. He is fifty years old, married, has two children (one in college, one in high school), and lives
in a four-bedroom house in a suburb of New York City.

Mr. Eliot has been with Kid–Vid for ten years. He sells the
Kid–Vid line to department stores and toy store chains all over the
country, and he is well known and well respected by the store
buyers. Last year he earned $75,000 in salary and commissions.
Mr. Eliot has no written employment agreement with Kid–Vid and
the company has been having financial problems. Thus, he is
looking for a new job.

Mr. Eliot knows from preliminary conversations with other
toy companies that finding a good position will be difficult. His
age and experience are actually working against him. The big
companies usually hire youngsters whom they can train and pay
peanuts. Mr. Eliot is set in his ways—which, by the way, work—
and he has a family to support. On the other hand, it is time to
find something new. Mr. Eliot could wind up on the street.

Recently, Mr. Eliot had lunch with the CEO of Toydyno, Ms.
Baer. Toydyno has a novel product, the Knobot. Knobots are
amazingly dexterous and articulate robots which can be pro-
grammed to play with children. Toydyno wants experienced,
savvy, aggressive sales people to put Knobots into toy depart-
ments, where Mr. Eliot already has extensive contacts. It also
wants salespersons to develop contacts in bookstores, camera
shops, and sporting good stores. It doesn't have time to train
novices. At lunch, Ms. Baer said she thought Mr. Eliot fit the bill
and suggested he come to work for Toydyno. However, one of the
terms in the Toydyno contract concerns a covenant not to compete. The covenant provides that if the Employee leaves for any
reason,

> 1) The Employee is prohibited from
>
>> a) selling electronic toys to anyone anywhere,
>>
>> b) using lists of customers who buy Knobots from
>> Toydyno for resale to the public, and
>>
>> c) disclosing the "computer source codes" which
>> make the Knobots do what they do, or disclosing
>> the Employer's technique for making the "flange-
>> hinges" which give the Knobots digital flexibility.

2) The Employee must turn over all customer lists in his possession. The lists are not merely of the names of customers. They also will include pertinent data regarding credit, merchandise turnover, buying patterns, volume of sales, and merchandise returns. The data will have been gathered by Toydyno personnel, including Employee.

Mr. Eliot has asked you to research this issue in New York and determine if, and to what extent, the courts are likely to enforce such a covenant. He wants to know whether he should negotiate any of the terms of the covenant not to compete.

Case Law

Columbia Ribbon & Carbon Manufacturing Co. v. A–1–A Corp., 369 N.E.2d 4 (N.Y. 1977)

Defendant Trecker was employed by Columbia Ribbon as a salesman for several years. He signed an employment contract with the following restrictive covenant:

1. The employee will not disclose to any person or firm the names or addresses of any customers or prospective customers of the company.

2. The employee will not, for a period of twenty-four months after the termination of his employment, sell or deliver any goods of the kind sold by the company within any territory to which he was assigned during the last twenty-four months prior to termination.

After Trecker was demoted, he terminated his employment with Columbia Ribbon and took a job with a competitor, A–1–A Corporation. Columbia then sued to enforce the terms of the covenant.

In determining whether a salesman is bound in whole or in part by a covenant not to compete with an employer after termination of employment, the court said that restrictive covenants are disfavored in the law. Powerful public policy considerations militate against depriving a person of his or her livelihood. Thus restrictive covenants are enforced only if they are limited in time and geography, and then only to the extent necessary to protect the employer from unfair competition which stems from the employee's use or disclosure of trade secrets or confidential customer lists. If, however, the employee's services are truly unique or extraordinary, and not merely valuable to the employer, a court will enforce a covenant even if trade secrets are not involved.

The court said that the broad sweeping language of the covenant in this case had no limitations keyed to uniqueness, trade secrets, confidentiality, or even competitive unfairness. The affidavits made no showing that any secret information was disclosed, that Trecker performed any but commonplace services (his work did not require the highly developed skills of learned professionals like doctors or lawyers), or that any business was lost. Moreover, nothing in the purely conclusory affidavits by Columbia contravened the points in Trecker's own affidavit that no trade secrets had been involved in his employment, that he had taken possession of no customer lists, and that all customers were publicly known, or obtainable from an outside source.

Accordingly, Columbia's showing was insufficient to defeat summary judgment. The court therefore affirmed the order below denying enforcement.

Greenwich Mills Co. v. Barrie House Coffee Co.,
459 N.Y.S.2d 454 (App. Div. 1983)

Three salesmen worked for Greenwich Mills, a company that sold coffee, tea, and related products to hotels, restaurants, and stores. When they were hired, they entered into a restrictive covenant with Greenwich Mills. Eventually they left Greenwich Mills and began working for Barrie House, which engaged in a similar business. Their former employer, Greenwich Mills, sought an injunction to uphold the covenant.

In denying Barrie House's motion for summary judgment, the court held that restrictive covenants will not be enforced absent trade secrets or special circumstances, but that knowledge of the precise blends of coffee that various customers of their former employer preferred might be considered a trade secret. Information on the technology and manufacturing process of a product that is unique is a trade secret. The court further stated that any trade secret through which a party might gain an unfair advantage would be sufficient to make a covenant enforceable if it is reasonable in time and area and bans solicitation of former customers rather than a total ban on competition. The court said a trial was necessary to determine whether there were trade secrets justifying an apparently reasonable one year ban on solicitation of Greenwich Mills customers.

Scott Paper Co. v. John J. Finnegan Jr.,
476 N.Y.S.2d 316 (App. Div. 1984)

A regional sales manager signed a restrictive covenant with Scott Paper Company, a paper manufacturer. The covenant provided that the manager would not engage in any work that involved confidential information obtained at Scott within 150 miles of the manager's last assignment for a period of not less than six nor more than twenty-four months. When the manager left, the paper manufacturer sought to enjoin him from using this information.

The court said that confidential information includes any information relating to the company which is not known to the general public, such as pricing and promotional information, customer preference data and buying records, customer lists, product sales records, market surveys and marketing plans, and other business information. The court did not enforce this covenant not to compete, however, because most of this information was outdated or generally known within the industry.

Quandt's Wholesale Distributors Inc. v. Giardino,
448 N.Y.S.2d 809 (App. Div. 1982)

Quandt, a distributor of restaurant food, had salesman Giardino sign a restrictive covenant that provided that for six months following termination of his employment, he would not compete with Quandt in the area to which he had been assigned.

The court held the distributor's six-month, three-county restrictive covenant was reasonable. However, plaintiff distributor made no showing concerning the unfair competition criteria mentioned in Columbia Ribbon. Customer names were readily available from directories. Giardino was well-trained and effective, but his services were not unique. Nor had plaintiff suffered an irreparable injury. In fact, five weeks after Giardino left, the sales on his route were greater than what they had been when Giardino left. Therefore, the court held that the restrictive covenant was invalid.

———

In editing the following letter, consider the following:

1) the audience for the document,

2) the purpose of the document, and

3) the writing techniques adopted to serve that audience and that purpose.

More specifically, assess

— the effectiveness of the writer's persona and tone, particularly in the introductory and concluding paragraphs,

— the strategy, logic, and clarity of the writer's organization,

— the appropriateness of the letter's length, comprehensiveness, and use of supporting legal authority,

— the need for an objective or adversarial recitation of the facts.

———

Dear Mr. Eliot,

This letter gives you my opinion of how a New York court would rule on the restrictive covenant contained in your prospective employment contract at this moment in time. I cannot guarantee the court will agree with my analysis. In addition, the law upon which I am basing my analysis is always subject to change by the courts or possibly the legislature. Furthermore, I have written this letter for your benefit only and not for the benefit of third parties. The letter is not to be used for any purpose other than for your information. Finally, I have based my opinion in part on the facts that you gave me at our meeting. If you misstated them then, or have since remembered facts, please let me know since a change in facts might change my analysis.

In determining whether a covenant not to compete is reasonable, courts examine a number of factors. First, an employer has a legitimate interest in enforcing a restrictive covenant not to compete in order to protect himself from unfair competition resulting from the loss of an employee's unique services. Although an employee's extraordinary services can be justification for the enforceability of a covenant not to compete, enforcement usually is not granted merely on the basis of the uniqueness of the employee's services. Reasonable time and geographic restrictions must be set forth in a covenant in order for it to be enforceable. In Quandt, a covenant not to compete that contained reasonable time and territory limitations was not enforced because the salesperson's duties were not extraordinary in nature. The services of an employee who acts merely in the capacity of an effective and well-trained salesperson may be valuable but are not so unique that their loss would result in irreparable damage or unfair competition to the employer. Quandt's Wholesale Distrib. v. Giardino, 448 N.Y.S.2d 809, 810 (App. Div. 1982). In fact, in Quandt, the sales in the employee's territory were equal if not greater once he terminated his employment.

The salesperson being hired by Toydyno will be expected to solicit new customers to promote the Knobots. However, this is not an extraordinary job requirement that any salesperson would not be expected or able to fulfill. The anticipated duties of this salesperson are not so unique that performance by another individual would cause Toydyno to incur a loss.

Although an employee's skills may not be classified as unique, a restrictive covenant may be enforced in order to prevent the use or disclosure of confidential customer information or trade secrets. It is highly likely that the "source codes" and the technique for making "flange-hinges" would be considered trade secrets. Not only is this information highly technical and probably the result of long hours of costly research, but it is so intrinsically related to the manufacture of the Knobot that its exploitation would cause Toydyno considerable harm. Therefore, it is likely that a court would uphold the provision of the covenant that prohibits you from disclosing this information.

The customer lists that you will be privy to may also be construed as confidential since they will contain business information that might give you an unfair competitive advantage. In Scott Paper Co. v. Finnegan, 476 N.Y.S.2d 316 (App. Div. 1984), a regional sales manager employed by a paper manufacturer signed a restrictive covenant prohibiting him from using business information including customer preference data, pricing and promotional information, customer buying records and other business information. When he left his employer and began working for another paper company, his former employer attempted to enjoin him from using this information. The court, however, held that it was either readily available from other sources like distributors in the paper industry or, as was the case with the pricing information, no longer relevant.

It is not clear if the business information on the client lists that you will have possession of would be obtainable from different sources. Assuming that it would not be—particularly the credit information—it is possible that you could gain an unfair advantage were you to use it. Hence, the information will most probably be deemed confidential and you will not be able to keep the lists.

Even though you will not be able to keep the lists, you will be able to maintain your customer contacts. The test applied by the courts in deciding when the identity of a customer is confidential is whether the customer's name is readily obtainable from an outside source. Columbia Ribbon v. A–1–A Corp., 369 N.E.2d 4 (N.Y. 1977). The customer contacts you will make will not be confidential. Your customers will include camera stores, bookstores, and sporting goods stores. Since the identity of these customers can be obtained in any business directory, a court would not consider them trade secrets. For the same reason, your original contacts in department stores in the region could not be construed as confidential either.

There is also the issue of the reasonableness of time and geographic restrictions. Here courts examine their scope and duration as well as a showing of unfair competition. If you were to use or disclose the business information on the customer lists, it would be reasonable only to enjoin you from competing in the area where that information would be relevant. It should be noted, however, that no geographical limitation could prevent you from selling electronic toys or anything else absent your possession and utilization of a trade secret or confidential customer lists.

To sum up, since Toydyno's "computer source codes," and the technique for making "flange-hinges" are trade secrets, the court may prevent you from disclosing or using them. Although you may have to return the customer lists because they contain confidential business information, you will be able to maintain your customer contacts since they are readily obtainable from other sources. Thus, you will be able to compete with Toydyno as long as you do not use any trade secrets or confidential information.

Ultimately, therefore, you should agree to clauses 1(c) and 2. Not only is Toydyno within its rights in demanding this information be kept confidential, but in all frankness, your employment prospects are not so bright that you can flatly reject all restrictions. However, you should not agree to 1(a) and (b), at least in their present form. I will write to Toydyno proposing these terms. Please call me if you have any questions.

Very truly yours,

2. Rewrite the advice letter to Mr. Eliot.

3. Assume Mr. Eliot has agreed to your course of action. Write an "advocacy" letter to Toydyno introducing yourself and attempting to advance your client's cause.

Exercise 15–C

Often when you counsel a client about a proposed transaction, you discuss the transaction with the client in person, rather than by letter. You might, for example, meet with a client about a proposed contract. Review the facts and cases described in Exercise 15–B, in which you are an attorney representing Timothy Eliot in a transaction involving an employment contract that includes a covenant not to compete. Assume that Mr. Eliot is going to come to your office for advice. Plan the counseling meeting.

Ordinarily you would review each of the proposed terms of a contract, even if you do not intend to discuss every term with the client. For purposes of this exercise, the counseling meeting will focus on a single term of the contract, the covenant not to complete.

How would you explain this contract term to Mr. Eliot? What are Mr. Eliot's likely objectives? What options does Mr. Eliot have? What are the pros and cons of each? What are the risks? What is likely to be most important to Toydyno? What aspects of the covenant might be successfully renegotiated?

How would a personal meeting look and sound different from a letter? What kind of relationship would you hope to establish in the meeting? Would the result be the same? Does one method of counseling (by letter or in person) seem to be more effective in this situation? If you decide meeting with Mr. Eliot in person would be more effective, can a letter play any role in the process?

Chapter Sixteen

Writing to the Court:
An Introduction to Advocacy

I. Introduction

In Chapter Seven we discussed how to write a legal memorandum that would be used within a law office to analyze a legal problem. The purpose of such a memorandum is to analyze the problem in an objective, exploratory way and to reach a conclusion based on that analysis. When you are writing to a court, however, your purpose is very different. You are then writing as an advocate representing one side in a dispute, and your purpose is not to explore, but to persuade the court to decide the case for your client.

A. The Purpose of Trial and Appellate Briefs

Attorneys submit many documents to trial and appellate courts. Important among those are trial and appellate briefs in which the attorney tells the court about the case and argues the case for the client. Both trial and appellate briefs seek to persuade the court of the validity of one point of view, but they differ in some important respects. A document written for a trial court (called a memorandum of law, an advocacy memorandum of law, or a trial brief) is frequently submitted in support of or in opposition to a motion, which is a request to the court for a ruling on a legal question. Attorneys may also submit a trial brief to present their side of any disputed issue, to summarize the evidence, to support or oppose post-trial motions, and to request particular instructions to the jury. Finally, attorneys may file extensive post-trial briefs at the end of the litigation to present the court with their final arguments based on the facts adduced at trial. A trial brief tends to be shorter than an appellate brief and less rigid in format.

An appellate brief is a more formal document submitted to an appellate court by which an advocate presents a case to a court for review. An appellate brief differs from a trial brief in that it is written from a record on appeal, and is written to convince an appeals court to affirm or reverse a lower court's decision. An appellate court does not hear evidence in the case as does a trial court. Rather, the appellate court reviews the trial court's decision and determines whether, based on the record below, the trial court committed error in hearing or deciding the case. An appellate court's review is limited by the power of the court to review particular questions, by the standard of review that is appropriate to the court and to the case, and by the record in the court below.

B. *Court Rules*

Whether you are filing a motion before a trial court or filing an appeal before an appellate court, you must familiarize yourself with the applicable court rules. Some rules apply to all courts of a certain type, such as the Federal Rules of Civil Procedure (governing civil cases filed in all federal trial courts), or the Federal Rules of Appellate Procedure (governing cases filed in all federal appellate courts). Other rules apply to particular local courts. Often, more than one set of rules will be relevant. For example, an attorney suing in federal district court in the Eastern District of New York will have to be aware of the Federal Rules of Civil Procedure, the applicable local court rules of the Eastern District, and any rules of individual judges. An attorney filing an appeal in the United States Court of Appeals for the Second Circuit would be bound by both the Federal Rules of Appellate Procedure and the rules of the Second Circuit.

Rules cover a variety of points, some substantive and some technical. For example, Rule 23 of the Federal Rules of Civil Procedure establishes the prerequisites for a class action, but Rule 6 is only technical, describing the method for computing periods of time under the Federal Rules. Local rules governing motion practice may prescribe the content of a memorandum in support of or in opposition to a motion, set out time and page limitations, or require attorneys to confer with opposing attorneys before bringing any motion to compel discovery.

You should learn the applicable court rules at the start of your case. Failure to do so could be disastrous.[1] You do not want to

---

1. For example, see this excerpt from   (Minn. App. 1984):
Swicker v. Ryan, 346 N.W.2d 367, 369

discover the night before you submit a 75 page brief that the page limit for your type of brief is 65 pages, and that an application to file a longer brief had to be submitted 15 days ago. Nor do you want to miss a deadline for filing a brief because you thought you had 20 days to file a reply brief, and the correct period of time is 14 days.

II. *Advocacy*

A. *Audience*

The audience for both trial and appellate briefs is a judge (or judge's law clerk), who reads many briefs every day and who decides many cases. A secondary audience is the opposing party. Since judges play the crucial role in litigation, it is worth your time and effort to consider carefully what information they need from your trial and appellate documents, and how that information can be clearly and quickly communicated. When you write an interoffice memo, you write to a person who makes important decisions about your own career. But when you write to a judge, you write to a person who makes important decisions affecting someone else, your client.

Unless you are told differently for your particular assignment, you should assume the judge is a generalist, that is, the judge sits on a court of general jurisdiction rather than on a specialized court, such as a bankruptcy or tax court. And although a judge most likely is familiar with some aspects of the case, such as procedural rules, you should still include information such as the burden of proof or the standard of appellate review where appropriate. Your most important task, however, is to introduce your case. Whether you are responding to a motion or entering an appeal, remember that the judge probably will know nothing about the facts of your case except those you include in your documents, and may know little specifically about the legal rules and arguments involved, except those you formulate and develop. Therefore, the documents you

While we are mindful of ... the court's discretionary authority to consider the matter on the merits irrespective of legal procedural defects, the case load before Minnesota appellate courts in 1984 requires a firm application of the new rules of appellate procedure. The bench and bar had sufficient time since August 1, 1983, the effective date of the new rules, and November 1, 1983, the effective date of the implementation for the Court of Appeals to become aware of the necessity for firm judicial and calendaring administration. Failure of counsel to follow the rules, or to timely make appropriate motions cannot be countenanced. Unfamiliarity with the rules, a heavy work load, or overwork is not good cause. The rules must be viewed as the guideposts for efficient court administration. We intend to apply them firmly and reasonably.

Failure of appellant to process an appeal, appealing from a non-appealable order and failure to timely order a transcript, are sufficient grounds to grant the motion of dismissal. This matter is dismissed.

submit to the court will be its first (and sometimes only) source of this information, and your preparation must be meticulous. Although oral argument is the second source of this information, not all cases are argued before a judge, and those that are may be allotted only a short time.

B. Persuasion

When you write to a court, you write to inform the court about the case. You also write to persuade, that is, to convince the court to decide in favor of your client. For lawyers, the importance of effective, persuasive writing cannot be overstated. Many principles of persuasion come from classical rhetoric, as conceived long ago by Aristotle. He identified three components of persuasion:[2] appeals to ethics, to emotion, and to reason. Each plays a role in lawyers' communication.

1. Ethics

The ethical appeal concerns the lawyer's credibility, not only by reputation, but gleaned from the document itself. For example, the document may make arguments with ethical implications. The document will also reveal whether the speaker is intelligent, and a person of good moral character and good will.[3] The ethical appeal also comes from a sense of trust and of shared values. An attorney who has not earned the trust of the court has little chance of success in that court.

Some values that attorneys share come from the special ethical obligations imposed by professional codes of conduct.[4] Indeed, the Code of Professional Responsibility imposes the obligation to maintain "the integrity and competence of the legal profession."[5] Both codes require candor to the courts. For example, under the Model Rules, an attorney must not make false statements of material fact or law[6] and must disclose material facts and legal authority.[7] Although an attorney also owes the client a duty of zealous advocacy,[8] that duty stops short of inaccuracy. In addition to compliance

---

2. Aristotle's theory of rhetoric applied to oral persuasion but applies as well to persuasive writing.

3. Translation in W. Ross Winterowd, Rhetoric, A Synthesis 31 (1968). See also Edward J. Corbett, Classical Rhetoric 94 (1977) ("sound sense, high moral character, and benevolence").

4. States have adopted either the ABA's Code of Professional Responsibili-ty (MC), or the Model Rules of Professional Conduct (MR).

5. MC Canon One.

6. MR 3.3 (a) (1);

7. MR 3.3 (a)(2)(3). Under § 3.3 (a)(3) a lawyer must disclose legal authority in the controlling jurisdiction that is directly adverse and that is not disclosed by opposing counsel.

8. MC Canon 7.

with professional codes of conduct, the lawyer's duty to the court as an officer of the court requires compliance with court rules.

Your credibility also depends on some more mundane concerns. If your work is careless, for example, if you cite cases incorrectly or if you inaccurately describe the decisions you rely on, the court may not trust any of your work. Once you lose credibility with the court, you have not only damaged yourself professionally, but you have injured your client.

2.   *Emotion*

Many people believe that emotion is inappropriate for a lawyer, at least for certain types of argument. But an appeal to emotion can be proper and effective, if it is restrained. You can evoke sympathy for your client's suffering, anger at the defendant's cruelty, or respect for the values of fairness and justice. An emotion that is inappropriate is hostility towards the opposing counsel and parties. Most important, you should convey your conviction for the merits of your client's case, and positive feelings towards your client. You want to make the judge, even an appellate judge, care who wins the case.

3.   *Reason*

Of course, reason is what we most associate with successful advocacy. Your appeal to reason is an appeal to the shared expectations of the legal profession about how arguments are structured and the kinds of support you need for your claims. A good deal of the material in this book is relevant to your appeal to reason. In trial and appellate briefs, the most explicit appeal to reason is in the Argument section of the document. Thus, the rest of the information in this chapter provides an introduction to techniques for writing a persuasive Argument in a brief and memorandum, that is, for an effective appeal to reason. The following two chapters provide more detailed information about writing each type of document.

The Argument in the trial and appellate brief is the analog of the Discussion in a memorandum. The term "argument" is not used to mean a pugnacious statement, but is used in the more traditional sense of a presentation of reasons that support a conclusion. In the Argument section of the document, you analyze the law and apply the law to the facts of your case. However, an Argument differs from a Discussion in terms of the audience, which is a court, and the purpose of the document, which is to persuade the court to decide the case favorably for your client. So you will write in a more assertive tone, that is, as an advocate.

In the Argument, you develop reasons why your client should prevail in order to convince the court to accept your conclusions. The reasoning that you engage in involves the same types of legal analysis you have been doing all year. For example, you may be applying fairly settled law to the facts of your case, and your conclusions depend on how you interpret the precedents and how you analogize and distinguish them. Or, you may initially analyze a question of law, for example, how to interpret a statute, and then apply that statute to the facts of your case. The difference is that in an Argument you always interpret the law and its application as requiring a conclusion favorable to your client.

Another difference is that you *must* come to a conclusion, and tell the court what that conclusion should be. This is not the place to engage in neutral presentations and even-handed analysis. For example, in a brief you would not write, "the courts are divided over how to read these statutes together: one way is unfavorable to the defendant, and one way favorable." Instead, you tell the court how to read the statutes in the way favorable to your client. "The provisions of Statute X must override those of Statute Y because X is more specific to the subject matter of this dispute."

An important tool of the advocate is the topic sentence. The topic sentence should be a conclusory one, such as the sentence above about Statute X overriding Statute Y. By using topic sentences in this way, you make your argument clear to the court. You then go on to provide the reasons that support your conclusion.

In addition, a successful argument requires you to explain away the points against you. The judges know there is another side to this dispute, for example, that statutes X and Y may be read in more than one way, or the case would not have been litigated and would not have been appealed. To ignore the case against you diminishes your credibility and the strength of your argument. Thus, even if you are the party who submits the initial brief, that is, you are the moving party of a motion or the appellant in an appeal, your analysis should include rebuttal of the other attorney's arguments. By framing those arguments in the way you want the court to understand them, you help the court understand the case, and you "innoculate" the court against the opposing attorney's memorandum or brief.

The kinds of arguments you emphasize will depend in large part on the court to which they are addressed. Arguments to lower courts are more factual and precedent oriented, because the lower courts are bound by the decisions of the jurisdiction's higher courts. Appellate arguments may be more policy oriented and concerned with the impact of a proposed decision. The jurisdiction's highest court has the power to overrule its own decisions and change a rule.

C. Choosing Precedent

The persuasive power of your Argument will also depend on your choice of precedents. Begin your discussion of the precedents with the strongest cases supporting the proposition you need to advance your argument. As a general rule, you should try to discuss and apply favorable precedents and come to an affirmative legal conclusion before raising and distinguishing unfavorable precedents.

You will not be able to discuss every authority that you have found, nor should you try to. Instead, you have to make judgments about their relevance. Several factors must be considered in determining which cases would best promote your argument. First consider the weight of authority. Whenever possible, base your argument on previous decisions of the highest court in the jurisdiction of your problem, especially decisions of the Supreme Court of the United States if you are analyzing constitutional or federal issues. Even if that court has not ruled yet on the particular issue in your assignment, relate your arguments to prior decisions of that court in analogous areas of the law, and to statements that the court has made in dicta.

Besides the decisions of the Supreme Court, the most important cases are always the controlling precedents of the jurisdiction. A court always wants to know the law of the jurisdiction. Rely on these decisions and show how they are consistent with the higher court's decisions and policy. Then, you may need to use persuasive decisions on the same point by a court that does not bind your court.

Choose cases because they are particularly relevant, first as binding authority, then because they are factually similar or the reasoning is otherwise appropriate. The reader should not be wondering why you have chosen a particular case to write about.

Many first-year students get caught up in trying to be persuasive and forget the basics of using legal sources. Remember, the first step to persuasion is to include information that the court needs in order to understand the issues. Quote the controlling statutory language and tell the court what the cases are about, in whatever detail is necessary. Do not try to analyze a case and also explain the facts within a single sentence. Remember that quotes and case names are not a substitute for thorough explication. A strong argument instead requires you to marshal many sources, to work out their meaning, and to apply those sources carefully to your client's case.

If you want the court to be aware of a number of cases, none of which requires individual discussion, group them together with parenthetical explanations—do not merely string cite.

Example

Gold did nothing more than push a shopping cart on a public street in broad daylight. This innocuous conduct does not even create an "objective credible reason" for the police to request information. People v. De Bour, 40 N.Y.2d 210, 213, 352 N.E.2d 562, 565, 386 N.Y.S.2d 375, 378 (1977). Indeed, it is hard to imagine a less remarkable picture on the urban landscape than a person pushing a shopping cart. Accord People v. Howard, 50 N.Y.2d 583, 408 N.E.2d 908, 430 N.Y.S.2d 578 (1980) (man carrying shopping bag does not justify stop); People v. Lakin, 21 A.D.2d 902, 251 N.Y.S.2d 745 (2d Dept. 1964) (man carrying woman's purse does not justify stop).

D. The Theory of the Case

One important skill of the advocate is that involved in creating a theory of the case. Your theory of the case is the story you tell about the case, and the framework within which you want the court to understand it. A good theory of the case is a theme that will win over your reader, and it will explain all the parts of your Argument.

The theory of the case combines two elements: the legal framework from which you present your client's position, and the facts in your client's "story" that justify relief under that legal framework.[9] It summarizes the reasons why your client deserves to win. For example, the plaintiff's theory in a libel case may stress how the defendant magazine damaged her career and her life by its defamatory story about her, and why there is minimal social value in protecting the magazine and its sleazy practices. The defendant's theory of the case, its defense, will stress first amendment values and the important role the media plays in a democratic society. In an employment discrimination suit, the plaintiff's theory of the case may be that affirmative action for blacks and latinos is necessary to achieve real racial equality, while the defendant company would characterize such relief as reverse discrimination.

In order to develop a theory, you must first become familiar with the facts, and with the controlling law. Think about the possible strategies available to you, and determine which is the strongest and most appealing presentation you can make. Often, you need to know which judges you will be arguing to in order to determine the strategies that work best with that judge.

9. *See* Marilyn J. Berger, et al., *Pretrial Advocacy: Planning, Analysis &* Strategy 18 (1988).

The following chapters explain in detail how to write persuasive trial and appellate briefs.

III. Principles of Style

A. Achieving Tone

The tone of your brief should reflect the serious responsibility that you have assumed as your client's advocate. You are not going to place that client at risk by irritating the court with flippancy, informality, or hysterical overstatement. Nor are you going to lecture the judges by telling them what they must or must not do. Therefore, you should avoid imperative sentences, since it is inappropriate to issue commands to a judge. You should also avoid being belittling or sarcastic, especially in regard to other judges. You may say that the judge below misapplied the law, or found the facts incorrectly, or reached an incorrect decision, but you should say it respectfully. In addition, avoid using exclamation points or italics. Your readers will more readily believe what you say if you sound reasonable.

To be persuasive, you need to sound objective, preserving at least the appearance of calm neutrality about the facts of the case, but revealing a firm concern and determination that no miscarriage of justice occurs. You want to impress upon the court the thought you have given to your client's problem, your commitment to your client's representation, and your respect for the court. In other words, you want to exhibit candor, conviction, and intelligence to serve your persuasive purpose and achieve an ethical appeal.

Tone in large measure results from the interplay between diction (word choice) and attitude. Irony is a clear example of this interplay in that the words convey a message belied by the speaker's tone of voice. Lacking tone of voice in the written medium, you can convey tone by skillful use of diction, juxtaposition (or context), and syntax (sentence structure).

B. Diction

Diction is a basic means of conveying attitude or tone. Many words have both explicit and implicit meanings. Select words on the basis of both their denotation (their explicit meaning or stipulated properties) and their connotation (their implicit meaning or overtones that have evolved from usage). To refer to a person as an informant, for example, is far more neutral than to label that person a snitch, which connotes double-dealing and self-interest. If you use the term "snitch" throughout your brief, however, a court might infer that the defendant's feelings about informants are largely your own. To suggest the unsavory character of the victim once might be productive; to hammer away at it might be counter-productive.

Pay particular attention to verbs because they, without a lot of embellishment, immediately and forcefully characterize an action. "Ogling" connotes a lasciviousness that "staring" does not capture. "Jab" minimizes an action that "wallop" maximizes. Because you want your prose to move, let your verbs, not only your adjectives, describe.

Certainly, an adjective or adverb is sometimes in order. In this regard, note that one apt adjective is often preferable to a series of them because it focuses the reader on the most telling detail. It is enough to know someone was accosted by a man screaming racial epithets. To add they were bigoted, insulting, and demeaning is unnecessary. If the adjectives do not materially refine the point, they dilute the impact of any given description. Understatement is, therefore, often more forceful than overstatement because of its bare concentration on the essential. It also acknowledges your readers' abilities to grasp your point while allowing them to draw their own conclusions. Out of a similar respect, you should avoid using qualifiers and intensifiers (very, clearly, possibly, absolutely) since insistence without substance is more irritating than persuasive. For example, to say simply that "this case arises from a tragedy," can be more forceful than "this case arises from a tragedy of a truly and clearly terrible magnitude."

C. *Context*

Context and juxtaposition are other good ways to establish tone. Instead of stridently denouncing testimony as incredible, juxtapose conflicting statements and calmly remark on their discrepancy. Similarly, you can juxtapose an opposing argument with facts or precedents that cast doubt on its validity or applicability. In the following example, the prosecution marshals a series of facts to undermine defense counsel's contention that there was insufficient proof that defendant intended to cause damage to the building, an element of second degree arson.

> In October 1989, Dick Terney ignited five separate fires on a sofa cushion and on the mattress on which Beth Lot's body was lying and then fled from the building, leaving the blaze to consume all of the mattress, to char Lot's body beyond recognition as a human being, to create an opaque wall of thick, black smoke from floor to ceiling inside the apartment, and to generate heat intense enough to deteriorate the bedroom door. Yet the defense contends the evidence is not legally sufficient to prove beyond a reasonable doubt that Terney intended to

damage the building and not simply to destroy his girl friend's body.

D.   *Sentence Structure*

The principles of good English sentence structure set forth in Chapter Ten and Appendix A apply to persuasive writing. Particularly important are those principles which promote clear and affirmative expression.

1.   Active voice is more forceful than passive voice. Active voice points the finger ("The defendant held Ms. White at gunpoint"). However, use passive voice to deemphasize the actor in the sentence ("Ms. White was held at gun point"). Also use passive voice when you want to direct your reader to the facts ("Acting as an arm of the prosecution, hindering the presentation of the defense, and giving unconstitutional jury instructions are all acts of judicial misconduct"), and to promote continuity between sentences ("The plaintiff supported his evidence with a 1996 study of environmental hazards. This environmental study was conducted in three counties.")

2.   Affirmative sentences are more dynamic than negative sentences.

3.   Shorter sentences adequately related to each other are preferable to longer sentences. They flow more fluidly. Long sentences slow the reader down if they contain a series of interrupting phrases or clauses that separate the subject and predicate. However, a series of short, staccato sentences can be abrupt and choppy.

4.   Transitional sentences or phrases should be used so that your reader can clearly comprehend the logical development of your argument.

5.   Rhetorical questions should be avoided. They raise questions that you should answer explicitly.

E.   *Quotations*

Whenever you use language that is not your own, quote the language exactly, place the words within quotation marks, and cite the source of the quotation. Failure to do so is plagiarism. Whenever a quotation is fifty words or more, use a block quotation, that is, indent and single space the quote and do not use quotation marks. Place the citation as the first nonindented text after the quotation.

Be selective in choosing quotations. Use them principally for statutory language and statements of the rule of a case or cases, or for particularly apt language that you cannot equal yourself. When you do quote an authority, do not immediately just repeat it in your own words. Instead, tell the reader how the quotation relates to

your point. If the quotation is long, however, you help your reader
if you forecast its essential point.

Do not employ quotations where you can convey that information just as well or better in your own words. It is often difficult to
integrate quotations smoothly, and even if this is done successfully,
differences in style may be distracting. Moreover, too many quotations will slow the flow of your argument, and a reader may decide
to overlook them. A reader might also ignore a lengthy quotation
because the quotation is visually oppressive. Try, therefore, to use
your own words, but be sure to supply a citation to the source. (See
Appendix A, section B for further information on quotation.)

Chapter Seventeen

The Trial Brief:
Memorandum of Law in Support of
or in Opposition to a Motion

I. Introduction

When you have a case before a trial court, it is often necessary or advisable for you to file one or more motions with the court. A motion is a request to the court for a ruling on a legal question. The court will respond to a motion with a ruling called an order. You may make the motion on your own initiative or the court may request that all parties file memoranda on a legal question that has arisen in the course of litigation. Motions are usually accompanied by 1) a "notice of motion" which will notify the other side that a motion has been filed, 2) a memorandum of law which supports the motion,[1] and 3) a proposed order (a ruling in your favor which the judge could sign). Supporting documents, like affidavits (a person's written statements either sworn to or affirmed), may also be appropriate. The attorney opposing the motion will submit a memorandum in opposition to the motion.

Attorneys make motions at many different stages of litigation. You will probably discuss these motions in your Civil Procedure class. Motions may be made before trial, during the trial, or post-trial. The plaintiff's attorney may file a motion for a preliminary

---

1. Some attorneys combine the motion with the supporting statements, known as a speaking motion, and do not file a separate supporting memorandum.

injunction at the same time that the complaint is filed. The defendant's attorney may respond to the complaint with a motion to dismiss the complaint for failure to state a claim. If the case proceeds, the plaintiff's attorney may move for certification of a class. Either party's attorney may move for summary judgment. Either attorney may move to compel discovery, or move for a directed verdict[2] at the close of the evidence offered by an opponent at trial. Finally, a party who has lost after a trial may move for a new trial or to alter or amend the judgment.

II. *The Essentials of a Memorandum of Law*

In this section we describe a particular type of trial brief, the memorandum of law in support of or in opposition to a motion, especially those filed with motions to dismiss and motions for summary judgment. When you write this type of memorandum, you need to think especially about how to be responsive to your audience, to the rules that govern the motion, and to the purpose of the motion.

A. *Audience*

The primary audience for these memoranda is a trial judge,[3] who is an extremely busy person and who may not have a law clerk. Therefore you need to make your point and make it quickly. At the stage of these motions, most judges will not be familiar with the case and the particular area of the law involved, and will look to your memo for explanations. Besides being very busy, most trial judges share other characteristics. For example, they are bound to follow the precedents of that jurisdiction, and they want you to tell them, reliably and clearly, what those precedents are. The judges also want to reach a fair result. You have the opportunity to influence their sense of fairness by how you present your facts and your legal arguments. Another characteristic is that most judges do not like to be reversed. Thus, you must convince the court that you have strong arguments on your side. And judges are lawyers, often successful lawyers. They have developed questioning minds and healthy skepticism. Thus, you must carefully support what you write.

When you are in practice, you will learn the individual characteristics of the judges that you come before. In your first year of law school, however, the role of the judge is usually filled by the legal writing faculty.

---

2. The Federal Rules of Civil Procedure, Rule 50(a), now calls this motion a Motion for Judgment as a Matter of Law.

3. The audience is also the opposing party, who will look carefully for flaws in your memo.

B. Governing Rules

The memorandum should include the technical standards by which the court judges the motion. For example, under Fed. R. Civ. P. 56, a federal district court judge will grant a motion for summary judgment if there are no genuine issues of material fact and the moving party is entitled to judgment as a matter of law. The memorandum should include these requirements. You should also include the case law within each jurisdiction imposing additional requirements; for example, the court must resolve ambiguities and draw reasonable inferences in favor of the party opposing the motion. When you analyze your case, it is important to remember that the court is going to review the facts from this perspective.

C. Purpose of the Motion

Next, the substance of the memorandum must be responsive to the type of motion it supports or opposes. For example, a defendant files a motion to dismiss in response to the complaint, so this motion is decided very early in the litigation. It challenges the legal sufficiency of the complaint. The defendant must accept as true the facts alleged in the complaint, so the memorandum will not challenge the accuracy of those facts. Instead, the defendant wants to show that under no state of facts and no interpretation of the law can this plaintiff be entitled to relief. For example, if the plaintiff is the legal representative of a minor who claims loss of consortium of a parent, the defendant will argue that no interpretation of the facts regarding his negligence would permit the plaintiff to succeed, because that jurisdiction recognizes only the loss of consortium of a spouse.

Because a motion to dismiss responds to a complaint, the defendant's memo sets out the plaintiff's claims in that complaint. If the complaint includes more than one claim, organized by counts, the defendant's memo sets out each count of the complaint and identifies the count or counts at which the motion is directed. Each count should be placed under a separate heading of the memo.

Another common motion is the motion for summary judgment, which may be submitted by either party. This motion is submitted after the pleadings are filed and the parties have developed the facts, for example, through discovery and affidavits. A successful motion will dispose of the case or a part of the case obviating the need for a trial. A memorandum in support of or opposition to this motion also must explain the plaintiff's claims as set out in the complaint, and the count or counts towards which the motion is directed.

Because the motion can be granted only if there are no disputed material facts, an important part of the moving party's memorandum is to show why the material facts are not disputed. The party opposing the motion, of course, will try to show that there are disputed material facts. The party weaves a narrative that shows the facts are either disputed or undisputed, identifies the relevant facts of record from sources such as depositions, and cites to the record. For example, a defendant employer in an Americans With Disabilities Act (ADA) case may move for summary judgment on the ground that the company did not have to provide the disabled plaintiff her requested accommodation. Under the ADA, an employer must reasonably accommodate only known disabilities of the plaintiff and the parties must engage in what the courts call "an interactive process" to determine those accommodations. The defendant would claim that it did not know of the plaintiff's disability at the relevant time. The defendant's memorandum in support of its motion will garner all the facts that are learned from discovery and affidavits relevant to show that it did not know of the plaintiff's disability. The plaintiff's memorandum will do the same to contradict the defendant's memorandum and emphasize facts that show that the defendant knew the plaintiff was disabled. If the memos reveal disputed facts on that question, the court will deny the motion so that the issue will be resolved at trial. The parties will do the same for the facts regarding whether the parties engaged in an interactive process. Many courts require the parties to list the disputed and the undisputed facts in their memoranda.

The moving party must also show that it is entitled to judgment as a matter of law. Thus in this section of their memoranda, the parties' legal arguments will apply the ADA as interpreted in that circuit to the facts of the case. This requires building arguments in the ways explained in Chapter Eleven, on arguing questions of law, and in Chapter Eighteen, on argument in a brief.

A last point that applies to memoranda also applies to all your work: avoid insults to opposing counsel and outlandish statements about the quality of that person's work. You will gain no points with the court with those tactics. And, of course, never insult the judge.

III. *Format of a Memorandum in Support of or in Opposition to a Motion*

The remainder of this chapter explains a suggested format of a memorandum of law. In the following chapter we explain appellate briefs. Much of the information in the next chapter is also relevant to writing these memoranda.

Although there is no required format for the memorandum of law, courts generally require that the moving party set forth both the grounds for the motion with citation to supporting authorities, and the specific relief sought. Memoranda may be divided into the following sections: the Caption and Title, the Introduction, the Statement of Facts, the Question(s) Presented, the Argument, the Conclusion, and any supporting affidavits or appendices.

A. Caption and Title

The first page of a memorandum contains at a glance the basic information about the case: the caption includes the name of the court, the names of the parties, the docket number, and the initials of the judge to whom the case has been assigned. It also includes the title of the memorandum in support of or in opposition to the motion. The cover page of the memorandum will usually contain the same information along with the name, address, and phone number of the attorney. A sample caption and title follows.

IN THE UNITED STATES DISTRICT COURT FOR THE
SOUTHERN DISTRICT OF NEW YORK

JANE SMITH, JOAN JONES,	)	
and MARY DOE, individually	)	
and on behalf of all others similarly	)	
situated,	)	94 Civ. 284
Plaintiffs,	)	(M.R.W.)
-against-	)	
	)	
CONSOLIDATED ELECTRIC	)	
CORP.,	)	
Defendant	)	

MEMORANDUM OF LAW IN SUPPORT OF
PLAINTIFFS' MOTION FOR DETERMINATION OF THE CLASS

B. Introduction

An Introduction is designed to provide a context for the motion and to provide the court with basic information about the case. The Introduction should at least identify the kind of case, the parties, the nature of the motion, the relief sought, and the reason. The court must be told the complete procedural history of the case, which can be in the Introduction or in a Statement of Facts. The Introduction to a memorandum in opposition to a motion would explain in one or two sentences why each basis of the moving party's motion should fail.

The following is a sample Introduction to a Memorandum in Support of a Plaintiffs' Motion to Certify a Class.

Plaintiffs Jane Smith, Joan Jones, and Mary Doe sued defendant Consolidated Electric Corporation alleging discrimination in employment on the grounds of sex in violation of Title VII of the Civil Rights Act of 1964, as amended, 42 U.S.C. § 2000e et seq. (1988). This memorandum of law is submitted in support of plaintiffs' motion pursuant to Rule 23(c)(1) of the Federal Rules of Civil Procedure for an order:

> (a) allowing this action to be maintained as a class action pursuant to Rules 23(a) and 23(b)(2) of the Federal Rules of Civil Procedure, and
>
> (b) defining the class represented by plaintiffs as all female employees of Consolidated Electric Corporation who have unsuccessfully sought or who, but for the discriminatory acts and practices of the defendant, would have sought management positions with Consolidated Electric Corporation.

The party opposing the motion might write the following Introduction.

> This suit is brought under Title VII of the Civil Rights Act of 1964, as amended, 42 U.S.C. § 2000(e) et seq. (1994). Plaintiffs allege that Consolidated Electric Corp. discriminated in violation of the Act. The plaintiffs have moved for certification as a class under Rule 23 (c) (1) of the Federal Rules of Civil Procedure, and for definition of the class. The plaintiffs' motion fails because
>
> (1) the alleged class is not so numerous that it is impracticable to join all members (Rule 23 (a) (1)),
>
> (2) there are no questions of law and fact common to the alleged class (Rule 23 (a) (2)),
>
> (3) the plaintiffs' claims are not typical of the claims and defenses of the class they allege (Rule 23 (a) (3)), and
>
> (4) the plaintiffs cannot fairly and adequately represent the class they allege (Rule 23 (a) (4)).

Exercise 17–A

Which Introduction to the Memorandum in Support of Defendant's Motion to Dismiss is better and why?

1. The plaintiff filed a complaint on September 1, 1998, alleging that General Corp. discriminated against her in violation of the Americans With Disabilities Act, 42 U.S.C. § 12101 et seq. (ADA or the Act). General Corp. has moved to dismiss, under Fed. R. Civ. P. 12(b)(6). This memorandum is filed in support of that motion.

In Count I, the plaintiff, who is an employee of General Corp. and a diabetic, alleges that she is disabled as defined in § 12102 (2) (A), and that the defendant has not accommodated her disability.

In Count II, plaintiff alleges as an alternative, that she is disabled because General Corp. regarded her as disabled in violation of § 12102 (2) (C) of the Act.

Both counts of the complaint fail to state a claim and should be dismissed. As to Count I, plaintiff is not disabled as defined under § 12102 (2) (A) of the Act because her diabetes is controlled by medication. Count II fails to state a claim because, even if General Corp. regarded her as disabled, under the law of this Circuit, General Corp. is not under a duty to accommodate.

2. This memorandum is filed under Fed. R. Civ. P. 12(b)(6) in support of defendant's motion to dismiss plaintiff's complaint. The plaintiff has no claim under the American With Disabilities Act (ADA or Act), because she is not disabled. Plaintiff has diabetes, which is controlled by her medication. Thus, General Corp. does not have to accommodate her condition. Moreover, General Corp. has not regarded her as disabled and even if it did, it does not owe her the duty to accommodate in this Circuit.

Thus the court should dismiss the complaint for failure to state a claim.

Exercise 17–B

Evaluate the following Introductions.

1. Memorandum of Law in Support of Defendants' Motion for Summary Judgment:

Introduction

Come now the defendants by their counsel with their motion for summary judgment. Pursuant to the order of this Court entered July 28, 1997, defendants/counterclaim-plaintiffs Tonetic, Inc. and Dr. Steven Nickel (collectively referred to hereinafter as defendants) submit this Memorandum of Law in further support of their motion seeking dismissal of all of plaintiff's copyright infringement claims on the grounds that, inter alia, in accordance with prior rulings by the Court of Appeals for the Second Circuit, plaintiff's description of defendants' software is too vague and insufficient to provide a basis for any injunctive and/or monetary recovery.

2. Memorandum of Law in Support of Motion of Defendant Pressman, Inc. to Dismiss for Forum Non Conveniens or in the Alternative to Transfer Venue:

Introduction

In a classic example of vexatious litigation, plaintiff Davis Corporation has filed this action in California—purportedly based on tort and contract claims that arose in Illinois, will be decided solely by reference to Illinois law, and has little or no connection to California—in a blatant attempt to bully the defendant Pressman, Inc. into dropping or compromising its previously-filed collection action in Illinois state court. Davis Corp. is thwarted by the facts, however, which demonstrate that the Central District of California is not the proper forum for this lawsuit and that the action must be dismissed or, in the alternative, transferred to the Northern District of Illinois, a more appropriate forum for deciding this controversy.

C. *Statement of Facts*

The Statement of Facts usually includes the procedural history of the case as it relates to the motion and the relevant facts. Keep two main points in mind as you write it. First, because the court is dealing with many different matters and cannot be expected to be familiar with the facts of your case, you must provide this information. Second, because you are looking for a favorable ruling, you want to present the facts of your case in such a way that the court will be inclined to decide the motion in your favor.

If your Memorandum contains an Introduction, you will need to decide which information should be provided in the Introduction and which in the Statement of Facts. The procedural history in the discrimination claim mentioned above could be written as follows:

Statement of Facts

On February 21, 1998, plaintiffs Jane Smith, Joan Jones, and Mary Doe filed a complaint individually and on behalf of others similarly situated challenging a course of conduct by defendant Consolidated Electric Corporation. Plaintiffs alleged that the defendant discriminated on the basis of sex in the terms and conditions of employment relating to hiring and promotion for management positions.

Plaintiffs have moved for certification as a class pursuant to Fed. R. Civ. P. 23.

After the procedural history, you would present the facts of the case that support your motion. To do this effectively, you must be familiar with the legal standards that govern the motion that you are bringing. A class action motion in federal court, for example, is governed by Rule 23. This Rule outlines certain prerequisites for class certification, including the requirements in Rule 23(a) that

(1) the class is so numerous that joinder of all members is impracticable, (2) there are questions of law and fact common to the class, (3) the claims or defenses of the parties are typical of the claims or defenses of the class, and (4) the representative parties will fairly and adequately represent the interests of the class.

Therefore, you would include facts that support the requirements of numerosity, commonality, typicality, and representativeness. These facts would likely come from pleadings, discovery documents (interrogatories and depositions), and affidavits, which you should cite. In the sex discrimination case, for example, you could include facts showing that the class is so numerous that joinder of all members of the class would be impracticable because Consolidated Electric has offices in five different states and because more than 80 women are potential members of the class.

In addition to the legal standard, you should think of how you can present the facts in a way that would be most convincing. Although it is inappropriate in the Statement of Facts to adopt an argumentative tone, it is still possible to arrange facts and choose words in such a way that they incline the court to see the case and the motion from your perspective. More detailed suggestions on writing a Statement of Facts are contained in section IV of Chapter Eighteen.

Exercise 17–C

1. Rewrite sentences (a) and (b) as the criminal defendant's lawyer to use more vivid language. Rewrite sentence (c) as the plaintiff's lawyer.

    a. The policeman stood in between the defendant and his car.

    b. He was experiencing fear of imminent harm to himself from his father.

    c. At the age of seven years, the plaintiff was involved in an automobile accident, being hit by a car, which resulted in the loss of use of his leg.

2. Read the following list of facts from a case involving the claim of a biological father for a hearing to prevent his nonmarital child from being placed for adoption. The standard for determining the father's right to a hearing is whether the father had established a relationship with the child or a family unit including the child.

The Facts

_____ Frank Rock and Mary Hall met in 1987

_____ Frank and Mary lived together 1990–92

_____ Baby born 1992

_____ Mary told people, including welfare office, that Frank was the father

_____ Frank visited Mary in hospital, after baby's birth

_____ Frank did not know where Mary and child were after Mary left hospital

_____ Frank never supported baby

_____ Mary married

_____ Frank found Mary in 1994 by hiring a detective

_____ Mary did not permit Frank to visit the baby

_____ Mary and husband filed petition for adoption Dec. 1994

_____ Frank filed petition to establish paternity Jan. 1995

Write a Statement of the Facts of one or two paragraphs for a memorandum of law for Frank, supporting his petition for a hearing, and then write one in opposition to Frank's claim (for the state agency).

D. Question Presented (Statement of Issues)

Some memoranda of law include a section in which the attorney states the legal questions that the motion raises. A memorandum could have one or more Questions Presented. This section could either precede or follow the Statement of Facts, or come at the end of an Introduction, or be omitted altogether.

The Question should both focus the court's attention on the basic issues in your motion and suggest an answer that would support a decision by the court in your favor. The Question combines the relevant facts of a case and a legal rule. For example, a person seeking to intervene in an action in federal court pursuant to Fed. R. Civ. P. 24 must make a "timely application". Therefore, one ground on which to oppose a motion to intervene is that the motion was not timely. A Question Presented raising this issue could be stated as follows:

> Is the agency's motion to intervene timely when it was made more than three years after the action was commenced and almost ten months after the judgment was entered?

To intervene as of right pursuant to Fed. R. Civ. P. 24(a)(2), an applicant must also show a legally protectable interest. A party opposing the motion could state the following:

> Did a preliminary injunction remedying racial discrimination against non-whites create a legally protectable interest, within the meaning of Fed. R. Civ. P. 24(a)(2), for white persons who seek to intervene as plaintiffs to obtain union membership for themselves?

The question in both of these examples focuses on a legal issue that the court must consider in deciding whether to grant or deny the motion (timeliness, legally protectable interest) and is framed in such a way that the attorney's argument is clear. More detailed suggestions on writing a Question Presented can be found in section III of Chapter Eighteen.

Exercise 17–D

Write a Question Presented for a memorandum for Frank Rock and one for the state opposing Frank's petition.

E.   *Argument*

The Argument is the heart of your memorandum. In it you provide the facts, citations to authority, and reasoning to convince the court to rule in your favor on the motion. The Argument is often divided into sections representing the main legal arguments or the counts in the plaintiff's complaint, although a short memorandum may have only one basic argument.

Each section of the Argument usually begins with a point heading that states the conclusion that you want the court to reach on that legal point. The point heading is a conclusory sentence that combines the facts of the case with the legal principles analyzed in that section. The headings help the court find your arguments and tell the court what your point is.

Example:

> All Counts of the Complaint Must Be Dismissed Because the Communications Complained of Are not Defamatory Per Se.

The heading should be followed with a thesis paragraph that tells the court the conclusion you want it to reach (the complaint should be dismissed) and why. If your motion is based on a rule that is divided into required elements, then you may have a separate section in your memorandum for each of these elements. As noted in the section on the Statement of Facts, a plaintiff who wishes to bring a class action must satisfy all four requirements of Rule 23(a). It may be appropriate, then, to discuss each requirement in a separate section.

As to the order of arguments, you should begin with any threshold arguments. Then, if the claim is defined by elements, as in certification of a class, discuss each in the order of the definition. If not, then begin with the strongest argument supporting your position on the motion.

Make your arguments affirmatively as an advocate, use persuasive language and remember to interweave the facts of the case with the legal points. Extensive suggestions on writing an Argument are contained in Chapter Eighteen.

Exercise 17–E

1. Assume you are representing an employee-at-will. An employee-at-will can be fired at any time for any or no reason. Rewrite the following statement so that it is more persuasive.

> Although the Pennsylvania Supreme Court has never held there is an exception to the employment-at-will doctrine, the lower courts have recognized a limited exception to the doctrine when an employer's discharge violates a clear mandate of public policy.

2. Assume you represent two children in a loss of parental consortium claim (loss of intangibles like love, companionship, solace). Rewrite the following argument so that it is affirmative.

> In all but thirteen jurisdictions that have recently considered the issue, children cannot sue for loss of parental consortium.

3. Assuming you want an exception to the statute of limitations to apply, phrase more effectively.

> While a mere post-traumatic neurosis is not enough to toll the statute, a "post-traumatic depression" coupled with "severe depressive reaction" has been held to constitute the requisite insanity that tolls the statute of limitations.

4. Assuming you want to invoke an exception to government immunity from liability, phrase more persuasively.

> Generally a municipality is not liable to an individual for failing to provide police protection. However, there is an exception if the police

assume a "special relationship" or "special duty" towards an individual.

F. *Conclusion*

The Conclusion is a brief statement, often one sentence, reminding the court of the relief you are seeking. It is often followed by a phrase like "Respectfully submitted," and then by the signature and name, address, and telephone number of the attorney of record. For example,

> For the foregoing reasons, plaintiff's motion for preliminary injunction should be granted.

Respectfully submitted,

Attorney's Name
Attorney's address
Attorney's phone number

Attorney for Plaintiff Jane Doe

Chapter Eighteen
Writing the Appellate Brief

I. Introduction

The purpose of an appellate brief is to convince a court to grant relief to your client for the issues on appeal by affirming or reversing the decision of the court below. Thus, your task as a brief writer is to present persuasively those arguments and that evidence which would convince a court that your client's position is the only one that comports with law and justice and that the lower court or courts either correctly or incorrectly decided the case. An appeal is not a re-trying of a case. Appellate courts do not hear evidence in the case as do trial courts. Rather, an appellate court's review is typically limited to a review of the trial court's decision to determine whether, based on the record of the evidence, the court below committed error in hearing or deciding the case. The function of the appellant's attorney is to search the record to determine what errors the trial court may have committed, to select the issues that have the best chance of convincing an appellate court to reverse the decision below, and to shape the arguments as convincingly as possible. The primary function of the appellee's attorney is to argue in favor of affirming the judgment below and to rebut the appellant's arguments.

A. Selecting Issues for Appeal

Usually, the first step in preparing an appeal is to review the record closely and research the law carefully in order to narrow the issues to those that are truly arguable. Because you want your brief to be credible, you need to avoid making both frivolous claims and too many claims. As the Supreme Court has observed, "a brief which treats more than three or four matters runs serious risks of becoming too diffuse and giving the overall impression that no one claim of error can be serious." Jones v. Barnes, 463 U.S. 745, 752 n.5 (1983).[1] In the Court's estimation, if you cannot win on the merits of your stronger points, you will not win on your weaker points; an attorney should, therefore, winnow out the weaker arguments. Id. at 751–52.[2] In the first-year legal writing courses, the issues may have been selected for you by your teachers. You should be aware nonetheless of some of the considerations that go into selecting issues for appeal.

For a real appeal, you would begin by reading the record to get a feel for the case.[3] Since the facts surrounding each legal issue give rise to initial impressions about your client's claims, appraise the record first from this viewpoint. Read carefully the decision appealed from. Also examine as possible grounds for appeal each motion or objection made by trial counsel and decided adversely to your client. Then try to grasp the trial counsel's and the opposing counsel's theories of the case. After this, research the legal issues thoroughly.

On the basis of this initial research, begin to plot out your strategy. Ascertain which facts are material, which arguments are consequential (that is, which arguments would give your client the greatest relief, like a dismissal of charges), and which arguments are persuasive (that is, which are likely to convince a court to rule in your favor but which will not necessarily give your client the same degree of relief, like a new trial or a modified sentence). After you identify those arguments for which there is a basis of appeal, decide which combination of persuasive and consequential arguments would most help your client. You have now, at least tentatively, selected your issues.

B. *Standard of Review*

An attorney must also consider the standard of review that is appropriate to each case. The standard of review that an appellate

---

1. Quoting the Committee on Federal Courts of the Association of the Bar of New York, Appeals to the Second Circuit 38 (1980).

2. Note also that the Code of Professional Responsibility, DR–102A(1), says, "A lawyer shall not bring or defend a proceeding, or assert or controvert an issue therein, unless there is a basis for doing so that is not frivolous, which includes a good faith argument for an extension, modification or reversal of existing law." See also Model Rules of Professional Conduct, Rule 3.1.

3. The suggestions offered here are paraphrased from William E. Hellerstein, "Appeal to Intermediate Appellate Courts," in Basic Criminal Law Practice (1985).

court uses will depend on a number of factors, including the court itself (federal, state, intermediate appellate, highest appellate), the nature of the case (civil, criminal), and the type of error alleged. It is important, though not always easy, for the attorney to determine the appropriate standard of review. The standards of review cover a wide range:[4]

- review of questions of law

    An appellate court does not have to defer to the trial court's decision on a question of law and can decide the issue de novo (without regard to the lower court's determination).

    E.g., Can an unmarried cohabitant sue for loss of consortium?

    Did a school board violate its students' first amendment rights by denying them access to their high school for meetings after school?

- review of questions of fact

a) jury trials–

    An appellate court will give great deference to a jury verdict and will generally not reverse that verdict. In civil cases, a jury verdict will be reversed only if it is unsupported by any evidence. If the verdict is supported by some evidence, however, to get appellate review of the weight or the sufficiency of the evidence, the attorney must have made a timely motion below. In criminal cases, the verdict will be set aside if the appellate court determines that no rational jury could have found the elements of the crime beyond a reasonable doubt.

b) trials by the court

    Findings of fact made by a trial court are also given significant deference, though not as great as that given jury verdicts. Under the Federal Rules of Civil Procedure Rule 52(a), for example, a federal trial court's findings of fact will not be set aside unless they are "clearly erroneous."

    E.g., Was the trial court's finding that the promotions were not the result of discriminatory intent clearly erroneous?

- review of mixed questions of law and fact

4. The categories were taken from the discussion of the Standard of Review in Ursula Bentele and Eve Cary, Appel-late Advocacy Principles and Practice: Cases and Materials 84–187 (3d ed. 1998).

The standard of review is difficult to characterize because the courts have not adopted a single approach as to whether these questions should be treated more like questions of law or questions of fact.

E.g., Was the plaintiff constructively discharged from his job?

● discretion of the trial court

Trial courts have discretion to determine certain issues. For example, many statutes give the trial judge discretion to award attorneys' fees. A discretionary decision by the trial court may be reversed for abuse of the discretion, for improvident exercise of the discretion, or for a failure to exercise discretion. The extent of the trial court's discretion will depend on the matter at issue.

E.g., Did the trial court abuse its discretion in denying the plaintiff back pay in an employment discrimination suit?

In analyzing your case and in writing your brief, you should include a reference to the appropriate standard of review, and, if necessary, an argument as to the correct standard. The standard of review that the appellate court uses can determine the outcome of the case. Therefore, in writing an appellate brief, the attorney should be aware of the strength of the issues not simply in terms of the merits, but also in terms of how likely the appellate court is to reverse the trial court's decision.

C. *Choosing Arguments in Support of an Issue*

Once you have decided which issues to appeal and the standard of review that applies, you must decide which arguments to raise in support of your claims. Usually your research will suggest the legal arguments and the policy arguments you ought to put forward. Limit your brief to your best arguments. When considering your options, be careful not to raise contradictory, inconsistent claims. You can argue, for example, that a court improperly denied a request for an adjournment because, although trial counsel exercised due diligence, he was unable to interview a key witness who was in the hospital. If you make this point, however, you cannot also argue that a court improperly denied a request for an adjournment because a key witness was never interviewed due to ineffective counsel who failed to exercise due diligence.

Also, consider whether raising an argument in the alternative is strategically appropriate. Alternative arguments are common tools of an attorney, and are appropriate when your client could materially benefit from the alternative argument. Assume, for example, that a child defendant in a negligence suit was held to an adult standard of reasonable care because the child was engaged in an adult activity. On appeal, you might argue first that the lower court applied the wrong standard because an exception to the rule applied. Under that exception, very young children can be held to a child's standard regardless of their participation in an adult activity. You would go on to show that your client is not liable under the child's standard of reasonable care. Then, if you think the facts would warrant a reversal even under the adult standard, it would be appropriate to raise this as an alternative argument.

D. *Ordering Issues*

After selecting your issues, you must decide how to order them. Generally, a brief follows the order of importance, that is, you begin with the most persuasive and consequential argument and move in a descending order down to the least important argument. There are two primary reasons for organizing your brief this way. First, the realities are such that a judge might not read your entire brief; in order to ensure that your most important argument will at least be read, you will want to put it in a prominent place in the brief. Second, by beginning with your most important argument, you set a positive tone for your brief as well as establishing yourself as a serious, credible, and thoughtful advocate. Of course, to organize a brief in order of importance, you must determine which of your arguments is the most important. Logic and strategy must be considered.

Strategy involves weighing the merits of your most persuasive argument (that which is most likely to succeed) against the merits of arguments affording your client greater relief. You must come to a realistic decision about whether your client is best served by beginning with the most persuasive argument or with the most consequential. When your arguments are of unequal strength, most attorneys advise beginning with your most persuasive argument, i.e., that argument which has the greatest chance of success based on the law and the facts. When your arguments are of comparable weight, however, most attorneys advise that you begin with your most consequential argument, i.e., the one which will most benefit your client. Common sense dictates that if you can argue a point that will give your client substantial relief as convincingly as a point that gives less relief, you begin with the argument that has greater consequences.

There may be times, of course, when you wish to depart from these established conventions. If, for example, your most persuasive argument really will not materially assist your client, you might decide to begin with the argument which would most benefit your client. You might also consider whether your client has expressed a strong preference for one argument, or whether the court to which you are appealing is more receptive to one kind of legal argument than another. An intermediate court of appeals, for example, would probably be more receptive to a fact-centered or doctrinal argument. A state supreme court, however, might be more open to a policy-centered argument (one which focuses on the purpose of the rule and the desirability of the end) or to an institutionally-directed argument (one which focuses on whether a legislative body or a court should create a rule).

Strategy is not the only factor in ordering your issues. You must also consider logic. Discuss threshold issues before other issues. Threshold questions–involving, for example, jurisdiction or a statute of limitations–take logical priority over other issues because the court's decision with respect to the former may obviate and preclude the court from considering the latter. If you have interdependent issues such that one question must be resolved before another question can be meaningfully addressed, logic dictates that you treat the initial question before the dependent question. For example, a decision must be rendered on whether a party consented to a search before an argument can be made about whether that party revoked consent.

Other problems will present you with different types of legal questions, for example, a constitutional and a statutory question. Barring special considerations, you would deal with the statutory question first and the constitutional question second. For example, a state sodomy statute would be scrutinized first for whether the defendant violated the statute. If the defendant did not violate the statute, then the court need not decide whether it is unconstitutional.

The interrelation of some issues might also be a factor in ordering issues. You might decide to shift a persuasive argument into a less prominent position in order to follow one point with discussion of another related point. Assume, for instance, that you have a persuasive argument that the trial judge unduly interfered with the cross-examination, a moderately strong argument that someone was improperly excused for cause during jury selection, and a weak argument that the prosecutor made an inflammatory summation. You might decide to follow the argument on the prejudicial conduct of the judge with the argument on the prejudicial conduct of the prosecutor if the two issues involve similar facts and legal questions.

These, then, are some of the factors you consider in ordering your issues. To check on the order and organization of issues and subissues, many people prepare an outline, which helps to clarify the logical relationships among ideas (rules of outlining are discussed in the section on Point Headings). Once you have decided upon an order, make sure your Questions Presented, Point Headings, and Arguments adhere to that order.

II.   *Format of an Appellate Brief: Introductory Information*

A.   **Title Page**

The Title Page is the outside front cover of your brief. At the top of the page you identify the court to which the case is being appealed and provide the index number to your case. The Title Page also includes the name of the Appellant and Appellee and may identify the Plaintiff and Defendant below. Under this information, you name the court from which the case is being appealed, the party whose brief this is, and the name and address of the attorney representing that party.

B.   **Table of Contents**

The Table of Contents should contain page references for each section of your brief, including the other introductory tables. These sections usually include the following:

Table of Authorities

Question Presented

Statement of the Case

Summary of Argument

Argument

Conclusion

Appendix (if any)

In addition, the Table of Contents includes the point headings (and subheadings, if any) for the sections in the Argument. The outline of the point headings gives the court a quick summary of the content of the Argument and permits the court to find the page at which any particular point begins. Type the headings in the Argument in upper case; type the subheadings in upper and lower case, indented and underlined.

C.   **Table of Authorities**

In the Table of Authorities, you provide page references in your brief for the authorities you relied on in the Argument. Ordinarily, you divide the authorities into categories. Put cases in alphabetical order with citations. (If a case is repeatedly cited, use passim instead of a page reference.) Then list the Constitutional and Statutory Provisions and the Administrative Regulations. Other authorities may be put under the heading of Miscellaneous, or you may set out other categories.

Some schools will require that their students' briefs conform to the format required by the Rules of the Supreme Court of the United States. Under these Rules, the brief should also include sections entitled Opinion Below, Jurisdictional Statement, and Constitutional and Statutory Provisions Involved. See Sample Appellate Brief, Appendix F.

III. *Question(s) Presented*

The Question Presented sets out the legal issue that the parties will argue, incorporating the key facts of the case, in order to tell the court what the appeal is about. Like all other parts of the brief, the Question Presented is also intended to persuade the court of the correctness of your client's position. You can use the Question Presented as a way of getting the court to see the issues in the case from your client's point of view by framing the question so that it suggests a response in your favor.

Under most court rules, the Questions Presented must appear at the beginning of the brief. Thus, the Questions Presented are in effect the introduction to your brief and will be the first part that the judges read. The Question or Questions must introduce the case to the court by setting out the legal issues that the parties will argue and by providing a factual context that explains how those issues arose. Rule 14 of the Supreme Court of the United States requires that the questions be "short and concise." They should also be understandable, preferably on first reading.

If your topic contains more than one issue, then you must pose more than one Question. Put your Questions in the order in which they will be argued. Each Question should be written in the same form, either as a statement beginning with "whether" or in question form, beginning, for example, with "may" or "does."

Some suggestions for writing the Questions follow.

A.   The Questions should include a reference to the constitutional provision, statute, or common law cause of action under which the case arises, as in the following example.

> Is the decision by a private nursing home to transfer a patient from a skilled nursing care facility to a health-related facility subject to the procedural requirements of the due process clause of the fourteenth amendment?

This Question identifies the due process clause as the constitutional provision at issue in this case. It tells the Court what the case is about. For a lesser known cause of action, for example, one that arises under a statute, you may want to include the operative statutory language in the Question.

> Did a person violate 18 U.S.C. § 1071, which prohibits harboring or concealing a person for whom a federal warrant has been issued, when, on four occasions, he gave a fugitive money and lied to the authorities about the fugitive's whereabouts?

B.   Unless you are dealing with a pure question of law, the Question should also provide the facts of the case as they relate to the issue. Because a judge must decide each case according to its facts and must apply the established principles of law to those facts, the Question should include some of the factual aspects of the case which gave rise to the legal question. Try, therefore, to avoid "label" or abstract questions that identify the type of action that is before the court but tell nothing about the particular facts of the case, as in the question below.

> Did the police seize the evidence in a search of petitioner's residence that violated his fourth amendment rights?

This Question labels the case as a search and seizure problem, but does not indicate the particular nature of the fourth amendment problem. The sentence could be the issue in almost every fourth amendment case. The writer of this Question should have identified why the police seizure of evidence may have violated the fourth amendment.

> Was the evidence seized in a search of petitioner's residence inadmissible on fourth amendment grounds when petitioner gave his consent to search only after the police officer implied he had legal authority for the search regardless of consent?

Similarly, the nursing home question provides the facts of the case as they relate to the requirements of the fourteenth amendment. When you provide a factual context, you help the court by defining the particular issue your case poses.

Note, however, that appeals based on questions of law (rather than on questions involving application of law to facts) need not include the particular facts that gave rise to the dispute. Instead they should include details about the rule under judicial scrutiny.

> Does a statute violate an advertiser's first amendment right to free speech if it bans the advertisement of tobacco products in places offering "family" oriented entertainment?

Or again, in the question below, it is unnecessary to relate specific facts establishing the child witness's likely trauma if forced to testify in front of the accused because the question is about the constitutionality of the statute, not its applicability to the particular child witness in this trial.

> Is a statute valid under the sixth amendment right of confrontation if it allows a child witness in a sex-offense prosecution to

testify outside of defendant's presence by one-way closed-circuit television when the statute can be applied only upon a showing of individualized, clear, and convincing trauma to the witness?

C.   State the Question as a general principle that would apply to anyone in the particular situation of these parties. One consequence of placing the Questions Presented first is that the reader knows nothing about the parties. Therefore, you should identify the parties by general description rather than by name. In the following example, the appellant is identified as a member of the bar, not as "appellant" or by name.

Do the first and fourteenth amendments protect a member of the bar from disciplinary action when she advises members of an organization of their rights and discloses the price and availability of legal services?

Another consequence of placing the Questions first is that you must avoid general and vague references to facts that the reader has not yet been given, as in the Question below.

Under the circumstances of this case, were the petitioner's fourth amendment rights violated by the manner in which police secured consent?

Instead, flesh out the "circumstances."

Is an individual's consent to a search of his premises coerced and involuntary under the fourth amendment when that consent follows a statement by a law enforcement officer implying legal authority for the search regardless of consent?

D.   Let the Question suggest an answer favorable to your client, but do not overstate your client's case. The Question that follows is overstated and will lose credibility with the court.

Does a person violate 18 U.S.C. § 1071 if he does absolutely nothing to help a fugitive except to let him walk off with a few pieces of old clothing and to feed him to prevent starvation?

Most court rules require that the Question not be argumentative. The Question should, therefore, appear neutral. Probably the best way to write a persuasive Question that is not unduly slanted is to incorporate favorable facts without any shrill commentary on them. For example, a Question that is posed favorably but which is not unduly slanted might be as follows:

Under 18 U.S.C. § 1071, which prohibits harboring a fugitive so as to prevent his discovery, does a person harbor a fugitive by providing him with some worn clothing and an occasional dinner?

Incorporating the facts into the Question ensures a measure of objectivity by telling the court what the parties actually did. In the Question above, the writer suggests the evidence is insufficient to establish a violation of the statute, but the court is given room to come to its own decision.

Some writers disagree with the advice that the Question Presented should be framed to suggest the answer favorable to the client, but instead advise that you formulate the issue so neutrally that the opposing counsel will accept it.[5] The nursing home question would meet this criterion.

E.   Do not usurp the function of the court by coming to conclusions that assume a favorable resolution of legal and factual issues that the court must decide. The underlined phrases in the examples below are improper because they are conclusions of law.

> Did the respondent Disciplinary Commission's reprimand of the petitioner for actions not likely to cause substantial harm violate the petitioner's rights to freedom of expression and association under the first amendment?

> Is the evidence obtained from a warrantless search conducted pursuant to consent inadmissible on fourth amendment grounds where the consent is not voluntarily given and where the search conducted exceeds the scope authorized by that consent?

In these Questions, the author assumes the very point that is at issue: whether the actions were likely to cause substantial harm; whether the consent was voluntary; and whether the search exceeded the scope authorized by that consent.

Be equally careful not to give away your case in the Question by conceding arguments to the opposing party and then trying to recapture them. The following Question does this:

> Whether a search, conducted pursuant to consent by the defendant, is unreasonable merely because it exceeds the bounds of the consent given.

By concluding that the search exceeded the defendant's consent, the writer has conceded that the search was not valid. The word "merely" will not retrieve the lost case.

F.   Although you should not concede an argument, your Question may pose alternative arguments. You may appear to concede a contested point in order to argue the next issue that follows logically from the first point. When you use this sort of alternative argument, you are implicitly saying, "but even if I am wrong on the first point, then the other party still should not prevail because of my arguments on point two." Utilizing this technique, the writer concedes the first point only for the purpose of meeting opposing counsel's next argument.

In the fourth amendment search and seizure problem, for example, the appellant can make an alternative argument: even if

---

5. See, e.g., Robert J. Martineau,   vocacy 145 (1985).
Fundamentals of Modern Appellate Ad-

he did consent to the search initially, he then withdrew that consent. Appellant admits to the consent only for the limited purpose of making his second argument. Such a Question might look as follows:

> Even if the petitioner initially consented to a search, is the evidence obtained from that warrantless search nonetheless inadmissible on fourth amendment grounds because the petitioner withdrew his initial consent to that search?

G. Finally, to make questions readable, keep related ideas together. For example, use the first half of the sentence to pose the legal question. Then use the second half to raise the legally relevant facts. Take particular pains to keep the subject of the sentence near the verb since this type of construction is the easiest to understand. Do not separate the subject of the sentence from the verb with a series of interrupting clauses or modifiers. The following question is hard to comprehend because eighteen words (those modifying the main noun) intervene between the main noun (statute) and the verb.

> Whether a <u>statute</u> allowing a child witness in a sex-offense prosecution to testify outside of defendant's presence by one-way closed-circuit television <u>is</u> valid under the sixth amendment right of confrontation when the statute can be applied only upon a showing of individualized, clear, and convincing trauma to the witness.

The question is more readable if the main noun of the sentence is near the verb, as in our earlier version of this question.

> <u>Is</u> a <u>statute</u> valid under the sixth amendment right of confrontation if it allows a child witness in a sex-offense prosecution to testify outside of defendant's presence by one-way closed-circuit television when the statute can be applied only upon a showing of individualized, clear, and convincing trauma to the witness?

Exercise 18–A

1. The following Questions Presented have been prepared for appellant, Alice Bell. Ms. Bell is suing her husband Alan Bell for civil damages under a federal statute popularly known as the federal wiretapping act or Title III of the Omnibus Crime Control and Safe Streets Act of 1968. Alice Bell claims her husband wiretapped her business telephone. Which is the best Question and why? What is wrong with the other Questions?

    a. Did the trial court err in dismissing Ms. Bell's claim against her husband for damages for using an extension telephone to intercept her private communications without her consent?

    b. Does Title III of the Omnibus Crime Control and Safe Streets Act prohibit the appellee's interception of the appellant's telephone conversations?

    c.   Did the trial court err in dismissing the appellant's claim since her husband's unauthorized actions of intercepting her oral telephone communications are clearly prohibited by Title III of the Omnibus Crime Control and Safe Streets Act and do not come within the exceptions to the Act?

    d.   Does Title III of the Omnibus Crime Control and Safe Streets Act, which prohibits an individual from intercepting any wire or oral communication, provide a cause of action for a wife against her husband who eavesdropped on an extension telephone and secretly recorded her private telephone conversations?

2.   The following Questions Presented have been prepared for Juliet Stone's appeal of the trial court's dismissal of her wrongful life claim against Dr. James Eagle. Juliet Stone is a child who was born with birth defects. Dr. Eagle is the obstetrician. The issue is whether there is a legal remedy for the injuries she has sustained. (For more information, see section VII(E).) Which is the best Question and why? What is wrong with the other Questions?

    a.   Whether infant Juliet Stone may sustain a claim for wrongful life against an obstetrician who negligently failed to inform the infant's parents of the advisability of having an amniocentesis test, thereby depriving them of the choice to abort, when the infant has suffered legally cognizable injuries.

    b.   Whether an infant born with severe congenital birth defects has a legally cognizable claim against her mother's physician.

    c.   Can an infant born with severe birth defects sustain a claim for wrongful life when the obstetrician failed to inform the parents of the risk of Down's Syndrome and the availability of amniocentesis, and thereby deprived them of making an informed choice about terminating the pregnancy?

3.   Assume you are a prosecutor appealing a pre-trial order suppressing evidence of the photographic identification of a robber by the only eyewitness to a bank robbery. The judge had found the photographic identification procedure conducted by the police was (1) "unduly and unnecessarily suggestive" and (2) the identification itself was not "independently reliable." Your student intern has written two versions of the Question Presented. You find one of them conclusory and both of them unpersuasive and unreadable. Using the information they provide, write a persuasive and readable question.

    a.   Whether the court properly suppressed the eyewitness's photographic identification testimony where photographs, each one basically resembling the others, were shown to the witness from which she identified the accused as the perpetrator of the crime without any influence from the police officer, and where during the course of the crime, the witness, who had an excellent opportunity to view the criminal, attentively observed the criminal for about a minute in strong light, thus enabling her to give a detailed description of the criminal that closely resembles the accused, on the ground that the procedure was unduly and unnecessarily suggestive and the identification itself was unreliable.

b.   Whether the pretrial photographic identification was unnecessarily and impermissibly suggestive when, weighing the various factors which affected the reliability of the witness's description of the perpetrator against the level of suggestiveness of the photographic procedure, there does not exist, in light of the totality of the circumstances, a substantial likelihood of irreparable misidentification, given the facts that the witness, although terrified, had seen the robber at close quarters and the officer's only comment after she tentatively identified the defendant's photo was that she was "doing just fine, a good job."

IV.   *The Statement of the Case*

Few attorneys dispute the importance of the Statement of the Case. The Statement is your opportunity to focus only on the facts and to present your client's version of those facts so convincingly that a court is ready to rule in your client's favor even before reading the Argument.

The Statement of the Case frequently includes two components: an opening paragraph and a Statement of Facts. The opening paragraph, often called the Preliminary Statement, includes procedural information about how the case got to that court. It describes the nature of the action, the parties involved, the wrongs alleged, the losses sustained, the decision below, and the relief requested. It also tells the court the type of order from which the appeal is taken.

In the Statement of Facts, you should present the material facts of the case, but in a way that inclines the court to your client's perspective. By selecting and arranging the facts, and by artful writing, you may accurately portray the events giving rise to the litigation, yet still present those events from your client's point of view.

The contrast between the appellant's and the appellee's Statements of the Case in most appeals illustrates that the same transcript can be used to convey very different impressions of the facts. These different impressions result from the attorney's judicious selection and arrangement of facts and are legitimate advocacy as long as you also honor your obligation to state your facts accurately and fairly. A lawyer who knowingly misstates the facts violates the Code of Professional Responsibility.[6] You must not only be accurate

---

6.   Canon 7, DR7–102A(5) says in pertinent part, "In his representation of a client, a lawyer shall not knowingly make a false statement of law or fact." See also Model Rules of Professional Conduct, Rule 3.3(a)(1) (which have been adopted in some jurisdictions and

about the facts which you include, but you must include all the known facts that are material to the case so as to avoid giving a distorted impression of the events. If you misrepresent the facts or allow a misleading inference to be drawn, you will lose credibility, and will be quickly corrected by opposing counsel–to your client's disadvantage.

Before you write this section, ask yourself what a reader who does not know the case would have to know, and in what order. Some students become so preoccupied with writing the facts to persuade that they omit important information and confuse the reader as to what the case is actually about or what happened. Be careful, therefore, that you include and logically order all the material facts, favorable as well as unfavorable, so that the court need not rely on the opposing brief to understand the dispute.

Nonetheless, the significance of a fact or event may well become apparent only after you have put it in a meaningful context; facts do not speak for themselves. Thus, although your portrait should ultimately be fair and understandable, you should arrange the facts in a context which is as advantageous to your client as possible.

Your initial selection of facts and interpretation of their significance should, therefore, be provisional. The interpretation, the selection, and the ordering of facts may need to be changed to reflect your growing understanding of how they can be used in your legal arguments, and how your facts set the stage for your theory of the case. If you write your facts with this purpose in mind, the court, after reading the Statement of the Case, ought to be aware not only of the boundaries within which it must work, but of the legal arguments to come.

A.   *The Opening Paragraph or Paragraphs*

Many brief writers begin the Statement of the Case with a brief synopsis of the case from a procedural point of view. Procedural history is essential to an appellate judge, who has to know how and why the case is before the court. The overview should be given in the opening paragraph of the Statement and include procedural information about how the case reached that court as well as information about the nature of the action, the parties involved, and the relief requested. Make sure you explain the background of procedural issues if your appeal involves any. For example, if you are appealing a judge's refusal to give an instruction to the jury, include in the procedural facts the party's request for the instruction and the judge's denial of the request. Some lawyers also summarize the lower court decision in the opening paragraph(s).

prohibit a lawyer from making false
statements of material fact or law).

Others, however, conclude the Statement of the Case with this information (see section IV, C).

Some attorneys separate the procedural history from the summary of relevant evidence by having separate headings for each. The procedural history may go under the heading "Preliminary Statement." The summary presenting the facts goes under the heading "Statement of Facts."

Example of a Preliminary Statement

This is an appeal from a judgment of the Supreme Court, New York County, rendered October 9, 1986. A jury convicted the appellant, Sam Mann, of burglary in the third degree, N.Y. Penal Law § 140.20 (McKinney 1975), and the court sentenced him to a prison term with a maximum of seven and a minimum of three-and-a-half years.

Mr. Mann filed a timely notice of appeal, and on November 19, 1986, this Court granted appellant leave to appeal as a poor person on the original record and typewritten briefs. On July 14, 1987, Una Bent, Esq., was assigned as counsel on the appeal.

B. *Developing the Facts*

1. *Organization*

To sustain your reader's interest, you want to develop the facts in a coherent and sympathetic narrative. Usually, a chronological order works best. Before you begin this chronological narrative, however, it is sometimes appropriate to have a paragraph recounting significant emotional facts, if there are any, which might elicit the reader's sympathy or antipathy. If you are a prosecutor, for example, you might want to begin with the details of the murder. If there are many issues and the Statement of Facts is somewhat lengthy, you may want to use a topical organization instead of a simple chronological organization. If you divide the facts into topics, you may use short topical headings before each new section. You might organize the facts into topics like the evidence at trial, the rulings of the trial court, and the charge to the jury. These subsections summarize and organize the facts pertinent to a legal issue you intend to address in the Argument section of the brief. If you are including witnesses' trial testimony, include that testimony under the appropriate topic, not in a witness-by-witness summary. You would still organize the facts relevant to each topic chronologically.

Before you write the Statement of the Case, you may want to identify the events to be covered and the facts material to them. Work out a structure that frames and maximizes the facts most favorable to your client and that limits the impact of facts damaging to your client. Bury damaging facts in the middle of a narrative and in the middle of paragraphs and sentences; juxtapose unfavorable facts with favorable facts; place favorable facts in positions of emphasis (at the beginning and end of sentences, paragraphs, and the narrative). Finally, allocate space according to importance. For example, as attorney for appellant in a criminal case, you would emphasize, even repeat, facts establishing your client's innocence or the closeness of the case, but condense and bury unfavorable material.

2.   *The Narrative Approach*

Although the Statement of the Case is not an occasion for displaying talent in creative writing, it is a prose narrative and should unfold logically.   To promote the narrative flow, you should usually refrain from parroting the record in a witness-by-witness procession and instead concentrate on integrating the testimony of the witnesses and using that testimony to describe events.   It is perfectly legitimate to mix direct and cross examination if doing so strengthens and clarifies the narrative flow.

To avoid monotony, you may also want to include quotations from the record.   Although direct quotation should be used sparingly because it threatens to interrupt the continuity of the narrative, testimony that seems to capture the true significance of an event can have a dramatic impact on the narrative.   It may, for example, be worth quoting the following statement in a prosecutor's brief, "When the officer said he was going to write out a speeding ticket, the appellant said, 'maybe there is something I could do to make you change your mind, maybe you're short of cash or something'."

Direct quotation should be buttressed by summaries of the record.   Indeed, summaries are preferable to frequent quotation because they promote continuity.   Make sure, however, that your summaries are borne out by the record.[6]   Remember, although you are trying to create a narrative, you are not creating fiction.   You must be accurate: you cannot add to or change the record; your direct quotations must be meticulously correct; and you must support your assertions in the Statement of the Case with reference to the page or pages in the record (R.) where the supporting facts

---

6. The New York Bar Association, Practitioners Handbook for Appeals to the Court of Appeals gives the following good advice on page 60:

If inference is relied on, a summary should make that clear and not simply cite a record page in the expectation that the reader will draw the same

inference. Moreover, all of the record references supporting the inference should be cited so that a reader disagreeing with the inference from the first reference may nevertheless accept it because the other references bear it out.

can be found, or to the page or pages in the opinion below from which the facts came.

One last technique for promoting narrative continuity and coherence is to supply visual details. Visual details help the reader to conceptualize the events. If you are trying to discredit an eyewitness's identification of a suspect, for example, you should describe how far away the witness was, the dim lighting conditions, the shadows cast by an adjacent scaffold, etc.

3. *Persuasive Writing Techniques*

Several writing techniques will help you to shape this section of the brief persuasively.

a. If the record allows, include emotionally significant facts and significant background facts—even if they do not have any strict legal significance—since such information might influence a court to look favorably on your case by establishing a context for understanding the events, by personalizing your client, or both. (Defendant's Statement of the Case on page 318 makes use of significant background facts.)

b. Personalize your client. Even if the record for your class assignments does not reveal any personal information about your client, you can help the court view him or her as a person deserving of fair treatment by referring to the client in a dignified way, as, for example, "Mr. Gonzales" rather than "Gonzales" or "Petitioner." This sort of personalization was achieved in the following paragraphs:

> Ms. Maria Fox, the petitioner in this case, was charged by the Attorney Registration and Disciplinary Commission of the State of Illinois for "soliciting employment" in violation of Disciplinary Rule 2–103(A). (R.1).

> Ms. Fox has practiced law for ten years and has successfully resolved legal problems for the Northwest Community Women's Organization (NCWO) of which she is a member. (R.2). Ms. Fox followed up a request for business cards with personal letters to NCWO members who attended a counseling session at which Ms. Fox was asked to speak. (R.3).

c. Characterize facts favorably. In the following example, the writer suggests the possibility of police coercion by first characterizing the officer's words as a threat and then restating the exact words of the officer:

> Officer Brown wanted permission to enter and to search the apartment. When Mr. Gonzales refused, Officer Brown threatened to seek a warrant and to leave an officer outside the door until his return. He said, "I can always go ask for a

warrant. I'll leave the other officer outside till I get back."
(R.1.) Mr. Gonzales then acquiesced to the search.

    d. De-emphasize unfavorable facts.

      i. You may de-emphasize unfavorable facts about your client's activities by using the passive voice. Passive voice will create a distance between your client and the activity described in the sentence. For example, instead of saying, "Ms. Fox mailed her letters to all the people who had signed the sheet," you would say, "The letters were mailed to the women whose names were on the sign-in sheet." By using passive voice, the writer avoids naming Ms. Fox as the person who mailed the letters.

      ii. Another way to de-emphasize your client's conduct is to use the other parties involved as the subjects of the sentences. For example, instead of saying that Gonzales had the stolen bank money in his apartment where it was found, you can focus on the police activity and say, "The police seized crucial evidence, money stolen from a bank, without a warrant."

      iii. You can also emphasize or de-emphasize a fact by using independent and subordinate clauses carefully. An independent clause is a sentence containing a complete thought, such as "Sam Paley is an excellent lawyer." That clause can be joined in a sentence with a subordinate or dependent clause which has a subject and verb but is an incomplete thought, such as "Although Paley's memory is poor." Because a subordinate clause depends on the independent clause for meaning, a reader's attention focuses on the independent clause. Therefore, it is helpful to put unfavorable facts into a dependent clause which is joined to a more favorable independent clause, such as "Although Paley's memory is poor, he is an excellent lawyer." This sentence leaves the impression of Paley's excellence as a lawyer. If you reverse the information in the clauses, "Although Paley is an excellent lawyer, his memory is poor," or "Even if Paley is an excellent lawyer, his memory is poor," you emphasize the negative information about Paley's memory.

    e. Vary sentence length. After several long sentences, a short sentence can have a dramatic impact.

    f. Choose your words to take advantage of their descriptive power. In a brief, you may describe events using loaded words that would not have been appropriate in a memorandum. It is legitimate, for example, to describe a boy as having applied "emotional blackmail" when he threatened to find a new girlfriend if his present one continued to resist his sexual advances, although such a description would be inappropriate in a memo.

    You should also use vigorous verbs (smash rather than hit) and pointed adjectives and adverbs for facts you want to emphasize.

On the other hand, use colorless verbs and few adjectives or adverbs for facts you wish to de-emphasize.

Do not interpret this advice to mean, however, that you should write in an openly partisan manner. The Statement of the Case should be written to appear neutral—even if it is not. Partisan characterizations and partisan choice of language must be subtle, or not attempted at all.

Other persuasive writing techniques are described in Chapter Sixteen.

————

The following paragraphs show how the appellee and appellant might each have presented the facts of the case on appeal. In the initial suit, plaintiff had sued Gothic Memorial Chapel for the negligent infliction of emotional anguish and distress, claiming that the defendant's conduct was negligent, that the negligence was the cause-in-fact of her emotional anguish and distress, and that her anguish was severe and disabling. At trial, the court held that although the defendant had been negligent and Miss Morte had suffered severe emotional distress, her distress was not the result of defendant's actions but of her grief at the loss of her father. Defendant was held not liable. The issue on appeal is whether defendant's negligence was the cause-in-fact of plaintiff's distress. Each statement of facts illustrates the writer's theory of the case.

The plaintiff's lawyer might present the facts as follows. (Procedural paragraphs and citations to the record are omitted.)

> On the day of George Morte's funeral, in full view of the decedent's daughter, Maria Morte, the hired bearers of defendant undertaker dropped the coffin in which the body lay, causing the lid to spring open and the corpse to crash to the ground. With greater alacrity than diplomacy, the employees heaved the dead man's body up and swung it back into the coffin. In the process, they banged George Morte's head against the side of the coffin, smashing his nose and ripping open his right cheek as it caught on the lock mechanism.
>
> This disruption took place as the funeral party was watching the pall bearers load the coffin onto the hearse for the motorcar procession to the graveyard. At that time, Maria Morte was standing less than four feet from the coffin and the hearse. Her horror at witnessing the defendant's employees manhandle her dead father's body was quickly apparent. She fell into hysterics and began to vomit convulsively. Among the assembled friends and mourners who immediately attempted to assist and soothe Miss Morte was a physician. He insisted on administering a strong tranquilizer

to Miss Morte in order to calm her sufficiently to accompany her beloved father's body to his grave.

For several months after this incident, Miss Morte suffered from a dramatic loss of appetite and weight. She had trouble concentrating, wept easily, and seemed alternately depressed and anxious. She was frequently awakened by recurring nightmares about graveyards, mangled corpses, and open coffins.

———

The defendant's lawyer might present the facts as follows.

Plaintiff in this action is an unmarried woman of 58 who for the last several years of her 85-year-old and ailing father's life served as his constant companion and nurse. Her mother had died when she was a child and she had no other surviving relation. Miss Morte had never married and had always lived in her father's house. The relationship between this elderly, dying father and his aging, spinster daughter has been described as exceptionally close.

The accident which is the basis for this action took place as the funeral party for George Morte was preparing to leave for the cemetery. The employees of Gothic Memorial Chapel inadvertently dropped the casket in which the deceased lay as they were sliding it into the hearse, requiring them to recover his fallen body from the ground. In the process of lifting the body back into the casket, the decedent's face was disfigured.

After the accident occurred, plaintiff appeared shaken. Friends came to her assistance and one of them, a physician, gave her a tranquilizer. In a short while, she was able to accompany the deceased to his final resting place.

For several months after the accident, Miss Morte suffered from the symptoms of grief and mourning which are the natural aftermath of losing a beloved parent. She cried easily, felt depressed, and experienced nightmares and loss of appetite.

Although most cases will not offer you such dramatic and gruesome possibilities, these two versions of the facts illustrate the very different impressions you can convey even when working from the same transcript. Miss Morte's account portrays the employees of Gothic Memorial Chapel as crassly negligent and unfeeling. The narrative begins with a detailed description of the pall bearers' actions and the resulting disfigurement to her father. The verbs are evocative, the nouns blunt, the tone intentionally macabre. The last paragraph, which describes the rather ghoulish content of Miss Morte's nightmares, suggests that her distress is directly tied to the pall bearers' activities. In the middle is buried the somewhat unfavorable fact that Miss Morte was not so distraught as to be unable to proceed to the cemetery. By suggesting that it was only the doctor's administration of the tranquilizer which made it possible for Miss Morte to carry on, this fact is minimized.

Miss Morte's attorney does not dwell in the statement on the close relation of this father and daughter or on her subsequent solitariness because to do so would portray Miss Morte's distress as the natural mourning of an unmarried, middle-aged daughter. On the other hand, appellee's attorney begins with these emotionally significant background facts as a way of minimizing the impact the incident in question had on her mental state. The last paragraph reiterates the idea that Miss Morte experienced nothing more or less than the natural grief of a daughter upon the death of her sole parent. Buried in the middle is the incident itself, which is rather quickly summarized and neutrally reported. The nouns are euphemistic, the verbs colorless, the tone factual. Miss Morte's rather immediate reaction to the manhandling is minimized by the suggestion she recovered rather quickly.

C.   *The Closing Paragraph*

You may end the Statement of the Case by relating the facts back to the legal issue before the court and by giving a short summary of the decision of the court below. The appellee will ordinarily want to place greater emphasis on the decision of the court below than the appellant would, since that decision was favorable to the appellee.

Contrast these examples from appellant's and appellee's briefs. Notice that the appellant summarizes the arguments made before the trial court while the appellee summarizes the trial court's reasons for its decision.

Appellant

> The defendant appealed his conviction on two grounds. The first was that his consent to the search was not voluntarily given in that he "was coerced into agreement by the threat inherent in Brown's language that a future search was inevitable." (R.2.) The second was that the evidence was seized after he had clearly indicated a desire to terminate the search. Id. A divided court of appeals affirmed the conviction. Id. This Court granted certiorari on the question of whether the police officer's search violated the fourth amendment.

Appellee

> The United States Court of Appeals for the Twelfth Circuit affirmed the defendant's conviction and rejected the defendant's claims that his consent was coerced. Instead, the court held that defendant's consent was freely and voluntarily given

in an attempt to allay suspicion and on the assumption that nothing would be found. (R.2) The court also found that the defendant's attempt to stop the search was an attempt to "obstruct the search" in the face of discovery of the evidence. Id.

Exercise 18–B

1. In the following examples, the defendant is appealing the trial court's decision granting closure of the courtroom during the testimony of a thirteen-year-old victim of a brutal assault on the ground that his sixth amendment right to a public trial had been violated. Which Statement for the defendant is more persuasive and why? Citations to the record are omitted.

Example A

Daniel McGee was indicted for Attempted Murder in the Second Degree and for Assault in the First Degree on June 15, 1986. Five days prior to the indictment, Mr. McGee allegedly assaulted thirteen-year-old Sheila Merta. Although only the defendant was apprehended, he acted in concert with others not apprehended.

The thirteen-year-old complaining witness, Sheila Merta, had testified before a Grand Jury and in two separate pretrial hearings, although no spectators were then present. During her testimony at trial, Ms. Merta began to cry. The prosecutor suggested the courtroom be closed because Ms. Merta was afraid of the spectators and embarrassed about having to testify to the details of the assault.

The trial judge held an in camera hearing to determine if there were sufficient reasons for removing spectators from the courtroom. When the judge asked Ms. Merta if closure would make it easier for her to testify, she responded in the affirmative. Ms. Merta then stated that she knew that McGee's mother, who had been a family friend and was in the courtroom, hated her. The trial judge then closed the courtroom because Ms. Merta was fearful of testifying before the spectators. The judge concluded that closure would assure Ms. Merta's testimony. The trial court weighed the equities and decided that it would not be an injustice upon the defendant to have the testimony of Ms. Merta taken without spectators being present. Defendant took exception to the ruling.

On January 13, 1987, defendant was convicted of assault with a deadly weapon, but was acquitted on the attempted murder charge. On February 12, 1987, McGee was sentenced to a prison term of five to fifteen years for the assault.

The Intermediate Appellate Court affirmed the trial court's decision that the defendant suffered no sixth amendment violation. The defendant was then given leave to appeal to this court.

Example B

The Appellant, Daniel McGee, is a resident of York, who, with other unnamed males, allegedly assaulted Sheila Merta, a young girl from their neighborhood, on June 10, 1986.   Only McGee was apprehended and charged with the assault.

On June 15, 1986, the Grand Jury of the County of Kings indicted McGee on two counts: Attempted Murder in the Second Degree and Assault in the First Degree.   Prior to the indictment, Merta testified before the Grand Jury and at two pretrial hearings.

At trial, Merta began her testimony, but then paused and started to cry.   The prosecutor asked to approach the bench where he suggested the court be closed during Merta's testimony because although she had not been threatened in any way, she was frightened about testifying.   The court noted that Merta had already testified before the Grand Jury and at two separate pretrial hearings and indicated that Merta "should be an old pro at testifying."

The defense counsel immediately objected to closure, acknowledging that every witness experienced some fear at the prospect of giving testimony at trial but that this "mild anxiety" was not enough to justify closure of the courtroom.

The trial court held a brief <u>in camera</u> hearing with Merta to decide whether to close the courtroom to all spectators during her testimony. The judge asked Merta what was the problem, as she had been a very able witness so far.   She answered that she did not know, but felt discomfort at the thought of Daniel's mother and neighbors looking at her as she testified.   She did not indicate that she would not testify nor did she express a preference for the courtroom to be closed.   The judge asked her if it would help her to testify if McGee's mother and other spectators were not in the courtroom.   She replied: "I guess so."   The judge then decided to close the courtroom.   The defense counsel objected, but the judge interrupted, saying he had made his ruling.   Defense counsel's exception was noted for the record, but counsel was not given the opportunity to be heard on the motion for closure.   The judge then ordered the courtroom to be closed to all spectators, including defendant's relatives, friends, and the press.

McGee was convicted on the assault charge and acquitted on the murder charge.   He was sentenced to an indeterminate sentence of five-to-fifteen years.

On Nov. 13, 1987, the Intermediate Appellate Court affirmed the trial court's decision in all respects and held that there was no sixth amendment violation.

Permission to appeal to this Court was granted to McGee on Dec. 1, 1987.   Awaiting appeal, Daniel McGee remains incarcerated pursuant to that judgment of conviction.

2.   In the following exercise, the legal question is whether the testimony of defendant's expert witness on the battered woman's syndrome should have been admitted into evidence because it satisfies the test for relevance in the jurisdiction.   Read the excerpts.   Then write a State-

ment of Facts first from the appellant's point of view (Joan Brown), then from the appellee's point of view (the State of Abbott). Assume the procedural history has already been written. Before you begin to write, consider these questions.

1. Which facts would form the focus of a Statement of Facts written from the appellant's point of view? from the appellee's point of view?

2. Which facts are legally relevant?

Excerpt of Testimony by Joan Brown

Q: (by Defense Counsel William Blake): Please give us your name and address.

A: My name is Joan Brown and I live at 600 Boston Place in Abbottsville.

Q: How old are you?

A: I'm 29 years old.

Q: Were you married to the deceased, John Brown?

A: Yes.

Q: How long were you married?

A: Nine years.

Q: Did you have any children?

A: Yes. We have a son who is 8 and a daughter who is 5.

Q: Do you have a job outside of the home?

A: No, I never finished high school, and since the kids were born, I stopped getting waitressing jobs.

Q: Did your husband ever strike you?

A.D.A. Robert Canon: Objection, your Honor. The deceased is not on trial in this case. I fail to see the relevance of this testimony.

Defense Counsel William Blake: Your Honor, the deceased's violence towards Mrs. Brown is highly relevant to her claim of self-defense.

The Court: Objection overruled. You may proceed, Mr. Blake.

Q: Mrs. Brown, did your husband ever strike you?

A: After my daughter was born, my husband started to beat me up a lot. Before then, he would push me around sometimes, but after Amanda was born, it got much worse and much more frequent.

Q: Can you be more specific?

A: Once John took me outside the house and beat my head against a tree. Another time he stabbed me in the foot with a pencil.

Q: Were there other episodes?

A: John pushed me down a flight of stairs in the house and I broke my arm and had to go to the hospital to have it set and put in a cast.

Q: Did you go to a hospital on any other occasions?

A: Last February I went to the hospital because I kept vomiting and blacking out after he beat me. There were a lot of times that he would punch me and shove me around. Sometimes he would hit the kids, too. Then other times he would be peaceful for a while.

Q: Were there any other instances in which you went to see a doctor because of your husband's beating you?

A: Two years ago John hit me in the face with a bottle and I went to the doctor to have stitches because my face was all cut up.

Q: Did you ever leave your husband?

A: Yes, last March I left John after one bad night and took the kids to a Women's Shelter on Foster Street. The next day John came to see me and said that he wanted me to come home and that things would be different. I went back with him. He was nice for a week and then he started pushing me and the kids around again.

Q: What happened on the day of April 28?

A: In the morning on the way out the door, John said he had it with me and that when he got home he was going to really finish me off. He said I humiliated him by going to the shelter. I was petrified all day. I knew he meant it. Whenever he said he would do something to me, he would always do it. Just before I knew John was coming home at six-thirty, I went to the drawer in the bedroom where John kept a gun. I took the gun downstairs, and when John came through the door I shot him.

Q: (By A.D.A. Canon) Mrs. Brown, do you have any family in Abbottsville?

A: Well, my husband's sister lives in Abbottsville, but she and I were never really close.

———

Excerpt of Testimony of Dr. Susan Black

Q: (By Defense Counsel William Blake) Dr. Black, please tell us something about your background.

A: I am a certified psychoanalyst and have spent many years studying the battered woman's syndrome. I have. . . .

A.D.A. Canon: Objection, your Honor. May we approach the bench?

The Court: Yes, you may. The jury is excused. (The members of the jury exit.) Mr. Blake, for what purpose do you intend to introduce expert testimony on the "battered woman's syndrome"?

Mr. Blake: Your Honor, we believe that expert testimony on the battered woman's syndrome is relevant to Joan Brown's claim of self-defense. The testimony would help the jury understand why she reasonably believed that she was in imminent danger on the day of the shooting and why deadly force was necessary to avoid this danger. In addition, this testimony would explain why she did not leave her husband, despite his brutality.

The Court: Mr. Canon?

A.D.A. Canon: I object to any testimony regarding a so-called "battered woman's syndrome." The testimony is irrelevant as it does not explain why, at the particular time that the shooting took place, Joan Brown reasonably believed that this force was necessary to prevent imminent death or great bodily harm to herself. In addition, the jury has already heard extensive testimony from both Joan Brown and her neighbor on the alleged violence of John Brown. I see no purpose in further discussion of this issue.

The Court: Mr. Blake, do you have a response?

Mr. Blake: Yes, your Honor. Dr. Black is a well-known authority on battered woman's syndrome. Her testimony will describe this syndrome and show how, in her opinion, Joan Brown displayed the classic signs of the syndrome. This testimony will explain Ms. Brown's state of mind and support her claim of self-defense.

The Court: Well, I would like to hear from Dr. Black and then I'll make a decision on whether her expert testimony will be admissible. Could you please describe the battered woman's syndrome?

A: Certainly. The battered woman's syndrome is a three stage form of family "disease". In stage 1, the battering male engages in minor physical abuse and verbal abuse. In this tension-building stage, the woman often attempts to placate the male to avoid more serious violence. Stage 2 is characterized by acute explosions of brutal violence by the battering male. In stage 3, the battering male expresses remorse for his behavior and asks for forgiveness, promising to change. The woman is hopeful during the third stage that her husband will indeed change. This is one reason why she stays with him despite the cycles of abuse. There are other reasons as well. One expert has described the demoralization experienced by some women because they cannot control the violence as "learned helplessness" or "psychological paralysis". They become incapable of taking action to change their situations. Of course, they may also be fearful of what will happen to their children, or fear that their husbands will find them and abuse them even more if they try to get away. And they may not have any money or way of earning a living.

Q: Dr. Black, have you interviewed the defendant, Joan Brown?

A: Yes, I have.

Q: Do you have an opinion on whether Joan Brown is subject to the battered woman's syndrome?

A: Yes, in my opinion, Joan Brown is subject to the battered woman's syndrome.

Q: As a battered woman, how did Joan Brown perceive her situation on the 28th day of April?

A: Joan Brown was terrified that her husband would kill her when he returned from work. He said he would, as he put it, "finish her off," and she believed, knowing him, that he would do it.

Q: I have no further questions. Thank you Dr. Black.

The Court: I have decided not to admit Dr. Black's expert testimony. I do not think it is relevant to the issue of self-defense in this case. In the state of Abbott, the jury applies an objective standard in evaluating a self-defense claim. According to the Abbott statute, which is not being challenged here, the jury must consider how an ordinary, intelligent, and prudent person would have acted under the circumstances existing at the time of the offense.

The jury may return.

V. *Summary of the Argument*

The Summary of the Argument is a short affirmative statement of the reasoning in the Argument that supports the advocate's view of the case. In this section, the neutral tone of the Statement of the Case gives way to open advocacy. You should set out your theory of the case, that is, you should explain the way you want the court to understand the case. In addition, present the law you want the court to apply and your interpretation of how that law applies to the facts. Include only the arguments favorable to your case.

The summary can be your first opportunity to argue your case to the court. Many busy judges read only the Summary before they hear the case, so that the Summary makes an important impression.

Begin the Summary with an introduction that provides the context of the case and sets out the conclusion you want the court to accept, such as "the state may proscribe an attorney from soliciting clients by mail." Tell the court what the conflict is, and the decision of the lower court you are asking it to affirm or reverse. Then state the rule and apply it to the facts. Explain briefly the reasons for your conclusion and try to craft them into an argument that supports your theory of the case. Do not just put together a list of topics like "this court's decisions interpreting analogous issues, cases interpreting the statute, decisions in other jurisdictions, and social policy all support recovery by the plaintiff." Instead, mention succinctly which analogies and policies support the claim.

Generally, you should write the Summary without reference to specific case names and without case citations, although sometimes it is necessary to name and cite to a crucial case if that decision controls the analysis of the problem. You should always include relevant statutory language and citations, however. In addition, you should always explain the controlling rules before you apply them. The Summary should be written so that it can be understood on its own. You should not refer to cases, rules, or theories that you do not explain. The Summary is not, however, an abstract discussion of the law. Unless you are dealing with a question of law, the Summary should be specific to the case, that is, you should relate the law to the facts of the case before the court.

Because this section is a summary of your Argument section, it should be conclusory and it should include only the very important points. As a rule of thumb, the Summary should not exceed two pages for a ten to fifteen page Argument; one page should be sufficient for most briefs. Finally, since this section summarizes your Argument, most attorneys write it only after they have completed the Argument section.

——————

What follows are sample Summaries from briefs on the question of whether the Sioux Falls School District Rules on religious holiday observances comply with the establishment clause of the first amendment.

Petitioner's Summary of the Argument

The Sioux Falls School District violates the neutrality mandated by the establishment clause of the first amendment by adopting a Policy and Rules that permit the observation of religious holidays in public school assemblies. To test the constitutionality of state-authorized rules and statutes under the establishment clause, the Court has developed a three-part test. First, the rules must have a secular purpose. Second, their principal or primary effect can neither advance nor inhibit religion. Third, they must not give rise to excessive entanglement between government and religion. Lemon v. Kurtzman, 403 U.S. 602, 612–13 (1971). The Policy and Rules violate all three parts of this test.

The Court has not hesitated, especially in cases concerning religious exercises in public schools, to look behind the purported purpose of a statute in order to discern the actual motivations giving rise to the enactment. Because the Rules allow the presentation of Christmas carols, religious skits, and nativity scenes, it becomes obvious that the respondent's purpose in adopting these Rules was not a secular one, but was to allow for the celebration of the religious aspects of Christmas and to advance sectarian ideals.

The Sioux Falls Rules also violate the second part of the Lemon test by having a principal effect that advances religion. Since devotional exercises, which the Rules permit, are inherently religious and their effect is to advance religion, they have no place in the public schools. Due to the devout nature of many Christmas carols, and the undeniably religious impact on a youngster from seeing a nativity scene on the public school stage, the direct and immediate effect of the Rules is the advancement of religion.

Finally, the Rules result in excessive entanglement between the schools and religion because they involve the secular authorities who execute the legislation in surveillance of religious activities. In addition, the Rules foster political divisiveness in the community along religious lines. For example, Assistant Superintendent Nicholas—assigned to monitor the implementation of the Rules—is on the public payroll. Also, both Nicholas and the school board must make discretionary judgments about the religious nature of particular activities. Finally, the amount of time and money devoted to the preparation and presentation of the annual Christmas programs is likely to give rise to divisive issues in local politics. Because the Policy and Rules violate all three parts of the Lemon test, they are unconstitutional.

Respondent's Summary of the Argument

The Sioux Falls School District adopted the Policy and Rules to assist teachers and administrators in fulfilling the duties imposed by the establishment clause to keep religious influences out of the public schools. To test the constitutionality of state-authorized rules and regulations under the establishment clause, the Court has developed a three-part test. First, the rules must have a secular purpose. Then, their principal or primary effect can neither advance nor inhibit religion. Finally, they must not give rise to excessive entanglement between government and religion. Lemon v. Kurtzman, 403 U.S. 602, 612–13 (1971). The Policy and Rules comply with each part of the Lemon test and are constitutional.

The Court has consistently accepted the stated legislative purpose of enactments in evaluating the first part of the Lemon test. The stated legislative purpose of the school district—"to foster understanding and mutual respect"—is undoubtedly secular. The Policy and Rules serve no religious purpose. The function of the Rules is to provide guidelines for the school district's teachers in the execution of their constitutional duty to keep purely religious influences out of public schools.

Second, the principal or primary effect of the Policy and Rules neither advances nor inhibits religion. The primary effect is the advancement of a secular program of education. The schools seek to teach the students about the customs and cultural heritage of the world. Thus, there is no constitutional barrier to the inclusion of this material in the schools.

Finally, the Policy and Rules do not excessively entangle government and religion. On the contrary, the Rules seek to limit the introduction of religious material into the classroom. This case presents none of the entanglement concerns which the Court has expressed that arise from government aid to religious institutions. When government aids religious institutions, then the character and purpose of the institution, the form of aid, and the resulting relationship between government and religious authority may entangle the state with religion. These forms of entanglement do not apply to public school cases.

Nor do the Rules provide any potential for political divisiveness that may arise from religious-oriented legislation. The Rules provide no money for religious activity and require no on-going implementation. Thus, the Rules prevent ongoing political controversies on the subject and remove the religious issue from the local political sphere.

Exercise 18–C

1. Criticize this opening sentence of a Summary of the Argument.

Since the circuit courts are split on the issue of whether a pro se attorney is eligible for an award of attorney fees under § 552(a)(4)(E), an analysis of that statute's language, legislative history, and policy objectives is necessary.

2. Father Molloy was convicted in April of willfully transporting firearms across state lines. Last week, he was sentenced to four years in prison. His sentence has been stayed pending his appeal. A summer associate in the firm representing Father Molloy has written the following Statement of Facts drawn from the trial transcript and a brief summary of the applicable law. Read these materials and then write a clear and persuasive Summary of the Argument. The only issue is whether Father Molloy was entrapped as a matter of law.

Statement of Facts

Father Molloy runs a soup kitchen and homeless shelter in the parish house of St. Bridget's Church in Brooklyn, New York. A dedicated and outspoken advocate of the poor and oppressed, Father Molloy is much in demand as a speaker at conferences and rallies all over the country. He first came to the attention of the F.B.I. last winter in connection with the arrest near St. Bridget's of suspected terrorist Seamus O'Rourke. No charges have been filed against Father Molloy in New York, but the investigation continues. When Father Molloy (a law school graduate) took a leave from St. Bridget's to teach a course at a law school in Washington ("Faith, Empowerment, and the Law"), he became a target of Prayscam, an F.B.I. "sting" operation.

Calling himself "Kieran Houlihan," Agent William Smith attended a "Housing Now" rally at which the priest spoke ("We cannot rest until all the oppressed are free—Blacks in South Africa, Catholics in Northern Ireland, the poor and homeless everywhere . . .") and signed up to audit Father Molloy's course.

On February 14, 1990, "Houlihan" approached Father Molloy after class and asked whether he might speak with the priest privately. Smith took Father Molloy to Casey's Pub, where he told Father Molloy that he needed help to save his family in Northern Ireland. Through security leaks, a Protestant terrorist organization had learned the names of all those suspected by British Intelligence of having IRA sympathies. The group was systematically executing everyone on the list. In the town where "Houlihan's" uncles and cousins lived, five people had already been killed, including one of his cousins. His family had begged him to help; the Catholic townspeople needed guns to protect themselves. At that point, Father Molloy said "I can't help you with guns, my son, but my prayers are with you and your people."

After the next class, on February 16, "Houlihan" again sought out Father Molloy. He told the priest that he had been able to obtain two dozen unregistered rifles and had been put in touch with an underground "expediter" who could smuggle them onto a flight from Kennedy Airport to Belfast, where his cousins would pick them up. Now, "Houlihan" said, his problem was to get the guns to New York; he was an illegal immigrant without a driver's license and couldn't take the chance of driving his car 300 miles. "I'm sorry, my son, but I can't drive your cargo to Kennedy for you," Father Molloy replied.

On February 21, "Houlihan" once more took Father Molloy to Casey's. "Houlihan" said he was close to solving his problem: he had arranged to ship the guns to New York on Amtrak, packed in a coffin. At Penn Station, a hearse would pick up the coffin and take it to the "expediter" at Kennedy. But Amtrak would not ship an unaccompanied coffin: would Father Molloy accompany the coffin and see that it was safely delivered to the "expediter"? "This is no easy matter, my son," began Father Molloy. "I know, Father, and I am ready to express my family's gratitude in meaningful terms. We will contribute $5,000 to St. Bridget's shelter if you will help us." Father Molloy stared into his glass without speaking. Finally, he said, "Very well, my son, I'll do it."

Father Molloy was arrested a week later on 33rd Street in Manhattan as he supervised the transfer of a coffin full of Remingtons into a hearse driven by Agent Robert Jones.

At trial, the court refused to find that Father Molloy was entrapped as a matter of law. The question thus became one for the jury. Molloy was convicted. On appeal, the only issue is whether the judge should have found there was entrapment as a matter of law.

Brief Summary of Applicable Law
(Full Citations are Omitted)

A court will find entrapment as a matter of law only when there was "some evidence" of government inducement to commit the crime charged, and the prosecution failed to prove beyond a reasonable doubt that defendant was predisposed to commit that crime. United States v. Kelly.

When the undisputed evidence, with all inferences drawn in favor of the government, indicates to any reasonable mind, "some evidence" of inducement, then the court can determine that there was inducement as a matter of law. Id. Inducement is an objective inquiry measuring whether the government's behavior was such that a law abiding citizen's will to obey the law could be overcome. Id. Although government agents may use "stealth and stratagem" to entrap criminals, they may not attempt to lure law-abiding citizens into the commission of crime. See Sherman v. United States; Sorells v. United States; United States v. Kelly.

Government agents do not entrap if they approach or solicit the defendant to engage in criminal activity. United States v. Burkley. Rather, there must be some undisputed evidence indicating that government agents employed "persuasion, fraudulent representations (beyond offering opportunities to one predisposed to commit a crime), threats, coercive tactics, harassment, promises of reward, or pleas based on need, sympathy," or "friendship" in order to show inducement as a matter of law. Id. Thus, in Sherman, the Court held that there was inducement as a matter of law when the government informer sought to persuade the defendant to procure narcotics with three repeated pleas based on sympathy and mutual experience as drug addicts. Similarly, in United States v. Owens, because the government agent posed as a fellow drug user and resorted to friendship to convince the defendant to sell the drugs, the court found inducement as a matter of law.

However, the mere promise of money is insufficient to show inducement. In Kelly, the court did not find inducement as a matter of law even though government agents, posing as businessmen, offered Kelly an initial $25,000 to attend a meeting. It should be noted, however, that in Kelly, the defendant did not testify "that his will was overborne by any insistent importunings" by government agents. Id.

Once a defendant shows inducement, the prosecution must introduce evidence beyond a reasonable doubt of the defendant's predisposition to commit the crime charged in order to defeat a claim of entrapment. Burkley. Thus, the prosecution must prove that the defendant had a "state of mind which readily respond[ed] to the opportunity furnished by the officer ... to commit the forbidden act for which the accused is charged." Id. The defendant's predisposition is determined from the entirety of the events leading up to the commission of the crime. Kelly.

When predisposition is at issue, the major inquiry is thus whether the defendant was "ready and willing to commit the crimes." Kelly. In Kelly, the predisposed defendant was aware of the purpose of the meeting and neither protested nor registered surprise at the initial bribe offer, "coolly" assuring the FBI agents that he would do their bidding, without repeated and insistent government pleas. Id.

Predisposition may also be proven by evidence of a defendant's bad reputation, previous criminal convictions, rumored activities, and response to the inducement. Russell. However, in Owens, although the defendant was a drug user and often in the company of drug sellers, the court found no predisposition to sell narcotics, as distinct from a predisposition to use narcotics. The court indicated that the facts that Owens had no prior record for selling drugs and did not show up the first time the agent requested the drugs tended to support its finding of no predisposition. Id.

VI. *Point Headings*

Unlike an office memorandum, a brief requires headings that divide the Argument section into its main and subordinate components. These headings, called point headings, are more than just topical headings used for easy transition from one topic to another, such as "the first amendment and commercial speech" or "the consent exception." Instead, they are persuasive summaries of the main arguments of the brief arranged in logical order. A point heading should be a conclusory statement about the legal issue which is favorable to your client.

In addition to a heading for each main argument, many writers use subheadings to introduce the subordinate parts of that argument. When read together—as they appear under the Argument section in the Table of Contents, for example—the headings and subheadings should provide a meaningful outline and summary of the entire Argument section. Because the point headings appear in the Table of Contents at the beginning of the brief, they are the reader's introduction to the substance of the Argument.

A.   *Organizing Headings in Outline Form*

Point headings provide an outline of the Argument section of a brief. The main point headings should summarize independent, unrelated legal arguments, each of which is an independent ground for relief. These point headings need not be logically connected to each other, although they should be in the order you have determined is the best and most logical order for your issues. Subheadings, however, must relate to the main point heading in a logical and consistent way because they are the components of a single argument. An argument that is subdivided is almost always ordered from the general to the specific. The main heading should state your general contention. The subheadings should supply specific reasons supporting the general contention. Any additional divisions should focus on the specific facts supporting the contention of the sub-heading above it. Thus, the outline organizes all the parts of your argument by how they relate to each other.

You need not achieve symmetry of organization among the major headings of the argument. Even if Section I has two subdivisions, Section II may have three subdivisions, or none at all. Where you do have subdivisions, indent and underline the subheadings and lay out the divisions in accordance with the established rules of outlining.

1. Main issues or grounds for relief are introduced by point headings which are preceded by roman numerals (e.g., I, II, III).

2. Subissues are introduced by subheadings which are preceded by capital letters (e.g., A, B, C).

3. Divisions of subissues are introduced by subheadings which are preceded by arabic numerals (e.g., 1, 2, 3) and then lower case letters (e.g., a, b, c).

You should not have single subdivisions, that is, a subissue A without a subissue B, or a subdivision 1 without a subdivision 2. Because a subdivision indicates that the main issue above it is divided into more than one point, you should not use a subheading unless you have at least two entries. If there is only one point to make about issue I, then incorporate your subissue into your dominant point heading. This needs to be done in the following outline of a contempt problem.

I. Paley did not act willfully or intentionally.

    A. Paley did not realize that Spence's trial was scheduled that morning.

II.   Paley did not act recklessly.

    A.   Paley followed standard office practice.

    B.   Paley inadvertently did not record the trial date.

The outline should be rewritten.

  I.   Paley did not act willfully or intentionally because he did not realize Spence's trial was scheduled that morning.

  II.   Paley did not act recklessly.

    A.   Paley followed standard office practice.

    B.   Paley inadvertently did not record the trial date.

When you use subheadings, be careful not to subdivide the arguments excessively. Too many subdivisions will break up the flow of an argument and result in a choppy product. Thus, when the subject matter is not too different, you should avoid using a new subheading for discussions running only one or two paragraphs in length. Instead, incorporate the material in those paragraphs into the text of the preceding or subsequent subheadings and write those subheadings to include the added material. On the other hand, do not be afraid to subdivide a complex argument that depends on several different types of legal support. Without subdivision, it might be difficult for the reader to understand and differentiate the multiple legal arguments being offered.

Exercise 18–D

Reorder these headings so that those which are logically subordinate to a dominant heading are arranged under that dominant point heading. Correct the outlining of these point headings so that the subordinate points are properly labelled, put in the lower case, underlined, and indented.

  I.   DR. PLATT'S TESTIMONY ON THE BATTERED WIFE SYNDROME WOULD AID THE JURY IN ITS SEARCH FOR TRUTH BECAUSE THE SYNDROME IS SO DISTINCTLY RELATED TO SCIENTIFIC AND MEDICAL KNOWLEDGE THAT IT IS BEYOND THE KEN OF THE AVERAGE JUROR.

  II.   THE TRIAL COURT ERRED IN EXCLUDING EXPERT TESTIMONY ON THE BATTERED WIFE SYNDROME BECAUSE THAT TESTIMONY SATISFIES THE THREE–PART TEST OF RULE 230 OF THE STATE OF KENT WHICH GOVERNS THE ADMISSIBILITY OF EXPERT TESTIMONY.

  III.   DR. PLATT IS A LEADING AUTHORITY ON THE BATTERED WIFE SYNDROME AND HER OPINIONS CAN THEREFORE AID THE TRIER OF FACT.

  IV.   THE PROBATIVE VALUE OF DR. PLATT'S TESTIMONY ON THE BATTERED WIFE SYNDROME SUBSTANTIALLY OUTWEIGHS THE DANGER OF UNFAIR PREJUDICE BECAUSE THE JURY NEEDS TO UNDERSTAND SUE GRANT'S MEN-

TAL STATE AT THE TIME OF THE MURDER TO EVALUATE HER CLAIM OF SELF–DEFENSE.

V. THE BATTERED WIFE SYNDROME IS GENERALLY ACCEPTED IN THE SCIENTIFIC COMMUNITY AND HAS BEEN THE SUBJECT OF AN INCREASING AMOUNT OF RESEARCH AND PUBLICATION.

B. *Writing Persuasive Headings*

Since point headings provide your reader with an outline and summary of your argument, they should be coherent, logical, and persuasive thesis sentences. In order for them to exhibit these characteristics, you must provide the reader with several kinds of information: the issue, the pertinent rule of law, the legally significant facts, and your conclusion on the issue. When you are employing only a single main point heading, all this information must be included in a single, coherent sentence. When you use subheadings, however, the main point heading need only state your legal contention concerning the application of a rule. The subheadings will supply the reasons for that contention and show their relevance to your client's situation.

A point heading should be one sentence, not a string of sentences. To promote ease of comprehension, try to keep each heading and subheading to a readable length so as not to deter the reader from giving attention to its substance. This is especially important for dominant point headings because they are typed entirely in capital letters, which often make for difficult reading. Although subheadings are printed in ordinary type (and are often underlined), they too should be kept reasonably concise (no more than 25 words) so that their thesis can be easily absorbed. Other suggestions follow.

1. When dealing with a factual question, your headings should not be abstract statements of the law (unless clearly supported by subheadings that supply reasoning and relevant facts). Rather they should combine the law with the relevant facts of the case. For example, the following heading is only a statement of the law:

THE FOURTH AMENDMENT GUARANTEES THE RIGHT OF ALL PEOPLE TO BE SECURE IN THEIR HOMES FROM UNREASONABLE SEARCHES AND SEIZURE.

The heading should demonstrate the law's application:

THE POLICE VIOLATED MR. BAXTER'S FOURTH AMENDMENT RIGHT TO BE SECURE FROM UNREASONABLE SEARCHES AND SEIZURES BECAUSE THEY ENTERED AND SEARCHED HIS HOME WITHOUT A WARRANT AND WITH THE CONSENT ONLY OF MR. BAXTER'S HOUSEGUEST.

Remember, briefs are written to persuade a court to rule in a particular way, for a particular party, in a particular situation;

they are not abstract discussions written for the general edification of a judge. If you have not related the law to the facts, your heading is unpersuasive.

2. Unless supported by sub-headings that supply your reasoning, headings should not merely state a legal conclusion favorable to your client but should supply supporting reasons. The following heading states a conclusion only:

> THE TRIAL COURT'S EXCLUSION OF SMITH'S POST-HYPNOTIC TESTIMONY DID NOT VIOLATE SMITH'S CONSTITUTIONAL RIGHT TO TESTIFY IN HER OWN BEHALF.

The writer should supply some support for this conclusion:

> THE TRIAL COURT DID NOT VIOLATE SMITH'S CONSTITUTIONAL RIGHT TO TESTIFY IN HER OWN BEHALF WHEN IT EXCLUDED HER POST-HYPNOTIC TESTIMONY BECAUSE THAT TESTIMONY WAS UNRELIABLE.

In other words, a heading should be an explanation, not merely an assertion. An assertion can be rejected as easily as it can be accepted; an explanation is more persuasive because it at least provides some basis for the assertion.

3. When dealing with a legal question, you do not need to include the facts of your case, but you do need to supply your reasons.

> THE GRANDPARENT VISITATION STATUTE IS CONSTITUTIONAL BECAUSE IT PROTECTS THE WELFARE OF CHILDREN WITHOUT UNDULY INTERFERING WITH PARENTS' FUNDAMENTAL RIGHT TO RAISE THEIR CHILDREN ACCORDING TO THEIR OWN BELIEFS.

4. Headings should clearly articulate relevant legal principles rather than cite cases or statutes. You must not assume your reader knows the rule of law established in a case or statute. For your thesis to be comprehensible, you must supply the rule. The following heading is uninformative:

> UNDER THE RULING OF ROSS v. BERHARD, 396 U.S. 531 (1970), THE FEDERAL DISTRICT COURT PROPERLY STRUCK A DEMAND FOR A JURY TRIAL IN AN ACTION FOR DAMAGES AND INJUNCTIVE RELIEF STEMMING FROM A NUCLEAR POWER PLANT ACCIDENT.

The heading should be rewritten so that the legal principle established in Ross is clear.

> BECAUSE A JURY DOES NOT PROVIDE AN ADEQUATE REMEDY FOR COMPLEX CASES THAT ARE BEYOND ITS PRACTICAL ABILITIES AND LIMITATIONS, THE DISTRICT COURT PROPERLY STRUCK A DEMAND FOR A JURY TRIAL IN AN ACTION FOR DAMAGES AND INJUNCTIVE RELIEF STEMMING FROM A NUCLEAR POWER PLANT ACCIDENT.

5. Point headings should be easily understood. Because so much information gets packed into point headings, you will have to work hard to make them intelligible. Two helpful suggestions are to keep the subject of your sentence near the predicate and to put the facts and reasoning at the end of the sentence. In the following heading, the author's reasoning intervenes between the subject and the predicate.

> A PARENT–CHILD PRIVILEGE, LACKING CONFIDENTIALITY, AN ELEMENT CENTRAL TO ESTABLISHED PRIVILEGES, IS NOT JUDICIALLY RECOGNIZED, AND THE DISTRICT COURT, THEREFORE, PROPERLY DENIED THE DEFENDANT'S MOTION TO QUASH THE SUBPOENA.

The heading should be rewritten:

> A PARENT–CHILD PRIVILEGE LACKS THE ELEMENT OF CONFIDENTIALITY CENTRAL TO ESTABLISHED PRIVILEGES, AND THUS, THE DISTRICT COURT PROPERLY DENIED THE DEFENDANT'S MOTION TO QUASH THE SUBPOENA.

6. Whenever possible, headings should be written as positive statements, rather than as negative ones. The following is a negative heading:

> PETITIONER MAY NOT SOLICIT CLIENTS BY MAIL UNDER THE GUISE OF EXERCISING HER FIRST AMENDMENT RIGHTS.

Instead, the respondent might have written:

> BECAUSE SOLICITATION IS INHERENTLY COERCIVE, THE STATE PROPERLY PROSCRIBED PETITIONER'S SOLICITATION OF CLIENTS THROUGH DIRECT MAILINGS.

Affirmative sentences are clearer and more forceful than negative sentences.

7. You should use active instead of passive voice constructions, unless you want to dissociate the subject of the sentences from the action expressed by the verbs. In the following heading, there is no tactical reason for using the passive voice.

> THE PROSECUTORIAL MISCONDUCT WAS SO PREJUDICIAL THAT THE INHERENT SUPERVISORY POWERS OF THE COURT SHOULD BE INVOKED AND THE GRAND JURY INDICTMENT DISMISSED.

This heading could be rewritten in the active voice.

> THE COURT SHOULD INVOKE ITS INHERENT SUPERVISORY POWERS AND DISMISS THE GRAND JURY INDICTMENT BECAUSE THE PROSECUTORIAL MISCONDUCT WAS PREJUDICIAL.

If a party wants to emphasize prosecutorial misconduct by beginning the sentence with that language, the party could still end the sentence in the active voice.

THE PROSECUTORIAL MISCONDUCT WAS SO PREJUDICIAL THAT THE COURT SHOULD INVOKE ITS INHERENT SUPERVISORY POWERS AND DISMISS THE GRAND JURY INDICTMENT.

The following point headings illustrate the petitioner's and respondent's arguments on Ms. Bell's claim against her husband for unauthorized eavesdropping and wiretapping of her telephone.

PETITIONER'S POINT HEADINGS

I. ALICE BELL STATES A CLAIM AGAINST HER HUSBAND UNDER 18 U.S.C. § 2510 BECAUSE HE EAVESDROPPED ON AND SECRETLY TAPE RECORDED HER TELEPHONE CONVERSATIONS FOR SIX MONTHS.

A. The respondent's secret tape recording of Ms. Bell's telephone conversations violated the plain language of 18 U.S.C. § 2510, which prohibits any person from intercepting any wire communication.

B. The legislative history of 18 U.S.C. § 2510 supports the plain meaning that Congress intended the statute to apply to private individuals and did not intend to exempt interspousal wire tapping.

II. ALICE BELL STATES A CLAIM UNDER 18 U.S.C. § 2510 BECAUSE THE RESPONDENT'S INTERCEPTION OF MS. BELL'S TELEPHONE CONVERSATIONS ON HER BUSINESS LINE DOES NOT FALL WITHIN ANY EXCEPTION TO THE STATUTE.

A. Because the respondent's eavesdropping and wiretapping were not conducted in the ordinary course of Ms. Bell's consulting business, they were not exempt under 18 U.S.C. § 2510(5)(a).

B. The respondent eavesdropped on his wife's private conversations without her consent.

RESPONDENT'S POINT HEADINGS

I. THE COURT PROPERLY DISMISSED PETITIONER'S COMPLAINT BECAUSE HER HUSBAND'S INTERCEPTION OF HER TELEPHONE CONVERSATIONS IS EXPLICITLY EXEMPTED FROM THE PROVISIONS OF THE OMNIBUS CRIME CONTROL AND SAFE STREETS ACT.

A. Mr. Bell used the business extension phone in the ordinary course of business when he overheard conversations establishing his wife's infidelity, and thus, his conduct is explicitly exempt from the statute's provisions.

B. Mr. Bell's original conduct was inadvertent and thus not willful interception as required by the statute.

II. THE PETITIONER'S COMPLAINT WAS PROPERLY DISMISSED BECAUSE HER HUSBAND'S INTERCEPTION OF TELEPHONE CALLS WAS WITHIN AN IMPLIED EXCEPTION

FROM THE OMNIBUS CRIME CONTROL AND SAFE STREETS ACT FOR INTERSPOUSAL WIRETAPS.

A. Congress did not intend that the Crime Control Act extend to disputes between spouses because domestic relations is an area traditionally reserved for state law.

B. The entire focus of the Omnibus Crime Control and Safe Streets Act is on law enforcement personnel and organized crime.

Exercise 18–E

1. These point headings were written for an appellant's brief arguing that a person who serves alcoholic beverages in his home (a social host) can be liable for serving a guest who the host knew was intoxicated when the guest later was injured. Which point heading is best for the plaintiff-appellant Joseph Nunn? What is wrong with the other headings?

A. JOSEPH NUNN STATES A CLAIM AGAINST SAMUEL TANN FOR SERVING HIM ALCOHOLIC BEVERAGES UNDER STATE V. SMALL.

B. DISMISSING JOSEPH NUNN'S CLAIM AGAINST THE DEFENDANT FOR SERVING HIM ALCOHOLIC BEVERAGES WHEN HE WAS ALREADY INTOXICATED WAS ERROR AND FAILED TO UPHOLD WELL–ESTABLISHED NEW HAMPSHIRE LAW PROVIDING PLAINTIFF WITH A CLAIM AGAINST THE DEFENDANT.

C. THE COURT BELOW COMMITTED ERROR IN DISMISSING THIS SUIT BECAUSE UNDER NEW HAMPSHIRE LAW THE DEFENDANT VIOLATED HIS DUTY TO HIS GUEST NOT TO SERVE HIM ALCOHOLIC BEVERAGES WHEN THE GUEST WAS INTOXICATED, KNOWING THE GUEST WOULD SOON BE DRIVING HIS AUTOMOBILE.

2. Another issue in the social host problem is whether, if the social host is under a duty not to serve the intoxicated guest, the host may be liable to the guest for the guest's injuries as well as to a person whom the guest injured (the more typical claim). Which is the best heading for the defendant-appellee (the social host)? What is wrong with the others?

A. EVEN IF THE DEFENDANT HAD A DUTY NOT TO SERVE THE INTOXICATED PLAINTIFF, THAT DUTY EXTENDS ONLY TO INNOCENT PARTIES WHOM THE PLAINTIFF FORESEEABLY INJURES, NOT TO THE PLAINTIFF FOR THE PLAINTIFF'S OWN INJURIES BECAUSE THE PLAINTIFF MUST BEAR RESPONSIBILITY FOR DRIVING WHILE UNDER THE INFLUENCE OF ALCOHOL.

B. THE DEFENDANT'S DUTY, IF ANY, ARISING FROM RSA § 175:6 EXTENDS ONLY TO INNOCENT THIRD PARTIES.

C. LEGISLATIVE POLICY AND SOCIAL WELFARE DICTATE THAT THE INTOXICANT HIMSELF CANNOT RECOVER FOR HIS INJURIES.

D. THE FACT THAT THE APPELLANT WAS HIMSELF THE INTOXICATED GUEST AT THE PARTY AND NOT A THIRD PERSON SHOULD BAR HIS RECOVERY FOR INJURIES RE-

SULTING FROM BEING SERVED DRINKS, WHILE OBVIOUS-
LY INTOXICATED, BY HIS SOCIAL HOST.

3. The following headings were written by a criminal defendant-appellant
    whose request for an instruction to the jury on entrapment was
    denied. Which is best? Why?

    A. THIS COURT SHOULD REVERSE THE DECISION OF THE
        COURT BELOW. ITS REFUSAL TO GRANT APPELLANT'S
        REQUEST FOR AN ENTRAPMENT INSTRUCTION TO THE
        JURY BECAUSE OF INCONSISTENT PLEADINGS CONSTI-
        TUTED REVERSIBLE ERROR.

    B. THE LOWER COURT ERRED IN NOT INSTRUCTING THE
        JURY ON ENTRAPMENT BECAUSE, ALTHOUGH THE DE-
        FENDANT PLEADED NOT GUILTY AND DENIED THE IN-
        TENT ELEMENT OF THE CRIME WITH WHICH HE WAS
        CHARGED, HIS PLEA IS NOT INCONSISTENT WITH A RE-
        QUEST FOR AN ENTRAPMENT INSTRUCTION.

    C. THE DEFENDANT WAS ENTITLED TO AN ENTRAPMENT
        INSTRUCTION.

4. The following point headings involve a father (Kent Carr) who was
    driving his pregnant wife to a doctor's appointment when he was in an
    accident. The first issue is whether he is immune to suit brought on
    behalf of the child (Jason). The child was born with birth injuries from
    the accident. The appeal is to the Illinois Supreme Court. Some Illinois
    intermediate appellate courts had held that, in cases alleging parental
    negligence in operation of a motor vehicle, the parent is immune from
    suit only if the parent was driving the car for a family purpose.

    These headings are taken from a good student brief. However, they
    can be even better. How can you improve them?

    I. KENT IS IMMUNE FROM LIABILITY TO JASON BECAUSE
        PARENTAL IMMUNITY DOCTRINE BARS AN UNEMANCI-
        PATED MINOR FROM RECOVERING DAMAGES IN AN AC-
        TION BROUGHT AGAINST A PARENT FOR INJURIES
        CAUSED BY THE PARENT'S ALLEGED NEGLIGENCE IN
        THE OPERATION OF A MOTOR VEHICLE.

    A. Holding Kent immune from liability to Jason for injuries caused
        by his alleged negligence is consistent with the overwhelming
        weight of authority in Illinois.

    B. Jason is barred from suing Kent for injuries caused by Kent's
        alleged negligence because allowing such a suit would subvert this
        state's policy of promoting family harmony and preventing tortfea-
        sors from benefitting by their own negligence.

    C. Jason should not be allowed to sue Kent because parental immuni-
        ty is the rule in a majority of jurisdictions, and any change in the
        doctrine on the basis of motor vehicle liability insurance should be
        made by the legislature.

VII.   *The Argument*

A.   *Introduction*

In the Argument section of your brief, you should develop the
reasons why your client should prevail in order to convince the

court to accept your conclusions. The Argument is divided into sections developing separate claims for relief. These main sections are introduced by dominant point headings, while the legal arguments supporting each claim are often introduced by subheadings when there is more than one argument. Within each section of the Argument, as in the Discussion section of a memorandum, you must thoroughly analyze the legal points and facts relevant to your claim. A thorough analysis requires you to identify the issue, explain the relevant law, work with the decision from the court below and the most relevant authorities you can find, argue your facts and compare cases, rebut opposing argument, and conclude. A brief will not be persuasive if the arguments in it are unsupported and insufficiently explained. Nor will it be persuasive if you avoid the essential hard questions that the court will want answered.

You must also organize your analysis carefully. To ensure that the structure of your argument is always apparent, build your analysis in terms of the legal conclusions you want to prevail and announce those conclusions and your reasons for the court to adopt them in headings and subheadings. Begin each paragraph introducing a new topic with a topic sentence that refers to the proposition that paragraph is advancing rather than to the facts of a case.

An analysis in the Argument section of a brief differs from an analysis in the Discussion section of an office memorandum mainly in how you frame it. In an argument, your tone is assertive rather than evaluative. The order and focus of your analysis is controlled by your persuasive purpose. Your presentation should be responsive, therefore, to the opinion below, the kind of legal argument you are making, and the type of support that you have.

Determining the type of legal argument you are making is important in brief-writing because how you structure the argument and what you emphasize will vary with the point you are trying to establish. Some cases lend themselves to particular kinds of arguments. Some arguments may be fact-centered; the rule of law is well established and what alone is at issue is its application to the facts. In this situation, the discussion might focus immediately on the particular facts of the case, and the thesis paragraph might key in on the important facts in some detail. After discussing the rule of law, you might even decide to marshal your facts before comparing them with analogous precedents.

Other arguments are more doctrinal; the issue is primarily a question of law about which precedent controls the case or how a statute should be interpreted. Here, your thesis paragraph might well lead off with the law you think should control and your authority for so arguing.

Some arguments are more policy-centered; the contentions involve the purpose of the rule and desirability of its end. In contrast to a fact-centered or doctrinal argument, a policy-centered argument might well treat the facts of the case in a somewhat summary fashion but discuss jurisdictional trends and secondary authorities at length. Thus, the type of argument you are making should influence how much space and emphasis to give to the various steps in your analysis. Be aware, however, that many legal problems, especially those you receive as moot court assignments, may present you with several types of arguments that are not exclusive of each other.

B. *Writing a Persuasive Thesis Paragraph*

Because the initial paragraph or paragraphs after a point heading are crucial in a brief, they should not simply duplicate the Summary of the Argument. Although you want to forecast the factual and legal points you will be developing, your first task is to get the court's attention. Thus, you may find yourself writing more creative openings than you would in an office memorandum and using your thesis paragraph to introduce the theory of your case.

The thesis paragraph should also be assertive and informative. You want to explain to the court what your client wants and why. You want to tell the court what the controlling law is and how the court should conclude about the issues in the case. Moreover, you want your points to flow naturally, logically, and inescapably to your conclusion.

The following are thesis paragraphs that set out the theory of the case, first in a question of law, then in paragraphs that apply rules to facts.

Example of a Thesis Paragraph on a Question of Law

I. A PRO SE ATTORNEY IS NOT ELIGIBLE FOR AN AWARD OF ATTORNEY FEES UNDER THE FREEDOM OF INFORMATION ACT BECAUSE HE HAS NOT INCURRED LIABILITY FOR FEES.

Arnie Frank has come to this court seeking a windfall. He wants this court to award him attorney fees that he has not incurred. Mr. Frank is an attorney, but has no client. Instead, he wants to force the government to become his unwilling client, subsidizing his pursuit of a matter of commercial interest to him. The court below correctly refused to allow him fees, holding that a pro se attorney is ineligible for an award of fees under the Freedom of Information Act (FOIA), section 552(a)(4)(E), which permits a court to award "reasonable attorney fees reasonably incurred" to a plaintiff who "substantially prevails" against the United States.

This court has already determined that a litigant who is not an attorney and who acts pro se is ineligible for attorney fees. DeBold v. Stimson, 735 F.2d 1037, 1043 n.4 (7th Cir. 1984); Stein v. United States Dept. of Justice, 662 F.2d 1245, 1263 n. 12 (7th Cir. 1981). It has not yet addressed whether a pro se litigant who is an attorney may be entitled to attorney fees under the FOIA. The reasoning of those cases, however, applies equally to Arnie Frank. The court below, moreover, properly followed the overwhelming weight of authority in determining that a pro se attorney could never recover attorney fees under the FOIA, since a litigant must actually incur responsibility for fees before the court may award them.

Many thesis paragraphs begin with a conclusion, as in this fact-based thesis paragraph concluding that a clothing store's dress code policy for female employees violates § 703(a)(1) of Title VII of the Civil Rights Act. This issue involves application of Title VII law to particular facts. Its theory is that the dress code violates Title VII because it requires a "uniform" and applies only to female employees.

Example of a Thesis Paragraph on Application of a Rule to Facts

Title VII of the Civil Rights Act of 1964 prohibits the dress code implemented by the petitioner because the petitioner forces its female sales clerks to wear an identifiable uniform, while it permits its male sales clerks to wear their own business clothing. Section 703(a)(1) of the Act declares that it is unlawful for an employer to "discriminate against any individual with respect to his compensation, terms, conditions, or privileges of employment because of such individual's ... sex.... " 42 U.S.C. § 2000e-2(a)(1) (1998). A dress code that requires women to wear a uniform while men may wear ordinary business attire constitutes discrimination in a term or condition of employment on the basis of sex. Carroll v. Talman Fed. Sav. and Loan Assoc., 604 F.2d 1028 (7th Cir. 1979), cert. denied, 445 U.S. 929 (1980).

You may decide not to begin the thesis paragraph with a conclusion, however, if the facts of the case are particularly interesting or compelling. For example, as the prosecutor of a defendant charged with murder, you might want to emphasize the gruesome facts of the murder. Therefore, your thesis paragraph might begin with a parade of facts relevant to the legal issue and end by tying those facts both to the legal principle upon which you are relying and to your conclusion. Be careful that your thesis paragraph is not merely a narrative of background information, or maudlin, or overwrought. It must include assertions about the case. Because the rest of the argument is devoted to explaining the reasons for your assertions and conclusions, a narrative which is not tied to your conclusion is confusing.

Example of Thesis Paragraph Beginning with Facts

I.   THE POLICE ACTED WITHOUT PROBABLE CAUSE AND VIO-
     LATED THE FOURTH AMENDMENT WHEN THEY ARREST-
     ED JOSEPH GOLD AND SEIZED HIS PROPERTY WHEN GOLD
     PULLED A SHOPPING CART WITH HOUSEHOLD ITEMS
     DOWN A CITY STREET AT MID–DAY AND REFUSED TO TELL
     POLICE WHERE THEY WERE OBTAINED.

When two New York police officers saw Joseph Gold pulling a
shopping cart down a Brooklyn street at mid-day, they leapt from their
car, grabbed him, and demanded to know where he had obtained the
items in the cart. The officers' extraordinary behavior had apparently
been precipitated by a report from two women that they had seen two
suspicious men in the neighborhood, neither of whom fits Gold's
description. When Gold's reaction to the police intrusion was to remain
silent, the officers then compounded that intrusion with a full scale
arrest—frisking, handcuffing, and placing him in the squad car for
transportation to the precinct to await a report of a burglary. In the
incident just described, Gold's constitutional rights were violated. On
the least possible evidence of crime, Gold was subjected to the greatest
possible intrusion on his personal privacy even though such an intrusion can be justified by nothing short of probable cause to believe a
crime has been committed. Accordingly, the evidence seized from him
under these circumstances must be suppressed. U.S. Const. amends.
IV, XIV; N.Y. Const. art. §§ 6, 12.

These examples of thesis paragraphs not only preview the
writer's theory of the case, they all include the rules that control
the litigated issue. The FOIA paragraph included the statutory
language about attorney fees, the dress code paragraph included
the relevant language of Title VII, and the fourth amendment
paragraph included the probable cause requirement.

If your argument is broken into subissues introduced by subheadings, place the thesis paragraph after the roman numeral
heading and before the first subheading. It should forecast the
arguments to be made in each subdivision, and it should relate
those arguments to your theory of the case. An argument that is
not subdivided because there is only one basic assertion being made
should begin with a thesis paragraph that summarizes the legal and
factual contentions you wish to establish.

Example of a Thesis Paragraph Introducing Subpoints

THE SIOUX FALLS RULES REGULATING AND PERMITTING
RELIGIOUS HOLIDAY OBSERVANCES IN PUBLIC SCHOOLS
COMPLY WITH THE ESTABLISHMENT CLAUSE OF THE FIRST
AMENDMENT.

The Sioux Falls Policy and Rules, which regulate permissible observance of religious holidays in the Sioux Falls public schools, are constitutional under the first amendment. The establishment clause of the first amendment has never been interpreted to mean that there can be no connection between government and religion. See Lemon v. Kurtzman, 403 U.S. 602, 612–13 (1971). Rather, the three-part test the Court has developed as the standard of analysis in establishment clause cases is intended to clarify the degree and type of connection that is permissible. To satisfy that test, "the statute must [first] have a secular legislative purpose; second, its principal or primary effect must be one that neither advances nor inhibits religion; finally the statute must not foster an excessive government entanglement with religion." Id.

The Sioux Falls Policy and Rules comply with each of these requirements. The purpose of the Rules is to advance secular educational objectives and to foster mutual understanding and respect. Moreover, the Rules have no direct immediate effect on religion. Rather than entangling the schools in religion, the Rules ensure that the schools stay clear of religious matters. Thus, the Policy and Rules are constitutional under the first amendment.

After this thesis paragraph, the writer should go to subheading A and focus on the first prong of the Lemon test, whether the statute has a secular purpose.

Exercise 18–F

1. The following thesis paragraphs introduce the State's arguments to the Second Circuit that there is no sixth amendment violation when a closure order enables a frightened witness to testify. Which example is better and why? What is wrong with the other example?

Example A

The sixth amendment provides an accused with the right to a speedy and public trial. Nonetheless, a court has the discretion to bar the public when it decides there is an interest sufficiently compelling to justify closure. United States ex rel. Lloyd v. Vincent, 520 F.2d 1272 (2d Cir.), cert. denied, 423 U.S. 937 (1975). Although closure is usually upheld only if the psychological well-being of a sex crime victim is at stake, United States v. Hernandez, 608 F.2d 741 (9th Cir. 1979), and Merta was only the victim of an assault, she is a minor. Moreover, Judiciary Law § 4, which gives a court the discretion to close the courtroom during specifically enumerated crimes (divorce, sex crimes), extends to any victim likely to be embarrassed or humiliated during testimony and Merta falls within that class of witnesses that the statute seeks to protect. Also the order was not too broad because it was the defendant's family who were the source of Merta's embarrassment. Finally, the findings were adequate because the court identified the reason for closure and the interest served. United States v. Brooklier, 685 F.2d 1162 (9th Cir. 1982).

Example B

The trial court properly closed the courtroom during the testimony of Sheila Merta, a thirteen-year-old assault victim who said the spectators frightened her. While the sixth amendment provides that a defendant in a criminal prosecution has the right to a public trial, that right is not absolute when a court concludes that other interests override a defendant's right to an open courtroom. United States ex rel. Lloyd v. Vincent, 520 F.2d 1272 (2d Cir.), cert. denied, 423 U.S. 937 (1975). In reviewing whether closure was proper, a court must determine whether: 1) the party advancing closure established an overriding interest; 2) the closure order was no broader than necessary; 3) the court examined reasonable alternatives to closure; and 4) the trial court made adequate findings in the record to support closure. Waller v. Georgia, 467 U.S. 39 (1984). The trial court's order satisfied the Waller test in the case at bar: the psychological well being of a young victim of a brutal assault is an interest sufficiently compelling to justify closure; the closure was limited to Merta's testimony; there were no reasonable alternatives to closure; and the findings made during an in camera hearing were sufficient to support closure. Therefore, the appellate court's order upholding the defendant's conviction should be affirmed.

2. What follows is one short argument from an appellate brief in People v. Nevin that was submitted to one of New York's appellate courts (full citations are omitted). The thesis paragraph has been omitted. Read the argument carefully and critically. Then,

    1) determine what kind of argument it is—a question of law, or of law applied to facts;

    2) write the missing thesis paragraph;

    3) write a point heading.

———

The term "dangerous instrument" is defined by the Penal Law as "any instrument, article or substance . . . which, under the circumstances in which it is used . . . is readily capable of causing death or other serious physical injury." P.L. § 10.00(13). It is long settled that the relevant inquiry is not whether an object is inherently dangerous, but whether, as actually wielded by the defendant, it constituted a real threat of grave or even fatal injury. See People v. Carter. Thus, a knife—an inherently dangerous object—has been held not to be a dangerous instrument within the statute when the defendant merely carried it in his hand. See People v. Hirniak. On the other hand, a handkerchief has been held to be a dangerous instrument when used to gag an elderly man. See People v. Ford. Similarly, an ordinarily harmless object used to beat a victim can be a dangerous instrument, because such use created a substantial and obvious threat of grave injury. See, e.g., People v. Carter (rubber boot);

People v. Ozarowski (baseball bat); People v. O'Hara (boots); People v. Davis (plaster cast).

However, when an object is put to a non-standard use that <u>may</u> cause serious physical injury, but is not very likely to do so, it is not a dangerous instrument—even if it does in fact cause injury. In <u>Matter of Taylor</u>, a teen-ager admitted throwing two rocks at a friend's head, one of which struck the friend, causing physical injury. However, the court dismissed a charge of assault with a dangerous instrument, stating

> [T]he criteria is the circumstance under which they were used. True, such a rock held in the hand and used to repeatedly pound a person on the head or vital organ could cause serious physical injury. Even a thrown rock coming in contact with some part of the body could cause such injury, but this is not to be considered "readily capable". The after effects of an act cannot be used to determine the legality or illegality of the act itself.

Id.

When the evidence at appellant's trial is viewed in the light most favorable to the People and measured against the statutory and case-law criteria detailed above, it is clear that no rational fact-finder could have concluded that the bar glass that injured bartender Bruce Flint was a dangerous instrument. First, the glass that injured Flint was small and thick rather than fragile. Further, the glass was not used as a bludgeon, nor was it broken and used to slash Flint—rather, the glass was aimed at Flint's back after Flint had turned away from Nevin. No one heard Nevin utter any threats, and when he threw the glass, he acted in an ill-conceived but purely impulsive effort to have the last word or to regain Flint's attention. Unfortunately, Flint turned back to face Nevin and the glass struck Flint in the face. More unfortunately still, the glass broke and cut him.

Although the glass concededly caused physical injury, under the circumstances it was not readily capable of causing serious or fatal injury. Like the rock in <u>Taylor</u>, the glass <u>could</u> conceivably have caused grave or fatal injury—to a person with an "egg-shell" skull, for instance—but under the circumstances, it was far more likely to miss Flint entirely, to glance unbroken off his back and fall to the floor, or at most, to strike and bruise him. Although Nevin may have acted foolishly and immaturely by throwing a small bar glass at the bartender, he did not use the glass as a dangerous instrument. Accordingly, his conviction should be reversed.

C. Synthesizing the Law and Precedents From Your Client's Perspective

1. Applying Law to Fact

If you set out the controlling rules in the thesis paragraph you need not repeat them all to begin the next paragraph. Instead, begin by explaining the rule or by analyzing and arguing your case by applying the first rule. For example, the writer of the thesis paragraph about the Sioux Falls Rules included the Supreme

Court's three-part <u>Lemon</u> test used to analyze a claim under the establishment clause. The writer then went on in the next paragraph under subhead A to analyze the first part of that test.

The topic sentence introducing the first issue often applies the rule to the facts of a case, or describes the rule by synthesizing the relevant cases to explain them in a way favorable to the client. Topic sentences are extremely important. They should not be written in the kind of objective, narrative, exploratory style you use in an office memorandum, but should synthesize cases favorably for your client. In addition to synthesizing cases by their facts, you may synthesize their policies. For example, a topic sentence in a brief opposing Freedom of Information Act (FOIA) attorney fees for pro se attorneys might be, "The same policies that have convinced this court to decline to award attorney fees to a pro se litigant who was not an attorney apply to an attorney who acts pro se." Then go on to explain the policies.

In the following (condensed) paragraphs on the first part of the <u>Lemon</u> test, the writer explained that the Supreme Court has almost always accepted the state's declared legislative purpose, and has not inquired further into purpose. The writer synthesized the cases to explain them favorably for the School Board client, and used that persuasive synthesis as the topic of these paragraphs. The paragraph begins with the writer's conclusion, and then summarizes the writer's interpretation of the important cases (the synthesis), before distinguishing the opposing cases.

> The purpose of the Sioux Falls Policy and Rules is a secular one: to foster understanding and mutual respect of different religions by exposing students to the various religious cultures and traditions in the world. The court need not inquire behind this statute's stated secular purpose and the lower courts correctly did not do so. Indeed, this Court has consistently accepted a state's avowed purpose. In <u>Wolman v. Walter</u>, 444 U.S. 801 (1979) the Court upheld provisions of an Ohio statute authorizing aid to non-public, primarily parochial schools. The Court's entire inquiry into legislative purpose consisted of a single reference to "Ohio's legitimate interest in protecting the health of its youth." <u>Id.</u> at 836.

> In the last twenty-five years, the Court has inquired beyond the stated legislative purpose only twice, for reasons that do not apply to the Sioux Falls Rules. In <u>Stone v. Graham</u>, 449 U.S. 39 (1980), the Court held that the state violated the establishment clause by requiring public schools to post the Ten Commandments in each classroom. And in <u>School District v. Schempp</u>, 374 U.S. 203 (1963), the Court held that the state violated the establishment clause by requiring Bible reading every morning in the public schools. The Court found that the purpose of these statutes was "plainly religious" even though each state had justified them on secular grounds. None of the factors that compelled the Court to look beyond the state legislative purpose in

Stone and Schempp exists in the present case. There are four important distinctions. [analysis of the distinctions followed].

To summarize the second part of the Lemon test, the writer again synthesized the cases and concluded that in cases involving public rather than private schools, the courts analyze only the principal effect of a regulation, not every direct effect.

As long as the principal or primary effect of a regulation neither advances nor inhibits religion, then that regulation is valid under the second part of the Lemon test. In cases involving public schools, the Court has always looked to the primary effect of a regulation rather than to every effect. "The crucial question is not whether some benefit accrues to an institution as a consequence of the legislative program, but whether its principal or primary effect advances religion." Tilton v. Richardson, 403 U.S. at 679 (emphasis supplied). The primary effect of the Sioux Falls Policy and Rules neither advances nor inhibits religion. Rather its primary effect is to effectuate the school district's secular purpose.

The cases involving aid to parochial schools provide the exception to the general rule that the Court will invalidate a regulation only if its principal or primary effect advances religion. Because of the character of these institutions, the Court's analysis must be particularly intensive. In those cases only, the Court has invalidated statutes with "any direct and immediate effect of advancing religion," Committee for Public Education v. Nyquist, 413 U.S. at 783. Since the Sioux Falls District Public School has no religious mission, this type of inquiry is unnecessary.

This type of case explanation requires you to read carefully and to pay attention to the facts, so that you will be able to distinguish the unfavorable precedents and use favorable precedents to your advantage.

Remember strategic use of cases may require you to interpret a precedent narrowly or broadly. If you want to distinguish a case, interpret it narrowly, that is, limit the holding of the case to its particular facts. For example, in the Sioux Falls Rules case, the respondent School District distinguished several cases by interpreting them to apply only to parochial schools, not to public schools. The respondent limited the holdings by considering the contexts in which the cases arose. If you want to analogize a case, characterize the facts and holding more generally so that your case falls under it.

Remember to choose the cases you rely on carefully. Use the cases from the jurisdiction of the appeal, and the most relevant persuasive authorities. Tell the reader the holding in the case and its important facts. Then explain how it applies to your case. You will not be able to include every case you have found. Instead, decide which cases require detailed analysis, which more cursory attention, and which you must omit.

If your case involves an unresolved issue, such as the FOIA issue above, or an application of law to an unusual set of facts, then identify the issue and, as did the writer of the FOIA issue, analogize to cases that have been resolved in a favorable way. The court will be concerned with how the reasoning of those decisions applies to your case. For example, a petitioner might pose an unresolved issue this way:

> Although this Court has not specifically considered whether a letter such as that written by Ms. Fox falls within the protection accorded newspaper advertisements in Bates, a situation similar to the present case came before the Court in In re Primus, 436 U.S. 412 (1978).

Exercise 18–G

A graduating high school student, Tim Jefferson, has sued in federal district court seeking to declare unconstitutional and to permanently enjoin the inclusion of prayer at graduation. The school board of Tim's school had authorized student elections to permit students to decide whether to include a voluntary, nonsectarian, student-led prayer in their graduation ceremony. By a majority of one, the students voted to have such a prayer.

The most recent decision on this issue is Lee v. Weisman, 505 U.S. 577 (1992). In Lee, a middle school principal had invited a member of the local clergy to offer a nonsectarian and nonproselytizing prayer at his school's graduation. The Court said that the principal's invitation represented governmental coercion to participate in religious activities, a form of establishment of religion barred by the first amendment.

1. Assume you are representing Tim Jefferson. Write a sentence or two interpreting Lee broadly so that it is analogous to your case.

2. Assume you are representing the school board. Interpret Lee narrowly to distinguish it from your case.

Exercise 18–H

1. The following paragraphs, which are addressed to the United States Supreme Court, argue that Fields Brothers' dress code requirements for employees are illegal under Title VII with respect to the "terms and conditions" of employment because different standards apply to men and women employees. Which example uses case law better and why?

Example A

This Court has consistently held that, under Title VII, an employer cannot impose one requirement on male employees and a different requirement on female employees. See, e.g., Phillips v. Martin Marietta Corp., 400 U.S. 542 (1971). By imposing the requirement that female employees must wear a store uniform, but that male employees need not, Fields Brothers violates Title VII by discriminating against women in their "terms and conditions of employment." See Carroll v. Talman Savings Ass'n, 604 F.2d 1028 (7th Cir. 1979).

Dress codes that impose burdens on employees of only one sex are suspect because they can be based on offensive sexual stereotypes and thus violate Title VII. In Carroll, the employer had imposed its dress code because it had decided that women tended to follow fashion trends and dressed improperly for work. Id. at 1033. Thus, the employer in Carroll issued clothing to women employees consisting of a choice of five pieces. The court found the clothing constituted a uniform and held that the defendant's practice of requiring females to wear these uniforms was prohibited by Title VII. Id. at 1029. The court stated that the dress code was based on an improper stereotype that women exercised poor judgment in selecting work attire but men did not. Id. See also EEOC v. Clayton Fed. Savings Ass'n, 25 Fair Empl. Prac. Cas. (BNA) 841 (E.D. Mo. 1981) (requiring only female employees to contribute to and wear uniforms is prima facie evidence of actionable discrimination under § 2000e–2(a)).

Example B

In two cases on point to the case at bar, the courts held that employers who imposed a dress code requirement only on female employees violated Title VII. Carroll v. Talman Savings Ass'n, 604 F.2d 1028 (7th Cir. 1979); EEOC v. Clayton Federal Savings Ass'n, 25 Fair Empl. Prac. Cas. (BNA) 841 (E.D. Mo. 1981). The dress code in Carroll required women to wear a uniform that consisted of choices among five items: skirt or slacks, jacket, tunic or vest. Male employees were required to wear ordinary business attire. Carroll, 604 F.2d at 1029–30.

The United States Court of Appeals for the Seventh Circuit held that the employer's requirement that women but not men wear a uniform violated § 703(a)(1) with respect to "terms and conditions of employment." Id. The court remanded the case for the entry of summary judgment for the female employee plaintiffs. A district court has followed the Seventh Circuit and held that a dress code imposed on female employees only is prima facie evidence of discrimination under § 703(a)(1). Clayton Federal, 25 Fair Empl. Prac. Cas. at 843.

Exercise 18–I

Read these case summaries carefully and write a persuasive topic sentence that synthesizes the cases to explain how the cases apply to the facts. Write a topic sentence first for one party and then for the other.

Facts: A child, Bart was born in 1994 to Carole Darin who was married and lived with her husband, your client Gerald Darin. Gerald is listed as the father on the child's birth certificate. Carole and Michael Hahn had had an extramarital affair for some two years before Bart was born and blood tests show to 98.5% probability that Michael is the father.

When Bart was four months old, Gerald moved to New York from California for business. Carole remained in California and lived with Michael for five months, although she and Bart visited with Gerald a few times.

Michael held Bart out as his child. Carole then returned to her own home, but when Bart was two she lived with Michael again for eight months. Carole has now reconciled with Gerald and they are living together again and have a child of their own. Michael has filed an action to be declared Bart's father and for visitation. California law imposes a presumption rebuttable only by the husband that a child born to a married woman is the child of the marriage. Michael claims that the presumption infringes his due process rights to establish paternity.

Case A

The state of Illinois brought a dependency proceeding on behalf of two minor children living with their father, Stanley. The mother and father had never married but had lived together with their two children for eighteen years. The mother died. The state declared the children wards of the state under an Illinois statute that provided that children of unmarried fathers, upon the death of the mother, are declared dependents without a hearing as to the father's fitness as a parent.

The court held that Stanley was entitled under due process to a hearing as to his parental fitness before his biological children could be taken from him.

Case B

Ardell Thomas had a nonmarital child that she raised in her own home. Ardell never married the biological father Quinlen and never lived with him. The father visited the child from time to time and brought gifts. Ardell married, and when the child was eleven, her husband petitioned to adopt. Quinlen opposed the adoption. The state statute provides that only the mother's consent is required for adoption of a nonmarital child who has not been legitimated. Under the statute, the father has no standing to object.

The court held that Quinlen's rights under the due process clause had not been violated because he had never taken any responsibility for the child, never acknowledged her, and never lived with her in a family unit.

Case C

The unmarried mother and the natural father, Caban, of two children lived together for five years, representing themselves as husband and wife. Caban was named on the children's birth certificates as their father. He and the mother supported the children. The mother moved out with the children to live with another man, not telling Caban where they were. The mother married one year later, and after two years her husband petitioned to adopt the children. Caban learned of their whereabouts only one year after their marriage and visited them several times. State law permits an unwed mother, but not an unwed father, to block an adoption by withholding consent.

The court held that Caban was entitled to a hearing to determine parental unfitness before his rights as a parent could be terminated.

2. *Questions of Law*

If your case involves a question of law, then analyze using the strategies explained in Chapters Two, Three, and Eleven. The strategies of statutory interpretation, for example, include inquiring into the statute's plain meaning, legislative history, and policies. It also may require using the canons of construction. As an advocate, marshal these arguments to interpret the language favorably for your client.

In the example that follows, the writer uses a plain meaning analysis, buttressed by the legislative purpose behind § 1963 of the Racketeer Influenced and Corrupt Organization Act (RICO). The example follows a thesis paragraph that concluded that the district court correctly denied appellant's pretrial motion for an order excluding the attorney's fees owed by appellant from forfeiture to the government under RICO. The RICO statute prevents an appellant from transferring criminally obtained assets to third parties in order to prevent forfeiture.

Example

The meaning of § 1963 of the Racketeer Influenced and Corrupt Organization Act (RICO), 18 U.S.C. §§ 1961–68 (1982 & Supp. II 1984), is unambiguous and does not exempt attorney's fees from forfeiture. Under § 1963(c), title vests in the government to forfeitable property at the time the criminal act was committed, rather than upon conviction of the defendant. Thus, the government may seek a special verdict of forfeiture of tainted assets that have been subsequently transferred to a third party. § 1963(c). The only way a third party may vacate or modify such an order is to show at a post-conviction hearing that he was "a bona fide purchaser for value" of such property "reasonably without cause to believe it was subject to forfeiture." Id.

Because under the plain meaning of the statute, Congress exempted only two groups of people from the reach of third-party forfeiture, tainted attorney fees are forfeitable. Parties who have acquired title to assets before the commission of a crime are exempt from forfeiture. This group would hardly encompass an attorney in the pretrial stage of a criminal proceeding. In addition, parties who are "bona fide purchasers for value reasonably without cause to believe that tainted assets are subject to forfeiture" are also exempt. § 1963(c). An attorney who "purchased" tainted proceeds in exchange for legal services could not be considered a bona fide purchaser under the statute. An attorney would necessarily be on notice of forfeiture after reading the client's indictment. In re Grand Jury Subpoena Dated Jan. 2, 1985, 605 F. Supp. 839, 849 n. 14 (S.D.N.Y.), rev'd on other grounds, 767 F.2d 26 (2d Cir. 1985).

The general legislative purpose behind RICO forfeiture also supports a plain meeting interpretation of § 1963. In Russello v. United States, 464 U.S. 16 (1983), the Court noted that the broad goal of RICO forfeiture provisions was to strip organized crime of its economic base and separate the racketeer from his illegally gotten gains. Id. at 26, 28. The relation-back provision of § 1963(c) furthers that goal by preventing pre-conviction transfers of forfeitable property. See Kathleen F. Bricket, Forfeiture of Attorney's Fees: The Impact of RICO and CCE Forfeitures on the Right to Counsel, 72 Va. L. Rev. 493, 496 n. 14 (1986). A construction inconsistent with the plain meaning of the statute would undermine this goal by allowing a RICO defendant to utilize what may be the fruits of racketeering activity to finance his criminal defense. See In re Grand Jury Subpoena, 605 F. Supp. at 850 n. 14.

If the question of law is one that asks the court to adopt a new rule, then your strategies involve liberal use of analogy to existing rules and of policy. This example uses historical material and persuasive authorities.

A de facto spouse's right to sue for damages for loss of consortium is the next logical step in the evolution of the doctrine of consortium. Under the early common law, only the husband or father could sue for loss of services of a member of his family. Courts now recognize that wives as well as husbands may bring claims for loss of consortium. In permitting a wife to bring a loss of consortium claim, the New York Court of Appeals identified the wife's loss as arising out of the personal interest she has in the marital relationship. Millington v. Southeastern Elevator Co., 239 N.E.2d 897, 899 (N.Y. 1968). The husband in Millington had been paralyzed from the waist down as a result of an elevator accident. The court reasoned that the woman's "loss of companionship, emotional support, love, felicity, and sexual relations are real injuries" that altered their relationship "in a tragic way." Id. In coming to a similar conclusion, the California Supreme Court focused on the shattering effect of a husband's disabling accident on the quality of his wife's life when her husband was transformed from partner to invalid. Rodriguez v. Bethlehem Steel Co., 525 P.2d 669, 670 (Cal. 1974).

Susan Webster has suffered damage identical to that suffered by a wife whose husband has been injured. Although she was never legally married to John Webster, the stability and significance of their relationship indicates that her emotional suffering will be as great as that of a married woman. Susan Webster's commitment to her relationship is apparent from its nine-year duration and shared parental obligations, and demonstrates that her loss was no less real than that of Mary Rodriguez, a bride of only sixteen months. Moreover, she has lived with and cared for John Webster since the accident and likely will continue to do so. The circumstances of Susan Webster's relationship compel a finding that she, like the plaintiff in Millington, has suffered in a "tragic way" as a direct result of the injury sustained by her de facto spouse. See Millington, 239 N.E.2d at 899. Accordingly, her consortium rights should be recognized and protected.

D. *Arguing Your Facts*

Your brief will not be convincing if you fail to argue your facts thoroughly. Regardless of whether you argue your facts before or after you analyze supporting authority, you should always paint your facts in such a way as to elicit a positive application of the law. Stress facts that align your case with favorable precedents. Stress facts that show injustices to your client. After you have dealt with your strong facts, work with damaging evidence. You should not ignore unfavorable evidence, as the opposing counsel will certainly present that evidence, and present it in a worse light. Instead, put that evidence forward, briefly and blandly, and provide an exculpatory explanation if possible. Emphasize both exonerating facts and mitigating facts. Downplay facts that distinguish your case from favorable precedents. Demonstrate the irrelevancy, if at all possible, of facts that may show your client as unworthy.

1. *Emphasize Favorable Facts*

Treat favorable evidence in depth. Do not describe supportive incidents in broad terms; parade each material detail.

Example (Citations to the record omitted)

The Supreme Court has said that, in the best of circumstances, "[t]he vagaries of eyewitness identification are well-known [and] the annals of criminal law are rife with instances of mistaken identification." United States v. Wade, 388 U.S. 218, 228 (1967). In Moore's case, the conditions made an accurate identification impossible and the court's description of the identification testimony as "highly reliable" is simply unrealistic.

The robbery took place in a parking lot on a dark October night. The complainant never identified Derek Moore as one of the robbers. The most he could say was that Moore "would fit the description" of one of the tall youths. Indeed, the complainant previously testified that Moore was not one of the robbers. Thus, the People's contention that Moore was one of the youths who committed the robbery depended solely upon the testimony of the Smith brothers, Tom and John, who claimed to have seen him at the robbery scene.

Although John Smith asserted that he had seen Moore climb the parking lot fence, this witness admitted on cross-examination that he had been fifty to sixty feet away and had only seen half of the person's face. Tom's identification testimony is also questionable. From a distance of ten to fifteen feet, through the dark, he said he saw Moore's face for a "split second." Although he asserted that this brief view was sufficient for him to recognize Moore, whom he had never seen before, he could not see whether the hood of Moore's light-colored jacket was up or down. Nor was he able to see an identifying mark on Moore's forehead—a two inch keloid scar. In sum, it is hard to imagine a less reliable identification that would still result in a prosecution.

2.   *Minimize Unfavorable Facts*

Learn to exploit paragraph structure so as to highlight favorable material and subordinate damaging material. Positive information should be advantageously located at the beginning and end of paragraphs. Damaging material should be buried in the middle of paragraphs—and sentences—and described generally. In this way, negative information is framed by the positive and is, to some degree, neutralized by the context.

Example (Citations to the record are omitted)

Upon seeing two white males round a corner armed with tire irons and chains, Derek Moore believed that he was about to become the victim of a racially-motivated assault. Because Derek knew nothing of the robbery these two youths had just witnessed, this assumption on his part was entirely reasonable. So was his decision to run in the opposite direction. The fact that the district court found the Smiths unassailably truthful in asserting that they had a different motive for chasing petitioner is irrelevant to Moore's belief. It is also believable that the Smiths might well have shouted racial epithets at someone they assumed had committed a robbery outside their very window. Thus, there is no significant conflict in these stories, although there is a plausible and exonerating explanation for why Moore took to his heels.

Exercise 18–J

1. The following paragraphs address the question of whether a trial court committed reversible error by failing to respond to the jury's request to have a portion of the testimony reread (Citations to the record are omitted). In which of the following examples are the facts used well? Why?

Example A

A question of fact existed as to whether the defendant and his friend were attempting to steal the complainant's wallet. The defendant testified that the intoxicated complainant initiated the altercation and that the complainant claims to have lost $80.00. Yet, the defendant and his friend did not have more than $20.00 at the time they were apprehended. The jury requested this testimony because it was in the process of determining whether the state had proved the elements of the crime charged. The court's failure to provide the jury with this testimony before it reached its verdict was extremely prejudicial. The defendant was denied a fair trial and impartial jury. The possibility that the jury may have returned a different verdict if it had been provided with a read-back of all the requested testimony, and not solely that of the People's witness, cannot be excluded. Thus, the court denied the defendant's right to a fair trial, and its error should be reviewed.

Example B

In the present case, there is neither compelling circumstantial evidence nor eyewitness testimony which discredits defendant's explanation of what happened. We have only the word of the complainant that he lost his wallet. He first testified that he had his wallet when he ran from the scene and later testified that it was returned to him by a police officer (that officer, however, did not testify). He also later testified that he did not know if the defendant took his wallet or if he lost it while he was running. The police officers who did testify did not hear defendant demand the complainant's money, nor did any of them see or retrieve complainant's wallet. In addition, the complainant was admittedly "high" on alcohol at the time.

In light of the questionable nature of the complainant's testimony, the weight of the evidence against the defendant is far from overwhelming. In combination with the taint to the proceedings created by the error of the court below, this court should reverse the judgment of the court below and remand this case for a new trial in the interest of justice.

Example C

The trial court's failure to provide the jury with the requested testimony did not prejudice the defendant's rights and, therefore, does not constitute reversible error. The information which the jury requested and which the court failed to provide did not pertain to a vital point. The jury requested a rereading of the defendant's testimony about what the complainant had said. This testimony amounted to three short lines. The defendant testified that "Hassler got very huffy, saying 'Who are you telling me where to walk?' and 'I'll walk where I damn please' ". Later, the defendant testified that the complainant "started saying we'd tried to rob him and all that bull." The substance of this testimony was not vital to the defendant. The testimony revealed only that there was a heated exchange of words between the complainant and the defendant and his friend, that the defendant claimed the complainant was the aggressor, and that the defendant denied trying to rob the complainant. These factors were already known to the jury from other evidence and a rereading of this testimony was not vital to the defendant. Therefore, the court's failure to reread it did not prejudice the defendant's rights.

2. Which example uses facts more persuasively as to whether an employer discriminates on the basis of sex when the store issues business suits to its women clerks only? (Citations to the record are omitted.)

Example A

Fields Brothers' dress regulations distinguish between the sexes but do not discriminate on the basis of sex because the distinctions are not based upon immutable sex characteristics nor do they impinge on a fundamental right. Summary judgment in favor of Fields is consistent with that two-prong test to determine sex discrimination in employment.

Fields Brothers' distinctions between male and female employees is not discriminatory as to conditions of employment because clothing styles are not immutable characteristics of a sex but can be changed at will like hair length. For that reason, a sex-differentiated hair length regulation was held not discriminatory. The employee was able to change his hair length in order to comply with his employer's regulations. The respondent in this case could easily have worn one of the suits issued to her and could have complied with the dress code. Her desire to wear her own choice of suit is not an immutable characteristic. Nor does Fields' code impinge upon an employee's fundamental rights such as marriage and child rearing. In cases in which regulations impinge on female employees' fundamental rights, the employers did not impose any restrictions on male employees. Fields, however, imposes dress regulations, albeit different ones, on its male sales clerks.

Example B

The Fields Brothers adopted a dress code policy for both male and female sales clerks in 1979. The store sells conservative business clothes and its customers are predominantly business people of both sexes. The store's president has explained in his affidavit that the store's management policy is to cater to its customers' preferences for conservatively dressed sales clerks. All members of the store's sales staff are therefore required to wear appropriate business attire.

The court below differentiated between the "uniforms" that the female clerks are required to wear and the "ordinary business" attire required of male clerks. In reality, there is no difference. The male clerks' suits are as much "uniforms" as the female clerks' suits. Male business attire has developed over the years into a recognized uniform of shirt, tie, suitcoat, and suit pants. A male clerk who deviated from this attire would not be appropriately dressed. Design of female business attire, on the other hand, is a relatively new industry, and the same similarity of appearance has not yet developed. The store's decision to supply its female clerks with suits was an attempt to solve the problem created by this difference.

The court also emphasized that female clerks must wear a patch with the store logo on their suits while the men are issued a pin. Yet no real difference exists between a patch and a pin. If a patch makes a business suit a uniform, then so does a pin. All sales clerks wear conservative business suits and the store logo; all are treated alike in the "terms and conditions of employment."

E. *Rebutting Opposing Arguments and Authority*

Establishing your own argument requires rebutting opposing argument. Yet you do not want to overemphasize those opposing arguments by setting them forth in all their untarnished glory and then scrambling to recoup your losses. Instead, address the argument opposing counsel is likely to make implicitly rather than explicitly, by answering it as you present it. In other words, make your counter-argument affirmatively and as an integral part of your case, rather than as a separate section devoted only to counter-argument.

When you rebut your adversary, avoid topic sentences that overemphasize the other party's arguments. Weak introductions frequently include statements like

— It is (has been) argued that . . .

— Respondents assert . . .

— The courts rejecting this claim have said . . .

Such expressions highlight the opposing argument by opening the paragraph with it. For example,

> It has been argued that awarding a child damages for loss of consortium would result in speculative and uncertain damages. However, damages for injuries sustained by the Jones children are no more difficult to ascertain than they are in other classes of injury involving intangible losses where the courts have allowed recovery.

If the author of this example had simply omitted the first sentence, her topic sentence would have focused on the reason why the opposing argument is not sound. She would have suggested the avenue her opponent would take, without giving it undue emphasis.

> Damages for injuries sustained by the children in this case are no more speculative than they are in other classes of injury involving intangible losses where the courts have allowed recovery.

Or again, in arguing that the first amendment's guarantee of freedom of association protects not only activities of an organization but also the activities of attorneys who assist that organization, the petitioner should not say:

> One may argue that Trainmen, Mine Workers, and United Transportation Workers can be distinguished from petitioner's case since in those cases the union was the party charged with violating a statute, while in this case the party charged with violating the statute is the attorney. However, the Court has held that lawyers accepting employment under a constitutionally protected plan of referral have a constitutional protection like that of the union which the state cannot abridge. Trainmen v. Virginia, 377 U.S. at 8.

A more effective advocate might say:

> This Court has long recognized the right of an organization to request an attorney to assist its members in asserting their legal rights. In United Mine Workers and Brotherhood of Railroad Trainmen, the Court held that a state could not proscribe a range of solicitation activities by unions seeking to provide low cost, effective legal representation to their members. Lawyers who accepted employment or acted at the request of these unions were also protected because their actions helped the unions further their members' rights.

In addition, potential weaknesses in your theory of the case should not be discussed at the beginning of an issue or subissue or at the end of such a discussion. Deal with them in the middle of the argument concerning that point. The reader will tend to remember the beginning and ending of a section more than the middle.

Although you should deal with supporting authority first, you must disclose authority in the controlling jurisdiction that is directly adverse. This is an ethical responsibility imposed by the American Bar Association's Code of Professional Responsibility Disciplinary Rule 7–106(b). In addition, the newer Model Rules of Professional Responsibility, as adopted by each state, also require an attorney to disclose legal authority in the controlling jurisdiction known to be directly adverse to the position of the client if it is not disclosed by opposing counsel.[7] Although it is probable your opponent will find and include these contrary decisions, you should address them anyway. There are also strategic reasons to acknowledge unfavorable law. Your brief will be taken more seriously if you go below the surface to rebut adverse authority with reasonable arguments. By doing so, you show the strength of your client's position. If you are the appellant, you may "innoculate" the court to opposing counsel's argument by putting it in a context favorable to your client. In addition, you assist the court by setting out the conflict and in doing so, add to your credibility.

The easiest way to overcome contrary authority is to distinguish the cases on the facts. If you cannot distinguish the cases, however, there are a number of other ways to minimize the significance of an unfavorable precedent and to convince a court that a rule should not be extended to include the circumstances of your case. You could explain, for example, that the reasoning of an unfavorable decision does not apply to your facts and would, therefore, create an injustice unless an exception was made. Or you could ask a court to overturn a decision because it is no longer sound public policy. Here you might look at persuasive precedents from other jurisdictions that have rules you believe are more indicative of current public policy. You might examine developments in allied fields that support changes in the field of law with which you are concerned. You could also demonstrate that, as a practical matter, a rule is not working well—it is too difficult to administer or too vague.[8] Remember that you might also need to diminish the impact of an unfavorable statute. Here you might try to show that the statute does not control the subject matter of your

---

7. Model Rules of Professional Conduct 3.3(a)(3) say, in pertinent part, that an attorney must not "fail to disclose to the tribunal legal authority in the controlling jurisdiction known to the lawyer to be directly adverse to the position of the client and not disclosed by opposing counsel."

8. See Board of Student Advisors Harvard Law School, Introduction to Advocacy, 139–40 (4th ed. 1985).

case, that the language of the statute is ambiguous enough to permit a construction more favorable to your client, or that the statute is unconstitutional.[9] Chapter Eleven, on questions of law, explains these strategies of argument.

The following paragraphs are representative examples of arguments attempting to neutralize adverse decisions. The examples are based on the following problem.

Stone v. Eagle

The parents of Juliet Stone, an infant born with severe birth defects, brought a wrongful life action on behalf of the infant against an obstetrician. They allege he negligently failed to inform them that the mother's age made her fetus vulnerable to an increased risk of Down's Syndrome and that amniocentesis, a procedure by which the presence of Down's Syndrome in the fetus can be discovered, was available to her. John and Mary Stone allege that they were deprived of the choice of terminating the pregnancy and that they would have terminated the pregnancy if they had known their child, Juliet, would be born with Down's Syndrome. The suit is for damages to the child. (Wrongful life claims are distinguishable from wrongful birth claims. In a wrongful birth claim, the parents, on their own behalf, sue the physician whose alleged negligence resulted in the birth of an unwanted or deformed child.)

Defendant moved for summary judgment and dismissal of Juliet Stone's wrongful life action on the grounds that she failed to state a claim upon which relief can be granted. The court granted the motion on the grounds that Juliet Stone had not suffered a legally recognizable injury. It reasoned that no life could not be preferable to an impaired life, that neither the court nor a jury would be able to ascertain an appropriate measure of damages, and that defendant did not cause Juliet Stone's impairment. In fact, she could never have been born a healthy child.

In appealing the dismissal of her wrongful life claim, Juliet Stone must overcome the fact that most courts, like the district court in her case, have rejected actions on behalf of infants who have attempted to sue for wrongful life. Recently, however, a few courts have permitted partial recovery in wrongful life claims, allowing the infant to recover as special damages the extraordinary medical expenses which the infant's condition would require. No court has as yet, however, granted recovery for general damages compensating the infant for being born with birth defects, for pain and suffering, or for an impaired childhood.

Example 1:   Precedents are not followed universally

The California Supreme Court has recognized wrongful life as a new cause of action. Turpin v. Sortini, 31 Cal. 3d 220, 643 P.2d 954, 182 Cal. Rptr. 337 (1982). The Turpin court held that a doctor was liable for

9. See Handbook of Appellate Advo-   cacy, 44–45 (UCLA 2d ed. 1986).

negligently depriving expectant parents of information that they needed to determine whether birth would be in the best interest of a severely malformed fetus. Id. The court approved of a lower court decision, Curlender v. Bio-Science Laboratories, 106 Cal. App. 3d 811, 165 Cal. Rptr. 477 (1980), recognizing the claim of an infant plaintiff afflicted with Tay–Sachs disease. This child suffered mental retardation, blindness, pseudo-bulper palsy, convulsions, muscle atrophy, susceptibility to other diseases, and gross physical deformity. The Turpin court recognized that the child in Curlender had a "very limited ability to perceive or enjoy the benefits of life, [and that] we cannot assert with confidence that in every situation there would be a societal consensus that life is preferable to never having been born at all." Id. at 229, 643 P.2d at 963, 182 Cal. Rptr. at 346.

Example 2: Precedents conflict with sound public policy

Two fundamental tenets of tort law are that there should be a remedy for every wrong committed and that future harmful conduct should be deterred. Both these goals are furthered by recognizing a claim for wrongful life. Social interests are advanced when a physician's duty to an unborn child extends to providing expectant parents with the genetic counseling and prenatal testing that enables them to make informed decisions about what is in the best interest of the fetus. The wrongful life claim complements professional practice by requiring all physicians to exercise proper diligence and skill in caring for patients both living and unborn. Curlender v. Bio-Science Laboratories, 106 Cal. App. 3d at 828, 165 Cal. Rptr. at 487. Because physicians have the medical expertise and knowledge to detect fetal abnormalities, they should be responsible for testing for them and counseling parents about them. Neither the state nor the parents should be burdened with the care and maintenance of children suffering from detectable genetic malformations while the physician who failed to exercise diligence and skill remains immune from liability.

Example 3: Precedents are inconsistent with trends in related fields

Many of the issues in a wrongful life action have been recognized in other medical malpractice actions. The prenatal injury cases have established an unborn child's right to sue. The wrongful birth action has found proximate cause and imposed liability on physicians for negligence in counseling and testing for genetic defects. The right to die cases have given the individual a right of self-determination which overrides social assumptions about the sanctity of life. These extensions in tort law reflect its responsiveness to changing social values and establish grounds for recognizing a wrongful life claim.

In a case of first impression or in a case where the application of existing law would produce substantial injustice, or where policy arguments, supported by secondary authorities and persuasive authority, make good sense, they should be pursued. There are and always will be circumstances in which the attorney argues that fairness demands that the court re-examine the law.   Be aware, however, that many litigators discourage policy arguments at the intermediate level of the appellate court system.   Intermediate court judges may see the highest court as the only policy-making court.   In addition, since the courts are overburdened, the judges may prefer to decide cases on the basis of existing law.

Exercise 18–K

1.   Identify these writers' techniques for minimizing unfavorable precedents or facts.   Evaluate each writer's success.

Example 1   The court below relied heavily on Carroll v. Talman Savings Ass'n, 604 F.2d 1028 (7th Cir. 1979).   Yet Carroll is the only decision from a court of appeals that has held a dress code discriminatory.   Not only is the case ten years old, but it was decided only by a 2–1 vote over the vigorous dissent of the respected Judge Vest.

Example 2   In Carroll, the court overturned an employer's sex-based dress code policies which required its female employees to wear a uniform but permitted male employees to wear a wide variety of attire, including sport coats and leisure suits.   The Carroll dress code is easily distinguishable from the one required by Fields, where both men and women must dress in conservative business suits.   In fact, in Carroll, the court said that Title VII does not prohibit uniforms in the workplace but only requires that a "defendant's similarly situated employees be treated in an equal manner."   Fields Brothers accomplishes the very thing that the court suggests: it treats its employees equally.

Example 3   Fields Brothers has urged that the proper comparison is to cases involving personal grooming regulations in which the courts have held that grooming standards, such as hair length regulations for male employees that differ from the permitted hair length for females, did not constitute sex discrimination under Title VII.   In Knott, for example, the court permitted reasonable grooming standards for its employees that included minor differences for males and females that reflected customary grooming styles.

These grooming codes are markedly different, however, from Fields' dress codes.   First, Fields' disparity of treatment between the sexes is more severe.   Fields requires female clerks to wear a clearly identified uniform in a limited style and color range while permitting male clerks their own choices.   In Knott, each sex was required only to meet a customary standard of good grooming.   The limitations on their grooming were minor.   Second, grooming regulations merely maintain a standard of conventional grooming for employees to follow.   In Knott, men with long hair were unconventional and inappropriately groomed for their employer's business.   Fields Brothers, however, fired the plaintiff for wearing her own conventional and entirely appropriate business suit because it was in a different dark color from the one issued.   Finally, some courts have justified grooming regulations because they are not based on immutable characteristics. This Court, however, has never limited the reach of Title VII to regulations based on immutable characteristics but has inquired more broadly as to whether the employer imposed disparate treatment on male and female employees.

Example 4   Although several courts have recognized an exception to Title III for interspousal wire tapping, some federal courts have held that a cause of action exists between spouses for violation of the Act. In Jones v. Jones, the court applied Title III to a husband who had tapped a telephone at his estranged wife's residence, and in White v. White, the court held that there is a cause of action for a wife whose husband had hired an investigator to tap her telephone. In these cases, however, the parties had gone beyond a domestic dispute. In Jones, the parties were already estranged. The telephone was located outside of the marital home. In White, a third party to the relationship was the agent of the intrusion. Neither of these cases involved the special nature of an ongoing domestic relationship within a marital home.

Example 5   Those courts that have decided that Title III does not apply to interspousal wiretapping have misinterpreted the policy behind the statute. As the legislative history shows, Congress repeatedly heard testimony about the frequent use of electronic surveillance between spouses in divorce cases. In fact, one committee witness, echoing the testimony of others, said that "private bugging can be divided into two categories: commercial espionage and marital litigation." Several Senators stated in the Congressional Record their understanding that the bill prohibited private surveillance.

2.   Rewrite Example 2 so that the paragraph begins more persuasively.

3.   Rewrite Example 3 so that the paragraph begins more persuasively.

4.   Rewrite Example 4 so that the paragraph begins more persuasively.

VIII.   Conclusion

The conclusion is very brief. It is not another summary of the arguments. Instead it specifies the relief which the party is seeking. It is followed by a closing, like "Respectfully Submitted," and then your name and address as attorney of record.

IX.   The Appellee's Brief

Many attorneys who represent appellees underestimate the importance of the appellee's brief. They reason that because they won in the court below, and because more cases are upheld on appeal than are reversed, all that remains to win again is to explain the lower court's decision to the reviewing court. Indeed, many attorneys believe that because the appellant often turns their arguments against them, the less said the better. Careful attorneys, however, never rest on their laurels. A good appellee's brief requires the same care and creativity as an appellant's brief.

The opinion below is, of course, strong authority in your favor. It is generally advantageous, therefore, to refer to that opinion and to choose quotes from it. Do not, however, rely upon it exclusively, especially if the opinion is poorly reasoned. Because lower court opinions, especially in a moot court problem assignment, often need bolstering, you should argue your case in the way that you think is most effective. You need not confine yourself to the structure of the decision used by the court below.

In appellate practice, you would always begin by reading the appellant's brief carefully and outlining the appellant's arguments. You would also read the cases that the appellant relies on if you are not already familiar with them and update those cases. Make sure that you meet each of the appellant's arguments in your own brief. If some of the points are frivolous, dispose of them quickly.

You need not confine yourself to the structure used in the appellant's brief. The appellee's Argument section may be organized completely differently from the one in the appellant's brief. If the appellee has stronger arguments for one issue than for another issue, the Argument section should begin with the appellee's strong issue, not the appellant's strong issue. Put your best argument in the most prominent position in the brief.

The Questions Presented, Statement of Facts, Summary of the Argument, and Point Headings should similarly reflect the appellee's orientation rather than the appellant's. As a general rule you should put your side's view of the case first in every section. It is usually more effective to state your view and then refute the appellant's view than it is to put the appellant's viewpoint first and leave your reader waiting to hear your client's arguments. You should also choose those arguments that will create sympathy for your client. While some student advocates are hesitant to do that when representing the government, the effective attorney will find ways to make sympathetic the point of view of her client, regardless of the particulars of the case. In other words, an appellee's brief should not be a negative document that merely argues against the appellant's brief, but should be an affirmative document.

Indeed, as counsel for the party that won below, your style should be positive and assertive. Emphasize your main points; do not be defensive. Nonetheless, be certain to answer every colorable argument that the appellant has raised. Except for clearly frivolous points, you cannot afford to ignore the appellant's weak or strong arguments. Give the judges your side of each point. Dispose of the appellant's weaker arguments quickly; label the frivolous arguments as such. (See section VII, E for suggestions on how to handle opposing arguments.) Be sure to cite to the appellant's brief if you refer to the appellant's argument.

There may be some significant differences between moot court programs and the situation you would face writing the appellee's brief in practice. In an actual appellate case, you would have the benefits of the appellant's brief, the briefs already written for lower courts, and the complete record when you write your own brief. Typically a case that reaches a supreme court has been briefed at least once before. The attorneys know their opponent's arguments and their own weaknesses well. You would know exactly which arguments your opponent relied upon and you could play off your opponent's choice of cases and words.

In moot court programs, however, the parties may not have briefs submitted to lower courts and the appellee may not have the appellant's brief. You may only have the opinion below, the references in that opinion to the arguments raised by each side in the lower courts, and an abbreviated record to help you frame your arguments. In that case, imagine an appellant's brief written by an opposing counsel. Decide how you would write the appellant's brief, and, however hard it is to tear apart your own arguments, respond in a positive fashion by asserting the appellee's best arguments and rebuttals.

Finally, you should note that in a true case, the appellant may have a parting shot. After the appellee's brief has been filed, the appellant may file a reply brief. The appellee, then, must choose arguments as carefully as the appellant did to avoid giving the opposing counsel an opportunity to tear apart the appellee's arguments unanswered in writing. In moot court, however, the appellee's brief is usually the last written word.

Exercise 18–L

A. Read the following background materials so that you are able to edit the argument based on these materials that appears in part B of this exercise.

DEPARTMENT OF INSURANCE v. STALWART

Background

Simeon Stalwart is a partner in a well-known law firm. He is executor of the estate of Martin Met, a former client of the firm. Met died on April 3, 1977. He was president and controlling shareholder of a number of insurance brokerage companies.

Since Met's death, Stalwart has been deluged with suits based on Met's misappropriation of corporate funds. Neither Stalwart nor the other members of his firm knew about the transactions on which the lawsuits are based.

In August 1977, the Superintendent of the Department of Insurance began to investigate Met's affairs. On September 9, 1977, the Superintendent obtained an Order of Liquidation from the Surrogate's Court (i.e., he was to settle the affairs of Met's companies, and distribute whatever was left over to the remaining shareholders). As liquidator, the Superintendent took control of the books and records of Met's companies.

In February 1978, the Superintendent served a complaint on Stalwart, as executor of Met's estate. The complaint alleged that Met had plundered the assets of the companies, and defrauded the minority shareholders. It sought $2,684,935 in damages.

Stalwart had no idea what the Superintendent was talking about. So he served interrogatories * on the Superintendent. The interrogatories were 30 pages long, and contained 125 separate questions, of which many had several parts. They included numerous questions like the following:

> Identify the documents on the basis of which the Superintendent claims that Martin Met wrongfully appropriated $16,000 of the assets of National Insurance Company in June and July of 1974.

The Superintendent returned written answers in which he stated, in response to all questions concerning documents,

> The answers are contained in the books and records of the various companies involved. Inspection of such records will be available on request.

Stalwart sent his associate, Harry Hopeful, to inspect the documents. Harry was shown to a room with 30 carton boxes of files, and a pile of 17 books of receipts and disbursements from the different companies. No attempt had been made to show which portions of which documents related to which interrogatories.

Stalwart moved for an order to compel discovery. The Superintendent cross-moved for a protective order. The Supreme Court, N.Y. County (Anderson, J.) granted Stalwart's motion and denied the Superintendent's cross-motion. The Superintendent appeals.

Statutes

CPLR § 3124 ... motion to compel disclosure ...

If a person, without having made timely objection ... fails to answer ... interrogatories ... [the other party] may ... apply to the court to compel disclosure.

CPLR § 3103 Protective orders

(a) Prevention of abuse. The court may at any time ... make a protective order ... limiting ... the use of any disclosure device. Such order

----

* Interrogatories are written questions which one party may serve on another. The party served must give written answers under oath.

shall be designed to prevent unreasonable annoyance, expense, embarrassment, disadvantage, or other prejudice to any person or the courts.

Cases

Schertzer v. Upjohn Co.,
42 A.D.2d 790, 346 N.Y.S.2d 565 (2d Dep't 1973)

The court granted the defendant the option of furnishing copies of relevant records instead of providing written answers to interrogatories, as long as the defendant (a) specified which interrogatories were being answered in this manner, and (b) identified each of the copies so supplied to show to which particular interrogatory it related.

Harlem River Consumers Cooperative, Inc. v. Associated Grocers of Harlem, Inc.,
64 F.R.D. 459 (S.D.N.Y.1974)

A party answering interrogatories could not refer to aggregations of material, but had to specify the portions on which he relied.

Blasi v. Marine Midland Bank,
59 A.D.2d 932, 399 N.Y.S.2d 445 (2d. Dep't 1977)

Motion to strike certain interrogatories granted: The interrogatories, consisting of 49 pages, are unduly prolix, vexatious, and unreasonably oppressive.

Commissioners of the State Insurance Fund v. News World Communication, Inc.,
74 A.D.2d 765, 425 N.Y.S.2d 595 (1st Dep't 1980)

Motion to strike interrogatories denied. While "detailed and exhaustive" interrogatories "at first blush" seemed "unduly burdensome and oppressive," they were necessary to a resolution of defendant's affirmative defense. Having raised this claim, the defendant could not complain because interrogatories were directed to explore the basis of the claim. Merely because interrogatories were burdensome was no reason to strike them, although the court would find differently if "their use verges on harassment or seeks irrelevant information."

B. Edit the following argument. Consider whether it is persuasive. (Is the language persuasive? Are the cases arranged in the most helpful order? Are opposing arguments handled well?) Correct any spelling or grammar errors you find. Correct citation errors. If the correct form requires information you do not have, indicate the missing information with an underline. If there are places where citations are needed, indicate with an underline.

Superintendent v. Stalwart

Stalwart's Argument

Schertzer v. Upjohn Co., 42 A.D.2d 790 (2d. 1973) states that the Superintendent can furnish copies of relevant documents, rather than providing written answers to interrogatories. However, we must look further to determine whether the Superintendent has indeed complied with Schertzer. Schertzer sets forth requirements as to how the documents must be produced. In our case, the Superintendent failed to identify which interrogatory each document purported to answer. Therefore, he obviously did not comply with Schertzer, which requires him to a) specify which interrogatories are being answered by production of documents and b) identify each document to show to which particular interrogatory it related. Supra. This is also supported by Harlem River.

Although the Superintendent's answers are definitely inadequate, a motion to strike interrogatories may be granted if they are "unduly prolix, vexatious and unreasonably oppressive". See Blasi, (59 AD 932), in which the interrogatories consist of 49 pages. However, such a motion is clearly not justified in the case at bar, and is a blatant attempt by the Superintendent to avoid compliance with the requirements of the CPLR.

Defendants interrogatories, although 30 pages long and consisting of more than 100 questions, can be easily distinguished from the set of interrogatories referred to in Blasi. Plaintiff's complaint is 26 pages long and charges Martin Met with numerous types of misconduct, including conversion of corporate assets, fraud, and breach of fiduciary duty. Plaintiff seeks $2,684,935 in damages. The interrogatories do no more than track plaintiff's complaint. Defendant is Executor of the Estate of Martin Met. He is therefore a defendant in this case only by virtue of his fiduciary capacity. He has no personal knowledge of the allegations contained in the complaint. Interrogatories seeking further information on each and every allegation in the complaint are therefore essential to allow defendant to defend himself in this case. Compare Commissioner v. News World, 74 A.D.2d 765, 425 N.Y.S.2d 595 (1st Dept.1980). The Court should have no difficulty in finding that the interrogatories are not unduly long; and that the Superintendent's answers were inadequate.

———

Editing Checklist: Brief

I. Questions Presented

A. Do the questions combine the legal claim and the controlling legal principles with the key facts that raise the issues?

B. Are the questions framed so as to suggest an affirmative answer?

C. Are the questions persuasive without being conclusory?

D. Do the questions read clearly and succinctly?

II. Point Headings

A. Do the Point Headings provide a sound structure for the Argument section of the brief?

B. Do the headings set out legal contentions favorable to your client and support those contentions with reasons and relevant facts?

C. Do the headings have a conclusory tone favorable to your client?

D. Are the headings clearly and concisely written?

E. Is each heading a single sentence?

III. Statement of the Case

A. Did you include the procedural history?

B. Are the facts set forth in a narrative that will be easy for a reader unfamiliar with the case to follow?

C. Is the statement complete, accurate, and affirmative?

    1. Are all essential facts included and irrelevant facts omitted?

    2. Are unfavorable facts included without being overemphasized?

    3. Are favorable facts effectively placed in positions of emphasis?

    4. Is the statement accurate?

    5. Are record references included for all facts?

D. Does the statement include any legal conclusions or editorializing that properly belong in the Argument section?

IV. Summary of the Argument

A. Did you answer the Question Presented?

B. Did you summarize from the Argument the main reasons for your answer?

C. Can the Summary be understood on its own?

V. Argument

A. Organization

    1. The Thesis Paragraph

        a. Does each issue begin with a thesis paragraph setting forth in affirmative (and conclusory) terms the major contentions?

        b. Does the thesis paragraph present an integrated statement of the theory you are putting forth?

        c. Is its length proportionate to the argument?

    2. Large–Scale Organization

        a. Is each ground for relief a separate point heading?

      b. Is the Argument organized around issues and subissues?

      c. Wherever possible, is the first issue the one most likely to succeed? Are all points under it arranged in order of strength?

  3. Small–Scale Organization

      a. Is each issue or subissue introduced by a thesis paragraph or sentence?

      b. Is each issue or subissue developed clearly and logically?

      c. Is your argument made before the opposing argument is countered, i.e., do you make effective use of the positions of emphasis?

      d. If the topic sentences of each paragraph were arranged in an outline would a strong skeleton of the argument emerge?

      e. Does each paragraph advance the argument?

      f. Are there genuine transitions between paragraphs?

      g. Do the sentences within a paragraph coherently relate to each other and the topic?

B. Analysis

  1. Are the facts of the case argued effectively?

  2. Are the authorities cited appropriately described, explained, and applied?

      a. Are the rules of law stated clearly, accurately, and affirmatively?

      b. Are the facts of cases which are helpful to your client presented as consistent with the facts of your client's case, insofar as this is possible?

      c. Are "harmful" cases adequately distinguished or explained?

      d. Is the decision appealed from either supported or criticized?

  3. Are policy arguments effectively made?

  4. How have the arguments of the opposition been answered?

      a. Have you made sure that opposing arguments are not treated defensively?

      b. Are affirmative counter-arguments made convincingly?

  5. Is the argument logical, internally consistent, and thoroughly developed?

VI. Language

Is the language clear, concise, and chosen for persuasive impact?

VII. Grammar, Spelling, and Citation Form

Is an otherwise persuasive brief marred by technical errors?

Chapter Nineteen
Oral Argument

Like most students, you may approach your Moot Court oral argument with some trepidation. For the first time in a short legal career, completely alone and in public, you must face an oral examination of your legal knowledge of a complex problem. However, if you come to the Moot Court well prepared, you will probably enjoy the argument and gain confidence from the experience. For practicing attorneys, oral argument is an opportunity to clarify their case, to clear up any misunderstandings or doubts on the part of the court, and to make an impression that cannot be accomplished through a brief.

I. *Preparing the Argument*

There is no substitute for solid preparation. You must thoroughly know the Record on Appeal, your arguments, and the facts and reasoning of the relevant cases. Since you have already written a brief on the topic, you will know the strengths and weaknesses of your case. Your aim should be to impress the strong arguments upon the court, to shore up the weak points, and to answer the questions that the court may have. You should not read your argument from notes, so try to prepare a short outline with clear headings that will jog your memory about the points you want to make. You may want to prepare the beginning of your argument in more detail to get you started at the time when you are likely to be the most nervous. Some people advise that you prepare two arguments. One is the outline of the crucial points you must include even if the judges give you little time to make your own presentation. The other is the longer talk to use if your judges ask few questions and you must fill your time with your own presentation.

Anticipate the questions that the court will ask and be prepared for them. The court will probably ask about obvious weaknesses in your case. Therefore, know how to meet those weaknesses. If there are adverse cases, decide in advance how you will distinguish them or diminish their importance. But avoid dropping case names. Concentrate, instead, on the reasoning and analysis which shows why your position is correct and just. Think through your case so that before you give your oral argument, you know which points, if any, you can safely concede and why these points are not dispositive. Finally, be prepared to deal with the implications of the result you seek.

II. Selecting the Arguments

Oral argument is not a spoken version of the written brief. You do not have the time, nor is this the place, to argue every point of your case. Instead, crystallize the issues. Select and make the arguments that you think will probably control the judge's decision for or against you and that will make the court want to rule in your favor.

Make clear the basic points that you want to establish. Do not try to make complex arguments. Oral argument is a poor time for explaining subtle intricacies of the law or of case analysis. Leave that for your brief. Arguments based on fairness, simplicity, and common sense are often more effective than those based on esoteric complexities.

Choose among the types of arguments you included in your brief, for example, policy arguments, doctrinal arguments, and arguments based on the equities of the facts of your case. Remember, though, that these arguments are not mutually exclusive. You can focus on doctrinal arguments and yet humanize the case by relating these arguments to your client's situation. You should also choose among consequential and persuasive arguments and decide which ones to stress.

Once you have selected your main points, decide which premises and authorities you need to establish those points. Then, plan your outline according to that structure. Present your strongest and most important argument first. Focus the court's attention on your most effective arguments. Attack your opponent's weak points, but do not be defensive and use up your time explaining why your opponent's position is wrong before you make clear why you believe your position is right.

III. *Introduction and Argument*

In an oral argument, the appellant (or petitioner) argues first. Then the appellee (or respondent) argues. In many Moot Courts, the appellant may then have a short rebuttal.

A standard introduction which both appellant and appellee can use is, "Your Honors, my name is _____, counsel for the _____ (appellant/appellee or petitioner/respondent)." In some Moot Court programs, students are advised to preface this statement with "May it please the Court." If your Moot Court rules provide for rebuttal, the appellant should reserve time for rebuttal during this introduction.

After the introduction, the appellant should begin by setting out the context and issues for the court. For example, an appellant might begin, "The issue in this case is whether a clothing store that requires only its female sales employees to wear a prescribed uniform during work hours violates Title VII of the Civil Rights Act of 1964 by discriminating on the basis of sex in the terms and conditions of employment." The appellant might then briefly state the key facts of the case on which this issue of law revolves. Then the appellant could outline the main arguments. "Field Brothers does discriminate on the basis of sex for these three reasons." The brief outline of the argument will provide the judges with a "road map" that will help them follow the development of the argument. Moreover, the outline gives a framework within which to work and to which it is useful to return, especially in the face of interruptions by questioning from the judges. After giving the judges the legal context of the appeal and an outline of the main arguments, the appellant should present the first argument.

The appellee, on the other hand, need not be tied to the same format. The appellee has the opportunity to capture the court's attention with the opening, either by using vivid facts or a persuasive statement of the issues. If the appellee is the prosecutor in a particularly vivid criminal case, the appellee might follow the introduction by saying, "Your Honors, the defendant has been tried and convicted by a jury of the first degree murder of his wife of fifteen years who was pregnant with his third child at the time of her murder." In the Field Brothers case, the appellee might begin, "The Field Brothers Clothing Store requires all its sales personnel, men and women, to wear a business suit at work. The store requires all its sales personnel to wear the store's logo on the suit. The store requires all its sales personnel to wear suits in a dark, conservative color. Thus, Field Brothers does not discriminate on the basis of sex because it treats all of its employees alike."

However, the appellee might also decide to begin as the appellant has by setting out the issues in the case and then outlining the arguments. For example, the appellee might begin, "Your Honors, the issue is whether a clothing store that requires all its sales personnel to wear a conservative business suit and the store's logo during working hours violates Title VII by discriminating on the basis of sex." If the appellant has misstated any facts of the case, the appellee will want to correct them if they are relevant to appellee's case.

In general, the appellee's argument should not be a point by point refutation of the appellant's argument. Instead, appellees should present their arguments in the order that the arguments seem most effective. However, an appellee must listen carefully to the appellant's argument and be ready to change the presentation to meet the appellant's points. Flexibility is essential. An appellee should also listen carefully to the questions that the judges ask the appellant. In this way the appellee may learn which aspects of the case particularly concern the court and speak to those issues.

The appellant's rebuttal is the last word in the oral argument. The appellant should not include new information not made during the main presentation. Nor should the appellant use the time to rehash what has been said. Instead, the appellant should use the time to answer important points, not the small details, that the appellee seems to have raised, or to correct significant errors in the appellee's presentation, or to shore up those arguments that were weakened by the appellee or the judges' questioning. In other words, use the time to go for the big points. For example, if the appellee based her argument on a theme that she repeated with persuasive effect, the appellant could begin by redefining that theme in order to negate, or at least weaken, its impact.

In sum, although oral argument can be quite stylized, there is still a good deal of room for varying the format of the presentation. Your main concern as an advocate should be that the court knows what the issues are and gets the important information it needs to understand your version of the case.

IV. Questions by the Court

An oral argument is a conversation with the court, not a speech or a debate. The purpose of oral argument is to give the judges the opportunity to ask questions. Many first-year students, mainly because of nervousness, however, react to questions as if they were unwarranted interruptions or attacks. Instead of responding this way, you should try to welcome the judges' questions and be receptive and flexible. Use the questioning as an opportunity to find out the judges' thinking on the issues in the case and to resolve any problems the judges may have in deciding the case in your favor. Be sure to respond directly to the question a judge has asked. If it raises a thorny problem that you do not respond to effectively, you may have lost an opportunity to convince the court. Always answer a judge's question, even if, as will often happen, the question takes you away from your prepared outline. In that event, return to the structure of your argument when you have completed your answer so that you can retain control over the argument until the next question.

Expect the court to question you on the weaknesses of your case. Do not evade or misrepresent your case's weak points, but decide how you can limit their importance. You gain the court's confidence by knowing the law and presenting it fairly. If, by evasion or lack of candor, you lose the court's confidence, the judges will look to the other attorney to find out what the case is really about. Your frankness and integrity are essential.

Some questioners will ask you to discuss legal authority, others will be concerned with policy matters, and still others may be concerned simply with clarifying the facts of the case. A judge may ask a series of hypotheticals to try to define the limits of your claim. It is essential that you anticipate every possible area of questioning. Decide how to reply to cases against your position and work out acceptable responses before you go into the argument.

Do not be fooled if, as an appellee, you hear the court rigorously questioning the appellant and believe that the court is on your side and that your own argument will be uninterrupted. The court may do the very same thing to you.

Always remember that you are in an appellate courtroom. Address the judges as "Your Honor" or "Justice." When a judge asks a question, never cut the judge off before the judge has finished. Never indicate that you think the judge's question is unwise or irrelevant. If you disagree with a judge's statement, such as a judge's description of a case holding, do so politely. For example, you can say, "Your Honor, my reading of the case, which seems to differ from yours, is that. . . ." Some lawyers preface their disagreement with a phrase like "With all due respect, Your Honor."

Answer the judge's question directly and immediately. Do not tell a judge you will answer the question later even if the question is about a topic you wanted to put off until later in your presentation. If you can, use your response as a means of returning to the original topic of your argument. Frequently, returning to your argument will not be easy or possible, either because the judge has jumped ahead, or has returned to an earlier point, or because the judge has decided to take you down the slippery slope. Try not to allow yourself to be led too far afield, but do not openly resist a line of questioning. If you must abandon your outline, do so until the line of questioning ends or a subsequent question offers you an avenue of escape. When you have the opportunity, there is nothing wrong in saying "Now, Your Honors, returning to my earlier point . . .," or "Your Honors, the second reason that Field Brothers does not discriminate is. . . ."

Even if you have prepared your argument carefully, you may have difficulty responding to some questions.[1] Respond to a confusing question by requesting a clarification from the court. If you are asked a question and cannot think of an answer, or if the question relates to an area of law with which you are not familiar, first try to give a partial answer that in some way responds to the court's question and gives you a moment to think. If the court is still not satisfied, you would be better off simply saying that you do not know the answer rather than wasting the court's time giving an uninformed response. If you are asked about a case that you did not read or cannot remember, simply say that you are not familiar with the case. The judge may stop the line of questioning there or may explain the case to you and ask how it relates to your case.

Sometimes a judge will pursue a line of questioning that culminates in the request that you concede a point in your argument. Think carefully before conceding. Some points are peripheral and your arguments may be weak. Therefore, you may want to concede that point to maintain your credibility if a concession in no way diminishes your other arguments. Beware of conceding a point that is necessary for your case, however.

V. *Citation of Authority*

You may wish to refer to crucial cases in your argument, but you should limit severely the number of cases you mention. Use your time in oral argument to concentrate on facts, reasoning, analysis, and policy. Remember that your brief contains the cases and the citations. In addition, do not give the reporter citations to cases that you mention unless the court requests them. Reading case citations impedes the conversation with the bench and is awkward.

VI. *Speaking Style*

There is no one single way to present an oral argument. Instead there is a wide range of successful, yet different, styles. Your presentation will depend on your personality, skills, imagination, and your reactions to speaking in public and being questioned by a panel of judges.

---

1. For other suggestions on how to respond to difficult questions, see the   Handbook of Appellate Advocacy 31–35 (UCLA 3rd ed. 1993).

You should not read your argument. Try to maintain a conversational tone. Speak without notes as much as possible. Look at the judges when you deliver your prepared remarks and when you answer their questions. Do not punctuate your argument with phrases like "I think," "I believe," or "The Appellant would argue". Just state the arguments themselves.

Ideally, you should be poised, confident, and professional. You should speak slowly (nervousness tends to speed up one's speaking style) and clearly. But do not speak in a monotone. Vary your tone to give emphasis to your statements and to maintain the judges' interest. You should also try to stand straight and avoid distracting body movements, like extravagant gestures, or overly casual movements, like slouching over the podium. Do not interrupt the judges, even if they interrupt you. Be polite but not subservient. Above all, try to be relaxed. However, realize that very few law students can accomplish these goals without a good deal of practice and oral argument experience.

Even without much experience, however, you can accomplish the essentials: know your case, look at the judges instead of at your notes, and concentrate on the judges' questions. The best oral arguments are those in which advocates know their case inside out and have a dialogue with the judges in response to their inquiries.

Your speaking style should also convey conviction on behalf of your client's cause. If you are not convinced that your client should win, the court will not be either. As an appellate advocate, your argument may be the last step between your client and imprisonment or a burdensome damage award or fine. Your oral skills and legal ability may win the day.

VII. *Prayer for Relief*

Close your argument with a prayer for relief, such as "For the reasons stated, appellant respectfully requests this court to reverse the judgment of the court below" (or use the specific name of the court below). You may want to briefly remind the court of one central point before you state the prayer for relief, but you must not irritate the court by dragging on the argument or by giving lengthy summaries once your time has elapsed.

Appendices

Appendix A

Grammar, Punctuation, and Quotation

INDEX

A. Grammar and Punctuation

1. Comma Usage

a. Put a comma before a coordinating conjunction—and, but, or, nor, for, yet—when the conjunction is connecting two independent clauses (unless the sentences are short).

Example: A statute must provide fair warning to the public of the nature of the proscribed conduct, and it must provide explicit standards for the application of the statute by the people enforcing it.

b. Do not put a comma before a coordinating conjunction when that conjunction is forming a compound subject, verb, or object.

Compound Subject The wrench that flew out of defendant's hand and the box of nails

377

Example:	that the wrench dislodged lacerated plaintiff's face (no comma before "and the box of nails").
Compound Verb Example:	The wrench flew out of his hand and hit plaintiff in the mouth (no comma before "and hit").
Compound Object Example:	Counsel labeled the charges ridiculous and the decision laughable (no comma before "and the decision laughable").

c.   When a dependent clause follows an independent clause, put a comma before a subordinating conjunction connecting an independent clause to a dependent clause **only** when the dependent clause is nonrestrictive (that is, the dependent clause gives information that is descriptive but not essential to the sentence).

Non-restrictive Example:	The court upheld the decision, although there was a dissenting vote (comma needed).
Restrictive Example:	The plaintiff will agree to settle if the defendant accepts these conditions (no comma—the condition is essential).

d.   When a dependent clause or introductory phrase comes first, put a comma after an introductory phrase or dependent clause to separate it from the independent clause. You may omit the comma only if the introductory phrase is short and cannot be misread.

Introductory Clause Example:	If a court finds a contract is unconscionable, it may refuse to enforce it.
Introductory Phrase Example:	To establish economic duress, plaintiff must show three elements.
Comma for Clarity Example:	To clarify, the element requires a showing of involuntary submission to a person in authority. (Without the comma after "clarify," a misreading is possible.)

e.   Do not use a comma to separate a complex or compound subject from its verb. You may want to avoid long, complex subjects by rephrasing your sentence.

Example:	Relying on the employee-at-will doctrine may prove to be a mistake (no comma after the complex subject "relying on the employee-at-will doctrine").

f. Surround nonrestrictive, interrupting words, phrases, or clauses with commas. A nonrestrictive element contributes information to the sentence but does not limit or define the meaning of the word/s it modifies. A nonrestrictive modifier can be omitted without altering the meaning of the sentence. (See Chapter Ten, #8.)

Example: Jessica Stone and Michael Asch, while in their senior years at college, met and fell in love.

g. Do not surround restrictive phrases or clauses with commas. A restrictive modifier identifies or limits the word it modifies and is essential to the sentence. ("That" always introduces restrictive modifiers; "which" and "who" can be restrictive or nonrestrictive; "which" cannot refer to persons.)

Example: One jurisdiction that does not award pecuniary damages for loss of consortium is Kent.

h. Separate the elements of a series with commas. Although a comma before the conjunction joining the last element is optional, most grammar and usage books encourage its use because a comma before the conjunction connecting the last element can clarify the number of units you have in the series and their proper division.

Example: Since then, Mrs. Pascal has been suffering from depression, insomnia, recurring nightmares, and severe weight loss.

Example of an Ambiguous Series: He wrote to several department stores, including Macy's, Bloomingdales and Abraham and Strauss. (Do we have a series of two—Macy's, Bloomingdales & Abraham & Strauss—or a series of three—Macy's, Bloomingdales, Abraham & Strauss? What are the proper divisions—Macy's, Bloomingdales, and Abraham & Strauss? Macy's, Bloomingdales & Abraham, and Strauss? To avoid this ambiguity, put a comma before the conjunction introducing the last element.)

i. You may put a comma before a phrase or a word you wish to highlight.

Example: The vice-president had called for the meeting, then missed it.

j. Commas (and periods) are put inside quotation marks but outside parenthesis and brackets. (If the parenthetical material is a complete sentence, however, the period goes inside the parenthesis.)

Example: **Quotation** **Marks**	Once we recognize that "designed for use" means "intended by the manufacturer," the court's application seems reasonable.
Example: **Parenthesis**	Given the limitation on length (20 pages), we dropped that discussion.
Example: **Complete** **Parenthetical** **Sentence**	Given the limitation on length, we dropped that discussion. (The brief could not be longer than twenty pages.)

2. Semicolon Usage

a. Connect two independent clauses with a semicolon when they are not linked by a conjunction.

Example:	Her moods wavered between depression and hostility; she often expressed a wish to die.

b. When a conjunctive adverb (however, hence, therefore, etc.) or other transitional expression links two independent clauses, put a semicolon before the conjunctive adverb and a comma after it.

Conjunctive **Adverb:**	Bills are admissible if they comply with CPLR § 4533a; however, judges can relax those standards.
Transitional **Phrases:**	A formal defect may be waived by a guilty plea or by a failure to object at trial or on appeal; on the other hand, a fatal defect may always be challenged by a writ of habeas corpus.

c. When elements in a series are long or contain internal punctuation, use a semicolon to separate the elements.

Example:	There are three steps outlined in this section of the statute: first, the jury must decide the full value of the injured party's damages; second, they must decide the extent, in form of a percentage, of each party's negligence, with a total of all percentages of negligence of all parties equal to 100; third, the judge must mold the judgment from the jury's findings of facts.

d. Semicolons and colons go outside quotation marks.

Example:	The ex-husband felt entitled to a share of Jane's royalties for "Cases on Torts"; in response, Jane asked for a share of his stocks.

3. Colon Usage

a. Colons are used to introduce enumerations or lists, but you should not put a colon between a verb and its complement. Finish the sentence and then put the colon after the complement, as in the example below.

Example:	The contractor made three demands: first, Charo must fire Smith; second, Charo must enter an exclusive distributorship agreement with Champlow; third, Charo must fly to N.Y. to sign a contract to this effect.

b. Colons may be used to introduce and highlight a formal statement or example.

Example:	The jury had been out for twelve hours: this may account for the defendant's edginess.

c. Colons are used to introduce a long quotation.

4. Sentence Fragments and Run–Ons

a. Sentence Fragments

A sentence must have a subject and a predicate. Most sentence fragments do not result from the absence of a subject and a predicate; rather they are the result of punctuating a dependent clause as a sentence. A dependent clause does not express a complete thought and must, therefore, be combined with an independent clause.

Example:	Even though his contributory negligence may diminish damages.

You must either add a comma and finish the sentence with an independent clause or omit "even though."

Rewrite:	Even though his contributory negligence may diminish damages, he will recover.

b. Run–On Sentences

There are two kinds of run-on sentences. First, there are those in which two complete sentences are written as one, i.e., with no punctuation (fused sentence). Second, there are those run-on sentences in which two complete sentences are joined by a comma instead of a semicolon (comma splice).

Fused Sentence	Personal service upon Multitech Associates was not proper and Village

Example:	Realty's suit will therefore be dismissed.
Rewrite:	Personal service upon Multitech Associates was not proper, and Village Realty's suit will therefore be dismissed.
Comma Splice Example:	Multitech had not designated Sue Johnson to accept summons, she had neither express nor implied authority.
Rewrite:	Multitech had not designated Sue Johnson to accept summons; she had neither express nor implied authority.

5. Apostrophe Usage

Apostrophes are used to indicate possession or contraction.

a. Singular possessive nouns are formed with **'s.**

(The court's decision)

b. If a singular possessive noun ends in **s,** add an **'s.** (Some writers use an apostrophe only.)

(James's plea)

c. Plurals not ending in **s** take an **'s.**

(Women's rights)

d. Plurals ending in **s** take an apostrophe.

(The associates' employment handbook)

e. The possessive case of two closely linked nouns is formed by the addition of a single **'s** if, and only if, one thing is possessed by both. (The brother and sister's treehouse but the brother's and sister's workbooks).

f. *Note an important exception: possessive pronouns are not formed with apostrophes.*

"It's" is the contraction of "it is."

The possessive form of "it" is "its."

"Who's" means "who is." "Whose" is the possessive form.

6. Agreement Between Subjects and Verbs

A verb must agree in number with its subject.

a. If the subject is singular, the verb must be singular. (Everyone, everybody, each, either, nobody, one, and anyone are singular.)

b. If the subject is plural, the verb must be plural.

c. If the subject is third person and singular (he, she, it), the present tense verb ends in **s.**

d. If 2 singular subjects are connected by an **or** or **nor,** the verb is singular. (Either John or Jane <u>is willing</u> to speak to the professor.)

e. If 2 plural subjects are connected by **or** or **nor,** the verb is plural. (Either 1st-year or 2nd-year students <u>are</u> registering on Friday.)

f. If one singular and one plural subject are connected by **or** or **nor,** the verb agrees with the nearer form. (Neither Joan nor her classmates <u>want</u> to rewrite the memorandum.)

g. If the subject is a collective noun, like jury, the verb is plural if the writer is thinking of the individuals and singular if the writer is thinking of the group. (The jury [individuals] were [plural] fighting over the verdict. The jury [group] has rendered [singular] a guilty verdict.)

7. Agreement Between Pronouns and Their Antecedents

Just as subject and verb must agree in number, so subjects and pronouns must agree in number and person.

This line, for example, was the lead into an ad for a well-known Chicago store:

EVERYONE HAS THEIR PRICE

"Everyone" is singular, and "has" is singular. But "their" is plural and does not agree with the subject to which it refers. Of course, in correcting the "their," the copy writer should try to rewrite the ad without using sexist language. The writer could try "his or her" or could look for some other construction that attracts less attention. You could try an article, for example.

EVERYONE HAS A PRICE

The following rules govern subject-pronoun agreement.

a. If the antecedent is singular, the pronoun is singular.

b. If the antecedent is plural, the pronoun is plural.

c. If the antecedent is **everyone, everybody, each, either, neither, nobody, one or anyone,** the pronoun is singular.

d. If the antecedent is two nouns joined by **and,** the pronoun is plural.

e. If the antecedent is two singular nouns joined by **or** or **nor,** the pronoun is singular.

f.   If the antecedent is two plural nouns joined by **or** or **nor,** the pronoun is plural.

g.   If the antecedent is singular and neuter (neither masculine nor feminine), the pronoun is it or its.

> **Example:**   The court recessed for lunch.   It returned at 1:00 P.M.

8.   Pronoun Reference

a.   Avoid Vague Referents.   If the pronoun is **this, that, it, such,** or **which** and refers to a preceding noun or statement, the relationship between the pronoun and the noun should be clear.

— "This" is best used in combination with a noun so that it is absolutely clear what the "this" refers to.

> **Example:**   The defendant travelled west on Main Street at fifty miles per hour.   This violates the law.

Since the "this" could refer to travelling west as well as to the rate of speed, the word "this" needs a noun.

> **Rewrite:**   "This rate of speed violates the law."

— If the pronoun can refer to two preceding nouns, make it clear which noun the pronoun refers to.

> **Example I:**   The parent corporation and the subsidiary, which places great emphasis on loyalty, have a singularly responsive relationship.

> **Rewrite:**   The parent corporation, which places great emphasis on loyalty, has a singularly responsive relationship with its subsidiary.

> **Example II:**   Jim talked to John while he waited for the elevator.

> **Rewrite:**   While Jim waited for the elevator, he talked to John.

b.   The referent or antecedent for every pronoun should be present in the sentence or, at least, in the preceding sentence.

B.   Use of Quotations

Keep quotes short.   But if you do use a long passage of fifty words or more, you must set out the quote in block form, that is, indented and single spaced.   You do not use quotation marks when you set out a quote in block form.   Put the citation as the first nonindented text after the quotation.

When you do use quotations, it is important to use them accurately.   You must quote material exactly as it appears in the source from which you quote.   You may alter the quote, but if you do, you must indicate the alterations.   Use these devices.

1. Indicate omissions with an ellipsis (three periods).   Do not indicate omissions from the beginning of the quote.   When an omission indicated by ellipsis points occurs at the end of the sentence, you must add a fourth dot which is the period for the sentence.

    Examples: "and so ... ask not what your country can do for you, ask what you can do for your country."

    And

    "ask not what your country can do for you, ask what you can do...."

    But Not

    John F. Kennedy said, "... ask not what your country can do for you."

2. Indicate explanations and changes, such as changing a letter from upper to lower case, with brackets.   Put your own version inside the brackets.

    Examples: "[A]sk what you can do for your country."

    Or

    The court said, "he [the defendant] must have known the gun was loaded."

    In the first sentence, the writer used "Ask" to begin a sentence.   The writer had to capitalize the "a."   The writer of the second sentence decided to clarify the referent for the pronoun "he."

3. You may underline to add emphasis but you must explain your additions after the citation.   Use this device sparingly.

    Example: "The statute <u>applies to tort actions only</u>."   <u>Jones v. Smith</u>, 510 S.E.2d 53 (Fla. 1980) (emphasis supplied).

    If the underlining is part of the original quotation, put in parenthesis (emphasis in the original).

4. Use "[sic]" to indicate that you have quoted accurately and that the original contains a mistake.

    Example: "The statue [sic] applies to tort actions only."

5. Begin a quotation with a capital letter if it is introduced by a colon or if the quotation is syntactically independent of the rest of the sentence.   If the quotation is a syntactical part of the sentence, do not capitalize the first letter.

    Example: As the judge said, "The motion is denied."

    Example: He said that the cross-examination was "almost finished."

    Example: The testimony of the plaintiff was explicit: "At all times, I was free to leave the site of the polygraph examination."

Exercise A–1: Grammar and Punctuation

Correct the grammar and punctuation errors in the following sentences.

1. Every decision concerning the children were made jointly.

2. It is unlawful in N.Y. to confine a person against their will.

3. The filing fee violates Doone's right to be heard in court, therefore, this fee requirement should be invalid.

4. The aerial surveillance was a concentrated search undertaken for the express purpose of observing defendants activities.

5. Olympia Department Store denied they had committed outrageous acts.

6. As a general rule the court will refuse to enforce that part of the contract that is unconscionable.

7. The District Court following a hearing denied defendant's suppression motion.

8. A sufficient connection between the litigation and the forum state exist; therefore, the court possesses jurisdiction over the defendant, and they should hear the case.

9. Based on aerial surveillance, the police entered the premises seized certain evidence and arrested the three defendants.

10. The requirement, that interrogatories be answered by the production of the relevant documents, was not met.

11. CPLR § 3124 requires disclosure "if a person, without having made timely objection, fails to answer interrogatories".

12. The superintendent's answer was insufficient and the protective order was unjustified.

13. Neither defendants nor plaintiff contest the facts.

14. Its reasonable to take inflation into account.

15. When Mr. Lattimore refused to answer Mr. Smith, he upset a salad tray.

16. We needed to edit (given the twenty-page limitation.)

17. The court said that "the actor disregarded the probability that severe distress would follow . . ."

18. Once we recognized that "designed for use" means "intended by the manufacturer", the court's application seems reasonable.

19. The court denied the defendant's motion because they had not filed in time.

20. Given the limitation on length (twenty pages) we dropped that discussion.

21. There is no reason to strike burdensome interrogatories if they are ". . . necessary to a resolution of defendant's affirmative defense."

Exercise A–2: Grammar and Punctuation

Correct the errors in the following sentences.

1. The Board's refusal to act makes them liable.

2. When Jane Edwards sought to end the harassment her complaints were disregarded. First by her supervisor then by the Personnel Sub–Committee, and finally by the Board itself.

3. Church's are free to enter into contracts.

4. The statute does not begin to run if the defendant ". . . through fraud or concealment causes the plaintiff to relax his vigilance . . ."

5. Rev. Bryant who is sixty-five refers to himself as "the rock'n roll preacher".

6. After careful consideration I believe your sexual harassment claim is solid.

7. The Board failed to act therefore it will be held liable.

8. Jane Edwards threatened to complain to the Minnesota Department of Human Rights after which she was fired.

9. If there is no invocation at graduation, their right to free exercise of religion is violated.

10. He had a contractual agreement with Healthdrink Inc. not to discuss Healthdrink and it's deceptive advertising.

11. The first amendment protects churches from state intervention in church affairs and thus the court is unlikely to order your reinstatement.

12. Her complaints were ignored by Bryant by the Personnel Sub–Committee and then by the Board.

13. The chain of events, described in Mr. Miller's testimony, suggest an act of robbery.

Exercise A–3: Review Exercise—Coherence, Grammar, and Style

Diagnose errors and revise.

(1) "First, the conduct must be extreme and outrageous". (2) In <u>Davis</u> the court argued that if the tactics' used by the creditors have involved the use of abusive language, repeated threats of ruination of credit and threats to the debtor's employer to endanger his job, recovery could be sustained, citing authorities and previous cases in other jurisdictions. Id., at p. 407. (3) It is clear that based on these tests liability could be established by the various tactics used by the Department store. (4) Disregarding, for now, the fact that Augusta the plaintiff herein didn't actually owe money, the employee of the credit department used abusive language such as

"four-flushing bitch," sent letters with statements threatening to report Augusta's delinquency to the credit rating bureau which, if done, would substantially hurt her credit rating and, in addition, on numerous occasions threatened to report her "refusal" to pay to her employer which might be construed by a reasonable person as a serious impairment to her continued employment. (5) An argument that could be made by Olympia, at this juncture, is that some meaningless speech from a collection department employee would hardly be considered oppressive or outrageous. (6) One only has to look at the aforementioned decisions to see that the store's position is weak at best. (7) In finding only one instance of outrageous conduct in Davis, the number of extreme actions here are clearly distinguishable. (8) The second factor involves the foreseeability by the store that the severe emotional distress will occur. (9) "Liability extends to situations in which there is a high degree of probability that the severe distress will follow and the actor goes ahead in conscious disregard of it" is a direct extraction from the courts opinion. Davis, *supra*. (10) This standard can be used as a basis for the instant situation, thus, the letter written by Augusta to the store's president is evidence that the store knew of the situation in April, and the harassment was not stopped nor correcting the billing error. (11) If a letter to the store's president is not sufficient information, establishing foreseeability, and consequences that might result from the store's continued actions then what is?

Appendix B

Introduction to Citation Form

INDEX

I. INTRODUCTION

A Uniform System of Citation, commonly known as the Blue-book, is the generally accepted authority for citation form for legal writing, although other citation forms exist.[1] A citation is used to identify the authority for a statement and to tell the reader where to find that authority. Citations also provide other information, such as the kind of support that the cited source supplies for your statement. For example, the citation tells you which court decided the case, and thus, whether the case may be binding precedent or not.

In your first year of law school you will mainly write legal memoranda and trial or appellate briefs. In these forms of writing,

---

1. See, e.g., The University of Chicago Manual of Legal Citation (the Maroon Book).

389

you cite authority within the text rather than in footnotes, and you put the citation right after the text that you are citing to. In other forms of writing, such as law review articles, you cite authority in footnotes. The information in this Appendix is about citing in text. Moreover, because most of the authorities you will use for first-year memoranda and briefs are cases, statutes, constitutions, law review pieces, and books, only the rules for citing these authorities are included.

A citation can be in the form of either a sentence or a clause. A citation sentence comes after the sentence of text that it is the authority for and is punctuated as a separate sentence. You use a citation sentence if the authority you cite supports the entire sentence in your text. If the citation supports only part of your sentence of text, then use a citation clause following that part of the sentence it is an authority for. Set off the citation with commas.

> **Example:** (A case name represents the citation)
>
> Parents may be immune from a tort suit brought by their children. Jones v. Day. However, parents are not immune from suits for intentional torts, Red v. Green, or from suits brought by emancipated children, Fred v. Frank.

In this example, Jones v. Day is the case authority for the information in the sentence about parental immunity that precedes it. Jones v. Day is written as a separate citation sentence. There are two citation clauses in the next sentence. Each citation provides authority for a part of the sentence. The writer has cited Red v. Green for its holding that there is no immunity from intentional torts, and cited Fred v. Frank for its holding that there is no immunity from suits brought by emancipated minors.

II. CASE CITATIONS

A case citation identifies the case and gives the reader the information necessary to find the published form of that case. The first time you cite a case, you must include the name of the case, the reporter in which it is published (or, if not yet in a reporter, its place of publication, which may be a looseleaf service or computer database), the page on which the case begins, the date the case was decided, and, if necessary, the court that decided the case. The date and the court information are enclosed in parentheses. The examples in these materials are for citations of cases from the United States published in case reporters or available on computer databases.

Table T.1 in the Bluebook lists each jurisdiction in the United States. It tells you the names of the courts in that jurisdiction, the case reporters to which to cite, and the abbreviations for the jurisdiction, its courts, and the reporters.

Below is an example and explanation of a typical citation of a state case. State cases are cited to the regional reporter, in this case the Pacific Reporter, Second Series, abbreviated P.2d. (The supernumerals are not part of the citation, but are keyed to explanations below.)

1   2 3   4 5   6

Jones v. Day, 25 P.2d 100 (Okla. 1955)

1.   Name of case, italicized, or achieved by underlining if typed or written. Use the last names of the parties if the parties are individuals, and use only the first named of each party. Use the complete name of a business entity, but abbreviate as permitted in the Bluebook. For example, if "Day" were the Day & Smith Steel Company, Incorporated, write as Day & Smith Steel Co.[2]

2.   Comma after the case name.

3.   Volume number of the case reporter and name of the reporter, abbreviated. Leave a space between volume number and name of reporter.

Do not put a space between P. and 2d because there should be no space between adjacent single capitals, and the Bluebook considers "2d" a single capital. If the reporter were the South Eastern Reporter, Second Series, you would write as S.E.2d. If the reporter were the Southern Reporter, Second Series, however, you would write as So. 2d because "So." is not a single capital and thus requires a space before the numeral.

4.   Page number at which the case begins.

5.   No punctuation, but leave a space.

6.   Parenthetical that identifies the jurisdiction and court, and the year the case was decided. Because the Pacific Reporter includes cases from many states, you must identify the jurisdiction of the case. Identification by the abbreviation of the state means that the case was decided by the highest court in that state. If the case was not decided by the highest court, then identify the court if it is not otherwise identified (by the name of the reporter, see below). For example, if a case was decided by the Minnesota Court of Appeals in 1978, cite as (Minn. Ct. App. 1978). Bluebook Table T.1 lists the proper abbreviations for the courts in each jurisdiction. If the reporter publishes cases from only one jurisdiction, do not include the jurisdiction in parenthesis.

---

2. Bluebook rule 10.2.1(h) instructs that abbreviations such as "Inc." or "Ltd." be omitted if a party's name contains words such as "R.R.," "Co.," "Bros.," or "Ass'n," which indicate that the party is a business firm.

You will cite most state court decisions according to the format in the Jones v. Day example, subject to the following exceptions.

A.   Parallel Citations to State Cases

Some states publish their court decisions in an officially published reporter. These cases are thus published in two case reporters: the state's official reporter and the regional reporter.

Before 1991 (the publication date of the 15th edition of the Bluebook), rules of citation required citation to both reporters for all citations to all state cases for which the state publishes an official reporter. Citation to both reporters is called a parallel citation.

The Bluebook now requires parallel citations only for documents submitted to state courts for citations to cases decided by courts of that state if that state publishes an official reporter. However, you will still see parallel citations in other materials that were written according to the previous Bluebook rules.

For parallel citations, cite the official reporter first, followed by the cite to the regional reporter, as in the examples below.

Blue v. Green, 85 Wis. 2d 768, 270 N.W.2d 390 (1980).

[This case is from the Wisconsin Supreme Court.]

Black v. Gold, 85 Ill. App. 2d 768, 270 N.E.2d 390 (1980).

[This case is from the Illinois Appellate Court, which is not the highest court in the state. However, the Illinois case reporter identifies the court so that it need not be identified in the parentheses.]

B.   Parallel Citations to California and New York Cases

Documents submitted to California and New York courts should provide a parallel citation to a third reporter for cases decided by the highest court of the state and cited to that state's courts. West publishes an additional reporter for each state, the California Reporter (Cal. Rptr.) and the New York Supplement (N.Y.S.).

Blue v. Green, 46 N.Y.2d 401, 186 N.E.2d 807, 413 N.Y.S.2d 895 (1978).

Black v. Gold, 50 Cal. 3d 247, 786 P.2d 375, 266 Cal. Rptr. 649 (1989).

Cases from the lower courts of these two states do not appear currently in a regional reporter and are cited to the state official reporter and to the West reporter for that state. See Table T.1 for specific parallel citation requirements.

C. Citation to Federal Court Cases

1. The Supreme Court of the United States

Supreme Court cases are cited to the official reporter, United States Reports, abbreviated U.S. Example:

Nathanson v. Victor, 300 U.S. 52 (1980).

If a case is not reported yet in United States Reports, you may cite to the Supreme Court Reporter (S. Ct.) or the Lawyer's Edition (L. Ed.), in that order. If the case is not yet reported in any reporter, cite to United States Law Week (U.S.L.W.) or to a computer database. Do not give parallel citations.

2. United States District Courts and Courts of Appeals

There are no official reporters for decisions from these courts; cases are cited either to the Federal Supplement (F. Supp. or F. Supp. 2d), which report cases from the district courts; Federal Reports (F., F.2d, or F.3d) which report cases from the courts of appeals; and Federal Rules Decisions (F.R.D.) which report cases concerning federal procedural issues.

Because the citation does not identify the court in which the cited case was decided, you must always identify the court, by district or by circuit, in the parentheses.

John v. Marshall, 400 F. Supp. 12 (W.D. Va. 1976). [This case is from the United States District Court for the Western District of Virginia.]

John v. Marshall, 400 F. Supp. 12 (D.R.I. 1976). [This case is from the United States District Court for the District of Rhode Island. Rhode Island comprises one federal district.]

John v. Marshall, 400 F.2d 12 (2d Cir. 1976). [This case is from the United States Court of Appeals for the Second Circuit.]

John v. Marshall, 400 F.2d 12 (D.C. Cir. 1976). [This case is from the United States Court of Appeals for the District of Columbia Circuit.]

D. Unreported Cases

To cite cases that are not reported or are reported only in slip opinions (individual court decisions published separately soon after they are rendered), cite by the case's docket number, the court, and the full date of the decision.

Silver v. Gold, No. 92–28 (E.D. Mich. June 9, 1993).

To cite cases available only on electronic databases, give enough information to allow the reader to find the case. Include the case name, the case docket number and court and the full date. Identify the LEXIS or WESTLAW database, using its identifying code or number for cases after 1986, and all relevant identifying information for cases before that year.

> Silver v. Gold, No. 81–45 (N.D. Ill. June 5, 1982) (LEXIS, Genfed library, Dist. file).

> Silver v. Gold, No. 89–45, 1990 WL 1000 at *4 (N.D. Ill. June 5, 1990).

The asterisk precedes the page or screen number.

E. Case History

Because parties to litigation may appeal losing decisions, many cases build up a litigation "history." This history may include a decision on a motion or trial, one or more appeals, and one or more rehearings. Some or all of this prior or subsequent history of a case may be relevant authority for your analysis and should be cited.

Give the prior history (usually the trial court decision) only if significant to the point for which you cite the case. The entire subsequent history (usually appellate decisions or denials of further review) should be included, unless the cite is for a denial of rehearing or for the case history on remand if these are not relevant to your analysis.

Subsequent history citations should be preceded by a word or phrase that explains the history, such as aff'd, which means that the higher court affirmed the decision below, or rev'd, which means that the higher court reversed. These explanatory words and phrases are quite stylized and are explained in the Bluebook. Note that the explanatory phrases are underlined and some are followed by a comma.

> Blue v. Green, 100 F.2d 25 (7th Cir. 1962), cert. denied, 312 U.S. 420 (1963).

This citation means that the Supreme Court of the United States denied review of the case that had been submitted by a petition for a writ of certiorari. If the date of the two decisions were the same, both 1963, then omit the date in the citation to the earlier decision.

The Maroon Book does not require prior or subsequent history unless the citation shows the strength of that case as an authority or shows if the case is continuing. Thus, you would use cert. denied only for a recent case to show finality.

III. CONSTITUTIONAL AND STATUTORY CITATIONS

A. Constitutions

Cite constitutions by country or state and abbreviate constitution as "Const." Do not include a date unless the constitution you are citing has been superseded.

U.S. Const. art. III, § 1, cl. 2.

N.M. Const. art. IV, § 7.

B.   Statutes

1.   Codes

Statutes are published in codes and are cited to the current official code volumes. The basic citation form includes the abbreviated name and volume of the code in which the statute appears, the section number (or whichever identification is used) of the statute, and the year the code was published. Statutes are also published by private publishing companies in codes that are annotated. Cite to this code only if there is no official code cite; do not use parallel citations. You will find the title of each jurisdiction's codes as well as other compilations and their abbreviations in Table T.1 of the Bluebook. Example:

42 U.S.C. § 1985(3) (1988).

The cited statute is found in Title 42 of the United States Code as section 1985(3). The date is the year the code was published, not the year the statute was passed.

If the statute is published entirely in the supplement because it was enacted after the code was published in hardcover, then cite to the supplement:

42 U.S.C. §§ 2000f(a–b) (Supp. I 1989).

If you are citing to an amended statute where the original version appears in the code and the amendment is in the supplement, cite to the code and the supplement:

42 U.S.C. §§ 2000e(k–m) (1988 & Supp. I 1989).

2.   Session laws

If a statute has not yet been published in the code, then cite it as an act in the session laws (laws enacted by a legislature during one of its annual sessions that are published and bound in the order of their enactment). Give its name and public law number, the volume and name of the session laws (for state laws, begin with the name of the state) and page. Example:

Public Debt Act, Pub. L. No. 86–74, 73 Stat. 156 (1986).

Also cite to the act if you are using material that is not published in the code, such as the statement of legislative purpose.

Some statutes that have been codified are commonly still cited by the name and identification from their original passage as a public act, in addition to their current code citation. Example:

The Omnibus Crime Control and Safe Streets Act of 1968, Title III, 18 U.S.C. §§ 2510–2515 (1988).

IV. PERIODICALS

Your most common citations to periodicals will be to law reviews. To cite law review material in your text, first give the author's full name as it appears in the publication. Include designations such as "Jr." and shorten a middle name (or names) to an initial, unless the author uses an initial for a first name. If so, use that initial and the full middle name.

Follow the author's name with the title of the material underlined or italicized. Then give the abbreviated name of the periodical in roman type (not large and small capitals), the page on which the piece begins, and the year of publication in parentheses. See Table T.13 of the Bluebook for the abbreviations for periodicals, and Table T.10 for geographic abbreviations.

A. Lead Material

Lead articles, usually written by faculty and practicing attorneys, are cited by the author's full name, as indicated above. Example:

> Phil J. Friday, Jr., Just the Facts, 50 J. Crim. L. & Criminology 78 (1980).

B. Student Material

Cite signed student work by the author's full name in the same manner as other signed law review articles. Student work is signed if the author is credited with the piece anywhere in the issue in which it appears, for example at the end of the piece. If only the author's initials are provided, the piece is unsigned.

In order to indicate that a student wrote the material, cite the designation of the piece, for example, Comment or Note, before the title. Example:

> Moira Standish, Comment, Will Thanksgiving Never Come?, 50 Nw. U. L. Rev. 5 (1986).

Short commentary, such as on recent developments, and unsigned student pieces are cited by the designation used in the periodical, followed by the title, if there is one. However, if the title is merely a long, digest-like heading, or a series of keywords, it should be omitted and the work cited solely by its designation. Example:

> Richard Martin, Recent Case, 46 Nw. U. L. Rev. 357 (1982).

NOT: Richard Martin, Recent Case, Constitutional Law—Right of Privacy—Abortion—Family Law—As Applied to Immature, Unemancipated and Dependent Minors, a State Statute Requiring a Physician to Notify a Pregnant Minor's Parents Prior to the Performing of an Abortion is Constitutional, 46 Nw. U. L. Rev. 357 (1982).

C. Abbreviations and Spacing

The general rule is to close up adjacent single capitals. However, for abbreviations of names of periodicals, do not close up single capitals if one or more refers to a geographic or institutional entity. In that case, set off with a space the capitals that refer to the entity from the adjacent single capital. Example:

Moira Standish, Comment, Will Thanksgiving Never Come?, 50 Nw. U. L. Rev. 5 (1986).

This article is in the Northwestern University Law Review. Because the "U." is an abbreviation of part of the name of the institution, it is set off from the "L.," which is the abbreviation for "Law."

V. BOOKS

Cite books with the author's full name as it appears on the publication. Follow the rules about initials as stated under periodicals. Next, cite the title of the book (italicized or underlined), as it appears on the title page (including the subtitle only if particularly relevant), the page, section or paragraph from which the material is taken, and, in parentheses, the year of publication and edition, if more than one edition. Example:

Benjamin Cardozo, The Growth of the Law 16 (1924).

If the book has an editor, give the editor's full name in the parenthetical before the date. Example:

2 Page on Wills, § 152 (Bowe M. Parker ed. 1991).

The "2" indicates the second volume of a multi-volume set. If the book has two authors, provide both names, using full names. For books with more than two authors, use the first author's name, followed by "et al." Example:

W. Page Keeton et al., Prosser and Keeton on the Law of Torts § 10, at 59 (5th ed. 1984).

VI. GENERAL CITATION INFORMATION

A. Citation to a Particular Page

If you quote from a source or discuss material on a particular page or pages in the source, you must cite the page or pages on which the quotation or material can be found. If you are citing the source for the first time, put the page citation after you cite the page at which the material begins. This page citation is often called a jump cite; the Bluebook calls it a pinpoint citation. Example:

Blue v. Green, 200 So. 2d 108, 110 (Ala. 1975).

In this example, the quotation from <u>Blue</u> is on page 110 of the Southern Reporter. If this cite were to appear in a document submitted to an Alabama court, it would also have to include a parallel pinpoint cite to the official state reporter, hence:

<u>Blue v. Green</u>, 50 Ala. 100, 104, 200 So. 2d 108, 110 (1975).

The parallel cite informs the court that the quotation can also be found on page 104 of the official state reporter.

In the following example, the material cited appears from page 161 through page 164 of the A.L.R. Annotation.

Michael S. Corwin, Annotation, <u>Patentability of Computer Programs</u>, 6 A.L.R. Fed. 156, 161–64 (1971).

Examples of the jump cite in citations after the first full citation are given below.

B. Short Citation Form

Once you have cited an authority with a complete citation, you may use a short citation form for subsequent citations if the short form does not confuse the reader as to what the cite is for, the full citation is in the same general discussion, and the reader can locate the full citation easily.

1. <u>Id.</u>

<u>Id.</u> is a citation form that refers to the immediately preceding cited authority, and can be used to refer to any kind of authority. If the second citation is to material on the same page as the preceding cite, use just <u>id.</u> Note that the underline to italicize should extend under the period after <u>id.</u> Example:

Citation one: <u>Green v. Blue</u>, 233 A.2d 562, 564 (Pa. 1967).

Citation two: <u>Id.</u>

If the citation is to a different page, use "<u>id.</u> at" the page number. Example:

Citation one: Benjamin Cardozo, <u>The Growth of the Law</u> 16 (1924).

Citation two: <u>Id.</u> at 25.

If the citation is to a case that requires a parallel citation, use "<u>id.</u> at" the page number for the first reporter cited and then the parallel citation. Example:

Citation one: <u>Blue v. Green</u>, 426 Pa. 464, 233 A.2d 562 (1967).

Citation two: <u>Id.</u> at 473, 233 A.2d at 581.

Do not capitalize <u>id.</u> if you use it within a sentence as a citation clause. Example:

Because the thirteenth amendment does not require state action, <u>id.</u> at 104, the court should hold that a private conspiracy violates that amendment.

2. Supra

Supra is used as a short citation when the authority has been cited previously but is not the immediately preceding citation. Do not use supra to cite to cases, statutes, or constitutions. For these, use id. where appropriate or the form discussed below. Use supra to cite to books and articles. Example:

> Cardozo, supra, at 10. [This refers to Cardozo's previously cited book, cited for material at page 10.]

3. Short Form for Cases, Statutes, and Constitutions

a. Cases: The necessary short form consists of the case reporter volume and page number (for each reporter if a parallel citation is required). The Bluebook provides a choice as to how much of the case name to include. You may omit the case name and cite to the reporter and page when it is perfectly clear which case you are referring to, or you may shorten the case name to the name of one party, or you may provide the full case name. If in doubt, use at least one party's name. Example:

Grey v. Pink, 270 N.W.2d at 390.

or

Grey, 270 N.W.2d at 390.

or

270 N.W.2d at 390.

If this citation were to appear in a document submitted to a Wisconsin court, the jump cite to the official state reporter would also be included. Examples:

Grey v. Pink, 85 Wis. 2d at 768, 270 N.W.2d at 390.

or

Grey, 85 Wis. 2d at 768, 270 N.W.2d at 390.

or

85 Wis. 2d at 768, 270 N.W.2d at 390.

When you discuss a case in text, as opposed to citing the case, you may always refer to the case by the name of a party if you have already cited the case. Do not identify a case only by the governmental party, such as "In United States...." Example:

> To invalidate an agreement, one court has required actual fraud. Blue v. Green, 35 P. 220 (Okla. 1910). Later courts have limited Blue to its specific facts, however.

or

> Fraud under the FTC requires intentional conduct. United States v. Green, 35 F. Supp. 12 (E.D.N.Y. 1960). Later courts have limited Green to its facts.

b.   Statutes: You may use a short form to cite a statute in the same general discussion in which you have cited the statute in full as long as the citation is clear to the reader.   For example, if you are discussing the Civil Rights Act, 42 U.S.C. § 1983, you may cite it as § 1983 in that discussion, or as the Civil Rights Act, or as 42 U.S.C. § 1983.   When you discuss a statute in text, you may also use the short designation.   Most people probably use the section designations.

c.   Constitutions: Do not use a short form citation except id. where appropriate.

4.   Hereinafter

You may devise your own short form for particularly cumbersome citations to any kind of material.   After you cite the material in full, follow with "hereinafter" and the form you will use. Enclose this information in brackets.   Example:

Paul Bator et al., Hart and Wechsler's The Federal Courts and the Federal System 300 (2d ed. 1973) [hereinafter Hart and Wechsler].

Do not use hereinafter for case names or for any statutes unless the name is extremely long.

C.   String Citation

A list of citations to several authorities for a particular point is called a string citation.   You will see string cites used in judicial opinions and in memoranda and briefs, but you should use long ones sparingly.   Unless your purpose is to actually list every case or other authority on point, or to literally show overwhelming authority, a string cite is usually not necessary and is difficult to read. The reader will tend to avoid it.

A citation of just a few authorities, however, is fairly common. The authority or authorities that are considerably more helpful or important than the others should be cited first.   The others should follow in the order listed in the Bluebook—enacted law first, international agreements, case law, and others as listed in Rule 1.4. If no authorities stand out, this ordering scheme governs the entire string cite.   The Bluebook also provides a correct order within each type of authority.   For case law, the order is federal cases, state cases, listed alphabetically by state, and foreign cases.   Within each jurisdiction (all federal courts are one jurisdiction), cite cases from highest court to lowest court, and within each court level, most recent to least recent.   Use the same order of jurisdictions to cite constitutions and statutes.   Separate the citations with a semicolon.

Example:

Sosa v. Grace, 350 F. Supp. 80 (N.D. Ill. 1987); Weiss v. Guillen, 400 S.E.2d 10 (Ga. 1986); McGee v. McGuire, 430 S.W.2d 85 (Mo. 1986); Jeter v. O'Neill, 500 N.E.2d 3 (N.Y. 1985); Alou v. Biggio, 150 S.W.2d 82 (Tex. 1979).

Remember that not all authorities are equal in weight. A string cite obscures the differences in the importance of the authorities listed. A case or statute from the jurisdiction of your assignment, for example, should be more important than those from other jurisdictions, and these citations should precede the others. While the Bluebook allows such an authority to be listed first in a string cite, you should also consider citing controlling authority alone, after the proposition it supports. Then, use an introductory signal (see below) to cite supporting cases from other jurisdictions, as is done in this example from an Illinois problem.

A parent is not immune from suit brought by an emancipated minor. Oscar v. Green, 350 N.E.2d 10 (Ill. 1971). See also Roosevelt v. Franklin, 390 A.2d 50 (N.J. 1965); Kit v. Carson, 41 N.W.2d 200 (N.D. 1962); Black v. Hills, 460 N.W.2d 80 (S.D. 1964).

D. Introductory Signals

Introductory signals are the italicized or underlined words that often precede citations to authority. Signals are used to show what type of support the citation supplies for the author's statement.

1. Direct citation without a signal: Use no signal before a citation if the authority

a.   is the source of a quotation, or

b.   identifies an authority referred to in the text.

2. Introductory signals

a. See is the signal most often used. It means that the cited authority is a basic source material for the proposition in the text. See is used if the proposition is not stated in the cited authority (use no signal if it is) but follows directly from it.

See also is used to give additional support, especially after other supporting authorities have been cited and discussed.

Because Jones did not act intentionally or recklessly, she is not guilty of criminal contempt. See Yellow v. Orange, 100 F. Supp. 58 (S.D.N.Y. 1951).

Because Jones did not act intentionally or recklessly, she is not guilty of criminal contempt under the rule of Yellow v. Orange, id. See also Gold v. Brass, 394 F.2d 42 (D.C. Cir. 1971); Silver v. Copper, 285 F.2d 512 (D.C. Cir. 1968).

b. E.g. means "for example." Use it to give one or more examples of support for the proposition in the text. E.g. may be combined with other signals. E.g. is followed by a comma.

Most state statutes require that the defendant act intentionally or recklessly. E.g., N.Y. Penal Law § 50 (McKinney 1980); Or. Rev. Stat. § 32 (1985); Utah Code Ann. § 12 (1981).

A defendant, therefore, should not be guilty if he acted negligently. See, e.g., Blue v. Green, 400 F.2d 12 (7th Cir. 1972) (defendant "just careless"); Gold v. Brass, 394 F.2d 42 (D.C. Cir. 1971) (defendant "merely inadvertent"); Yellow v. Orange, 100 F. Supp. 58 (S.D.N.Y. 1951) (defendant's "mere oversight").

    c. Cf. means that the proposition in the cited authority is different from, but analogous to, the proposition in the text, and so supports the proposition. Cf. can show comparisons, as does the signal "Compare."

    d. Show authority in contradiction to your proposition with a signal introduced by "but," such as "but see", and "but cf."

Either intentional or reckless disregard of a court order constitutes criminal contempt. Gold v. Brass, 394 F.2d 42 (D.C. Cir. 1971). But see Lead v. Pipe, 512 F.2d 65 (12th Cir. 1980) (requiring intentional conduct for criminal contempt).

A signal may be used with an explanatory parenthetical as in the examples above. The Bluebook encourages parenthetical information to be added to the basic citation in order to explain the relevance of the authority cited with an introductory signal. The parenthetical information should relate to the material discussed in your text. Generally, a parenthetical should be a phrase, not a sentence, and should begin with a present participle (example 2(d)). However, if you do not need a complete participial phrase, use a shorter parenthetical (example 2(b)).

You may also supply other parenthetical information, such as information that explains the weight of the cited authority. Examples:

Gold v. Brass, 394 F.2d 42 (D.C. Cir. 1971) (Bork, J., dissenting).

Lead v. Pipe, 512 U.S. 65 (1980) (per curiam).

BLUEBOOK EXERCISES

Rewrite these citations correctly. If the correct form requires information that you do not have, such as a page number, indicate the information with an underline.

1. Johnson et al. v. Smith 312 N.E.2d 600 (Il. 1964).

2. Michaels v. Jordan, 100 F.Sup. 5 (R.I.1941).

3. Jordans v. Marsh Corp. Inc., 206 So.2d 3 (Miss. 1959).

4. Marsh v. Metropolitan Housing Institute, 6 F.3d 9 (CA 2 1992).

5. Simon v. Pauls, 210 U.S. 15, 200 S. Ct. 7, 190 L.Ed. 16 (Sct. 1965).

6. In this appeal, the defendant has raised an error he did not raise at trial. See U.S. v. Carter, 230 F.2d 62 (1971) quoted on page 64. See also, State v. Brown, 400 P.2d 10 (Calif. 1990), State v. Wallace, 100 So.2d 7 (Ala. 1951), State v. LaFollette, 100 Wisc.2d 48 (1985), 312 N.W.2d 30 (1985).

7. In Ryan v. Quinn Brothers Corporation, 318 N.E.2d 6 (Mass. 1964), the court held that the defendant had violated Section 12 Mass. Annotated Laws Chapter 5. However, the plaintiff received only nominal damages. Ryan, supra on page 10.

8. Title 15 Section 552 Part a4 of The United States Code published in 1989 permits a court to award attorney fees "reasonably incurred" to a successful litigant [my emphasis].

9. The appellee has distinguished Maryland law from the cases that the appellant has relied on. (a) For example, the appellee distinguishes Pioneer Lands Inc. v. Agnew, 400 A.2d 36, 390 Md. Repts. 165 (Md. 1981). (b) The Environmental Preservation Act, Md. Code Annot. [Environ.] § 36 (1992), the statute at issue in Pioneer Lands, is different from the one at issue here. (c) Pioneer Lands at 38. [Correct the citations at (a), (b), and (c).]

10. The statute requires that three witnesses sign the will. § 15 Miss. code Ann. Only two witnesses signed the decedent's will, and the will is invalid. See, Macabre v. Macabre, 150 So.2d 35 (Miss. 1972), Rigor v. Mortis, 182 So.2d 10 (Miss. 1979). This court has said, "It is more important that the statue [error in original] be enforced than the will be valid," Macabre, at 37.

11. You are citing to the book Learned Hand, The Man and the Judge, by Gerald Gunther, published by Alfred Knopf in 1994, for information in footnote 148 on page 37. Cite this source.

12. You have just read a law review article "Videotaping Wills: a new frontier in estate planning." The author is Alfred W. Buckley. It appeared in volume 11 Ohio Northern University's law review in 1984 on pages 271–287. Cite it.

BLUEBOOK QUICK INDEX
(Sixteenth Edition)

Appendix C

Sample Office Memorandum

TO: Assistant State's Attorney

FROM: J.B.

RE: People v. Keith

DATE: November 1, 1989

Facts: Roger Keith was indicted for murder in a hit-and-run killing in Silver Stone, Colorado. At a preliminary hearing on September 30, 1989, Keith's defense attorney moved for dismissal of the murder charge on the ground that the state had lost the alleged murder weapon, and that the loss constituted suppression of exculpatory evidence and denied Keith the right to a fair trial. The court has asked for a memo in opposition to the motion.

The murder indictment stems from a hit–and–run accident on September 2, 1989, at 6:30 P.M. Two witnesses observed a young white man they could not identify start a car, take off at high speed, and swerve onto the sidewalk, striking the victim. The witnesses said the car was a red hatch-back that had a rear license plate that said "GUMSHOE."

Keith is a newspaper reporter and was investigating allegations of corruption in the Silver Stone Police Department at the time. The stories already published had named the arresting officer in his case as involved in some minor illegal activities. Keith owned a red hatch-back with "GUMSHOE" license plates. Keith was arrested the night of the killing and insisted that he was home alone all evening and that his car was not in operating condition. He also claimed that his car was missing its front license plate. The police found Keith's car in his garage and towed it to the police impoundment yard. It was stolen that night from the police yard and has never been recovered.

Police Officer Miller, the arresting officer, testified at Keith's pre-trial hearing that the police impounded Keith's car according to usual police practice. Miller last saw Keith's car at the police impoundment area on the night of the killing. His partner, Police Officer Jaeger, was to have secured the impoundment area that night, but Miller was unable to testify that Jaeger in fact did so. Unfortunately, Jaeger died the next day, which, obviously, precluded him from testifying. Miller returned to the impoundment area the following day and found the gate open and the defendant's car gone. There was no damage to the locks on the gate and Keith's car was the only one missing. Miller also testified that he did not start or examine the car the night of the arrest because the forensic team was going to examine it the following morning. However, Miller said that he did not observe any evidence that the car was involved in a hit-and-run killing, and did not notice if the car was missing its front plate.

The defendant's mother, Estelle Keith, supported Keith's assertion that his car was inoperable, testifying that the car needed to be jump-started in order to run. She also testified that Keith's front license plate had been missing for "a week or so before Roger was arrested."

Question Presented: Whether a hit-and-run murder charge against a criminal defendant should be dismissed on the ground that his car, stolen from police custody before the police could examine it, was material exculpatory evidence, and that under the federal and Colorado constitutions, he cannot receive a fair trial without it.

Short Answer: No. Although the police suppressed Roger Keith's car when it was stolen from police custody, and Keith is unable to obtain comparable evidence, he has no concrete evidence that police acted in bad faith, or that the police were aware of the exculpatory nature of the evidence.

Discussion: Under the federal and Colorado constitutions, a criminal defendant's due process right to a fair trial may be violated as a result of the state's failure to preserve potentially exculpatory evidence. See People v. Enriquez, 763 P.2d 1033, 1036 (Colo. 1988). However, the evidence must possess exculpatory value that is apparent to the state before its loss, and it must be of such a nature that the defendant cannot obtain comparable evidence by other means. Id. Furthermore, for a due process violation under the federal constitution, the state must have acted in bad faith when it failed to preserve the evidence. Arizona v. Youngblood, 488 U.S. 51, 58 (1988). The record here reflects that the state suppressed the evidence, and that Keith cannot obtain comparable evidence by other means. However, the record is not clear whether the police were aware of the exculpatory nature of the automobile before its loss, or that the evidence was lost as a result of bad faith on the part of the police, although the inference is strong that it was. Moreover, even if the state does not require police bad faith, Keith's due process right to a fair trial will not be violated under Colorado law unless the police were aware of the exculpatory nature of the automobile.

When evidence can be collected and preserved in the performance of routine procedures by the state, failure to do so is tantamount to suppression of evidence. People v. Humes, 762 P.2d 665, 667 (Colo. 1988). In Humes, the court held that because there are routine procedures for collecting and preserving blood samples, the police's failure to preserve the samples constituted suppression of evidence by the prosecution. Id. Similarly, in People v. Sheppard, 701 P.2d 49 (Colo. 1985), the state was responsible for the loss of a car that was evidence in a vehicular homicide case. Without authorization from the state police, the body shop that was holding the car crushed it for scrap metal. The court held the state responsible for the loss. Under the circumstances, the failure to collect and preserve the automobile was "properly attributable to the prosecution." Id. at 52. However, when the state fails to preserve evidence in its possession, through no fault of its own, the state does not suppress evidence. People v. Greathouse, 742 P.2d 339 (Colo. 1987). In Greathouse, the blood samples in question were not lost as a result of police action or inattention, but apparently by a natural process of decay. Thus the state had not destroyed the evidence. Id.

In the present case, as in Humes and Sheppard, the loss of evidence is attributable to the state. Miller testified that it is standard procedure for police to impound automobiles involved in hit-and-run cases. Moreover, the circumstances surrounding the car's disappearance indicate that Jaeger failed to lock the impoundment area gate. His dereliction of duty contributed to the car's disappearance, and therefore, it can be concluded that the state suppressed the evidence.

However, the suppressed evidence must have possessed exculpatory value apparent to the police before its loss. California v. Trombetta, 467 U.S. 479, 489 (1984); People v. Sheppard, 701 P.2d at 54. In Sheppard, the court dismissed the case on due process grounds when the exculpatory nature of the evidence was clear to the police as a result of its own preliminary evaluation of the evidence. Sheppard's car had gone off the side of the road and down an embankment, killing a passenger. A policeman had inspected the car after the accident and reported it to have mechanical defects that could have accounted for the accident. Id. Conversely, the state does not have the duty to preserve apparently inculpatory evidence. People v. Gann, 724 P.2d 1322 (Colo. 1986). In Gann, the defendant's due process rights were not violated by the failure of the police to preserve the apparently inculpatory telephone number of an anonymous informant. Id.

There is some evidence that Keith's automobile may have had apparent exculpatory value. Miller said that the car bore no evidence of a hit-and-run killing. Nonetheless, Miller's superficial examination is probably not sufficient to establish that the police were aware of the exculpatory nature of the automobile before it was stolen. Had the police noticed whether the front license plate was missing or had they confirmed that the car was not in working order, then the evidence would have had apparent exculpatory value. Since they noticed neither, the evidence was not apparently exculpatory.

Furthermore, if the defendant can obtain comparable evidence by other reasonable means, the loss of exculpatory evidence does not violate the defendant's right to a fair trial. Trombetta, 467 U.S. at 489. In Sheppard, 701 P.2d at 54, the defendant, charged with vehicular manslaughter, claimed that an examination of his car would have revealed that mechanical defect and not driver negligence caused the accident. The destruction of the physical evidence deprived Sheppard of the opportunity to examine the car. Concluding that, despite the police preliminary report tending to support the defendant's claim of malfunction, the defendant had no adequate evidentiary substitute for his destroyed vehicle, the court held that Sheppard's due process right was violated. Id.

Like the defendant in Sheppard, Keith has no evidence "comparable" to the stolen vehicle itself. Instead of objective evidence like the policeman's report, he has only his own and his mother's testimonies that his car was inoperable, and that his front license plate was missing. He also has Miller's statement that he did not notice damage consistent with the crime. This statement is even less authoritative than the preliminary report in Sheppard, and certainly does not carry the same weight as, for example, a forensic finding to the same effect. See People v. Palos, 930 P.2d 52 (Colo. 1985) (forensic ballistics report provided exculpatory evidence comparable to defendant's lost gun). Thus, because Keith is unable to obtain evidence comparable to his car, he should be able to satisfy this element.

Finally, a due process violation under the federal constitution requires that the police have acted in bad faith when they failed to preserve the evidence. Youngblood, 488 U.S. at 58. It is insufficient to show that the loss was a result of mere negligence on the part of the police. Rather, the defense is limited to those cases in which "the police themselves by their conduct indicate that the evidence could form a basis for exonerating the defendant," and, acting in bad faith, failed to preserve it. Id.

The Colorado courts have not yet had occasion to consider Youngblood's addition of a bad faith requirement. However, the court must do so to determine Keith's federal due process claim. A failure to follow routine practice may indicate bad faith. In Youngblood, 488 U.S. at 56, and Trombetta, 467 U.S. at 488, the defendants' cases were weakened because the police had followed their normal practices. In contrast, normal procedures were not followed here. Since there is no evidence of a break–in, Keith's car must have been lost because Jaeger failed to lock the gates, and by failing to do so, he did not follow standard police procedure. Only Keith's car was stolen. The police had reason to frame Keith because one of Keith's newspaper stories had named Miller in connection with minor illegalities. The police did not know if future stories would name not only Miller again, but others in the department. Jaeger may have left the gate open in solidarity with another officer. The inferences from these facts are strongly in Keith's favor.

However, at this point, Keith has only inferences. There is no concrete evidence about the missing front license plate, the unlocked gate, the vehicle's disappearance, and even Jaeger's death. He has nothing to link these events to prove police bad faith. Moreover, bad faith will turn on whether the police knew that Keith's car was exculpatory evidence. "The presence or absence of bad faith by the police for purposes of the Due Process Clause must necessarily turn on the police's knowledge of the exculpatory value of the evidence at the time it was destroyed." Youngblood, 488 U.S. at 56 n.2. Officer Miller's credibility will be crucial because he is the only officer who looked at Keith's car before he impounded it.

Nevertheless, it is not clear whether Youngblood requires concrete evidence of bad faith, or whether the court will be allowed to infer bad faith from these rather suspicious circumstances. In Youngblood, the defendant had neither concrete evidence nor inferences because the police laboratory personnel acted negligently by not preserving evidence before the police had any information linking the defendant with the crime. Miller and Jaeger, however, identified and charged Keith before they impounded his car. Because the lost car is so crucial to Keith's defense, the inference of bad faith may be enough to make this criminal trial "fundamentally unfair," id. at 61 (Stevens, J., concurring) unless Miller offers credible testimony that he was not aware of the exculpatory nature of the car.

Moreover, even if the police did not act in bad faith, it is possible that the indictment may be dismissed under the due process clause of the Colorado Constitution. The Colorado Supreme Court's last decision on this issue was Enriquez, decided just before the Supreme Court of the United States decided Youngblood. The Colorado court may decide that bad faith is not required, and that the Colorado Constitution affords greater due process protection than does the United States Constitution. Then, under Enriquez, the crucial issue will be whether the police were aware of the car's exculpatory value before the car was stolen. 763 P.2d at 1036. Keith's story would be corroborated if Miller cannot credibly testify he did not notice if the car was missing its front plate. If he did notice, then the police would have known that the car was exculpatory evidence. That fact and the loss of the car would require the court to dismiss this case. Without that information, however, it is likely that Keith's motion will fail.

Appendix D

Sample Office Memorandum

TO: Senior Attorney
FROM: Law Clerk
DATE: November 21, 1994
RE: Emily West Contract Litigation

FACTS: Emily West is president of the newly formed Aunt Em's Natural Heartland Bake Company, a producer of goods baked without additives or preservatives. While searching for a source of very high quality wheat, West was referred to Abel Prentice, an experienced wheat farmer with an excellent reputation as a knowledgeable grower and dealer. Prentice grows wheat on a 3,000 acre farm he owns and operates in this state. For over thirteen years he has been selling his own wheat and wheat grown by other farmers to manufacturers.

West visited Prentice in May 1994 and described the kind of bread she wished to produce. Prentice assured West that he knew a great deal about the bread business. In fact, Prentice told her that he probably knew more about her business than she did. After thinking it over, West signed a contract to buy wheat from Prentice. The written contract contained the terms of quantity, price, delivery, and payment schedules. No description or warranty as to the quality of the wheat, however, was included. After signing the contract, Prentice said: "You won't be sorry. I grow the finest wheat money can buy."

When the wheat was delivered in July, West found that 15–20% of it was blighted and unusable. West rejected the wheat and refused to pay Prentice. On August 5, 1994, Prentice filed suit against West's company for breach of contract.

QUESTION PRESENTED: Can West, a buyer of wheat, successfully defend a breach of contract suit on the grounds that the seller, Prentice, breached both express and implied warranties under the Kansas Commercial Code, Kan. Stat. Ann. §§ 2-313, 2-314, 2-315 (1983), when 15–20% of the wheat Prentice delivered was blighted and unusable?

CONCLUSION: West has a strong defense based on breach of implied warranty of merchantability, Kan. Stat. Ann. § 2–314 (1983), since the goods sold to her were neither of fair average quality nor fit for the ordinary purpose of baking bread. She can also prove a breach of the implied warranty of fitness for a particular purpose, Kan. Stat. Ann. § 2–315 (1983), since she informed Prentice of her particular use for his goods, that of baking breads without additives or preservatives, and he knew she was relying on his judgment to select suitable goods. However, she probably cannot successfully use breach of express warranty, Kan. Stat. Ann. § 2–313 (1983), because Prentice's statement to her was an opinion and not an affirmation of fact.

APPLICABLE STATUTES:

Kan. Stat. Ann. § 84–2–104. Definitions: "Merchant"; "Between Merchants"; "Financing Agency"

(1) "Merchant" means a person who deals in goods of the kind or otherwise by his occupation holds himself out as having knowledge or skill peculiar to the practices or goods involved in the transaction or to whom such knowledge or skill may be attributed by his employment of an agent or broker or other intermediary who by his occupation holds himself out as having such knowledge or skill.

. . . .

Kan. Stat. Ann. § 84–2–313. Express Warranties by Affirmation, Promise, Description, Sample

(1) Express warranties by the seller are created as follows:

(a) Any affirmation of fact or promise made by the seller to the buyer which relates to the goods and becomes part of the basis of the bargain creates an express warranty that the goods shall conform to the affirmation or promise.

(b) Any description of the goods which is made part of the basis of the bargain creates an express warranty that the goods shall conform to the description.

. . . .

(2) It is not necessary to the creation of an express warranty that the seller use formal words such as "warrant" or "guarantee" or that he have a specific intention to make a warranty, but an affirmation merely of the value of the goods or a statement purporting to be merely the seller's opinion or commendation of the goods does not create a warranty.

Kan. Stat. Ann. § 84–2–314 Implied Warranty: Merchantability; Usage of Trade

(1) Unless excluded or modified (Section 2–316), a warranty that the goods shall be merchantable is implied in a contract for their sale if the seller is a merchant with respect to goods of that kind.

. . . .

(2) Goods to be merchantable must be at least such as

(a) pass without objection in the trade under the contract description; and

(b) in the case of fungible goods, are of fair average quality within the description; and

(c) are fit for the ordinary purposes for which such goods are used;

. . . .

. . . .

Kan. Stat. Ann. § 84–2–315. Implied Warranty: Fitness for Particular Purpose

Where the seller at the time of contracting has reason to know any particular purpose for which the goods are required and that the buyer is relying on the seller's skill or judgment to select or furnish suitable goods, there is unless excluded or modified under the next section an implied warranty that the goods shall be fit for such purpose.

DISCUSSION: Abel Prentice's breach of contract claim is based on Emily West's wrongful rejection of the goods. However, if Prentice breached any of the three warranties under the Kansas Commercial Code, then West rightfully rejected the goods and has a successful defense. The Kansas Commercial Code provides three possible defenses based on breach of warranty: breach of implied warranty of merchantability, § 2–314; breach of implied warranty of fitness for a particular purpose, § 2–315; and breach of express warranty, § 2–313. West has a strong defense based on breach of implied warranty of merchantability. Moreover, she has a good defense based on implied warranty of fitness for a particular ,purpose. However, she cannot successfully defend the suit by claiming breach of express warranty.

The best defense against Prentice's suit is under § 2–314, the implied warranty of merchantability. This section provides that if the seller is a merchant, a warranty of merchantability is implied in a contract. Id. (1). Section 2–314(2) sets out minimum standards which goods must meet to be merchantable. Under these standards, goods must, *inter alia*, "pass without objection in the trade under the contract description," § 2–314(2)(a); and, in the case of fungible goods, be "of fair average quality within the description," § 2–314(2)(b); and be "fit for the ordinary purposes for which such goods are used," § 2–314(2)(c). Prentice is a merchant and the goods did not meet any of these standards. Therefore, Prentice breached the implied warranty of merchantability.

The statute itself defines merchant, in pertinent part, as "a person who deals in goods of the kind or otherwise by his occupation holds himself out as having knowledge or skill peculiar to the practices or goods involved in the transaction." Kan. Stat. Ann. § 2–104(1) (1983). One court in Kansas has addressed the question of whether a farmer is a merchant in a case involving the sale of hogs between hog farmers. Musil v. Hendrich, 627 P.2d 367 (Kan. App. 1981). The court concluded that the defendant farmer in the hog transaction was a merchant under either definition in the statute. First, as someone who had been in the hog business for thirty years and was selling 50–100 hogs per month, he was a dealer in hogs. Second, he held himself out as having knowledge or skill relating to the goods, since he had equipment and buildings related to hog farming and sold hogs to private individuals, as well as to a slaughterhouse. Id. at 373. Prentice, like the hog farmer in Musil, is a merchant under either definition. Prentice is a dealer because he is a wheat farmer who sold manufacturers not only his own wheat, but also the wheat of other farmers. He also held himself out as having knowledge relating to the goods, since he has been a wheat farmer for thirteen years, runs a 3,000 acre farm, and stated to West that he knew more about her business than she did. Prentice is therefore a merchant, and it is appropriate to apply § 2–314.

Under the standards of merchantability provided in § 2–314, the warranty was breached first because the 15–20% blighted wheat was of lesser quality than would "pass without objection in the trade" and was not of "fair average quality." § 2–314(2)(a)(b). Fair average is described as "the middle belt of quality . . . not the least or the worst . . . but such as can pass without objection." § 2–314 Comment 7. According to regulations from the Kansas Department of Agriculture, to be of fair average quality, a wheat shipment can contain no more than 10% of a blighted or inferior product. Kan. Admin. Regs. 397.41 (1981). Since the wheat Prentice shipped was 15–20% blighted, it did not meet this standard.

The implied warranty of merchantability was also breached because the wheat was not fit for its ordinary purposes. Under Kansas law, the buyer must show the ordinary purpose of the goods involved and show that the goods are not fit for that purpose. Black v. Don Schmidt Motor, Inc., 657 P.2d 517, 525 (Kan. 1983). The ordinary purpose for wheat is to make flour for bread. Since wheat that is 15–20% blighted would not make acceptable flour, the wheat is not fit for its ordinary purpose. Accordingly, Prentice breached the implied warranty of merchantability.

Prentice has also breached the implied warranty of fitness for a particular purpose. A warranty of fitness for a particular purpose is implied "when the seller, at the time of contracting, [knows] any particular purpose for which the goods are required, and [knows] that the buyer is relying on the seller's skill or judgment to select or furnish suitable goods." § 2–315. At the time the contract was made, Prentice knew that West required a high quality wheat for her all-natural bread, and that she was relying on his judgment to select and provide suitable wheat. Since the making of all-natural bread is a particular purpose, and since wheat that is 15–20% blighted is not fit for this purpose, Prentice has breached an implied warranty of fitness.

The first requirement is that the goods are to be used for a particular, as opposed to an ordinary purpose. In International Petroleum Services, Inc. v. S & N Well Service, Inc., 639 P.2d 29, 37 (Kan. 1982), the court described a particular purpose as more specific, narrow, and precise than an ordinary purpose. Id. The court also stated that a particular purpose meant a use peculiar to the nature of the buyer's business. Id. West intended to use the wheat to make all-natural bread and cakes using no preservatives. She would, therefore, need especially high quality wheat, not a product that could be used in making ordinary baked goods which could rely on preservatives for freshness.

In addition, Prentice had reason to know of the particular purpose she intended for the wheat. Prior to signing the contract, West described her business to Prentice and told him the kind of bread she wanted to produce.

Finally, West relied on Prentice's skill and judgment to select the appropriate goods. See Addis v. Bernadin, Inc., 597 P.2d 250 (Kan. 1979). In Addis, the plaintiff buyer, a manufacturer of salad dressings, informed the defendant seller that he needed jar lids for dressings containing vinegar and salt. Although the seller knew that the lids the buyer had ordered were incompatible with their intended use, he did not tell the buyer. Id. at 254. The court held the seller, who had superior knowledge, had breached the implied warranty of fitness for a particular purpose. The buyer had relied on the seller's knowledge of his product and on his judgment to select appropriate goods in conformity with the use the buyer described. Id. West, too, relied on Prentice's judgment to provide appropriate goods. She was just starting her business, but Prentice had been selling his own wheat for over thirteen years. Moreover, Prentice not only said he knew all about the wheat business, he boasted that he knew more about her business than she did. Therefore, a court would probably hold that Prentice breached an implied warranty of fitness for a particular purpose.

It is not likely, however, that an express warranty had been created. An express warranty is created by a seller's "affirmation of fact" about the goods, or a description, sample, or model of the goods given to the buyer, any of which is "made part of the basis of the bargain." § 2–313(1)(a)(b)(c). The seller need not use formal words of guarantee, or intend to create a warranty. § 2–313(2). However, a statement which is merely the seller's opinion of the goods does not create a warranty. Id. The written Prentice–West contract made no mention of any express warranty. That could only have been created in Prentice's statement to West that he grows "the finest wheat money can buy". However, as this statement is more opinion than an affirmation of fact, Prentice did not create an express warranty.

Kansas courts have held that express warranties can be created by oral statements if these statements are affirmations of fact and not opinions. Formal words of guarantee are not necessary, but an affirmation merely of the value of the goods is not sufficient to create an express warranty. Young & Cooper, Inc. v. Vestring, 521 P.2d 281 (Kan. 1974); Brunner v. Jensen, 524 P.2d 1175 (Kan. 1974). In Young, the defendant buyer purchased cattle from the plaintiff seller who told him that the cattle were "a good reputable herd . . . clean cows." 521 P.2d at 285. The court said that such statements are taken by cattlemen to mean that cattle are free of brucellosis. The seller thereby created an express warranty, which was breached when the cattle were found to have the disease. Id. at 293. The court classified these statements as affirmations of fact and not opinion, since they were representations of fact "capable of determination" or "susceptible of exact knowledge." Id. at 290. Similarly, in Brunner, another case concerning cattle, the seller's oral statement to the buyer that cows would calve by a certain date was not, the court said, an opinion. The court held that the seller's statements created an express warranty which was breached when the cows did not calve on time. 524 P.2d at 1186.

The facts in West, however, are distinguishable from those in Young and Brunner. A court would probably classify Prentice's statements about his wheat as opinion, rather than fact because his statement is neither "capable of determination" nor "susceptible of exact knowledge." The statement more resembles sales talk, and therefore, did not create an express warranty.

Appendix E

Sample Memorandum in Support of a Motion

IN THE CIRCUIT COURT OF COOK COUNTY, ILLINOIS
COUNTY DEPARTMENT, LAW DIVISION

PARK, INC., et al.,)
                  Plaintiffs,) No. 86 L 22939
        v.) N.W.
DAVID RYAN, et al.,)
                Defendants.)

MEMORANDUM IN SUPPORT OF MOTION TO DISMISS COMPLAINT AS TO WRIGLEY HOUSING, INC., JOE SAYERS, ANN CHRISTIE, AND MARGARET JAMES

INTRODUCTION

Plaintiffs PARK, INC. ("Park"), a real estate management company, and its President, Earl Marple ("Marple"), have sued more than thirty individuals and organizations active in the tenants' rights movement in the West Park section of Chicago. Plaintiffs' four-count complaint purports to state claims for libel and slander. On December 22, 1986, defendants Wrigley Housing, Inc. ("Wrigley"), Joe Sayers ("Sayers"), Ann Christie ("Christie") and Margaret James ("James"), filed a motion to dismiss the complaint as to those defendants pursuant to Rule 2–615 of the Illinois Rules of Civil Procedure. This memorandum is submitted in support of those defendants' motion to dismiss.

STATEMENT OF FACTS

Plaintiff Park is a corporation engaged in the business of managing and developing real estate. (Complaint ¶ 1.) Park has developed and manages more than 500 rental units in the West Park area of Chicago. (Complaint ¶ 12.) Plaintiff Marple is President of Park, and has been in the real estate business since 1969. (Complaint ¶¶ 1, 9.) This case arises out of a dispute between Park and Marple, on the one hand, and the West Park Tenants' Committee ("WPTC"), the Professionals for Better Housing ("PBH"), and Alderman David Ryan, on the other hand, concerning Park's real estate management practices. (Complaint ¶¶ 16–22.)

In April 1986, WPTC convened a meeting of tenants and former tenants of Park and of representatives of other tenants' rights organizations and block clubs, in response to complaints about Park's rental policies and practices. (Complaint ¶ 22; Exhibit A.) Park's tenants continued to meet, to distribute literature to Park tenants, and to picket at Park's rental office and at Marple's home. (Complaint ¶ 22.)

Plaintiffs allege that the communications thus published by WPTC and PBH were defamatory. (Counts I and II.) Specifically, in Count I, they allege that a newsletter attached as Exhibit A to the complaint contains the following defamatory statements:

> That in August 1985 (or on or about said time) there were complaints regarding Park as to "giant rent increases"; "failure to refund security deposits and pay interest"; "chronic heat and hot water problems"; "intimidation of tenants"; and "outrageous set of move-out policies."

(Complaint ¶ 30.)

Plaintiffs allege that a leaflet attached as Exhibit B to the complaint contains the allegedly defamatory statement that "the WPTC wanted to meet with Park 'to discuss the state investigation of Park.' " (Complaint ¶ 28.) They also allege that leaflets attached to the complaint as Exhibits C and D libel Park and Marple by stating, inter alia, that Park's tenants want to meet with Marple to discuss "problems relating to his mismanagement of ten buildings in West Park with nearly 500 apartments" and, specifically, "lack of water," "lack of heat," "poor building security," "unfair security deposit deductions," "lack of smoke detectors," "unresponsiveness to requests for repairs," "failure to pay security deposit interest," "electrical problems," "roaches," "intimidation and harassment of tenants," "infrequent garbage pickup," and "outrageous move-out policies." (Exhibits C–D; Complaint ¶ 31.) Plaintiffs allege that Exhibits A, B, C and D were authored by WPTC and PBH and that the authors "were one or more of the following Defendants," with Christie included on a list of thirteen names. (Complaint ¶ 25.)

In Count II, plaintiffs allege that various defendants, including Christie, picketed the offices of Park's rental agent. (Complaint ¶¶ 47–48.) Plaintiffs claim that various picket signs and oral communications included defamatory statements that Park and Marple were "in housing court," did not supply heat in their buildings, had a policy "not to return security deposits," "made bogus deductions" from security deposits, and that the buildings managed by Park had roaches. (Complaint ¶ 49.)

Counts III and IV concern a letter sent to the limited partners of Park on or about October 1, 1986. (Complaint ¶ 64.) The letter indicates that it was endorsed by Alderman Ryan and a number of tenants' and housing rights groups, including Wrigley Housing. (Exhibit E.)   Plaintiffs allege in Count III that the letter contains the following allegedly defamatory statements:

A.   Evidence exists documenting continuous complaints by tenants about maintenance problems and the indifferent handling of these complaints by Park, Inc.

B.   City inspection reports detail numerous instances of housing code violations in Park, Inc. properties.

C.   Park is not repairing housing code violations and is not making repairs in a workmanlike manner.

D.   Numerous outgoing tenants have complained about not receiving proper disbursement of their security deposits.

E.   Most tenants have not received the requisite interest on their security deposit interests.

F.   The buildings show serious signs of mismanagement and distress.

G.   Many tenants are not renewing their leases with Park, Inc. because they cannot deal with habitually poor management.

H.   The buildings are developing high vacancy rates and falling into disrepair.

ARGUMENT

The plaintiffs' complaint must be dismissed because the communications complained of in Counts I, II, III, and IV are not defamatory *per se* under Illinois law.   Even assuming that the statements are defamatory, Illinois law grants them a qualified privilege.   Furthermore, plaintiffs' prayer for punitive damages is unsupported and must be stricken from the complaint.   Finally, the complaint contains no allegations concerning defendants Sayers and James and should be dismissed as to those defendants.

I.   ALL COUNTS MUST BE DISMISSED BECAUSE THE COMMUNICATIONS COMPLAINED OF ARE NOT DEFAMATORY PER SE.

Under Illinois law, the defendants' statements are not defamatory *per se.*   To be considered defamatory *per se,* the language must be so obviously and naturally harmful to the person to whom it refers that damage is a necessary consequence and need not be specially shown.   Owen v. Carr, 113 Ill. 2d 273, 274, 497 N.E.2d 1145, 1147 (1986); Sloan v. Hatton, 66 Ill. App. 3d 41, 42, 383 N.E.2d 259, 260 (4th Dist. 1978).   Four classes of words, if falsely communicated, give rise to an action for defamation without a showing of special damages:

    1.   Those imputing the commission of a criminal offense

    2.   Those imputing infection with a communicable disease

    3.   Those imputing inability to perform or want of integrity in the discharge of duties of office or employment, and

    4.   Those prejudicing a particular party in his profession or trade.

Fried v. Jacobson, 99 Ill. 2d 24, 26, 457 N.E.2d 392, 394 (1983). With respect to corporate plaintiffs, moreover, the alleged libel must assail the corporation's financial or business methods or accuse it of fraud or mismanagement. American International Hospital v. Chicago Tribune Co., 136 Ill. App. 3d 1019, 1022, 483 N.E.2d 965, 969 (1st Dist. 1985); Audition Division, Ltd. v. Better Business Bureau, 120 Ill. App. 3d 254, 256, 458 N.E.2d 115, 118 (1st Dist. 1983).

In determining whether particular language constitutes libel *per se*, Illinois courts apply the rule of innocent construction:

> a written or oral statement is to be considered in context, with the words and the implications therefrom given their natural and obvious meaning; if, as so construed, the statement may reasonably be innocently interpreted as referring to someone other than the plaintiff it cannot be actionable *per se*. This preliminary determination is properly a question of law to be resolved by the court in the first instance.

Chapski v. Copley Press, 92 Ill. 2d 344, 347, 442 N.E.2d 195, 199 (1982). Thus, the court must examine the statements here within the context of the surrounding circumstances and events, and judge the words accordingly. Id.; Sloan v. Hatton, 66 Ill. App. 3d at 43, 383 N.E.2d at 261. Moreover, the trial court is required to make this determination in the context of the entire publication. Chapski, 92 Ill. 2d at 345, 442 N.E.2d at 199.

The following emerges clearly from an examination, in context, of Exhibits A through E to the complaint: As Exhibit A shows, tenants of buildings owned and managed by Park were meeting and organizing in early 1986. It is clear from Exhibits B through E that the tenants' goal was to meet with Park and Marple to discuss various problems the tenants perceived.

> "To plan other direct action to get Park to meet with us" (Exhibit B)

> "We want to meet with Earl Marple to discuss and get action on these problems" (Exhibit C)

"Quite simply we want Park to meet with us and begin to address our legitimate concerns" (Exhibit D);

"Therefore, we are asking that (1) you attend a special meeting of the West Park Housing Forum...and (2) that you encourage Mr. Marple to attend this meeting also" (Exhibit E, at 3).

Thus, the context of the communications here was clearly a dispute between tenants and a landlord about the manner in which he was managing his buildings.

Chapski requires that, in ruling on a motion to dismiss, the trial court must review the allegedly libelous documents to determine, as a matter of law, whether they are subject to a reasonable *non-defamatory* construction; if so, the documents are not actionable even if they may also be subject to a reasonable *defamatory* construction and even if the party receiving the communications understood them in a defamatory sense. Chapski, 92 Ill. 2d at 345, 442 N.E.2d at 199. Following this mandate, Illinois courts have repeatedly dismissed libel cases after finding that the statements complained of were susceptible of a reasonable innocent construction. See, e.g., Meyer v. Allen, 127 Ill. App. 3d 163, 165, 468 N.E.2d 198, 200 (4th Dist. 1984); Audition Division, Ltd. v. Better Business Bureau, 120 Ill. App. 3d at 257, 458 N.E.2d at 119; Cartwright v. Garrison, 113 Ill. App. 3d 536, 537–40, 447 N.E.2d 446, 447–50 (2d Dist. 1983).

Rasky v. CBS, Inc., 103 Ill. App. 3d 577, 431 N.E.2d 1055 (1st Dist.), cert. denied, 459 U.S. 864 (1982), is particularly relevant to this case. The Rasky plaintiff was a landlord whose building maintenance and business practices were criticized by a number of tenants' groups and a state representative, among others; CBS News then broadcast a news program describing the controversy and interviewing tenants. The appellate court, affirming dismissal of the case, found that the derogatory remarks by the news media and community groups could be interpreted innocently.

The overall thrust of the CBS news telecast was that citizens in the community were bitterly opposed to the way in which they perceived that plaintiff managed his buildings and that, through their representatives, they intended to explore available legal remedies for redress. In that context, the report noted that Edgewater citizens: have accused plaintiff of being a "slumlord"; have previously taken legal action against him; claim he does not make repairs. In our opinion, the CBS news telecast, taken as a whole, is capable of an innocent construction and cannot be considered defamatory as a matter of law.

103 Ill. App. 3d at 577, 431 N.E.2d at 1059.

The communications complained of in this case, read as a whole and in context, amount to no more than the statements found to be non-defamatory in Rasky. The thrust of Exhibits A through E is that numbers of citizens were "bitterly opposed to the way in which they perceived that plaintiff[s] managed [their] buildings and ... intended to explore available legal remedies for redress." Id. In that context, Exhibits A through E may reasonably be construed innocently and thus may not sustain an action for defamation.

Furthermore, it is not libel *per se* to state that complaints have been filed about a business. See, e.g., Audition Division, Ltd. v. Better Business Bureau, 120 Ill. App. 3d at 254, 458 N.E.2d at 119; American Pet Motels, Inc. v. Chicago Veterinary Medical Ass'n, 106 Ill. App. 3d 626, 628, 435 N.E.2d 1297, 1300 (1st Dist. 1982). Illinois courts have reasoned that a statement that customers have complained about a business is not equivalent to a statement that the business is incompetent, fraudulent, or dishonest. Thus, the statements complained of in Exhibit A—that in August 1985 there were a variety of complaints regarding Park (Complaint ¶ 30)—are not defamatory, as a matter of law.

Under Illinois law, it is also not libel *per se* to state that a plaintiff's business activities are under investigation. Cartwright v. Garrison, 113 Ill. App. 3d 536, 539, 447 N.E.2d 446, 450 (2d Dist. 1983); see also Spelson v. CBS, Inc., 581 F. Supp. 1195, 1205 (N.D. Ill. 1984), aff'd mem., 757 F.2d 1291 (7th Cir. 1985). Thus, the statement complained of in paragraph 28 of the complaint (that the WPTC wanted to meet with Park "to discuss the state investigation of Park") is not defamatory *per se,* as a matter of law.

In short, when considered as a whole and in context, the statements in Exhibits A through E are susceptible of a reasonable innocent construction, and do not constitute libel *per se.*

II. THE COMMUNICATIONS COMPLAINED OF ARE ENTITLED TO A QUALIFIED PRIVILEGE UNDER ILLINOIS LAW.

Even assuming, *arguendo,* that this Court finds the statements complained of defamatory, they are nonetheless not actionable, because they are privileged under Illinois law. Certain communications, even if false and defamatory, are afforded special protection—a qualified privilege—because the law recognizes their social importance. The elements of this qualified privilege are (1) good faith by the defendant, (2) a legitimate interest or duty to be upheld, (3) publication limited in scope to that purpose, and (4) publication in a proper manner to proper parties. See, e.g., Edwards by Phillips v. University of Chicago Hospitals, 137 Ill. App. 3d 485, 488, 484

N.E.2d 1100, 1104 (1st Dist. 1985); American Pet Motels, Inc. v. Chicago Veterinary Medical Ass'n, 106 Ill. App. 3d at 630, 435 N.E.2d at 1301.

The face of plaintiffs' complaint demonstrates that the privilege applies here. First, the defendants had a good faith, legitimate purpose for the communications challenged: to address a matter of shared concern—the availability of decent, affordable, safe housing in the West Park community—and to assist one another in dealing with problems they perceived in the management practices of one large landlord. The documents themselves, a newsletter and leaflets, show that defendants' purpose was entirely legitimate, i.e., to meet with Park to discuss those problems.

Moreover, the statements in Exhibits A through E were limited in scope to furthering these common concerns. The newsletter describes community efforts to improve housing conditions. (Exhibit A.) The leaflets and letter to Park's limited partners are directed at the goal of meeting with plaintiffs to discuss certain perceived problems in Park's rental units. (Exhibits B, C, D, E, at 3.)

Finally, the statements here were communicated in a proper manner and to proper parties. The newsletter and leaflets were distributed to Park's tenants and to other residents of the West Park community interested in improving their housing conditions. (Complaint ¶¶ 31, 54B.) Exhibit E was addressed only to the limited partners of Park. (Complaint ¶ 64.)

Similarly, the statements complained of in Count II, which concern the picketing of Park's rental agent, are privileged under Illinois law. The persons making these statements spoke in good faith and in the interest of promoting good rental housing; they limited their statements to Park tenants and prospective tenants; and they made the statements in furtherance of their purpose to persuade plaintiff to meet with them to discuss their perceived problems and complaints. (See Exhibit D: "Why we're picketing Park/Rental Express" ... "Quite simply, we want Park to meet with us and begin to address our legitimate concerns ....")

Under these circumstances, the qualified privilege clearly applies to all the communications complained of in plaintiffs' complaint, requiring dismissal as a matter of law, absent factual allegations that defendants abused the privilege. See, e.g., American Pet Motels, 106 Ill. App. 3d at 626, 435 N.E.2d at 1302.

III. PLAINTIFFS FAIL TO STATE A CLAIM FOR PUNITIVE DAMAGES.

Punitive damages may not be recovered without a showing of actual malice. Gertz v. Robert Welch, Inc., 418 U.S. 323, 349–50

(1974). Plaintiffs here seek an award of punitive damages based solely upon the bald assertion that defendants acted "maliciously, willfully, and with a conscious disregard for the rights of Plaintiffs." (Complaint ¶¶ 32, 52, 55, 60, 67, 71.) Bare allegations of actual malice in a complaint, however, do not suffice; "rather, conclusions of malice and intent must be clothed with factual allegations from which the actual malice might reasonably be said to exist." L.R. Davis v. Keystone Printing Service, Inc., 111 Ill. App. 3d 427, 433, 444 N.E.2d 253, 262 (2d Dist. 1982). Because plaintiffs do not adequately plead actual malice, their prayers for punitive damages should be stricken from the complaint.

IV. THE COMPLAINT DOES NOT CONTAIN THE NECESSARY FACTUAL ALLEGATIONS CONCERNING CERTAIN INDIVIDUAL DEFENDANTS AND SHOULD THEREFORE BE DISMISSED AS TO THOSE DEFENDANTS.

Finally, the complaint should be dismissed as to certain of the individual defendants, because it contains no allegations of wrongdoing on their part. The complaint contains no factual allegations whatsoever concerning the conduct of defendants Sayers and James, and should therefore be dismissed in its entirety as to them. Counts III and IV, which concern the letter to Park's limited partners, contain absolutely no allegations that defendants James, Sayers, or Christie participated in the composition or publication of that letter, and should therefore be dismissed as to those defendants. Additionally, Count II, alleging defamation based on picketing the office of Park's rental agent, is devoid of any allegations concerning the conduct of defendants James or Sayers, and should therefore be stricken as to those defendants.

Finally, plaintiffs fail throughout to allege defamation with sufficient particularity. In actions for libel and slander, a plaintiff is held to a high standard of specificity in pleading. Altman v. Amoco Oil Co., 85 Ill. App. 3d 104, 106, 406 N.E.2d 142, 145 (1st Dist. 1980). By contrast, plaintiffs here allege, for example, that the authors of Exhibits B, C and D "were one or more of the following Defendants," including defendant Christie in a list of thirteen names. (Complaint ¶ 25.) Unless plaintiffs can amend to specify the personal involvement of each named individual, the complaint should be dismissed as to those individual defendants.

CONCLUSION

For the foregoing reasons, defendants Wrigley Housing, Inc., Joe Sayers, Ann Christie and Margaret James respectfully request that this Court enter an order dismissing the complaint with costs, or, in the alternative, dismissing them as defendants in this case.

WRIGLEY HOUSING, INC.,
JOE SAYERS, ANN CHRISTIE
AND MARGARET JAMES

By: _____
        Their Attorney

Cynthia G. Bowman
Northwestern University
School of Law
357 E. Chicago Avenue
Chicago, IL 60611
(312) 503–8576

Appendix F

Sample Appellate Brief

IN THE
UNITED STATES COURT OF APPEALS
SEVENTH CIRCUIT
March Term, 1987
No. 87–551

ARNIE FRANK,
<u>APPELLANT</u>

v.

CENTRAL INTELLIGENCE AGENCY,
and
FEDERAL BUREAU OF INVESTIGATION,
<u>APPELLEES</u>

On appeal from the
United States District Court for the
Northwestern District of Illinois

<u>BRIEF FOR THE APPELLANT</u>

i

QUESTIONS PRESENTED FOR REVIEW

1. Does the 1974 amendment to the Freedom of Information Act, 5 U.S.C. § 552 (a) (4) (E), permitting a court to award attorney fees to substantially prevailing complainants, permit fee awards to pro se litigants who are attorneys?

2. If so, does a court abuse its discretion by denying an award of attorney fees to a plaintiff who substantially prevails in a Freedom of Information Act suit when the defendant government agencies had no reasonable basis in law for withholding a majority of the documents eventually released, and the information revealed by the suit exposes illegal government activities that the plaintiff intends to disseminate to the public?

TABLE OF CONTENTS

TABLE OF AUTHORITIES

Cases

Statutes

Legislative History

Miscellaneous Authority

OPINION BELOW

The opinion of the United States District Court for the Northwestern District of Illinois denying Mr. Arnie Frank's motion for attorney fees appears at 1000 F. Supp. 1 (N.D. Ill. 1987).

JURISDICTION

The United States Court of Appeals for the Seventh Circuit has jurisdiction to hear this appeal pursuant to 28 U.S.C. § 1291 (1983).

STATUTE INVOLVED

Freedom of Information Act, 5 U.S.C. § 552 (a) (4) (E) (1983)

> The court may assess against the United States reasonable attorney fees and other litigation costs reasonably incurred in any case under this section in which the complainant has substantially prevailed.

PRELIMINARY STATEMENT

The appellant, Mr. Arnie Frank, brought this action against the appellees, the Central Intelligence Agency (CIA) and the Federal Bureau of Investigation (FBI) to recover attorney fees under the Freedom of Information Act (FOIA), 5 U.S.C. § 552 (a) (4) (E). The United States District Court for the Northwestern District of Illinois declared Mr. Frank ineligible under the statute for an award, and denied him the fees he requested. Frank v. CIA, 1000 F. Supp. 1 (N.D. Ill. 1987). Mr. Frank now appeals this decision.

STATEMENT OF THE CASE

Mr. Frank is an attorney in private practice, and donates a considerable amount of his professional time to the service of the political leader Lyndon LaRouche and his supporters. (R.2) In 1972, Mr. Frank requested certain documents from the Department of Justice under the Freedom of Information Act, 5 U.S.C. § 552 et seq. (1983), concerning FBI and CIA monitoring of Mr. LaRouche's supporters. (R.3) Through those documents, Mr. Frank learned that he had been under government surveillance while he was a student at the Windy City School of Law in Chicago in 1968. (R.3)

As a student, Mr. Frank was the president of a student group called Law Students Against Tyranny (LSAT) that supported Mr. LaRouche. (R.3) When LSAT staged a demonstration outside the Democratic National Convention, the CIA and FBI assigned covert agents to spy on Mr. Frank and other members of LSAT (R.3) The FBI was also keeping several other political groups under surveillance, including the NAACP, the American Civil Liberties Union, and the Students Against the Vietnam War. (R.6) At the same time, the CIA was illegally wiretapping phone conversations and intercepting the mail of members of those groups. (R.7)

The discovery of the government's illegal activities prompted Mr. Frank to investigate the true extent of the government's surreptitious investigation of himself and other supporters of Mr. LaRouche. Mr. Frank then filed another request under the FOIA in 1974 for documents concerning the matter. (R.3) After protracted correspondence, the government responded by refusing to divulge the requested documents without offering any legal justification. (R.2) In order to obtain the documents, Mr. Frank was forced to sue the government under the provisions of the FOIA. (R.1)

Not until 1979, under an order from this court, Frank v. Department of Justice, 540 F.2d 2 (7th Cir. 1979), did the government produce approximately one-half of the documents Mr. Frank originally requested. (R.1) The further revelations of the government's shocking activities led Mr. Frank to sue the CIA and the FBI for invasion of privacy. (R.3) In order to prevent embarrassment from the wide-spread dissemination of information about the government's illegal activities, the government settled the claim before trial. (R.4) At the same time, however, the government continued its refusal to produce the rest of the documents. (R.2) Mr. Frank proceeded with his FOIA suit in spite of the government's recalcitrance, and finally in 1985 recovered thirty-five of the forty documents he originally requested. (R.2) That recovery marked the end of almost fifteen years of litigation. (R.2) Mr. Frank now plans to publish a book discussing the released documents and the government's illegal activities.

Mr. Frank requested the court below to award him attorney fees. During the entire pendency of his FOIA suit, Mr. Frank acted as his own attorney. (R.4) Mr. Frank estimates that he spent no less than 2 1/2 hours per week on his case for a period of fifteen years. He has requested an award computed at the hourly rate of $125. Because the FOIA provides that a court may award attorney fees to complainants who "substantially prevailed," Mr. Frank instituted this action in the court below to recover fees. (R.2) That court denied the award of attorney fees, holding that an attorney acting pro se is not eligible for an award of fees. In addition, although the parties stipulated that Mr. Frank "substantially prevailed," and that the government had no "reasonable basis in law for withholding a majority of the records eventually released," the court held that it would not have exercised its discretion to award fees even if Mr. Frank were eligible. (R.2) In response to the decisions of the court below, Mr. Frank now files this brief for review by this court to be argued orally on April 9, 1987.

SUMMARY OF THE ARGUMENT

The broad language of the 1974 amendment to the Freedom of Information Act (FOIA), 5 U.S.C. § 552 (a) (4) (E) (1983), allows the court to award "reasonable attorney fees and other litigation costs reasonably incurred" to complainants who "substantially prevailed" in suits brought under the statute. The conventional rules of statutory construction require that this language be interpreted to read that only litigation costs must have actually been incurred and attorney fees need not actually be incurred for a court to award them. Thus, because there are no exceptions to the statute, attorney pro se litigants are eligible for awards of fees pursuant to the Act although they incur no literal out-of-pocket expenses for counsel.

Congress originally passed § 552 (a) (4) (E) to facilitate private enforcement of the FOIA by removing the economic obstacles that previously prevented citizens from vindicating their rights. Attorneys, like other citizens, may face economic barriers when they choose to represent themselves in FOIA suits. The time they spend pursuing their claims diverts their professional skills from other income-producing activities. Because the cost of vindicating their rights is economically equivalent to incurring legal expenses, attorneys should not be excluded from eligibility to receive compensation under the statute. Moreover, an attorney who acts pro se has been represented by an attorney, thus distinguishing the attorney from a lay person acting pro se, whom this court has held is not eligible for fees.

Furthermore, Congress enacted the amendment to discourage government recalcitrance in complying with the FOIA by penalizing its bad faith with charges for fee awards. When the government harasses self-represented complainants, or withholds information in bad faith, the fee award serves as a penalty for its unreasonable behavior. Excluding attorneys from eligibility merely encourages the government not to comply with the Act whenever releasing information to attorney pro se litigants would cause government officials or agencies embarrassment.

In addition, because Mr. Frank is eligible for fees, the court below abused its discretion when it denied him an award. When he substantially prevailed in his FOIA action against the government, Mr. Frank exposed important information to the electorate about the misconduct of the two government agencies. The dissemination of that information through his suit and the book he will publish

3

provides a substantial public benefit by making citizens aware of the government's illegal activities. Although Mr. Frank may profit from his publication, the public benefits he has provided are substantially more important than any commercial benefit he might receive.

Moreover, the CIA and FBI withheld documents from Mr. Frank with no reasonable basis in law in order to avoid disseminating records revealing their illegal activities toward Mr. Frank and members of other political organizations. Mr. Frank had to litigate for almost fifteen years when the government should have honored his FOIA request immediately. The court should have exercised its discretion to award attorney fees to Mr. Frank to further Congress' goal of penalizing government agencies for their obdurate behavior.

Finally, Mr. Frank's request for fees was sufficiently documented and was reasonable considering the time and effort he was forced to expend over the fifteen years of litigation. This court should remand to the district court to exercise its discretion and award Mr. Frank the sum he requested for attorney fees.

4

ARGUMENT

I. AN ATTORNEY PRO SE LITIGANT IS ELIGIBLE TO RE-CEIVE AN AWARD OF ATTORNEY FEES AND LITIGATION COSTS UNDER THE FREEDOM OF INFORMATION ACT (FOIA) IF HE SUBSTANTIALLY PREVAILS IN A FOIA SUIT.

By enacting appropriate legislation, Congress has the power to alter the "American Rule" in which no attorney fees may be awarded to the prevailing party. Alyeska Pipeline Serv. Co. v. Wilderness Soc'y, 421 U.S. 240 (1975). In the 1974 amendment to the Freedom of Information Act, Congress did so by allowing citizens who "substantially prevailed" against the government in suits brought under the Act's provisions to receive awards in the court's discretion "of reasonable attorney fees and other litigation costs reasonably incurred." 5 U.S.C. § 552 (a) (4) (E) (1983). In enacting the amendment, one of Congress' primary goals was to remove the economic barriers that would preclude a complainant with a meritorious FOIA claim from pursuing it. S. Rep. No. 93–854, 1, 17 (1974) (hereafter S. Rep. 854).

The plain meaning of the amendment is that only litigation costs must have been incurred. However, even if the litigant must also have incurred attorney fees, Mr. Frank in effect incurred fees because an attorney who acts pro se in a FOIA suit faces economic barriers to pursuing the suit if he cannot be compensated for his time. The attorney has foregone other income-producing activities of his law practice. Thus the litigant in effect has incurred the fees of being represented by an attorney.

Thus, although this court has held that a lay pro se litigant is not entitled to attorney fees, DeBold v. Stimson, 735 F.2d 1037, 1043 n.4 (7th Cir. 1984), the reasoning of that decision does not apply to an attorney litigant because an attorney acting pro se is represented by a member of the Bar. Because the situation of attorneys who represent themselves in FOIA litigation differs from that of laymen acting pro se, they should be eligible for fees.

A. The language of the 1974 FOIA amendment is plain that attorney pro se litigants need not literally incur attorney fees in order to be eligible for an award of fees.

The 1974 FOIA amendment authorizes courts to "assess against the United States reasonable attorney fees and other litigation costs reasonably incurred." § 552 (a) (4) (E). The plain meaning of the words "reasonably incurred" is that they modify only the words "litigation costs" and not "attorney fees." A complainant thus need not actually incur attorney fees for a court to award fees under the amendment. In Holly v. Chasen, 569 F.2d 160 (D.C.

Cir.1977) and <u>Cuneo v. Rumsfeld</u>, 553 F.2d 1360 (3d Cir. 1981), the courts interpreted the words "reasonably incurred" to modify only "litigation costs." This interpretation is appropriate in light of the statute's plain meaning and the Doctrine of the Last Antecedent. The plain meaning of "reasonable attorney fees and other litigation costs reasonably incurred" is that "reasonably incurred" modifies "other litigation costs" alone. Were "reasonably incurred" interpreted to modify "reasonable attorney fees" the second "reasonable" would be redundant. This reading contradicts the presumption that every word in a statute is intended to have meaning.

Furthermore, the Doctrine of the Last Antecedent states that "qualifying words, phrases, and clauses are to be applied to the words or phrases immediately preceding and are not to be construed as extending to or including those more remote." <u>See Quinden v. Prudential Ins. Co.</u>, 482 F.2d 876, 878 (5th Cir. 1973). Under this rule, the phrase "reasonably incurred" modifies only "litigation costs" because it is the phrase immediately preceding it. <u>Id.</u> This resolution of the semantic issue makes it clear that a complainant need not actually incur attorney fees to be eligible for an award under § 552 (a) (4) (E). <u>See Cuneo</u>, 553 F.2d at 1366.

   B.   <u>An award of fees to attorney pro se litigants promotes Congress' goal of facilitating private enforcement of the FOIA by removing economic barriers to litigation confronting potential litigants.</u>

Congress passed the 1974 attorney fees and costs amendment to the FOIA to close "loopholes which allow agencies to deny legitimate information to the public." H.R. Rep. No. 93–876, <u>reprinted in</u> 1974 U.S. C.C.A.N. 6272, 6287. Before the amendment, many citizens with legitimate claims were unable to pursue them because of the obstacle of attorney fees, and Congress enacted § 552 (a) (4) (E) to remove that economic barrier from litigants. <u>Id.</u> Congress designed the FOIA so that individual citizens would ensure government compliance with the Act through private litigation without major economic barriers. <u>See Cazalas v. Department of Justice</u>, 709 F.2d 1051, 1057 (5th Cir. 1983), <u>cert. denied</u> 469 U.S. 1207 (1985).

Thus, even if the statutory antecedent "reasonably incurred" is ambiguous, the statute should be interpreted to promote the statutory policy. In representing themselves, attorneys face economic barriers when they seek to enforce the FOIA through litigation. Such barriers include the prospect of paying an attorney or foregoing the opportunity to earn a regular income for a day or more in order to pursue a pro se suit. <u>Crooker v. Department of the Treasury</u>, 634 F.2d 48, 49 (2d Cir. 1980) [hereafter <u>Crooker I</u>].

Accord Holly, 72 F.R.D. at 116 (pro se litigants face economic barriers). The opportunity cost of an attorney's spending time on his own case is no less real than the costs incurred by a litigant who must hire an attorney. Id. If they have to divert time from income-producing activities, attorneys may find themselves unable to vindicate their rights under the FOIA. Id. In economic terms, there is simply no difference between money paid out and income foregone, and both of them may represent the same economic burden. Richard A. Posner, The Economics of Justice 10 (1981).

Furthermore, by not permitting an attorney pro se litigant eligibility for fees, this court would encourage attorneys who wished to vindicate their FOIA rights to hire other attorneys to represent them. Such a response would result in an increase in total litigation costs. Attorneys capable of pursuing their own FOIA claim should not be penalized simply because they choose to do so. Moreover, unlike the lay pro se litigant in Debold, the attorney acting pro se has secured professional representation in order to enforce FOIA claims. See DeBold, 735 F.2d at 1043.

Not only is an award of fees to an attorney pro se litigant consistent with this court's decision in DeBold, it is also consistent with the court's policy of awarding fees to legal-aid and public interest organizations even where the litigant paid nothing for the services he received. Id. In both situations, attorneys must perform services without remuneration in order to pursue legitimate FOIA claims. It would be anomalous to allow citizens facing economic barriers to recover attorney fees when none were charged, but deny this benefit to attorneys facing the same barriers. See, e.g., Falcone v. IRS, 714 F.2d 646, 647 (6th Cir. 1983) (attorney fees permitted to legal service organizations, but not to attorney pro se litigants in FOIA suits). If the Congressional purpose of citizen enforcement of the FOIA through private litigation is to be achieved, the courts should not create economic disincentives to attorneys by denying them fees when they represent themselves. See Cazalas, 709 F.2d at 1056.

Finally, the circuits that have denied attorneys eligibility for an award of fees have reasoned that an allowance of these fee awards creates a "windfall," and that an award of litigation costs is a sufficient incentive to induce attorney pro se litigants to pursue their claims. See, e.g., Crooker v. Department of Justice, 632 F.2d 916, 921–22 (1st Cir. 1980) [hereafter Crooker II]. However, this analysis overlooks the fact that the time spent pursuing FOIA litigation precludes attorneys from receiving remuneration by representing clients in other actions. In such situations, attorneys might reasonably choose to represent another's FOIA claim rather than their own simply because in the former they would receive compensation for professional services. Such economic realities could keep an attorney from seeking what would otherwise be a meritorious FOIA claim. This frustrates the Congressional purpose of encouraging all persons to vindicate their statutory rights under the Act. S. Rep. No. 854 at 17.

C. Congress intended wide application of the 1974 amendment in order to discourage government recalcitrance in complying with the Act and to penalize the government for pursuing litigation without a reasonable basis in law.

By allowing eligibility for attorney fees to claimants who "substantially prevail," Congress sought to discourage government agencies from employing dilatory tactics to frustrate legitimate FOIA requests. Id. Fee awards are to be taken out of the agency's budget rather than from the general fund to ensure that agencies would litigate only cases where their position was supported by some "reasonable basis in law." Id. In fact, one of the four major criteria to determine whether a particular complainant is entitled to discretionary fees is whether the government's withholding of the records had a reasonable basis in law. S. Conf. Rep. No. 93–1200, reprinted in 1974 U.S. C.C.A.N. 6285, 6288; See Stein v. Department of Justice, 662 F.2d 1245, 1262 (7th Cir. 1981). Congress intended to penalize government agencies that are "recalcitrant in their opposition to a valid claim or [are] otherwise engaged in obdurate behavior." S. Rep. No. 854 at 19.

In order to achieve these important Congressional purposes, this court should not limit the application of § 552 (a) (4) (E). If attorney pro se litigants were not allowed to recover fees, government agencies could block one type of valid claim and stall the dissemination of legitimately requested documents with impunity. This would especially be the case where dissemination of the documents would lead to embarrassment of, or claims against, government officials and agencies. See Cazalas, 709 F.2d at 1055. The goal of penalizing the government's harassing and dilatory behavior in FOIA cases is as compelling when the claimant is an attorney acting pro se as when the claimant is an ordinary citizen. Indeed, if individuals are to be accorded full protection against abuses of the power of the government, then there is a strong incentive for this court to hold government agencies acting in bad faith financially accountable to all litigants who "substantially prevail" in FOIA suits.

Furthermore, the government has repeatedly withheld information illegally and litigated weak cases when litigants represented themselves. See, e.g., Cazalas, 709 F.2d at 1055 (government sought to harass and embarrass attorney pro se litigant); Barrett, 651 F.2d at 1089 (government withholding of documents was both "arbitrary and unreasonable"); Crooker II, 632 F.2d at 920 (government denied existence of requested documents). If the court imposes fee awards upon the government following bad faith behavior, those awards will discourage such tactics and force the government "to oppose only [in] those areas that it ha[s] a strong chance of winning." S. Rep. No. 854 at 17. Disallowing eligibility for fees under § 552 (a) (4) (E) would encourage the government to engage in that behavior Congress expressly sought to discourage. That this behavior is limited to pro se litigants is no consolation. By allowing pro se attorneys to recover, this court would help effectuate Congressional policy by discouraging government harassment of individuals with meritorious FOIA claims. Id. Accord Cazalas, 709 F.2d at 1055.

    D.   Pro se attorney eligibility under § 552 (a) (4) (E) will encourage vigorous advocacy in FOIA cases, but will not result in abusive fee generation.

Because the award of fees is within the discretion of the court, there is little merit to the concern that full awards for pro se litigants will encourage attorneys with inactive practices to create suits in order to generate fees. See, e.g., Falcone, 714 F.2d at 648 ("the United States could become an unwilling 'client' for inactive attorneys"). However, the mere fact that attorneys are eligible for awards does not mean that these awards are automatic. See H. R. Rep. No. 876 at 6–7. This court has already recognized this limitation when it said that "[f]ulfillment of the condition precedent [i.e., substantially prevailing] alone does not entitle a litigant to an award of attorney fees." Stein, 662 F.2d at 1262. See also Cox v. Department of Justice, 601 F.2d 6 (D.C. Cir. 1979) (eligibility does not mean entitlement); Chamberlain v. Kurtz, 589 F.2d 827, 842 (5th Cir. 1978), cert. denied, 444 U.S. 842 (1979) (awards left to discretion of district judge); Blue v. Bureau of Prisons, 570 F.2d 529, 533 (5th Cir. 1979) (eligibility does not create presumptive award under FOIA).

Unmeritorious awards are additionally unlikely because this court has adopted the four criteria suggested in the Senate version of the 1974 amendment that ensure discretionary awards of attorney fees only when there are valid claims. Stein, 662 F.2d at 1262. When using its discretion to determine awards, this court considers

    (1) the benefit to the public, if any, derived from the case; (2) the commercial benefit to the complainant; (3) the nature of the complainant's interest in the records sought; and (4) whether the government's withholding of the records had a reasonable basis in law.

Id. at 1256, citing S. Rep. No. 854 at 17.

Because only meritorious claims would receive awards, the fear of fee generation is unfounded. The stringent considerations listed above would allow a court to use its discretion to "weed out" those fees that an attorney purposely generated. Id. Also, a court is not bound to award the total amount of fees requested, but may adjust the size of the award in its discretion. See Jordan v. Department of Justice, 691 F.2d 514, 518 (D.C. Cir. 1982). The equitable powers of the court are broad enough that concerns over fee generation cannot serve as a rational basis for denying eligibility to all attorneys. Id.

Furthermore, the statutory requirement that a complainant "substantially prevail," § 552 (a) (4) (E), renders fee generation virtually impossible. An attorney bringing a frivolous lawsuit would be unable to generate fees since eligibility for an award is contingent on the suit's merit and necessity. See Cox, 601 F.2d at 6. (adverse court action must be necessary to substantially prevail). Thus, any complainant who has substantially prevailed has, by definition, brought a worthwhile suit. In addition, the government may avoid the prospect of having to pay attorney fees by releasing the documents it does not reasonably believe it has a right to withhold. Cazalas, 709 F.2d at 1056 (no fees necessary if government responds to justified requests). Hence, it is unrealistic to characterize a "substantially prevailing" attorney pro se litigant as trying to generate fees when illegal and unreasonable actions on the part of the government are necessary to receive an award.

Finally, attorneys who represent themselves in FOIA litigation provide the kind of vigorous advocacy Congress desired. S. Rep. No. 854 at 17–19. The determination and skill of attorneys dedicated to vindicating their rights would promote Congress' purpose of encouraging citizens to enforce the act. See, e.g., Cazalas, 709 F.2d at 1056.

II.   THE COURT BELOW ABUSED ITS DISCRETION BY DENYING ATTORNEY FEES TO MR. FRANK WHEN HE SUBSTANTIALLY PREVAILED IN HIS FOIA SUIT.

The parties have stipulated that Mr. Frank "substantially prevailed" in his FOIA suit, and that the government had no reasonable basis in law for withholding a majority of the records Mr. Frank sought. (R.2)

This court has adopted the four criteria of the Senate version of the 1974 amendment to be used in determining whether an award of attorney fees is appropriate. These criteria are

(1) the benefit to the public, if any, derived from the case; (2) the commercial benefit to the complainant; (3) the nature of the complainant's interest in the records sought; and (4) whether the government's withholding of the records had a reasonable basis in law.

Stein, 662 F.2d at 1262.

A careful consideration of all four criteria and the reasonableness of Mr. Frank's claim in light of the time he spent working on the FOIA suit show that the court below abused its discretion when it denied a fee award to Mr. Frank.

A. Because the public substantially benefitted from Mr. Frank's FOIA suit and the government unreasonably withheld its records, the court below abused its discretion by denying Mr. Frank's request for attorney fees.

The documents released as a direct result of Mr. Frank's FOIA suit provided substantial benefit to the public by exposing important information to the electorate. One of the principal goals of the FOIA is to promote "an informed and intelligent electorate" by ensuring public access to information concerning the activities of government officials and agencies. H.R. Rep. No. 1497, 89th Cong., 2d Sess. 12, reprinted in 1966 U.S.C.C.A.N. 2418, 2429. Mr. Frank's suit has furthered that goal by revealing information about the improper conduct of the CIA and FBI. (R.7) The information that the government unreasonably withheld exposed their embarrassing and illegal wiretapping and mail-censoring activities, not only of Mr. Frank, but of members of several other political groups, including the NAACP, the ACLU, and the Students Against the Viet Nam War. (R.7) Although these revelations are highly disconcerting, they provide an essential public service by informing the electorate of wrongdoing in the government. Disseminating the information that an agency of the government is "less than just" in its dealings surely benefits the public. See Cazalas, 709 F.2d at 1053 (pro se attorney revealed discriminatory employment practices of the Department of Justice). Mr. Frank's FOIA request has made available the kind of important information that the public needs to make responsible political decisions. See Aviation Data Serv. v. Federal Aviation Admin., 687 F.2d 1319, 1323 (10th Cir. 1982).

Moreover, Mr. Frank's commercial and personal interests in bringing his FOIA suit were slight in comparison to the public benefit derived from his FOIA request. Mr. Frank now plans to further disseminate his findings to the public by publishing a book discussing the released documents. (R.6) When the nature of a publication is "scholarly, journalistic, or public interest oriented," then it clearly accrues to the public benefit. See Des Moines Register and Tribune Co. v. Department of Justice, 563 F. Supp. 82, 84 (D.D.C. 1983). Only if the purpose of the FOIA request is to acquire information that profits only the recipient's business will the recipient's commercial and personal interest make an award of attorney fees inappropriate. For example, in Aviation Data Services, the plaintiff requested information from the Federal Aviation Administration that was used only for its business of collecting and selling information about the aviation industry to its clients. 687 F.2d at 1320. Mr. Frank, however, has no business clients to whom he will sell the information. Instead, he will use the information he requested only for scholarly publication.

Mr. Frank's use of the disclosed records is more like that of the journalist who published a newspaper article that the court held was not a commercial use of the materials he received from his FOIA request. Des Moines Register, 563 F. Supp. at 84. Mr. Frank's book is also an enterprise that he undertook to educate the public. Any remuneration that he receives from book sales no more detracts from his primary goal of promoting public awareness than a newspaper reporter's salary or a newspaper's sales detracts from the public benefits of news articles. Id.

Moreover, Mr. Frank's personal interest in the records is based on his active political involvement, not on commercial activity. Mr. Frank has always been involved in activities that educate the public. (R. 3–4) He donates his services to the political candidate he supports and has financed the present fifteen-year litigation out of his own funds. (R.4) Although Mr. Frank may have had a considerable personal interest in the litigation at its inception, that interest disappeared when the government settled his personal suit for invasion of privacy after it was forced to release the first set of documents. (R.4) After that settlement, Mr. Frank pursued the records in order to expose them to public scrutiny. This publication comes only at the end of fifteen years of opposition to government recalcitrance. (R. 4)

When the court below said that Mr. Frank's "commercial and personal interests in the matter outweigh any public aspect of the case," (R. 7), the court incorrectly balanced these criteria. A party's commercial benefit should not deprive him of attorney fees if the public benefits from the disclosure of the requested material, or if the agency acted in bad faith without reasonable basis in law. Aviation Data Services, 687 F.2d. at 1322; Cazalas, 709 F.2d at

1054. Not only are the disclosed materials of substantial public interest, but the court below accepted the stipulation that the government agencies acted without any "reasonable basis in law." (R. 2) The court below abused its discretion in denying fees on those grounds.

Moreover, a claimant's request for personal records does not disqualify him from a fee award. For example, in Cazalas v. Department of Justice, 709 F.2d 1051, the claimant requested documents related to her dismissal from the United States Attorney's office. The court decided that, although she had a strong personal interest in the documents, she was not disqualified from a fee award because her request benefitted the public by exposing sex discrimination in government. Id. at 1053. The public benefit from Mr. Frank's request for records is even greater than the plaintiff's in Cazalas. His request produced documents that went beyond information about himself and included information about government spying on other individuals and organizations.

Finally, when "government officials have been recalcitrant in their opposition to a valid claim or have been otherwise engaged in obdurate behavior," then fee awards are appropriate. S. Rep. No. 854 at 19. The government's spying on Mr. Frank is a prime example of the kind of behavior Congress had in mind when suggesting the fourth criterion. Indeed, the agencies conceded that they had acted without any "reasonable basis in law." The CIA and FBI engaged in reprehensible illegal activities against Mr. Frank and other members of political organizations. (R.3) They later sought to further harass Mr. Frank by refusing to comply with his legitimate FOIA request. (R.1) The agencies sought to prevent "wide-spread dissemination of the information in [Mr. Frank's] documents" by settling his privacy claim, and continued to unreasonably refuse to disclose documents for years. (R.4) Under the circumstances of this case, in light of the government's unreasonable withholding of documents, the court abused its discretion in not penalizing the government by awarding fees to Mr. Frank.

> B.   Mr. Frank requested a reasonable fee award from the court to compensate him for the time he spent working on his FOIA suit.

In his claim for attorney fees, Mr. Frank estimated that he spent no less than 2 ½ hours per week on the case for a period of fifteen years. (R.4) He also provided the court below with documentation attesting to the reasonableness of the hourly rate of $125 that he was requesting. (R.4) Yet, the court below denied any fees to Mr. Frank, leaving him with no compensation for over fifteen years of professional work. (R.4) "To decline any fee award whatsoever simply because of doubts of parts of the claim is, in any but the most severe of cases, a failure to use the discretion" of the court. <u>Jordan</u>, 691 F.2d at 521 ($125/hour fee not excessive with proper documentation). The court below abused its discretion when it refused to award anything to Mr. Frank. His fee estimate was conservative, and represented a large sum only because the government forced him to litigate for almost fifteen years. Mr. Frank deserves compensation for the time and effort he spent "fighting the government," and the fees he requested are a reasonable estimate of attorney fees for his work.

CONCLUSION

For the foregoing reasons, the decision of the United States District Court for the Northwestern District of Illinois denying plaintiff's motion for attorney fees pursuant to 5 U.S.C. § 552 (a) (4) (E) (1983) should be reversed and the case remanded for the district court to determine fees.

Respectfully submitted,
Counsel for the Appellant

*

INDEX

References are to Pages